THE WIZARD OF THE NORTH
The Life of Sir Walter Scott

Sir Walter Scott, 1820
By Chantrey. Original at Abbotsford.
By permission of Mrs Maxwell-Scott.

CAROLA OMAN

The Wizard of
the North

The Life of Sir Walter Scott

HODDER AND STOUGHTON
LONDON SYDNEY AUCKLAND TORONTO

To Dr James Corson, Honorary Librarian of Abbotsford, the greatest living authority on Scott, without whose constant kind advice this book might still be on the stocks.

Preface

I GREW UP IN A HOUSE IN THE VERY CENTRE OF OXFORD. IT HAD A
Norman pillar in a crypt under the kitchen, remains of cloisters in the
drive, an Elizabethan wing with Victorian accretions, and an early
Georgian wing. Naturally, it had ghosts. Discounting the sudden cold
draughts, hurrying footsteps, worried whispers, and knockings on doors,
inevitable in premises where central heating has been introduced unsuccessfully, there were three principal ghosts. Lady Hester Bourne saw "Old
Alison", a housekeeper type, we gathered. My niece Julia Trevelyan
Oman (Mrs Roy Strong), when three years old, was visited nightly by a
Lady. ("What's she doing now, baby?" "She's smiling behind a fan!")
But our nursery-maid, Ethel Stangoe, carried away the palm. She
repeatedly heard "the lame gentleman"—Sir Walter Scott. He came up
the stairs from the outermost hall, and paused; and if after that the
footfall faded, it was all right. It was only the Professor, working late,
gone on up to his study, in the Victorian wing. But if, after the halt, the
lame gentleman came on down the long passage of the Georgian wing,
Ethel drew the bed-clothes over her head and trembled. (Her mother had
the second sight.) He might be coming on, up the steep little flight of
stairs to the staff quarters. Nobody, apparently, ever told her that Sir
Walter Scott would not want to go anywhere except to the green room,
Mr Skene's room, at the bottom of the passage, and that Sir Walter
would have been the kindliest of visitants.

James Skene, perhaps Scott's dearest friend, lived in our house from 1844 to 1864. After trying Leamington, according to the *Dictionary of National Biography*, he settled happily in Oxford and "enjoyed the best literary society". One of his daughters sent an article, "Some episodes in a long life", to *Blackwood's Magazine* in 1896. She said that her father, whom she had left drowsing over his fire one evening, had called to her to come quick. "I want to tell you of such a delightful surprise I have just had. Scott has been here! dear Scott! He told me he had come from a long distance to pay me a visit, and he has been sitting here with me, talking of our old happy days together. He said it was long since we had met; but he is not in the least changed: his face was just as cheerful and pleasant as it used to be; I have so much enjoyed being with him." Needless to say, James Skene, who was in his ninetieth year, died soon after this experience. Scott had been dead for over thirty years.

I do not think that it was really the hope of meeting the lame gentleman that set me off on the long trail of a Scott enthusiast. We had gone to Scotland for summer holidays ever since I could remember. When friends ask me what made me want to write a life of Scott, or when I began to think of it, I am baffled. For I cannot remember when I was not collecting material for it. Twice, at seven-year intervals, we took a house outside Melrose, and once a house in Edinburgh. With my brother, I think I visited nearly every important site in the Scott story. We had no transport except bicycles, or the local railway, though I do once recall a family expedition when we accompanied a hired car to St Mary's Loch. We ascended the Eildons and lay on the top with maps and glasses. We went up the Rhymer's Glen, to Glenfarg, Smailholm and Sandy Knowe, Colmslie, Hillslap, Langshaw. We explored Selkirk, Jedburgh, Dryburgh, Borthwick, Niddrie, Hermitage, Roslin. I sketched every available pele tower and keep, set up my easel in Greyfriar's churchyard, and in Queen Mary's bedroom, Holyrood House. I paddled across the Tweed at Abbotsford in 1913.

As the years passed I collected every book about Scott that came out. I bought the Waverley novels gradually, in a lovely little edition: "The New Century Library", two and sixpence each, bound in soft leather, four sepia illustrations, india paper. When I am going for a long journey by air, I still choose one to slip in my pocket. That superb complete edition of Scott, the "Magnum Opus", we attribute to our Heriot Row great-grandfather. It occupied a large portion of the Chippendale, breakfront bookcase in the dining-room of the house where Scott had come to call on Skene. (This piece of furniture was so beautifully made that the doors sighed as you closed them after extracting a Scott.) I read all his articles, and was struck by his excellence as a reviewer. I bought Lockhart, and when I came to write a life, was startled to find how inaccurate he had been, and how he manipulated letters. But my first impression of him as a biographer was unchanged. He gave us the man; he got to the heart of the story.

It was a deprivation, during the First War years that there could be no more Scotland. But there could! I bought three severe guide books with good maps, and traced many Scott journeys. The end of that war brought a famous Scottish author to Oxford. With awe and wonder, in the train going up to London, I watched John Buchan correcting proofs. I cannot remember that any contemporary ever shared or encouraged my taste for Scott—only W. P. Ker, Professor of Poetry, who sent me a poem for my wedding, in 1922. I took an English husband to the Scott country for his honeymoon. It snowed: but it was April.

In 1932, a flood of books came out to celebrate the Centenary of Scott's death. Sad to say, most of the authors would have benefited greatly by seeing each other's discoveries before they published. Sir Herbert Grierson produced the invaluable collected edition of Scott's letters (and also an oddly disappointing small Life). The letters are the librarian's delight and nightmare. There are twelve volumes, and the spines have no numbers on them. John Buchan's Life held the field, in spite of the availability of many new manuscript sources, until the second outburst, the Bicentenary of Scott's birth, 1972. Then Professor Edgar Johnson's weighty two-volume *Sir Walter Scott, the Great Unknown* arrived from America—but not for the timid beginner. Both these leading Scott biographers included, I think mistakenly, careful descriptions and criticism of the novels and poems. These should ideally form a separate publication. I hope I am right in that I have not attempted to impose the novels on a generation with whom they are not yet popular. I also decided not to publish for the Bicentenary but to see what it brought forth—a flood of articles, two first-class exhibitions in Edinburgh and several subsidiary ones, an excellent short book by David Daiches—*Sir Walter Scott and his World*.

The author wishes to thank for information and permission to reproduce pictures, His Grace the Duke of Buccleuch, Mrs Maxwell-Scott, the Scottish National Portrait Gallery, the Hon. Mrs Conway, Mrs Somervell, Mr John Murray; and for information and visits to Scott sites, Mrs Maxwell-Scott (Abbotsford), Vice-Admiral Sir Conolly and Lady Mary Abel Smith (Ashiestiel), Sir Tresham and Lady Lever

(Lessudden), Mr F. Douglas-Whyte (Rosebank), Mr and Mrs Law (Lass-wade), Messrs Murray, Beith and Murray (39 Castle Street). Lady Henderson kindly lent unpublished lecture notes by the late Sir David Henderson, and Miss Clare Talbot, Archivist at Hatfield House, the late Kingsley Adams, author of the catalogue of the Hatfield House Collection, and the late Dr Elizabeth Dexter of Massachusetts, advised on portraits for the chapter "Who was Lady Scott?" Mrs G. G. Brocklebank and Sir Tresham Lever have most kindly read the proofs.

After great heart-searchings the author has followed Scott and Lockhart in the spelling of such place-names as Ashestiel, Sandy Knowe, etc.

Finally, she must admit that she has not been able to trace the origin of the title of her biography, *The Wizard of the North*. Mrs Grant of Laggan, in 1820 and 1821, referred to Scott as "the Wizard" and "the Wizard of Abbotsford". Anne Scott also used the expression. *The Literary Gazette* of July 14th, 1821, appears to have been the first to use the full title, followed in 1831 by *The Border Magazine*.

C. O.

Contents

Chapter		page
I	Lamiter, 1771–1778	17
II	High School to Advocate, 1778–1792	25
III	Greenmantle, 1790–1797	45
IV	Miss Carpenter of Carlisle, September to December, 1797	62
V	"Laughing Philosophy", 1798–1799	77
VI	The Minstrelsy, 1800–1802	87
VII	Experimental, 1802–1803	98
VIII	Ashestiel, 1804–1805	112
IX	"A Little Lion", 1806–1809	126
X	Publisher and Poet, 1809–1810	149
XI	The Flitting, 1811–1813	168
XII	The Author of *Waverley*, 1814–1815	182
XIII	"Conundrum Castle", 1816–1819	210
XIV	Crest of the Wave, 1820–1822	235
XV	Happy Days, 1823–1825	270
XVI	"The Muffled Drum", 1825–1826	288
XVII	"Right Hand", 1826–1827	309
XVIII	"We Must Take What Fate Sends", 1828–1832	331
Appendix Who was Lady Scott?		359
Index		367

Illustrations

Sir Walter Scott, 1820 *Frontispiece*
By Chantrey. Original at Abbotsford.
By permission of Mrs Maxwell-Scott.

Williamina Belsches *facing page* 48
Medallion by an unknown artist.
Lent to the Scottish National Portrait Gallery, 1945, by
Miss Adelaide Traill, her great-granddaughter.

Williamina Belsches Stuart, Lady Forbes 48
By Cosway.
With an inscription on the back by her mother, Lady
Jane Stuart—
    Even Cosway's flattering pencil cannot grace
      That dear, that charming form, that matchless face.
    Nature alone can justice do to these
      Tho' Cosway's pencil never fails to please.
By permission of Mrs Somervell, from the collection at Fettercairn
House.

Miss Charlotte Carpenter, 1797, and her father Jean
François Charpentier   64
Artists unknown. Originals at Abbotsford.
By permission of Mrs Maxwell-Scott.

Arthur Hill, second Marquess of Downshire   64
By H. D. Hamilton.
By permission of the Hon. Mrs Conway.

Walter Scott, 1805–6   96
By James Saxon.
With the dog Camp. Lady Scott's favourite portrait.
Engraved for the frontispiece of the first edition of *The
Lady of the Lake*, 1810.
By permission of the Scottish National Portrait Gallery.

Ashestiel   112
*Engraving by J. Horsburgh from sketch by J. M. W. Turner in the
Fitzwilliam Museum. Published in* Poetical Works *(1833–34)
Vol. VII. Photograph by the Fitzwilliam Museum, Cambridge.*

39 Castle Street, Edinburgh. "The town residence of Sir
Walter Scott for upwards of twenty-five years."   112
*Engraving by W. Miller from sketch by J. M. W. Turner,
reproduced in Lockhart's* Memoirs, *Vol. IV (1839). Photograph
by Department of Prints and Drawings, British Museum.*

Lady Scott   113
By James Saxon. Original at Abbotsford.
By permission of Mrs Maxwell-Scott.

Walter Scott, 1809   128
By Raeburn. Original at Abbotsford.
An 1808 version is at Bowhill, in the collection of the
Duke of Buccleuch, in which the background is of Her-
mitage Castle, and the dog Camp is at Scott's feet. In the
Abbotsford version the background is of the Yale of
Yarrow and Camp has for companion one of the grey-
hounds, Percy and Douglas. This is the picture housed
by Skene when 39 Castle Street was sold.
By permission of Mrs Maxwell-Scott.

Henry, third Duke of Buccleuch and family   160
By H. P. Danloux. Signed and dated 1798.
The figures from left to right are: Lord Montagu, Lady
Caroline, Duke Henry, Duchess Elizabeth, Lady Harriet,
Lady Elizabeth, Lord Courtown (son-in-law), Harriet,
Countess of Dalkeith (daughter-in-law), Charles, Earl of
Dalkeith, afterwards fourth Duke of Buccleuch, Lady
Courtown (born Lady Mary Scott).
*By permission of His Grace the Duke of Buccleuch, from the
collection at Bowhill.*

The Abbotsford family   176
By Wilkie.
"Mr. Wilkie, the painter, has made a capital picture of
the whole family which he intends to finish in London
for the Exhibition. We are all drawn in character. Anne
and I are two milkmaids with pails on our heads, papa
sitting, and Captain Ferguson standing looking for all
the world like an old poacher who understands his trade."
Letter from Sophia Scott to her governess Miss Millar,
November 25th, 1817.
Sir Walter wrote to Sir Adam, March 7th, 1827 (Letters,
X, 168) that the remaining characters were an octogenarian shepherd, and his own two sons, little Charles and
tall Walter, behind Sir Adam, left and right respectively.
The dogs were Maida and Ourisk.
By permission of the Scottish National Portrait Gallery.

John Gibson Lockhart (1794–1854)   177
By H. Pickersgill.
Private collection.

The Daughters. Sophia and Anne Scott, 1818   192
By William Nicholson. Originals at Abbotsford.
By permission of Mrs Maxwell-Scott.

Cornet Scott of the 18th Hussars   225
By William Allan. Original at Abbotsford.
By permission of Mrs Maxwell-Scott.

Harriet, wife of Charles, Earl of Dalkeith, afterwards
fourth Duke of Buccleuch   240
Artist unknown.
"My fair chieftainess" to whom Scott dedicated *The Lay
of the Last Minstrel*, 1805. Died 1814.
*By permission of His Grace the Duke of Buccleuch, from the
collection at Bowhill.*

Sir Walter Scott. A Study for "The Finding of the   241
Scottish Regalia", 1818
By Andrew Geddes.
By permission of the Scottish National Portrait Gallery.

Abbotsford, 1837   256
*By Thomas Allom (1804–1872), engraved by Thomas Prior
(1809–1880) for Vol. I of* Scotland *by William Beattie
(1838).*

Sir Walter Scott, 1822   289
By Sir Henry Raeburn.
By permission of the Scottish National Portrait Gallery.

I

Lamiter

1771–1778

I

DURING THE DARK DAYS OF FEBRUARY 1773 A SUCCESSION OF OLD
wives and solemn-looking gentlemen made their way up the two flights
of stairs in a tall gabled house at the top of College Wynd in Edinburgh
Old Town. It was near rather a sinister site—the Kirk of Field where
Queen Mary's second husband Darnley had been blown up and then
strangled. But socially it was still considered desirable—almost in the
University. The noise from outside on the upper floors, even when all
windows were closed, was distracting. The physicians were shown a fine
blond boy about eighteen months old and told a perplexing story. On the
night before he had been struck down by what they had thought to be a
teething fever, which had lasted three days, he had been so agile and full
of mischief that it had been a business to catch him and get him to bed.
On the fourth day, when he was bathed as usual he seemed to have lost
the power of his right leg. And that was how affairs stood. There was no
sign of dislocation or sprain. He just could not move his little leg. His
anxious-eyed parents implored guidance. They were fortunate in that the
child's maternal grandfather was Dr John Rutherford, Professor of
Medicine. Dr Rutherford had himself a young family, by a second wife.
His first wife had been a daughter of Sir John Swinton of Swinton, a
house famous for its warriors in mediaeval days.

Dr Rutherford considered the case of the little sufferer. His poor Anne had certainly been unlucky in her nursery. Of the first clutch of six boys and girls, born in Anchor Close, five had died before the move to College Wynd, and one since. They were going to move again. Mr Walter Scott was going to build a house in George Square, near the Meadows. He could afford to, for he was a respected Writer to the Signet, the highest rank in Scotland in the profession of solicitor, and he had added by careful toil to a good partnership bought for him by his father. He was a reliable man with regular features, not very joyful and at the moment absolutely miserable. The ailing child was the second to be named after him and had already escaped an untimely end. A wet-nurse engaged for him had gone to consult Dr Joseph Black, Professor of Chemistry, who had warned the Scotts that she was in an advanced consumption.

Mrs Walter Scott was by no means as handsome as her husband. She was low-statured and her features were undistinguished except by an expression of great kindliness. When she sat for her marriage portrait, in oils, to a local expert, she dressed in the height of fashion as befitted a lady of family—brocade stay-bodice, nosegay of artificial flowers tucked in, pearls, and a velvet cloak, ermine trimmed.[1] As a motherless girl great trouble had been taken to form her manners. She had been a pupil of the Honourable Mrs Ogilvie whose victims were taught never to let a back touch the back of a chair.

At length Dr Rutherford pronounced his opinion.[2] The child had better be sent to his grandfather, Mr Robert Scott who had a farm down in Roxburghshire. Young Walter had one more lucky escape before he settled in a demi-paradise. So that he should not be a care to the household at Sandy Knowe, a nurse had been sent with him. This character soon confided in old Alison Wilson, the housekeeper, that she had twice carried her charge up to the craigs, under what she realised was a strong temptation of the Devil. She must get back to her lover in Edinburgh. So she had intended to cut the child's throat with her scissors and push the body down into the moss. Alison instantly took possession of the precious lamb and the woman was sent back to Edinburgh. They afterwards heard that she had been pronounced a lunatic and confined.

<h2 style="text-align:center">II</h2>

The child's first memories were of Sandy Knowe. Amongst the strange remedies suggested by his well-wishers was that whenever a sheep was killed he should be stripped and wrapped up in the skin, while it was still warm. When he was thirty-six and very happy he wrote a memoir of his early life, and put it in a drawer. This was a shock, in due time, for his devoted son-in-law and biographer who had spent hours trying to make bricks without straw about a great man's infancy. For his hero had been a very noticing child, although, after so many years, not quite exact as to dates. He had never forgotten the sheepskin.

In this Tartar-like habiliment I well remember lying upon the floor, while my grandfather, a venerable old man with white hair, used every excitement to make me try to crawl. I also distinctly remember the late Sir George MacDougal of Makerstoun, father of the present Sir Henry Hay MacDougal, joining in this kindly attempt. He was God knows how[3] a relation of ours, and I still recollect him in his old-fashioned military habit (he had been colonel of the Greys) with a small cocked hat, deeply laced, an embroidered scarlet waistcoat and a light-coloured coat, with milk-white locks tied in a military fashion, kneeling on the ground before me, and dragging his watch along the carpet for me to follow it. The benevolent old soldier and the infant wrapped in his sheepskin would have afforded an odd group to interested spectators.

It was a tiny, brilliant vignette. Most of the scenes impressed on his memory were on a much larger scale—panoramic. They were destined to form for life a taste for a particular neighbourhood. At first the ewe-milkers used to carry him about among the craigs. He was very quick at the uptake and soon came to know every sheep and lamb by their head-mark. But the most important character in his day came to be "Auld Sandy Ormistoun", the cow-bailie, who had "the chief superintendence of the flocks that browsed upon the velvet tufts of loveliest green". He used to catch Sandy early to get a ride on his shoulder up to the tower above its little loch. When Sandy blew a certain note on his whistle the maids in the house knew that the boy wanted to be fetched down again. But he was perfectly happy, lying hour after hour on a springy sweet-scented hill, under a changing heaven, up on the top of his world. Behind him rose the ruined keep of Smailholm, and below the groves of Mertoun, the principal seat of the Scott of Harden family, and Dryburgh Abbey, where he had a right to be buried since Mr Robert Scott's wife was a Haliburton. (When the Earl of Buchan had bought the estate he had continued the right to burial to Captain Robert Scott.) Across Tweed came Lessudden, home for three centuries of the Scotts of Raeburn. There was a wonderful screen of unmistakable contours in the

rear view opposite Smailholm—the triple peaks of Eildon, cleft in three
by Michael Scott, magician. *Trimontium* had been a famous Roman camp
for three centuries. Behind them rose the shattered peel tower of Thomas
the Rhymer, who had gone inside them with the queen of the Faerie, and
a little further, the valley of the Leader and the bleak Lammermuirs.
There was Hume Castle, captured by Cromwell, on the eastward skyline
towards the majestic Cheviot, and quite close, only a few miles west-
wards, Melrose Abbey, and the waters of the Gala and Yarrow and
Ettrick Forest.

His days were spent watching his flock, and the shadows of clouds
bearing across the hills, and the kestrel hovering. For sounds there were,
in season, the bees in the heather and the curlews calling and the grouse
chuckling, and always the wa-ing of sheep. He was forgotten one day
when a storm came on and his auntie came running to fetch him home.
She found him lying on his back amongst the knolls, clapping his hands
at the lightning and crying out at every fresh flash, "Bonny! bonny!"
Later, when he was producing book after book which was received by the
world with the same cry, the incident was fondly produced as prophetic.

At what he called the "old rumble-tumble farmhouse" there was,
as in one of His Majesty's ships, never a still moment. There were voices
crying on a high note, and doors clapping in a high wind, and pails and
cans jangling, and sometimes Uncle Thomas, over from Crailing, trying on
his pipes his darling piece "Sour plums in Galashiels". At times the boy
led quite a procession of children, headed by his first cousin Annie, a
daughter of Thomas. He used a little crutch, which he never mentioned.
In the evening his grandmother sat with her spinning wheel at one side
of the fire and his grandfather (a good deal failed), in his elbow-chair on
the other, and the boy lay on the rug at their feet, listening to the Bible
or whatever good book his aunt was reading to them. There were two or
three old volumes which lay in the window-seat. Before he could read he
had learnt by heart the ballad of Hardiknute. He shouted this about the
house so loudly that Dr Duncan, Minister of Mertoun, mildly complained:
"One may as well speak in the mouth of a cannon as where that child is."
Sometimes, in the long winter evenings his grandmother would tell him
thrilling tales of his ancestors and the days of old—Wat of Harden,
Wight Willie of Aikwood, Jamie Telfer of the fair Dodhead, and other
heroes, all in the Robin Hood line. The only news from the outside
world came with Uncle Thomas's weekly visit. The little boy received an
impression that George Washington was a personal enemy, and must be
defeated. With the same fervour he loathed the name of the Butcher

Cumberland. Mr Curle of Yetbyre, husband of Barbara Scott, another of the Sandy Knowe aunties, had been present at some of the atrociously cruel executions of the followers of Prince Charlie, at Carlisle and in the Highlands, after Culloden. Some of them had been distant relations.

Winter brought excitements, such as the Tweed in spate; but the winds which blew the snow into drifts were fiercely cold, and nature rebelled at the thought of trimming a close lantern and setting out into a white world. Nevertheless such duties were punctually fulfilled and the lambing proceeded. During the hard weather of 1774–75 Robert Scott of Sandy Knowe sank and died. The grandson well remembered the writing and sealing with black wax of all the funeral letters to kith and kin and the solemn ceremony of the procession leaving the old thatched farm. The Goodman of Sandy Knowe had been highly thought of as a judge of stock. He had commonly worn a jockey-cap on a head as white as bog-cotton, and his grandson from Edinburgh was thought to resemble him. He had made a false start in life. He had volunteered as a sailor, but his experience on his trial passage of being shipwrecked off Dundee had made him vow he would never put to sea again. His father had been a full-blooded character known as "Old Beardie", and was such an ardent Jacobite he was not going to shave until the Stewarts came again. He had cast his son off, for a weakling. Robert replied by turning Whig. However, Mr Scott of Harden had offered him a lease of a farm.

It had been, not very kindly, remarked that Mr Walter Scott, W.S., never missed a funeral. He came to Sandy Knowe of course to play a leading role. His boy was a splendid little fellow, "a sweet-tempered bairn, a darling with all about the house". Bannock and kail, burn and brae had done their work.

Mr Walter Scott, after seeing his son, took local advice.

With the passing of the Goodman, changes inevitably came to Sandy Knowe. Uncle Thomas arrived to assist the widow. Miss Jenny was told she was taking the lame boy to try the waters of Bath. Dr Andrew Wilson, of Abbey Gardens, Kelso, had a helpful Scottish contact there, Dr Robertson.[4]

III

They sailed for London in the *Duchess of Buccleuch*, Captain Beatson, master. The name of the vessel seemed a happy omen, for the Scotts of Buccleuch were, if not the most ancient, now much the grandest of the clan. Looking back, the boy believed they had been at sea twelve days.

He had an air-gun and he perfectly remembered being persuaded to fire at one of the passengers, who fell apparently dead on the deck and would not get up and walk away until his little assailant had burst out crying. They made a short stay in London, but when he revisited the scenes with his bride, nearly a quarter of a century later, Walter Scott was surprised at the accuracy of his impressions of the Tower and Westminster Abbey.

At Bath they were settled in lodgings at 6 South Parade by Mr Robertson, and Miss Jenny made the necessary appointments at the pump-room and baths. Mr Robertson reported that Dr Gusthart had ordered the hot bath and held out good hopes as the patient was but four years old. When the little boy heard that Mr Robertson was writing to Kelso he poured out messages—how he had half a dozen young lady friends here, but loved Miss Carlyle best. He had kissed another man's wife! He was soon going to write a letter to Dr Wilson. At Sandy Knowe it had been held that although the laddie was not fond of his book, "Miss Jenny was a grand hand at keeping him to the bit." He was now sent to a dame school for a quarter, and with an occasional lesson from his aunt "came to read brawly". A splendid new relation arrived out of the mysterious east to the white glare of fashionable Bath in high summer, 1775. Captain Robert Scott of the Honourable East India Company's Service was on leave. The bachelor Captain took Walter to the theatre—*As You Like It*. This was the highlight of his Bath recollections. A warm relationship sprang up between uncle and nephew, and although he did not remember much about Bath the boy realised afterwards that he had been very happy there. He preserved a picture of the Avon winding behind the Parade, and the cattle lowing amongst the soft English hills opposite, and —equally magnificent—a toyshop near the Orange Grove. He was frightened by the statuary on the west front of the Abbey. This was neo-Georgian Britain and classical statues were likely to spring up everywhere. His wise uncle introduced him to a Neptune who presided benevolently where a pleasure boat crossed to Spring Gardens. The family party from Scotland found a little circle of friends. Mr John Home, the author of *Douglas*, was there with an invalid wife who took the lame boy for drives in her carriage on the Downs. Walter sat for his miniature, *en profile*, which showed that in his fifth year he had a shock of linty locks, a piercing eye and indeterminate features.[5] An Irish maid in the lodgings sang to him two old ballads, very gruesome, which he remembered word for word. But for him there was to be no history of a spectacular Bath cure. At the end of a twelvemonth it was plain that all the treatment had been "without the least advantage to my lameness".

IV

A short stay at his parents' house in George Square was a foretaste of something he was not to like nearly as well as Sandy Knowe. He made a great hit, however, with a lady of more than threescore, a poetess, a leader of Edinburgh literary society. Mrs Alison Cockburn was a grand-aunt of his mother. She wrote next day to Dr Douglas, Minister at Galashiels.

> Edinburgh, Saturday night, 15th November
> 1777
>
> of the gloomy month when the people of England hang and drown themselves.
>
> I last night supped in Mr Walter Scott's. He has the most extraordinary genius of a boy I ever saw. He was reading a poem to his mother when I went in. I made him read on; it was the description of a shipwreck. His passion rose with the storm. He lifted his eyes and hands. "There's the mast gone," says he; "crash it goes! They will all perish." After his agitation he turns to me, "That is too melancholy," says he; "I had better read you something more amusing." I preferred a little chat and asked his opinion of Milton and other books he was reading, which he gave me wonderfully. When taken to bed last night he told his aunt he liked that lady. "Which lady?" says she. "Why, Mrs Cockburn, for I think she is a virtuoso like myself." "Dear Walter," says Aunt Jenny, "what is a virtuoso?" "Don't ye know? Why it's one who wishes and will know everything."
>
> Now, sir, do you think this a very silly story? Pray, what age do you suppose this boy to be? Name it now, before I tell you, why, twelve or fourteen. No such thing; he is not quite six years old. He has a lame leg, for which he was a year at Bath, and has acquired the perfect English accent.[6]

Sea-bathing was the next thing tried. Early in 1778, still under the protection of his aunt, he went to Prestonpans. Here he made two new friends. An old veteran, by name Dalgetty, had come to end his days in the little resort. He drew the pension for an ensign but was called by all "Captain". The American wars were raging. Captain Dalgetty and Walter held different views as to the tactics of General Burgoyne. Somebody had shown the boy a map. The Captain indignantly refuted the suggestion that Burgoyne might not arrive in time. The news of his surrender at Saratoga Springs, when it came to Prestonpans, very late, rather shook the friendship. His other Prestonpans acquaintance was an old friend of his father, a retired lawyer, George Constable. Some forty years later his oddities were so vividly depicted in the character of Jonathan Oldbuck in *The Antiquary* that friends of Scott spotted who must have written this.

He had a charming little companion at Preston, "a very good-natured pretty girl . . . whom I laughed and romped with and loved as children love". She was Miss Dalrymple, daughter of David Dalrymple of Westhall, a Lord of Session.

He crammed himself with gooseberries in the little garden and he remembered his terror lest the spectre of Blind Harry of Fawdon should show his headless trunk at one of the windows of the old tower.[7]

NOTES

1. The marriage portraits of both Scott's parents, attributed to Robert Harvie, are at Abbotsford.
2. The word Poliomyelitis, according to the Oxford English Dictionary, entered the English language in 1880.
3. He was a second cousin of Robert Scott of Sandy Knowe.
4. There are five principal sources for the Sandy Knowe period—two in *Memoirs of Sir Walter Scott*, J. G. Lockhart, 5 vols, 1900 edition, hereafter cited as Lockhart. (Vol. I opens with a fragment of autobiography by Scott, dated Ashestiel 1808, hereafter cited as Ashestiel.) Lockhart, I, 64–73; Ashestiel, I, 12 et seq. Scott's own recollections were further detailed to Mrs Mary Anne Hughes of Uffington, *née* Watts (ed. H. Hutchinson 1904) 90, 244, hereafter cited as Hughes, and James Skene, *Memories of Sir Walter Scott*, Skene Papers, 1909, hereafter cited as Skene, 7, 168–9. Recollections of Miss Jeany Wilson of Kelso appear in *The Centenary Memorial of Sir Walter Scott*, ed. C. S. M. Lockhart, 1871, hereafter cited as *Centenary Memorial*. Dr Arthur Melville Clark, *Sir Walter Scott, the Formative Years* (1968), deals with his education and life up to 1797, but Dr Clark clings to his theory that Scott was born in 1770. An article by Dr James Corson (*Weekend Scotsman*, December 26th, 1970) argues satisfactorily that Dr Clark has not proved 1771 to be the wrong year or 1770 to be the right one. The theory is not new. James Glen and Sir Herbert Grierson (editor of Scott's Letters, 12 vols, 1932, hereafter cited as Letters) examined it about 1935. Glen's conclusions are available in the National Library of Scotland.
5. Now in the National Portrait Gallery of Scotland.
6. Lockhart, I, 71.
7. Sir Walter Scott's Journal, ed. David Douglas, 2 vols, 1890; II, 340; hereafter cited as Journal. Original manuscript is now in the Pierpont Morgan Library, New York. A revised version from the photostat in the National Library of Scotland by J. G. Tait was completed by W. M. Parker, 1950.

II

High School to Advocate

1778–1792

I

HIS GRANDMOTHER AT SANDY KNOWE HAD TOLD HIM STORIES OF ancestors who had performed doughty deeds. There had been Auld Wat of Harden who had married the Flower of Yarrow. When stores had run out in their household it had been the custom of this lady to present them at dinner with a pair of clean spurs on the dish generally furnished with meat. Their eldest son and heir, having been caught on a raid into the lands of Sir Gideon Murray, and given the choice of the gallows or Muckle-Mouth'd Meg, one of the three unmarried daughters of the house, had sadly chosen Meg. There was no record that the marriage was anything but successful. One of their sons, Scott of Raeburn, had become a Quaker, and suffered singular persecution. Two ancestors had been lame. There had been John the Lamiter, founder of the branch originally called of Sinton, and William the Boltfoot. He came six generations later, but had been one of "the prowest knights" of the genealogy.

Young Walter from Sandy Knowe was sent to stay with his kinsfolk the Scotts of Raeburn, and more than half a century later, returning from the funeral of an octogenarian, he wrote down in his Journal a sad incident.

I was staying at Lessudden, an old mansion, the abode of this Raeburn. A large pigeon-house was almost destroyed with starlings, then a common bird, though now seldom seen. They were seized in their nests and put in a bag, and I think drowned or threshed to death, or put to some such end. The servants gave me one, which I in some degree tamed, and the brute of a laird seized and wrung its neck. I flew at his throat like a wild cat and was torn from him with no little difficulty. I never liked him.[1]

He was also sent to Kelso where his grandmother now lived with Aunt Jenny. There was a much-loved playroom up in the top of the house, where together with his little cousin Barbara Scott, and Jeany Wilson the doctor's daughter, he fashioned puppets. Walter made the men. They were three inches high and clad in blue and their features were inked in.[2]

He was lucky in his uncles. Back at Sandy Knowe Uncle Thomas had got a pony for him, a little Shetland mare, no bigger than a Newfoundland dog—Marion. She walked freely about the house and fed regularly from his hand. He soon learnt to ride her well and gave his aunt fits by cantering over the rough ground around the tower. When he was a grandsire he gave an invalid grandson a little mount of the same breed, and she too was Marion.

His happiest hours after he rejoined his family were those spent with his mother. He read poetry with her—Pope's translations of Homer, the songs of Allan Ramsay, The Pilgrim's Progress, The Arabian Nights. He slept in her dressing-room and used to steal out of bed in his nightshirt to read Shakespeare by the light of the fire until the bustle of the company rising from supper warned him it was time to creep back to his bed next door. His most wretched memory was one written down years later concerned with the compulsory family walk, probably on the Meadows.

> There is the stile at which I can recollect a cross child's maid upbraiding me with my infirmity as she lifted me coarsely and carelessly over the flinty steps which my brothers traversed with shout and bound. I remembered the *suppressed bitterness* of the moment, and consciousness of my own inferiority, the feeling of envy with which I regarded the easy movements and elastic steps of my more happily formed brethren.

It would seem that in spite of all the treatments and cures he was not going to be able to walk like the rest of the world. He was lame. He was lame.[3]

The time had come when he must have some more regular education.

A series of experiments followed. He was sent first to a little private school in Bristo Port and when he did not seem to be getting on there, had a young tutor for the rudiments of Latin. Mr James French was destined for the Ministry. Walter Scott's mother dreaded the moment when he had to stand up for himself. He had been the pet lamb of Sandy Knowe, riding about on his pony like a little laird. Now he was the middle son in a collection of five. Robert was in his twelfth year and determined to follow the profession of his namesake uncle, but in the Royal Service. In vain Mrs Scott enticed an old sailor to come round and feed the boys with tales of the horrors and hardships at sea. Robert was rough with Walter, "haughty and imperious". Next came John, nine years old. He was going to be a soldier.[4] Thomas and Daniel were in the nursery still, six and four, but they could not be called docile. Mrs Scott in an ill-advised moment engaged a music-master for the family. Lady Cumming, a next-door neighbour, sent round to ask that when the young Scotts were to be flogged it might not be all on the same morning. Only Robert had the least talent, but they were all learning singing. The surviving daughter of Mrs Scott's last half-dozen of children was so unusual that she scarcely counted at all except as a liability. Anne attracted misfortune. She was accident prone. One of her hands was mangled for life by being caught in the gate of the iron railing leading to the area in the centre of George Square. She was nearly drowned in a quarry-hole filled with water on the south side of the same square. When she was six, left alone in a room with a candle, her cap caught fire, and she was severely burned before she was rescued. Her face swelled up with the slightest cold. Walter noted that like her brothers she had a peculiar temper. She was his junior by a year and died unmarried before she was thirty.

II

About April 1779 he was considered fit for Luke Fraser's second class —Edinburgh High School, and limped off swinging his satchel. The boys wore a costume which was almost a uniform—round black hat, white shirt, rather large cloth waistcoat and single-breasted jacket of glaring colour—royal blue, scarlet or grass green—and brown corduroy breeks. Their stockings were worsted in winter, and blue or (for best) white cotton, in summer.

Walter Scott the Lamiter from George Square decided that from the moment he entered the schoolyards he must be prepared to defend himself. A boy who said it was "no use to hargle-bargle with a cripple" was told that if he might fight mounted—strapped to a deal board—the cripple would try his hand with anyone taller. Before he left the school he was one of the nimblest climbers on the Cat's Neck of Salisbury Crags, and "the kittle nine steps", a passage projecting high from the shiny and precipitous black granite of the castle rock. He never forgot that he had once slipped there. He became one of the stoutest snowballers of Authority in the shape of the Town Guard.

He had about two years in the class of Luke Fraser, a flogger but generously allowed by him to be a good Latin scholar and a very worthy man. He denied stories that he had been a dunce but admitted to having been "an incorrigibly idle imp". He had glanced like a meteor from one end of his class to the other. He took trouble over just what attracted him. His next teacher was a great one, Dr Alexander Adam, Rector of the High School, one of those heroes of Edinburgh's Golden Age whose portraits by Raeburn glow on the walls of the Scottish National Portrait Gallery. (According to Henry Cockburn, nine years junior to Scott and a Whig, this truly excellent, discerning, and benevolent man taught "Latin, some Greek and all virtue".) He was patient with the timid and backward; he enthusiastically encouraged any suggestion of high promise. He never forgot an old boy. It was a proud moment in the story of a pupil who perhaps had not applied himself as he should when the Rector announced that although others understood Latin better, Gualterus Scott was behind few in following and enjoying the author's meaning.

But the curriculum at the High School prided itself only on the classics. Mr Scott sent Walter also for an hour a day to a writing and arithmetic school, and for some months of 1782 and the succeeding year engaged for his brood a resident tutor, another student of divinity who could also give instruction in French. Mr James Mitchell was a strict Sabbatarian.

Walter Scott, schoolboy, was already beginning to show marked signs of characteristics which were to develop. He was accepted in his circle as a story-teller. He had an irrepressible sense of humour. He had begun to collect friends and association objects of all kinds. In his thirteenth year he passed on normally to the University, but his parents were not satisfied with his looks. He was growing fast. He detested the confinement of city life. Great changes had taken place amongst his Sandy Knowe relatives. Old Mrs Robert Scott had been gathered. She had been living with her unmarried daughter in Kelso. Thomas reigned in the farm. It was nothing new for a Scott of their branch to own property in Kelso, five miles south. "Beardie" had kept a town house there. Miss Jenny now had a garden, which was perhaps what she had always wanted. Nobody knew much about her inmost thoughts, for her tongue was middling sharp. Walter believed that she might have had George Constable had she been so minded, for in her youth she had been very good-looking and she still had the most beautiful eyes and teeth. She had a very large garden. It occupied between seven and eight acres and had been laid out in the beginning of the century in the Dutch taste. It had long, straight walks between hedges of yew and hornbeam, a shrubbery, a bower, an arbour and a mass of contorted little walks called the labyrinth. There was a sizeable orchard; rustic seats were placed at strategic intervals; there was a banqueting hall. At the foot of the garden, separated from it by a path called Ford Walk, ran the Tweed, broad and strong. The churchyard and Lady Waldie's garden adjoined it on the north, and on the west the glebe of Mr Lundie, Minister. Walter had, on Friday, April 23rd, 1784, stood on a chair in the churchyard and beheld a venerable figure who spoke very colloquially, telling excellent stories. John Wesley had been staying with Dr Douglas and fallen down three pair of the doctor's stairs, but the Angels had guarded him.

Walter's father had decided to buy the property in which Miss Jenny now lived so doucely, with her young cousin Barbara Scott (who was going to become Mrs Meik) and just the one maid; for though the garden was so large, the house up in the north-west corner of it was very small. There was an idea that when Uncle Robert retired he might buy it and live with her. Meanwhile Walter might spend a season there and attend the Grammar School.

He thought Kelso was the most romantic village in Scotland. The neighbourhood was that on which he had looked down as on a promised land when he had lain with his sheep in a world as bright and unsubstantial as a soap-bubble. It included the meeting of two superb rivers, the Tweed and the Teviot, both renowned in song, the ruins of an ancient Abbey, vestiges of a castle, at the siege of which James II had been killed, and in a park nearby a mansion built for the first Duke of Roxburghe by Vanburgh. In the little dove-grey village more houses were thatched than slated, but the Tweedside coach from Kelso to Edinburgh passed Smailholm every lawful day at 9 a.m. going north and at 2 p.m. going south. On Mondays the Earlston carrier collected eggs and butter for the Edinburgh market. Kelso was famous for its damsons and pears. Queen Mary had stayed there two nights, and the Prince. His followers had raised the standard in the little square and proclaimed his father as James III and eighth.

Walter sat under the giant oriental plane tree in the centre of the garden and forgot dinner hour. He had discovered Bishop Percy's *Reliques of Ancient Poetry*.⁵ He was reading all he could lay hands on now—the novels of Richardson and Henry Mackenzie, of Fielding and Smollett; and anything in the way of Travel.

Lady Waldie (the title was honorary but universally bestowed) had a son at the Grammar School. She gave Walter the run of her library, small but choice. This gentle kindly widow was a Quakeress. (He remembered her gratefully in his first note to *Redgauntlet*.) The pedagogue at Kelso Grammar School was an original. He was enormous, very ungainly and rejoiced in the name of Lancelot Whale. Walter had other new companions at the school. James and John Ballantyne were the sons of a general merchant in the village. James was going to study the law; John was to be apprenticed to a London banking house. They were both rather undersized; James was theatrical and John a wonderful mimic. Walter was five months older than James; John was three years younger, and there was a third little boy, Alexander. Walter, as a pupil from the vaunted Edinburgh High School, was assigned a separate seat in the Kelso village school, and at the public examination he impressed the audience by spouting the speech of Galgacus from the *Agricola* of Tacitus. He thought that by most of the company not one word was understood. He generally finished his stint before the elder Ballantyne, and would whisper, "Come, slink beside me, Jamie, and I'll tell you a story." School occupied only four hours of the long light days. They went for rambles together by the banks of the river. Walter's fund of stories seemed to James inexhaustible, "Certainly the best story-teller I ever heard, either then or since."

III

Scott attended six sessions at Edinburgh University.⁶ He opened with Professor John Hill, in whose Humanity class he met again many old High School companions. His Professor of Greek was Andrew Dalzel, who had a winning manner; but there was the difficulty that most of Scott's fellow students had got some Greek already. After rather faint-hearted efforts during two sessions he gave up Greek. He entered his name for instruction in Logic and Metaphysics with Professor John Bruce who was going to retire to shine in politics. Moral Philosophy he studied under a most popular lecturer—Professor Dugald Stewart. His father had a legal career for him in mind, and for History he had the future Lord Woodhouselee—very dry. He was sent to an outside source for Mathematics.

But upon the whole his reputation at the University was no more remarkable than it had been at the High School and it was bedevilled by periods of ill-health during which he convalesced again at Kelso, missing Edinburgh friends as his years and inches increased. His first great Edinburgh friend was John Irving, who shared his tastes for authorship and the days of old. They made Saturday and Sunday expeditions together to read one another their effusions in verse and prose. They wisely chose the most secluded stretches of Arthur's Seat, Blackford Hill and Salisbury Crags, for declamations which were dramatic. They had begun by taking out books from Sibbald's Circulating Library in Parliament Square—the shop in which Walter first saw, from a distance, "Robert Burns, the boast of Scotland". They read *The Castle of Otranto*, Spenser, Ariosto and Boiardo. A blind poet, Dr Blacklock, who took young men as boarders, introduced Walter to Ossian and Spenser. He preferred *The Faerie Queene*. Walter read quicker and when they were devouring a book together John always remembered that Walter had to wait for him, with the wind rattling in the page. John was going to become a W.S. and so, it was supposed, was Walter. In the spring of 1786 when he was still three months short of fifteen he signed indentures for five years as apprentice to his father.

There were advantages and disadvantages in his new situation. The drudgery of the office was depressing. He felt "caged up like a cobbler's linnet". He never liked living in a town. "But I loved my father, and I felt the rational pride and pleasure of rendering myself useful to him. I was ambitious also; and among my companions in labour, the only way to gratify ambition was to labour hard and well." As a Writer's Apprentice he could make a little money—threepence a page. He said he had once written upwards of a hundred and twenty folio sheets at a sitting. The habit he then formed was for life. He automatically ended a page with a flourish. His family often heard him mutter: "There goes the old shop again!" The money he earned so hardly went on little luxuries—the theatre, coins, Italian lessons. He wanted to read Froissart and Brantôme and *Gil Blas* in the originals, *Don Quixote*, the *Guerras Civiles de Granada*, and the works of Dante and Tasso. At Greek he had been a total failure but he acquired a reading facility in French, Italian and Spanish. (His son-in-law only once witnessed him throwing his heart over and addressing a Monsieur in his native tongue. It was when some of the courtiers of the exiled Charles X were dining at Abbotsford. One of his admiring guests said that Sir Walter spoke the French of Joinville—that is of the Crusades of St Louis and the early fourteenth century.)

The money he spent on literature included a great many ephemerae dear to a young fellow with a quiet sense of humour—chapbooks. Eventually his library contained over two thousand items. He said he had bought a hundred and fourteen before he was ten. Their very titles were enjoyable, *The Whole Proceedings of Jockey and Maggy*, *The Buckingham Wonder*, *The Oxfordshire Tragedy*, *The Bride's Burial*, *A Dreadful Warning to Cruel Mothers*, *Captain O'Blunder's Observations on the Bloody War in America*. Not all were lurid or comical. He had some serious literary chapbooks: *Christ's Kirk on the Green* written by King James I, Allan Ramsay's *Gentle Shepherd*, Goldsmith's *Deserted Village*.[7]

It would appear that he got his first sight of the Highlands in the way of business and before he was sixteen. It was desirable that his father's clients should get to know him. (The vista from the Wicks of Baiglie went straight into *The Fair Maid of Perth*.) The gracious city, key to the Highlands, set amongst shining waters and green meadows and backed by blue hills, enchanted him. Two of his father's Jacobite clients were Alexander Stewart of Invernahyle and Duncan Stewart of Ardsheal and Appin. He was in charge of an eviction order against some Maclaren tenants of the second Stewart, and rode with an escort of six men from a Highland regiment quartered at Stirling, under a sergeant who reminded him of Sergeant Kite in Farquhar's *Recruiting Officer*, and had anecdotes of Rob Roy. It was something of an anticlimax to discover at Invernenty that the offending Maclarens had packed up and gone off, for America it was said. He wished them well. He had seen Loch Katrine. His son-in-law treasured an incident in Scott's description of his first Highland visit. It was either to the fastness of a Stewart or a Campbell.

> On reaching the brow of a bleak eminence overhanging the primitive tower and its tiny patch of cultivated ground, he found his host and three sons, and perhaps half-a-dozen attendant gillies all stretched half asleep in their tartans upon the heath, with guns and dogs and a profusion of game about them; while in the courtyard, far below, appeared a company of women, actively engaged in loading a cart with manure.

He was a little surprised that these useful females turned out to be the laird's lady and three of her daughters. When they reappeared from their "bowers" no trace remained of their morning's occupation except complexions glowing with a radiant freshness. The girls were not ill-informed and extremely agreeable. At dinner a gigantic haggis was borne into the hall in a wicker basket by two half-naked Celts, followed by a piper, and the evening ended with song and dance.

He was struck down by serious illness in the second year of his apprenticeship. His Rutherford grandfather had gone to his reward, but there was a stepbrother of Mrs Scott who was going to become President of the Royal College of Physicians of Edinburgh. Dr Daniel Rutherford pronounced Walter's recovery from a haemorrhage in his lower bowels as little short of miraculous, and judging by the patient's account of his treatment it seems indeed to have been so. In raw spring weather he was confined to bed with a single blanket; he was bled and blistered till he had scarcely a pulse left. He was not allowed to talk and he was restricted to a vegetarian diet. His only refuge was in reading, especially military history. He laid out little collections of shells and seeds and pebbles to represent contending armies. By an arrangement of mirrors he was able to watch the drilling of Edinburgh's modern troops in the Meadows Walks. John Irving was apprenticed to another firm, so he had not been seeing him quite so often, but now John came regularly to his bedside, and relieving Mrs Scott and the melancholy Anne, played chess interminably with him. A succession of crones were left within call to descend upon him with maledictions if he opened his mouth. He was recorded as a most amiable patient. He read Orme's *Indostan* and early monkish chroniclers in Latin, and Vertot's *Knights of Malta* and *Le Grand Cyrus*, "poetry and voyages and travels and fairy-tales, eastern stories". He scratched flowers on paper. Spending his copying money on two drawing masters had been a failure, but he never truly knew that he could not draw until he sat next to Will Clerk of Eldin at work. All of that family had it in their bones, and for good measure Will's mother was a sister of the Adam brothers—architects. The best that Scott ever achieved was a sketch of Hermitage Castle, a gaunt Liddesdale keep haunted by memories of Mary, Queen of Scots and Bothwell. He stood up to his middle in snow setting down that impression. And afterwards, under verbal instruction, Will Clerk put it into a regular form, and then Hugh ("Grecian") Williams, who was a professional, produced a revision which was engraved for the frontispiece of the first volume of *Minstrelsy of the Scottish Border* by Walter Scott, received with acclaim when he was thirty.

IV

Gradually he climbed back to health. As soon as possible he was sent down to Kelso, but this time to his uncle's "neat villa". Captain Scott had retired and was comfortably settled with all his nautical paraphernalia about him and niece Barbara Scott to look after him. "Rosebank", originally "Nicholstownfield", had been built by Dr Jackson of Kelso. His daughter, Dorothea, sold it to Captain Scott in 1788, and the Captain added some adjacent fields. It was the last house on the road out of Kelso to Berwick on Tweed and had a dazzling view of the Tweed at the bottom of a steeply sloping garden.[8] It was so far out that Walter told friends to send letters to his aunt's house, "Garden", where he went almost daily. He was in his eighteenth year, and an interesting-looking youth. He fell in love.[9]

Dear Jessie,

I hope you will pardon me thus addressing you, after so short an acquaintance, but in truth I cannot commence writing to you in any other way. I do regard you as my dear Jessie, and if you will only allow me that favour be assured you shall have no cause to regret having done so. I cannot sufficiently express the impression your lovely features have made on my heart, but I am certain it is one that can never be effaced. Your gentleness, your goodness, your kindness have filled me with the sweetest feelings I have ever known. Might I believe I am not indifferent to you I should enjoy a comfort nothing else could give. I scribbled the enclosed lines, which, though I am well aware they are quite unworthy of their subject, I hope will not be unfavourably received. They at least have one recommendation—the sentiments they contain are as sincere as any that ever influenced a human bosom. If you are not offended at my boldness I hope to see you tomorrow morning. Sweet dreams attend you!

Allow me to write myself
Your obedient admirer
WALTER SCOTT.

To Jessie

Lassie can ye love me weel?
    Ask your heart, and answer true,
Doth that gentle bosom feel
    Love for one that loveth you?

Say not out of mere compassion
    Say not out of idle sport
Ruth and folly lead a fashion
    Only for the foolish sort.

Lassie gin ye'el love me weel,
   Weel I'll love ye in return,
Whilst the salmon fills the creel,
   Whils't the flower grows by the burn.

Teviot and Tweed ne'er change their places,
   Nor Heav'n its stars on earth may rain,
But e'er I slight thy winning graces,
   Such must be and be again.

                                        W.S.

Jessie, according to the anonymous biographer of Scott who never succeeded in interesting a publisher, was the daughter of a small tradesman in Kelso and a year or two his junior. They made the discovery that they were both unhappy at home. Jessie's father was "an austere Presbyterian, who should he become aware of the young lawyer's intimacy with his daughter would have put an immediate stop to it. Walter Scott was soon taught the value of secrecy. Their meetings were not the less relished for being clandestine." It was awkward when Walter had to return to Edinburgh at a day's notice, without being able to say his goodbye in person. However, after a few months he was back again, but then she was "on a visit to a relative". He rained letters and poems upon her. "To the Flower of Kelso", "To the Pride of Teviotdale". They were dated dramatically "Tuesday midnight" and "Sunday morning, one o'clock". Some of their opening lines were charming— "When first I met thine eyes of blue", "Sometimes I lived, as you might see." He passed from being "Ever your devoted and attached WALTER" to "YOUR True WALTER". She told him she liked poetry.

Of Scottish songs you are sufficiently familiar—you would not deserve to be considered a Scottish lassie were you ignorant of them —but of ancient English ballads it is very possible you may not have heard once. Of ballads and romances I think I have held a longer acquaintance than have I with any other kind of learning, and lately I have managed to get hold of more than one collection of old songs native on the other side of the Border.

He told her he was destroying all her notes, "though very unwillingly", and he hoped she had already, or would, follow his example. (He was mistaken.) With so many interruptions it was perhaps not surprising that the affair went on for "three or four years at least". Then there came a day when he returned to Kelso to find that she had been called away to attend a sick aunt, and apparently so suddenly that she had not been able to warn him. Several months of silence passed. Perhaps it was all for the best; but he missed her. On his next Kelso visit he discovered that she had been in Edinburgh all the time and was likely to stay there. But he still knew not where. He met her as he came down the common stair of a house where he had been calling upon a friend. Her aunt occupied the flat above. He took up the affair again and it seemed with redoubled vigour; but the charm was gone. They were both older. And from being a romance it was unquestionably becoming an *opera bouffe*. For Jessie had to put him in what they called "a narrow closet" while she tended her mercifully deaf aunt; but it must surely have been quite a large larder though he complained he "dare na stir a leg".

> Here's haddocks dry and barley meal
> And Marmalade and jam,
> And high suspended by a hook,
> Above me hangs a ham.

Jessie hit upon the happy thought of supplying him with writing materials, and he produced *The Prisoner's Complaint*, "Come Jessie, I impatient grow" and *Law versus Love*, "Away with parchments, warrants, bills . . ." She hardly knew what to make of him. "He appeared to possess the proper ardour of a lover, yet there was so much drollery mixed up with his devotion, that it was difficult to say whether he was jesting or loving." He began to come less frequently and when he did he was met by reproaches. "The freedom of her language" after their final quarrel opened his eyes. Jessie believed that she had a rival and she was, in a sense, right, but treading on holy ground. He tried more than once to get his poems back, but failed. Jessie's aunt died leaving her a small property, and she married a medical student, with whom she went to London, and became the mother of a thriving family. But she regarded Walter's conduct "with a resentment that never subsided".

V

There were many doubts as to which of the characters in the Waverley novels were drawn from various members of the author's circle, but no one ever questioned that the elder Fairford in *Redgauntlet* was drawn from his father, and that there were decided likenesses in the elder Osbaldistone in *Rob Roy*. Nor was there ever much question that the younger Fairford was the younger Walter. But as to his brother-in-arms, Darsie Latimer, although Will Clerk carried off the palm, there were two other candidates.

Mr Saunders Fairford, as he was usually called, was a man of business of the old school, moderate in his charges, economical and even niggardly in his expenditure, strictly honest in conducting his own affairs and those of his clients, but taught by long experience to be wary and suspicious in observing the motions of others. Punctual as the clock of Saint Giles told nine, the neat dapper form of the little hale old gentleman was seen at the threshold of the Court hall, or at farthest at the head of the Back Stairs, trimly dressed in a complete suit of snuff-coloured brown, with stockings of silk or woollen as suited the weather; a bobwig, and a small cocked hat, shoes as black as Warren would have blacked them; silver shoe-buckles and a gold stock-buckle. A nosegay in summer, and a sprig of holly in winter, completed his well-known dress and appearance. His manners corresponded with his attire, for they were scrupulously civil and not a little formal. . . . Every profession has its peculiar honours and Mr Fairford's mind was constructed upon so limited and exclusive a plan that he valued nothing save the objects of ambition which his own presented. He would have shuddered at Alan's acquiring the renown of a hero, and laughed with scorn at the equally barren laurels of literature. It was by the path of the law alone that he was desirous to see him rise to eminence; and the probabilities of success or disappointment were the thoughts of his father by day, and his dream by night.

It was typical of Walter Scott, senior, that when somebody praised the soup he at once diluted his portion with water, and that when presented by his son with his Scots Law class notes, neatly copied and bound, he commented without intending the least irony that they would make very pleasant reading for his leisure hours.

The Sabbath at 25 George Square was dark indeed. It opened with the usual daily family prayers; it passed on through two services to catechising after supper on the sermons enjoyed. The house on which the young Walter came to look as almost a prison had been thought at the time of its erection to be elegant. Each residence was "finished within itself" or "self-contained"—no common stair. It was on the west side of the square, an austere, grey stone house with sets of three long sash windows on each floor, except the ground floor where the façade was relieved by a door flanked by two columns. The building of the south side of the square had begun in 1766, and by 1785 all four rows were complete. It was near enough for those with business in the Old Town, but a fair step when Princes Street and the squares behind that district began to receive fashionable inhabitants. It was, in fact, a comfortable mid-Georgian family house of the type being imposed in large numbers on the landscape of Great Britain regardless of whether they were to be set in towns or country villages. Walter Scott, junior, never cared for them. He saw them as unimaginative.[10]

Robert had long departed for the Navy (after being at a superior school, Closeburn, near Dumfries), and John for a Highland regiment. Walter was the eldest son at home and as the one destined for the law he received unremitting attention from his careful parent. He was, at some date after his severest illness, exposed to the Earth-Bath treatment of Dr Graham. This fellow was a showman who used to attend Greyfriars Church dressed in white and silver, with a *chapeau bras*, his hair marvellously arranged in a double *toupée*. He had a row with the magistrates when he came to Edinburgh, as they refused to allow him to lecture. He set up his Temple of Health, as in London (where the future Emma, Lady Hamilton, had been employed as an attendant). He had a fatal accident on the premises, and they were closed. Scott did not benefit from his treatment. Lockhart believed that the flamboyant Dr James Graham actually died of starvation. His crystal chandeliers went for a song on stalls on the South Bridge.

Walter Scott, law-student and Writer's Apprentice, was promoted to what he described as a spacious parlour, but his friend Francis Jeffrey (two years younger and with Whig leanings) wrote of "a small den, on the sunk floor of his father's house". Walter delighted in it, and it was soon filled with association objects—a painted cabinet of Scottish and Roman coins, a claymore and Lochaber axe, given him by old Invernahyle, a collection of pieces of wood, boughs from Crookston Castle, Falkland Palace, Holyrood House, etc., from which he was going, sometime, to have a set of chessmen fashioned. There was a little print of Prince Charlie and below it, hooked on the wall, "Broughton's Saucer". Mrs Scott, the best of wives and most discreet of women, was puzzled one autumn by a client who always came to see her husband after dark in a sedan chair, and muffled up in a mantle. At last curiosity triumphed and she ventured in with a salver, observing that the gentlemen had sat so long they would be the better of a dish of tea. The stranger, a person of distinguished appearance richly dressed, bowed and accepted a cup; her husband refused coldly, and the moment his guest had withdrawn threw up the window and cast out the valuable porcelain to perish on the pavement. "Neither lip of me nor mine comes after Mr Murray of Broughton."[11] His nocturnal caller was the secretary of Prince Charles, who had borne fatal evidence against his master's faithful followers and so saved his own life and fortune. Walter Scott, senior, had a surprising strain of the dramatic in him. His son thought that if he had not stuck to being a Writer he might have done well as a Special Pleader. Although so hard on sin, he had allowed his children to perform private theatricals in which Walter was Manager and, with the realism of youth, had cheerfully adopted the part of Richard III because if he had not the hump at any rate he could limp.

The news that Burns was expected in town aroused longings in his breast. One of his father's clerks, Thomas Grierson, said he knew Burns and thought he could manage a supper, but that came to nothing. In the end it was young Adam Ferguson whom he had known at the High School who invited him to his home, Sciennes Hill House, known as Kamtschatka because it was so far out of Edinburgh and inhabited by an owner who wore furred garments. Professor Adam Ferguson was expecting quite a large gathering. The venerable author of *Douglas* whom Walter had known at Bath was to be there, and Professors Joseph Black, James Hutton and Dugald Stewart—several ladies. The boy had his great moment. The poet paused and was moved to tears as he read the six lines of verse below a popular engraving of an incident of the war in Canada, a soldier lying dead in the snow with his dog sitting in misery on one side, and on the other his widow with a child in her arms. Burns asked who was the author of the verse. It was John Langhorne, quite unmemorable, nobody knew. "I whispered my information to a friend present, who mentioned it to Burns who rewarded me with a look and a word."[12]

Three years of toil in "the dry and barren wilderness of forms and conveyances" passed heavily. He generally had no transport except Shanks's pony, and very few companions with whom he could discuss his darling topics of high romance and antiquity, and always poetry. In 1787 he found himself, unexpectedly, the second surviving son. Robert, the sailor, had mistakenly concluded that after the Peace of Versailles there would be no promotion without "interest" in the Royal Service. He had exchanged into that of the East India Company and died at sea "a victim of the climate", aged twenty-three. It was borne in upon Walter that the company in his father's office was narrowing. He would not cease to be an apprentice until the spring of 1791. Long before that, in 1789 or 1790, he plucked up courage to tell his father that he did not want to go into partnership with him. "The Bar, though I was conscious of my deficiencies as a public speaker, was the line of ambition and liberty." Mr Scott was more than kind. He was all for a son with a rise in him. Tom, who was a good sharp lad, should go into the business—and incidentally although it was much diminished, would have an immediate prospect of a handsome independence.

So Walter set off to study Roman or Civil Law and secondly the Municipal Laws of Scotland. Will Clerk and he attended the same Scots Law lectures. They began by planning that they would come to each other's home every morning before seven for question and answer, but it soon ended in Walter walking the two miles between George Square and the west end of Princes Street every weekday for two summers. Will had style. He was fascinatingly talented and lazy. He had an uninhibited brother in the Navy, James, who took them out in a lugger (and said "the lamiter" was the first to begin a fight and the last to end it). He had an elder brother, John, who was already an advocate, and a cousin who had an ancestral home of surpassing beauty at Penicuik. Indeed, Will seemed to have well-placed relatives all over Scotland. Professor Robert Dick had a limited audience for his lectures, and the young men made heavy weather of Civil Law under his tuition. But Scots Law, surprisingly, was interesting in places. There were bits of history in it, and David Hume, nephew of the historian, was vigorous and knowledgeable. Walter's circle widened. He wrote down in his early autobiography "the persons with whom I chiefly lived at this period of my youth". Will Clerk and his cousin John Irving came first, and then there was James Edmondstone of Newton, a nephew of Sir Ralph Abercromby, and his cousin George, a son of the immortal General, and Professor Ferguson's son, Adam, and Thomas Douglas, later Earl of Selkirk, and David Boyle, later Lord Justice-Clerk. Lockhart added three more, George Cranstoun, who became Lord Corehouse, and two Murrays, cousins, Patrick of Simprim and Sir Patrick of Ochtertyre. Walter had now, allowing for the alterations brought by age, attained the appearance which was to become famous. The future Duchess of Sutherland, a recently married *belle*, well remembered him, quite young, in the Assembly Rooms. He had been "a comely creature". His shock of flaxen hair was now a light brown, and was to become white rather early. His features were somewhat heavy and homely, but when invaded by a smile, charming. He never forgot his pride, as "a great lubberly boy", at being invited to escort Lady Balcarres to her box at the theatre. His father's manners had been good, but formal; his mother's had avowedly been formed by a high priestess of etiquette.

He himself, when they were both middle-aged, told a devoted correspondent, "I am naturally rather shy, though bronzed over by the practice of the law, and a good deal of commerce with the world." His manners were easy and simple. "He greeted every man as a brother." When he had become a lion, and as a host in his own beloved house, the whole company lit up when he entered. Lockhart heard that he had been very attractive as a youth. He had a fresh, brilliant complexion, his eyes were clear, open and well set, he had particularly even and excellent teeth

> while the noble expanse and elevation of the brow gave to the whole aspect a dignity far above the charm of mere features. His smile was always delightful . . . His figure, except for the blemish in one limb, must in those days have been eminently handsome, tall, much above the usual standard, it was cast in the very mould of a young Hercules; the head set on with singular grace, the throat and chest after the truest model of the antique, the hands delicately finished; the whole outline that of extraordinary vigour . . . I have heard him, in this part of his life, say with an arch simplicity of look and tone which those who were familiar with him can fill in for themselves—"It was a proud night with me when I first found that a pretty young woman could think it worth her while to sit and talk with me, hour after hour, in a corner of the ball-room while all the world were capering in our view."

There is no firm evidence that he ever danced, though the family had dancing lessons. It would be necessary that a young man who meant to make his way in the world should know how to come into and leave company, make his bow, hand a lady to her chair; but his good mother might have looked after all that. He had women friends as well as men, of all ages. There were two particular old dames close by, Mrs Alison Cockburn, and Mrs Anne Murray Keith who lived in amity with her "chum" and cousin, old Lady Balcarres, in a flat and sunk storey actually in George Square. He had younger women friends too, sisters of George Cranstoun and Will Erskine. Both the Cranstouns were good-looking, but had Roman noses. Little Mary Anne Erskine, who like Jane Anne Cranstoun kept house for a bachelor brother, was also like a sister to Walter Scott. He said himself that the first woman of real fashion that took him up was the beautiful bride of his kinsman Scott of Harden, later Lord Polworth, "a daughter of Count Brühl, the famous chess-player half-sister to the Wyndhams". She kindly "set him right as to a thousand little trifles". He was five and twenty by the time she got to work, but he had already known her mother-in-law, Lady Diana Scott, daughter of the last Lord Marchmont, who could tell him tales of the brightest literary ornaments of the reign of Queen Anne.

It is difficult to decide how much he walked. He stated in his auto-biographical fragment that it was often twenty to thirty miles a day. They might start at 5 a.m. and get in at 8 p.m. He once breakfasted at Prestonpans, spent the forenoon at the ruins of Seton, and walked over the battlefield before walking home. He remembered going on a fishing ex-pedition with George Abercromby and Will Clerk to Howgate and seeing over Penicuik House where he found the host and hostess so kind that he forgot home for two or three days. It was his first Palladian Scottish country house and for three generations the Clerks of Penicuik had collected pictures and antiquities. He arrived with certainly no luggage or change of clothes and probably nothing in his purse.

There was an occasion when his mother began to worry, for Walter was a good brother and often took Tom, three years younger, along with him. "My dear Annie," said Walter Scott, senior, "Tom is with Walter this time; and have you not yet perceived that wherever Walter goes he is pretty sure to find his bread buttered on both sides?" John Irving said that in their early University days they visited all the old castles available within eight or ten miles of Edinburgh. Roslin was a place of which Scott was specially fond. "We frequently walked there before breakfast; after breakfasting there, we walked all down the river-side to Lasswade—and thence home to town before dinner. He used generally to rest one hand upon my shoulder when we walked together, and leaned with the other on a stout stick." Will Clerk rallied him on the shabbiness of his corduroy breeches, much glazed by the rubbing of his staff. He had once defended himself with it for an hour by the Tron clock against an assault by three ruffians. He was proud of his strength: "When actually at the oar no man could pull it harder than I." He could, before breakfast, lift a smith's anvil by the horn. He believed it said somewhere in the *Odyssey* that morning was the time.

The friends with whom he went for his tramps, though all of good family and connections, were few of them at all well off. Will Clerk was the son of a seventh son of a baronet; Cranstoun's father had been the son of a peer, but again a seventh son; Erskine, poorest of the lot, was son of a non-juring minister. They only once, as far as he could remember, got down to hips and haws and spring water. And as they had asked for a drink at a farmhouse they got beautiful milk. In Edinburgh society it was unusual to be rich, and tales of ostentatious London entertainments roused more mirth than envy. In London, society was very mixed and money mattered more.

Walter Scott and Will Clerk passed their Civil Law Trials on June 30th, 1791, and on July 6th, 1792, their Scots Law Trials. Five days later, on July 11th, they both assumed the gown, "with all its duties and honours".

> My progress in life during these two or three years had been gradually enlarging my acquaintance, and facilitating my entrance into good company. My father and mother, already advanced in life, saw little society at home except that of near relations, or upon particular occasions, so I was left to form connexions in a great measure for myself. It is not difficult for a youth with a real desire to please and be pleased, to make his way into good society in Edinburgh—or indeed anywhere—and my family connexions, if they did not greatly further, had nothing to embarrass my progress. I was a gentleman, and so welcome anywhere, if so be I could behave myself, as Tony Lumpkin says, "in a concatenation accordingly . . ."

With these words the fragment of Scott's autobiography breaks off. The anchor is up. The biographer is left to the evidence of the letters, the poems and novels, of Lockhart and other outside sources until the Journal opens thirty-three years later.

Lockhart believed that, like Alan Fairford, Walter Scott, advocate, stood his friends and family "a bit chack of dinner" on the occasion of July 11th, and that the old gentleman his father was, like old Fairford, very joyous. It was suspected that it was by his canny direction that the young man dedicated his obligatory thesis "On the Title of the Pandects Concerning the disposal of the dead bodies of Criminals" to the most influential of their legal neighbours in George Square, Lord Braxfield, a very coarse old dog, but President of the Supreme Criminal Court of Scotland. After the ceremony of their putting on the gown, the two new barristers mingled for a time with their companions in the Outer Court. Then Scott said to Clerk, mimicking the air and tone of a Highland lass waiting at the Cross to be hired for farm labour, "We've stood here an hour by the Tron hinny, and de'il an ane has speered our price." A friendly solicitor gave Walter a guinea fee before the Court rose. They walked down the High Street together, and Walter said, "This is a sort of a wedding-day for me, Willie; I think I must go in and buy me a new nightcap."[13]

NOTES

1. Journal, II, 325.
2. Centenary Memorial, 8–13.
3. From a contribution by Scott to *The Keepsake*, 1828: "My Aunt Margaret's Mirror". "My Aunt Margaret" was not a fictional character; she was Miss Margaret Swinton, an aunt of Scott's mother, and a great favourite with her young relatives. She was murdered by a supposedly devoted maid, when Scott was nine years old and the horrible incident made a great impression on him.
4. These two boys probably did not go to the High School. A composite letter home from them is headed "W— Hall". Wallace Hall, Closeburn, was an establishment for youths going into the services. (Dr Corson, *Weekend Scotsman*, 26.10.70.)
5. There is a plan of "Mr Walter Scott's Garden and Park at Kelso surveyed February 1783", facing page 155 in James Fleming Leishman's *Linton Leaves* (Edinburgh, 1937). The caption beneath the illustration mistakenly describes the property as "Plan of Sir Walter Scott's Garden at 'Rosebank', Kelso".
6. Classes attended by Sir Walter Scott at Edinburgh University:
   1783–84. Latin. Professor John Hill
   Greek (Classus tyronum). Professor Andrew Dalzel
   1784–85. Greek (Classis provectiorum). Professor Andrew Dalzel
   1785–86. Logic (Classis junior and also Classis provectiorum). Professor John Bruce
   1789–90. Moral Philosophy. Professor Dugald Stewart
   1790–91. Scots Law. Professor David Hume
   1791–92. Scots Law. Professor David Hume
   Civil Law. Professor Robert Dick.
7. The collection of chapbooks has been catalogued by Dr James Corson, Honorary Librarian at Abbotsford.
8. MS. possessed by Mr F. Douglas-Whyte of Rosebank, Kelso.
9. In 1932 *New Love Poems of Sir Walter Scott*, edited by Davidson Cook, F.S.A., were published separately and also in the Centenary Edition of *The Letters of Sir Walter Scott*. The letters and poems were noticed by Mr Cook in the Foster Collection in the Victoria and Albert Museum and formed a chapter in an undistinguished anonymous biography of two volumes, never published. Mr Cook failed to trace either the surname or identity of the biographer.
10. *The Book of the old Edinburgh Club*, vol. 26. *George Square*, ed. M. Tait & W. Forbes Gray (1948). 25 George Square is now occupied by the Catholic Students' Union.
11. Lockhart, I, 153.
12. Ibid., 115–17.
13. Ibid., 159.

III

Greenmantle

1790–1797

———

I

HE WAS IN LOVE AGAIN, AND HAD PROBABLY BEEN SO FOR TWO YEARS.
That was the date at which his friends began to notice that he had become
quite attentive to his dress. This time it was serious. According to one of
his own veiled allusions to the affair he had three years of dreaming and
two years of wakening. Lockhart was so discreet about Lady Scott's
predecessor that he never mentioned her name until 1848 when he added
a note to the first volume of his 1837 edition of the Life; and his whole
account of the affair, though as brief as possible, bristles with inaccuracies.[1]
He alludes to her as Miss Margaret Stuart, but her father did not take
that surname until a year after her marriage. She was Williamina Belsches,
and in 1790 she was barely fifteen. Scott was nineteen. When Sophia
Lockhart tackled Will Clerk, he told her by letter in 1835:

> Your father's *penchant* for the lady began I think about in the year
> 1790 (her mother Lady Jane was an acquaintance of his mother,
> which led to a visiting acquaintance). It was a prodigious secret at
> first which I discovered by observing that he wore a sort of medallion
> in the style of Tassie's heads about his neck which had been made for
> him by a Mons. Guidbert, a French tutor; and shortly afterwards he
> told me all about it. He certainly was very much attached to her.

Will Erskine, asked by Lockhart, while Scott was still alive, whether there had been any poems said disappointingly, "Oh! yes he made many little stanzas about the lady and he sometimes showed them to Cranstoun, Clerk and myself—but we really thought them in general very poor." He took down a volume of the *English Minstrelsy* and pointed out three verses, *On a Violet*, done just after the conclusion of the business, and afterwards included in Scott's collected works. The second and much longer poem, a manuscript in Scott's own hand, *To Time—by a Lady*, had initials on the back which seemed to show "that the authoress was no other than the object of his first passion". They appeared later, however, to have been merely copies of great favourites of hers—"the production of Mrs Hunter of Norwich, wife of the famous surgeon".[2]

Lockhart's account of the beginning of the romance was attractive. A shower had come on just as the congregation was dispersing in Greyfriar's churchyard after a Sunday morning service. Scott offered his umbrella to a young lady and escorted her to her home which proved to be quite near his own, in Nicolson Square. To return from church together "Mrs Scott being of the party" became a custom before they met in society. It then appeared that the mothers "had been companions in their youth". This is quite wrong. Lady Jane Belsches was only thirty-five, twenty years younger than Scott's mother, and in fact there was a relationship on her side of the family—Swinton. Scott could have claimed to be third cousin of Sir John Belsches. The first mention of the young lady as Greenmantle came in a letter to Scott from a friend of those days with whom later he almost lost touch, Charles Kerr of Abbotrule. "From the description of the blooming fair as she appeared when she lowered her *manteau vert*, I am hopeful you have not dropped the acquaintance. At least I am certain that some of our more rakish friends would have been glad of such an intro-duction." Greenmantle was the heroine, years later, of *Redgauntlet*, so many people believed the portrait was of Williamina Belsches. She was also identified as Matilda in *Rokeby*, a graceful ductile beauty with curling chestnut hair and hazel eyes. She was Margaret in *The Lay of the Last Minstrel*, a blue-eyed blonde. Di Vernon in *Rob Roy* and Catherine Seyton in *The Abbot* were amongst other suggestions.

Obviously, to this kind of fascinating detective work there could be no end, but Scott himself told Miss Edgeworth in a letter dated 1818 that Matilda "was attempted from the existing person of a lady who is no more". In *Redgauntlet* Darsie Latimer writes to Alan Fairford that he believes "a deep consuming passion once kindled in a breast so steady as yours would never be extinguished but with life." Lockhart was sure that his secret worship of his *princesse lointaine* was invaluable to Scott at a critical period of his early manhood, when he was by no means of a cold disposition.

> His friends, I have heard more than one of them confess, used often to rally him on the coldness of his nature. By degrees they discovered that he had, from almost the dawn of the passions, cherished a secret attachment . . . He had an instinctive delicacy about him which made him recoil with utter disgust from low and vulgar debaucheries.

Every year he seemed to arrive for his two months at Rosebank in time for the Lammas floods. He constructed a shelter in a large tree at the bottom of the garden which spread its branches horizontally over the river, and used to sit there watching the Tweed in flood roaring like thunder. He had two friends on the opposite bank, brothers of the owner, Mr Walker of Wooden, both officers and the possessors of a fine pair of greyhounds. Already he was a dog-lover. He made an attempt to import a canine companion to Rosebank. "If you continue to want a mastiff, I think I can procure you one of a good breed, and send him by carrier." He used to communicate by signals across the river to "the lobsters" as he called his red-coated friends, to plan the day's outings. They pursued hares, waded through the mosses after duck, and tried to keep down the heron, gulls, and cormorants. His father had suggested that he should attend the circuit at Jedburgh to make his bow to the Lord Justice Clerk, so he had done that, "and might have had employment, but durst not venture". "I am lounging about the country here, to speak sincerely, as idle as the day is long." Towards the end of September 1792 he went for an expedition through Hexham "which would have delighted the very cockles of your heart". He had seen an incredible number of Roman inscriptions built into barns, gate-posts, etc. They had all been dug up from the neighbouring Roman wall. Since last year, when he had gone with his old naval uncle, he had ridden on his fishing expeditions into Northumberland, "man Thomas behind with a portmanteau, and two fishing-rods fastened across his back much in the style of St Andrew's Cross". He had explored Flodden Field. This year he had not been so lucky. His Galloway had "thought proper (N.B. without a rider) to leap over a gate" and was consequently lame for the present. As he had made a similar *faux pas* in Northumberland, that time with his owner on his back and nearly drowned him, he would have to be replaced. So on a Sunday morning Walter had nothing to do but write so long a letter that his friend would have trouble to get through it. Uncle was engaged reading the naval tactics of Will's father, an antiquarian so erudite that his Essay on dividing the Line in sea-fights was believed to have inspired Admiral Rodney in Dominica. Dates did not support this, but a controversy had followed delightful to retired characters such as Captain Robert Scott of Rosebank, and it was afterwards very generally held that Clerk's theories had contributed much to England's successes at sea during the French Revolution.

Roman remains were a family hobby with the Clerks. There was a Roman camp on one of old Sir John's properties in Dumfriesshire, and his grandson's accounts of his enthusiastic discovery of a *praetorium* which an employee resignedly mentioned *sotto voce* he had himself dug, was treasured by Scott to attach to the character of Oldbuck in *The Antiquary*. Will Clerk's much older brother, John, took an impish pleasure in burying medals, and fashioning mutilated heads for the laird to discover and put in his museum. One was so remarkable that the Earl of Buchan carried it off to present to the Scottish Society of Antiquaries. The companions of his apprentice days in his father's office accused Walter Scott of deserting them "for the sake of Clerk and some more of those dons who look down on the like of us". He told them that Will Clerk was worth all of them put together. Actually Clerk was not going to come to much. He was too lazy. He was going to become a charming old bachelor who gave excellent little dinner-parties, and was the best of company, tenderly looked after by a spinster sister. He was not as literary as Erskine, he was not as robustly patriotic or as observant of nature or as keen a sportsman as James Skene of Rubislaw, who was yet to come; but he was the confidant of Walter Scott's romantic yearnings in the autumn of the year when they had both qualified. Scott drew towards the close of his Sunday morning screed of September 30th with the meaning phrase "I have no prospect of seeing my *chère adorable* till winter, if then." Sir John Belsches had an Edinburgh house but his lady and daughter spent the summer in their estate in Kincardineshire.

Within a few days of Scott writing that if his pony did not soon recover he was thinking of going into town, a new interest which was to enliven his holidays for the next seven years, and indeed determine his profession, presented itself. A racketty young friend, Charles Kerr of Abbotrule, introduced him to his kinsman the Sheriff-Substitute of Roxburghshire. Robert Shortreed "just your man" had many connections in the unexplored and remote passes of Liddesdale. With this local worthy as his guide, Scott "explored every rivulet to its source, every ruined *peel* from

Williamina Belsches
Medallion by an unknown artist.
Lent to the Scottish National Portrait Galley, 1945, by Miss Adelaide Traill, her
great-granddaughter.

Williamina Belsches Stuart, Lady Forbes
By Cosway.
With an inscription on the back by her mother, Lady Jane Stuart
Even Cosway's flattering pencil cannot grace
    That dear, that charming form, that matchless face.
Nature alone can justice do to these
    Tho' Cosway's pencil never fails to please.
By permission of Mrs Somervell, from the collection at Fettercairn House.

foundation to battlement". The district was without wheeled traffic, inns, public houses or regular roads. They passed from the shepherd's hut to the minister's manse. On these annual rambles which he described as his raids into Liddesdale, Scott collected at least one ballad for his *Minstrelsy of the Scottish Border*. "He was *makin' himsell* a' the time," explained his mentor, "but he didna ken maybe what he was about till years had passed. At first he thought o' little, I daresay, but the queerness and the fun." Shortreed believed that an upland sheep-farmer, Willie Elliot of Millburnholm, was the original of Dandie Dinmont, but there was a later candidate, Jemmie Davidson of Hindlee, who was known as Dandie to his dying day. Scott had heard of him but had never met him when he wrote *Guy Mannering*. He had celebrated terriers all called Mustard or Pepper according to their colours, but with no other distinction except "old", "young" and "little".[3]

Dr Elliot at Cleughead, where Shortreed and Scott slept (in one bed, which was the usual hospitality offered on their trips), was a goldmine. He had already a large manuscript collection of the ballads after which Scott had been questing, and he willingly promised to supply more. Of course the young intending author had to sing for his supper; or rather he had difficulty in evading more than his capacity of the whisky-punch manufactured in a small milk-churn at such ports of call as that of Auld Thomas o'Twizzlehope, famous also for his skill on the Border pipe. There was an unforgettably dramatic moment when on a Saturday night, while a young divinity student was reading aloud to the company from the Guid Book, the host started up from his knees shouting, "My —, here's the keg at last!" A supply of *run* brandy from a smuggler's haunt on the Solway Firth was carried in by two staggering herdsmen. The carouse was still in progress at daylight. Shortreed said that the fund of humour and drollery possessed by the young advocate was unbelievable. Wherever they stopped he just suited himself to the company—"daft or serious, sober or drunk (this however in our wildest rambles was but rare), drunk or sober, he was aye the gentleman".

Scott was notably temperate after his marriage, and repeatedly warned his sons against a fatal habit. He did not deny that in his early twenties when he was a member of clubs and societies at some of which drinking was hard, he had done his best to damage a fine constitution. He attributed the digestive disorders of his middle-age to this pernicious indulgence. He was one of the co-founders of the Literary Society at which he was known as "Duns Scotus" and "Colonel Grog" (an allusion to his grogram breeches, not to liquor). Will Clerk was "the Baronet", not because of his

grandfather but from Sir John Brute in Vanburgh's *Provok'd Wife*. The most
far-fetched nickname was that of tall Adam Ferguson who was "Linton"
because on one of their expeditions a Newhaven fisherman in a neighbouring boat, mistaking him for a crony, had called out "Linton, ye
lang bitch, is that you?" John Irving was "Crab", Launce's dog in *The
Two Gentlemen of Verona*. The Club originated after a ride to Penicuik and
was purely social, as was the Teviotdale which Lockhart held was less
select: it was probably also the most bacchanalian. When Scott joined the
Speculative where he was successively librarian, secretary and treasurer,
it was nearly twenty-five years old and in rather a poor way. Ironically,
it was the only one to survive.

There were theories that its membership was dwindling because in
1789, the first of its eight lean years, political speculation was unrewarding
if not dangerous. The Bastille had fallen on July 14th. Scott did not, like
Wordsworth, hail the French Revolution with ecstasy. ("Bliss was it in
that dawn to be alive, But to be young was very heaven.") A good many
of his circle did, however. They nicknamed themselves "The Mountain"
after the Montagnards, the extreme Democratic party led at first by
Danton (and sitting on the highest benches of the old royal riding school
on the north side of the Tuileries gardens, now the hall of the National
Convention). Old Doctor Adam, the most amiable and artless of men,
came out with a full heart for Liberty, Equality and Fraternity. It was a
mistake. For soon the clouds thickened and the revolutionaries deposed
their king, who tried to escape with his whole family to his wife's native
Austria. They were brought back ignominiously and imprisoned. In
January 1793 Louis XVI went to the guillotine. An authoress well known
as "the Swan of Lichfield" wrote in the *Gentleman's Magazine*: "O, that
the French had possessed the wisdom of knowing Where to Stop." Great
Britain declared war and four battalions of the Guards embarked for
foreign service. Scott was one of the five young Tories of the Parliament
House bound over to keep the peace after a riot in the theatre when a
party of Irish medical students had called for revolutionary airs and tried
to shout down the National Anthem. He told Simprim that he had three
broken heads laid to his charge. A new interest appeared in his letters,
"The Edinburgh Volunteers". His brother Tom enlisted in the grenadier
company—men above six feet. In Edinburgh the Speculative Society
debated six times with varying result according to the date, "Was the
putting of Charles I to death justifiable?" Scott did not hold that he
made very valuable contributions at his clubs or societies. He was never a
good speaker unless on some subject by which he was much moved and he

thought his literary essays very poor. He sent one on the origin of the
feudal system to Rosebank. His friends thought he was invaluable as a
harmoniser. As far as his profession went, Will Clerk cautiously affirmed
that he gradually crept into a tolerable share of such business as might be
expected from his connection with his father's firm. He became very well
known, however, amongst the lawyers of the Outer House as a teller of
good stories. Clerk complained that Scott took his anecdotes and totally
transformed them. Scott said he merely put a cocked hat on their heads
and a cane in their hands to make them fit to come into company.

He collected some glorious anecdotes in the Jedburgh Assizes, if not
anything more. "You're a lucky scoundrel," he whispered to a successful
client, a veteran poacher. "I'm just of your mind," was the reply, "and
I'll be sending you a maukin [hare] the morn, man." A housebreaker in
whose flagrant case he failed, gave him two pieces of advice in lieu of a
fee: never to keep a large watch-dog chained up out of doors—useless—
a terrier within was the thing. New locks are less trouble than old heavy
ones.

Looking back on those years he thought he could not applaud the way in
which their days were spent.[4] "There was too much idleness and sometimes too much conviviality; but our hearts were warm, our minds
honourably bent on knowledge and literary distinction." Like his young
lawyers in *Redgauntlet* and *Chronicles of the Canongate* he "swept the boards
of the Parliament House with the skirts of my gown . . . got no fees,
laughed and made others laugh; drank claret at Bayle's Fortune's or
Walker's, and ate oysters in the Covenant Close."[4] On his desk lay the
latest novel snugly entrenched beneath Stair's *Institute* or an open volume
of *Decisions*; and his dressing-table was littered with old play-bills, letters
about a meeting of the Faculty, Rules of the Speculative, etc., "in fact all
the usual miscellanea of a young advocate's pocket which contains everything except briefs and bank-notes".

In the autumn of 1793, with Adam Ferguson, he made the first of his
tours in Perthshire and Forfar and went to Tullibody, Cambusmore,
Blairdrummond, Ochertyre, Craighall. He stayed mostly at country
houses belonging to other Montagnards or their relations, and made
expeditions to the local sights. Glamis was visited from Patrick Murray's
estate at Meigle, and there, as Lord Strathmore was not resident, and the
distance was rather long, he gladly accepted the offer of a bed from Peter
Proctor, seneschal. He was awed by the apartment in which King Duncan
was said to have been murdered. "I must own that when I heard door
after door shut, after my conductor had retired, I began to consider myself

as too far from the living and somewhere too near the dead." It really was worse than seeing Kemble as Macbeth.

He went from Meigle also up to Dunnottar, and it was in the churchyard there that he saw, for the first and only time, Peter Paterson, the old character who made it his business to clean and refurbish the headstones on the graves of the Covenanters. The young advocate expressed himself to the Rev. James Walker, Minister of Dunnottar, as much interested in explorations in the well of the castle, and in a vitrified fort, Lady Fenella's Castle. It was close to the home of his lady-love, Fettercairn. He cut her name in runic characters at the gate of the castle at St Andrews.

She passed from seventeen to eighteen, to nineteen. William Scott, afterwards Laird of Raeburn, but at present seeking a fortune in the East Indies, wrote to enquire how things were going. He replied dubiously, "The lady you allude to has been in the town all winter, and going a good deal into public, which has not in the least altered the sweetness of her manners. Matters, you see stand just as they did." But August 1795, after consulting with Clerk, he had decided to send her a declaration in form. Someone else might get her if he never spoke. It was not an easy letter to write. As far as birth went there was not much disparity, though her mother, as a daughter of the Earl of Leven and Melville, might hope for something better than an unknown young advocate who wrote poems and was not earning much. His fee-book for the first of his years at the Bar disclosed less than twenty-five pounds, and for the next not much more than double. At the end of five years the total was about four hundred pounds. His first substantial fee was spent on a silver taper-stand for his mother which she always kept on her chimney-piece and loved to explain. So virtuous a woman could not have a favourite child, but it was noticeable that her second surviving son was always "Wattie, my lamb". There was another reason for gloom about his future as an advocate. He was beginning to discover that his taste was for a literary career. In 1795, he had been appointed one of the curators of the Advocates' Library.

Unfortunately, as they both grew older and the lady began to go into society, it was borne in upon him that she was an important heiress; and by the curious wording of a warrant granted by William III mentioning "heirs whomsoever" (which included females) "and their heirs male", she could transmit a baronetcy.

The fatal letter was sent and the answer came. Really, neither Scott nor his friends could make head or tail of it. It was "highly flattering and favourable". As to the future, she pointed out what was the most prudent line of conduct for them both "at least till better days". He clutched at that straw. He thought himself "entitled to suppose that she as well as I myself looked forward to them with pleasure". He had been so anxious, struggled so hard to expect disappointment, that the arrival of something so agreeable "*entre nous* terminated in a very hearty fit of crying". To be sure, on reading it through, ten times a day, and always with new admiration of her generosity and candour, he was still conscious of "mixed feelings". He said he had always been careful, as Clerk advised, to under- rather than over-rate the extent of their intimacy. His friends, privately, sometimes wondered how much he did know her? Was the love affair entirely one-sided? She had intellectual interests. She read aloud his poems. They corresponded, which was certainly something; but it rather appeared that the subjects were entirely literary. He could hardly wait for the winter season which would bring her to Edinburgh again. "O for November! Our meeting will be a little embarrassing one. How will she look, etc. etc. etc."

Nothing is recorded as having happened during the winter, and in May he had decided upon another bold move. He would go to stay with Patrick Murray of Simprim again, and this time offer to call. Lockhart thought that the extraordinary action of Scott's father in the affair had taken place at a much earlier stage. This may have been so, but it was upon hearing that his son contemplated an excursion to the vicinity of Fettercairn that he conceived it his duty to warn her parents.

> The young lady, who was very highly connected, had prospects of fortune far above his son's. The intimacy if allowed to go on, might involve the parties in future pain and disappointment. He wished no such affair to proceed without the express sanction of those most interested in the happiness of persons as yet too young to calculate consequences for themselves.

Sir John Belsches had inherited an East India fortune from his father, but what his mother had brought was even more valuable. She had been a kinswoman of the Invermay branch of his family. With her Stuart inheritance she had bought the estate of Fettercairn in the Mearns. Sir John was an advocate, and Clerk for the admission of Notaries. He was Member for Kincardineshire for several years; he was going to assume by royal licence the name of Stuart, and eventually be appointed a Baron of Exchequer. He told Mr Scott that he had heard nothing of his son's contemplated visit, and thanked him for his scrupulous attention. He added that he believed that Mr Scott was mistaken. "He appeared to treat the whole business very lightly." He had reason. He was a cold and gloomy man, suffering from a sense of inferiority. Even at this date, far from being affluent, he was heavily embarrassed. Walter, who did not hear of his parent's interference "till long afterwards", proceeded with his plans and wrote to the Rev. James Walker.

Miss Jane Anne Cranstoun came of a family reputed to be "the cleverest but the oddest people in the world". It struck her that Scott's suit might be helped if he was able to present himself to his lady-love in the character of a printed author. She called in Willy Erskine who happened to be on his way to London with a commission from Walter to see publishers on his behalf. The young poet's interest at the moment was in translations from the German. Her brother, Erskine, and others of their circle had been attending classes given by a medical Herr Doktor Willich, who had insisted that they must learn to walk before they could run. While they were burning to explore Goethe and Schiller, he detained them with Salomon Gessner's *Der Tod Abels*. Scott had also been encouraged by the lady of Scott of Harden, born the daughter of the Saxon Minister to the Court of St James's. She got him from Hamburg the ballads of Gottfried August Bürger. His old friend at Prestonpans, George Constable, got him a lexicon, through the mediation of a monk of the Scots College at Ratisbon. He set to work. He had one more ally, a new friend, James Skene of Rubislaw, three years his junior, who had bravely been sent abroad by his widowed mother to become proficient in languages two years after the opening of the French Revolution.

There were already at least half-a-dozen English translations of *Lenore* in existence, but nothing daunted, Scott began his translation early in April 1796 after supper one night, and startled Miss Cranstoun's maid at 6 a.m. next dawn by a request to see her mistress at once. He read it aloud to her and Miss Cranstoun announced "Upon my word, Walter Scott is going to turn out a poet—something of a cross, I think, between Burns and Grey."

He set off for his favourite haunts in Perthshire and Forfarshire, and reported fully to Erskine from Aberdeen in what can only be described as wild spirits. He misdated his letter "September 24th" instead of April, and he addressed it too late to catch William Erskine, Advocate, London, but it found its way back to Edinburgh. At one moment he described himself as a forlorn pilgrim, at the next as a knight of old.

> Monday was three weeks I left the ancient city of Edinburgh, my equipage two ponies and Boy—or if you will two palfreys and a footpage. Beside me pranced the doughty Baron of Newton, John

James Edmondstoune on a most splendid Bucephalus. Next day see the same party drawn up with the addition of Lieut. Drummond of the Scottish cavalry, and the Laird of Simprim, upon the field of Bannockburn. Next see us at John Ramsay's—then at Cambusmuir.

He set off north on "my solitary journey" up Loch Lubnaigh and round by Lochearnhead over roads so rough that he had to dismount and lead his steed a great part of the way. He had, as Erskine had told him he must, found the house of Aberuchil completely to his taste. At Perth he had met Mary Anne Erskine, Will's sister, who looked charmingly. "Like a Cloud upon a Whirlwind did I pass through the fat Carse of Gowrie, thro' Dundee, thro' Arbroath, thro' Montrose." "For a thousand reasons" he had deferred staying in that neighbourhood till his return . . . "tore myself from that quarter of the country, and sad and slowly trotted on to Aberdeen with many an anxious thought upon the shadows clouds and darkness that involve my future prospects of happiness . . . straining my eyes towards the distant Grampians." He had been kindly entertained by friends of his father at Aberdeen. There was a Circuit Court in progress there and his old tutor, James Mitchell, with whom he spent a night on his return journey at Montrose, believed he had attended it. He slightly horrified the good man by the interest he expressed in the supernatural—perhaps the result of his German studies. He told Erskine that he was leaving Aberdeen the next day, and should be in Edinburgh in about eight days. "I am you may believe anxious enough on one score and another, and may well adopt the burden of an old song 'If it werena my heart's licht, I wad die'."

Other people too were anxious about him. Miss Cranstoun had written to him to the Post Office, Montrose, and it had been forwarded to Aberdeen. The postmark was April 18th.

Dear Scott,

Far be it from me to affirm that there are no diviners in the land. The voice of the people and the voice of God are loud in their testimony. Two years ago when I was in the neighbourhood of Montrose we had recourse one evening for amusement to chiromancy, or, as the vulgar say, having our fortunes read; and read mine were in such a sort, that either my letters must have been inspected, or the devil was by in his proper person. I never mentioned the circumstance since, for obvious reasons; but now that you are on the spot, I feel it my bounden duty to conjure you not to put your shoes

rashly from off your feet, for you are not standing on holy ground.
I bless the gods for conducting your poor dear soul safely to
Perth. When I consider the wilds, the forests, the lakes, the rocks—
and the spirits in which you must have whispered to their startled
echoes, it amazeth me how you escaped. Had you but dismissed your
little squire and Earwig, and spent a few days as Orlando would
have done; all posterity might have profited by it; but to trot
quietly away without as much as one stanza to despair—never talk
to me of love again—never, never, never! I am dying for your
collection of exploits. When will you return? In the meantime,
Heaven speed you! be sober, and hope to the end.

An invitation to stay at Fettercairn also caught him, still at Aberdeen,
and on May 6th he wrote from an inn at Kinross to Mr Walker, to tell
him the extent of his explorations at Fenella's fort, and apologise that he
had not been able to do so before. "I was detained at Fettercairn House by
the hospitality of Sir John and Lady Jane two or three days later than I
expected, from which you will easily guess that Miss Belsches was recovered and able to see company." Many years later, in a castle in Styria,
Jane Anne Cranstoun told an old naval friend, Captain Basil Hall, who
published it, how her little scheme for Scott's courtship had succeeded.
The book of his poems arrived one day at Fettercairn after dinner, when
the tea-table was being brought in. He had called his translations of
Lenore and *The Wild Huntsman*, *William and Helen*, and *The Chase*. Alexander
Manners, one of the publishers, had been a member of his German class.
"Much curiosity was expressed by the party—the fair lady inclusive—as
the splendid little volume gradually escaped from its folds . . . Conceal-
ment was out of the question, and he was called upon by the unanimous
acclamation of the party to read the poem." This may have been so, but
he did not leave Fettercairn an accepted lover, and he wrote a dreadfully
ominous poem of ten quatrains, describing his yearnings as he looked
down in farewell on Fettercairn from the neighbouring hill of Caterthun.
It closed nobly—

> And ever thro' life's chequer'd years
> Thus *ever* may our fortunes roll
> Tho' *mine* be storm or *mine* be tears
> Be *hers* the sunshine of the soul.

By September 9th when he sent a long, facetious letter to Erskine from
Kelso, he knew beyond doubt that a very strong rival suitor had entered

the lists. "Dot-and-carry-one is certainly gone to Fettercairn." Sir William Forbes, the banker, had arrived in the end of August with his son and heir in tow. "I could be excessively foolish just now, as I have been whistling, halooing, and I verily believe almost crying this whole morning to the utter astonishment of my Uncle and Cousin." But he continued to hope against hope. He wrote another gloomy poem though, "By a thousand fond dreams my weak bosom betray'd", etc.

In his next letter to Erskine he begged him "if the subject is casually introduced to treat it lightly". Will too was being left in a howling wilderness. Mary Anne had made a happy match. As she was going, as Mrs Campbell of Clathick, to live nearby the Belsches of Invermay, it was possible she might meet Miss Williamina.

> I am sure she will like her for her own sake, and I need not say how much I should be delighted to see such a union take place between such kindred minds in each of whom I take such interest—that is if nothing has occurred from the campaign of the formal Chevalier and his son and heir Don Guglielmo. I endeavour to treat the recollection of this visit and its consequences with levity, and yet upon my word, Dear Erskine, it requires an exertion to do it. Down, busy devil, down.

He kept up his spirits, but on October 12th one of the Montagnards wrote to another, "Mr Forbes marries Miss Belsches. This is not good news. I always dreaded there was some self-deception on the part of our romantic friend, and now I shudder at the violence of his most irritable and ungovernable mind."

II

Sir William Forbes was one of the most respected figures in Edinburgh. Pitt took his advice on matters of finance and offered him an Irish peerage which he refused. His family had been prominent in Scottish history since the thirteenth century and he did not ask to be anything more than the sixth baronet of Pitsligo, His youth had been bitterly penurious. He had been brought up by a widowed mother of great piety with an iron will, of whom he wrote a touching memoir. He was an author, a member of The Club in London, together with Samuel Johnson; Boswell appointed him as literary executor. He had dedicated an autobiography, *Memoirs of a Banking House*, to his eldest son. This story was remarkable. At the age of fifteen he had entered the firm of Messrs Coutts, originally corn factors,

but by then chiefly bankers, living on the President's stair in Parliament
Close. He had not married until he was past thirty. Three years later he
was at the head of his old firm, renamed Forbes, Hunter and Co., later
Forbes, Hunter Blair. Coutts had settled in London. During the French
Revolution and Napoleonic campaigns, and consequent panics in Great
Britain, his house had stood firm. He gradually bought back the family
estate in Aberdeenshire, sold by his grandfather, and became a model
landlord. In Edinburgh he was a sagacious adviser to the High School,
the Merchant Company, the Morningside Asylum and the Blind Asylum.
He built the Episcopal Church of St John, and was, together with his
partner, a progenitor of the South Bridge.

By all accounts, including those of his unsuccessful rival in love, young
William Forbes was a worthy son of such a father. He was three years
younger than Scott, twenty-three, a fine horseman and sportsman, handsome, healthy and public-spirited. It was not extraordinary that the
parents of Miss Belsches considered him a desirable and prudent match for
their ewe-lamb. Lady Jane Stuart wrote to him, after the affair was
happily settled, "I shall never forget how much she was prepossessed in
your favour the first evening she met with you . . . the same thing has
never happened of any other, having never once heard her speak in the
same way of any one of all the young men we have seen and met with."
Over forty letters from Lady Jane and her daughter, preserved in the
Fettercairn papers, mostly of 1796,[5] show beyond doubt that the mother
encouraged young Forbes, who had not pressed his suit until he had heard
that Scott was not an accepted suitor. There was a letter to him from
Williamina in her usual highly involved style, dated October 6th, after
he had spent a month at Fettercairn, which might refer to Scott.

> I know that the warmth of my temper lays me open to errors
> innumerable, that I am apt to form hasty opinions of those whose
> insinuating manners or pleasing appearance prepossesses me in their
> favour. Altho' I have never experienced any serious disagreeable
> consequences from this fault, yet I have very often been much hurt
> and distress'd by finding that I had heedlessly contracted an appar-
> ent intimacy, with those whose ideas and conduct were very different
> from my own.

Her mother added four days later that nothing was so obnoxious to
Williamina as seeing a man intoxicated with drink. It is possible that
Edinburgh gossip had told them that amongst his fellow advocates young
Scott was known as "Colonel Grog". It would have been quite out of

character for young Forbes to have mentioned this, but then it was equally out of character for Scott, in his first pangs of jealousy, to write of young Forbes as "Dot-and-carry-one".

The marriage took place on January 19th, 1797. Sir John's debts already exceeded eight thousand pounds and soon rose to twenty thousand. Forbes Hunter helped him on a large scale, and his son-in-law personally made private loans.

After the birth of four sons and two daughters—of whom the fourth son became an eminent physicist—Williamina Belsches Wishart Stuart, Lady Forbes, died. She was thirty-five and although her husband had an Edinburgh house just round the corner from Scott's home in Castle Street, it does not appear that there was much communication between the families. This was the more remarkable as they had many and strong links; Scott's great friends, Skene and Macdonell of Glengarry, married two of William Forbes's sisters. In September 1806, writing to thank Forbes from Ashestiel for arranging credit through his bank, Scott sent best wishes for Mrs Forbes in her approaching confinement and his own wife's kind compliments. In his middle-age he spoke bitterly twice to James Ballantyne who had been jilted, about the inhumanity of such a thing; he told another unsuccessful wooer that scarcely one out of twenty persons marries his first love, and scarce one of those who does has cause to rejoice. "What we love in these early days is generally rather a fanciful creation of our own than a reality. We build statues of snow and weep when they melt."[6]

When Scott's financial crash came in 1826 William Forbes, "high-spirited noble fellow as ever", came to his rescue and behaved to the end with the greatest consideration and delicacy. But Scott remembered . . . "It is fated that our planets should cross, and that in the periods most interesting for me. Down, down, a hundred thoughts." He mused in his Journal at Abbotsford on a dark winter's night of 1825:

> What a life mine has been! half-educated, almost wholly neglected or left to myself, stuffing my head with the most nonsensical trash, and undervalued in society for a time by my companions, getting forward and held a bold and clever fellow contrary to the opinion of all who held me a mere dreamer; broken-hearted for two years, my heart handsomely pieced again, but the crack will remain to my dying day.[7]

In 1827 he got a shock. He received a letter "from one who had in former days been no stranger". Lady Jane Stuart wanted permission to print some ballads in his hand from an album which had belonged to her daughter. It was to him like a summons from the grave. He thought perhaps he ought not to have gone to see the old lady, but of course he did. She had written so strangely,

> Were I to lay open my heart of which you know little indeed, you would find how it was, and ever shall be, warm towards you. My age encourages me, and I have longed to tell you. Not the mother who bore you followed you more anxiously (though secretly) with her blessing than I. Age has tales to tell and sorrows to unfold.

He went again and again "and fairly softened myself, like an old fool, with recalling old stories, till I was fit for nothing but shedding tears and repeating verses the whole night . . . What a romance to tell, and told I fear it will some day be."

About this he was not quite right. Mystery still surrounds the story. Rumours that the Wizard of the North had not been fortunate in his first love were widespread in his later life, and somewhat ill-naturedly held to explain his choice of a wife "very different from what might have been anticipated". Certainly, so far as an idealistic and intellectual companion for life went, Scott's way was henceforward solitary.

NOTES

1. Lockhart I, 136–40 and Addenda (note) 505.
   Two manuscript collections which were not available to students until the Bicentenary year throw some light on the story of Scott's frustrated romance. The Forbes collection from Fettercairn was loaned to St Andrew's University Library by the late Dame Katharine Watson-Watt. Mrs Somerville has deposited the Fettercairn Papers in the National Library of Scotland. The story is most incorrectly reported by Lockhart (I, 138–40) who misses the significance of Scott's visit to Montrose and Dunnottar in Spring 1796 and supposes the events of April–May to have taken place in September. Lord Sands (Sir Walter Scott's Congé, 1929) devoted a whole book to the fragmentary evidence available about an affair of gossamer delicacy (not helped by Scott who himself wrote September for April). He quoted from one of the Fettercairn Papers. Miss F. M. Skene had quoted from five others in an article in the Century Magazine, July 1899. Grierson took trouble in his notes to Scott's Letters (I, 44–57) in the introduction to that volume, lvii–lix, and in his life of Scott, 28–44, but without reaching any satisfactory conclusion.
2. Forbes MS., IV, 10. Williamina's poetry notebook, a quarto leather-bound volume, contains pressed flowers and over forty poems copied by her.

3. Lockhart, I, 1666–71; Hughes, 85–89. Mrs Hughes when staying at Abbotsford heard that Davidson had at first been highly affronted at finding himself immortalised. He entered on his tax returns only two dogs—Mustard and Pepper.

4. Lockhart, I, 173–77; 194; 201–5; 208–12.

5. Fettercairn Papers. Box 67.

6. Letters, I, 246; V, 202; VI, 208.

7. Journal, I, 56: 96–97; II, 62–64.

IV

Miss Carpenter of Carlisle
September to December, 1797

I

HIS FRIENDS WERE MISTAKEN IN FEARING THAT FINDING HIS LONG years of devotion frustrated he might do something desperate. He had had some months in which to school himself. His first slender volume of translations from the German duly appeared, and he sent copies to his circle, from the giants of his schooldays to his many friends. They were all civil but he could not deceive himself that it had set the Thames on fire. "My adventure, where so many pushed off to sea, proved a dead loss and a great part of the edition was condemned to the service of the trunkmaker." His next new interest was much more rewarding. It had been a humiliation to him that because of "my infirmity" he had not been able to join any of the volunteers. The formation of a body of light cavalry gave him his chance. Fears of a French invasion were increasing. In February 1797 a number of young men in Edinburgh offered their services to government, to undertake duties in any part of the kingdom. Skene believed that Scott was the progenitor of the scheme. He and William Forbes were Cornets. Scott was Quartermaster, Secretary, and at first also Paymaster. Skene thought Scott had a remarkably firm seat on horseback and kept up the spirits of the whole corps. His first charger was a spirited animal—"Lenore". The ordinary hour for drill was 5 a.m. in that spring and summer, after which Scott, with others of his profession,

had to present himself in the Parliament House in wig and gown. Henry
Cockburn made fun of him:

> Walter Scott's zeal in the cause was very curious. He was the soul
> of the Edinburgh troop of Midlothian Yeomanry Cavalry. It was not
> a duty with him but an absolute passion. He drilled and drank and
> made songs with a hearty conscientious earnestness which inspired or
> shamed everybody. His troop used to practise, individually, with the
> sabre at a turnip which stuck on the top of a staff to represent a
> Frenchman. Walter pricked forward gallantly, saying to himself
> "Cut them down. The villains, cut them down," and made his
> blow, which, from his lameness, was often an awkward one, cordially
> muttering curses all the while at his detested enemy.[1]

In November, after his translations from Bürger were published,
he met again a companion of his earlier Kelso years who was to have a
great influence on his later literary projects. James Ballantyne had not
been very successful in practice as a solicitor in his native small town. He
had willingly agreed to print and edit a new local journal with a Tory slant.
He had been encouraged by two London authors, William Godwin (afterwards father-in-law of Shelley) and Thomas Holcroft, novelist and
dramatist (a good sixty). He was delighted on entering the Kelso coach,
after an expedition to Glasgow to buy types, to find Scott a fellow-traveller.
Such vehicles pursued their journey of forty miles in a very leisurely
fashion, with a halt to dine on the road. Scott described one such occasion
in *The Antiquary*. The result of that chance but prolonged meeting was to
be important. For the moment, Ballantyne found that Scott took up their
friendship just where it had left off. The young editor was sure he had
managed to interest the young poet.

The day on which the Edinburgh Light Dragoons offered their services
through the Duke of Buccleuch, Lord-Lieutenant of Midlothian, was one
in which history was being made elsewhere—Valentine's Day, 1797. The
enthusiasm roused by the news of the Battle of Cape St Vincent was
tremendous and infective. Scott's brother-officers were of distinguished
quality. His circle widened. In July, when the Court of Session rose, and he
set off for a tour of the English lakes, two of his companions wore, or at
least took with them, their military scarlet—his brother John, on leave
from Gibraltar, and "Linton", Adam Ferguson. It is fortunately possible
to learn exactly what Scott took in a portmanteau on his travels at this
date, as he left a list, dated April, eagerly fastened upon by his son-in-law
biographer.[2] It included shirts, blue pantaloons, flannel drawers, a spare

waistcoat, worsted stockings or socks. In the slip in the cover came shaving tackle, eating implements, pipe and tobacco bag, shoes or hussar boots, blue overalls, and for his steed, currycomb, mane-comb, horse sheet, spare girth and fore-front shoes. There was also a pistol. They went by Carlisle, Penrith, Ullswater and Windermere through majestic scenery, thrilling in the last splendour of summer, and on their homeward journey made a detour. Rough fields of late-ripening hay and oats gave way to sombre moorland, stretching towards the Scottish Border. The air was nimble. The Schaws Hotel (which had no private rooms) stood seven hundred feet above sea-level. Its little stone-bordered promenade overlooked the river Irthing, described by a medical visitor as being as brown and frothy as the best stout. Steps and paths led down to the Wells—chalybeate and sulphur springs patronised by the Romans and ever since. Gilsland was a little spa, small and remote but attractive.[3] That very odd and bogus characters haunted such places was not perhaps perfectly appreciated by Scott at twenty-six, though by the time he wrote St Ronan's Well he realised all the possibilities.

He was exactly in the mood to fall in love again (on the rebound), and it appears that he was much struck with the charms of one young lady staying in the same hotel, to whom he dedicated verses after an expedition to the Roman Wall.

> Take these flowers which, purple waving
>   On the ruin'd rampart grew,
> Where the sons of freedom braving,
>   Rome's imperial standards flew.
>
> Warriors from the breach of danger
>   Pluck no longer laurels there;
> They but yield the passing stranger
>   Wild-flower wreaths for Beauty's hair.

II

Gilsland was, as they had expected, a good centre from which to make the sort of excursions in which Scott delighted. There was a Roman camp at Birdoswald, only three miles distant; he saw again with pleasure and wonder the Wall, which lay like a spent snake amongst heather and sandstone for seventy-three miles from Newcastle to the Solway. In some places it still stood "high enough to break a man's neck". There were

Miss Charlotte Carpenter, 1797, and (below left) her father Jean François
Charpentier   *Artists unknown. Originals at Abbotsford.*
By permission of Mrs Maxwell-Scott.

Arthur Hill, second Marquess of Downshire
By H. D. Hamilton.
By permission of the Hon. Mrs Conway.

historic castles at Naworth, Triermain, and Askerton; there was a priory
at Lanercost. Bewcastle had a Runic column fifteen feet high in the
churchyard which puzzled antiquarians. For the older guests at the spa
there were cards—piquet and casino—for the younger "balls". About a
week passed agreeably and nothing more is heard of the first beautiful
fellow-visitor. But then, on a morning ride with Ferguson, a young lady
passed slowly across their vision, riding towards Gilsland. They kept her
in view until they had satisfied themselves that she was staying at
Wardrew House. There was a ball that night at The Schaws and Captain
John Scott put on his regimentals and tall Ferguson his uniform as an
Edinburgh volunteer. There was considerable rivalry as to who should be
the first to be presented to the unknown beauty of the morning ride, but
though both the gentlemen in scarlet could dance, it was Walter Scott
who succeeded in handing her in to supper.

Marguerite Charlotte Charpentier, although she now called herself
Charlotte Carpenter, was entirely French. There were of course charming,
and perfectly acceptable, French refugees in Edinburgh society. One had
been a valued member of the Speculative. Miss Carpenter was, very
properly, accompanied by a Dragon—Miss Jane Nicolson, an English
lady of uncertain age. She was (mistakenly) said to be a daughter of the
Dean of Exeter and a grand-daughter of a Bishop of Carlisle. The couple
were certainly friends of Dr Bird, perpetual curate of St Mary's, Carlisle,
and his wife, with whom they had come to the spa. There was watering-
place gossip that Miss Carpenter had been removed from the vicinity of an
undesirable suitor in the West Country at the insistence of her guardian,
the Marquess of Downshire. They had intended to settle in Carlisle but
had found the Birds just about to fly.[4] For some extraordinary reason, in
spite of her appearance, accent and broken English, Scott wrote to his
best-loved aunt that her parents were of English extraction. Her manners
were sprightly and friendly. A little circle formed and drank tea together.
Mrs Bird found that Mr Walter Scott knew her friend Major Riddell.
Dr Rutherford, step-brother of Walter's mother, and his lady, turned up
from Edinburgh.

Lockhart, who was not afterwards always a favourite with a middle-aged
mother-in-law, gallantly accepted that "A lovelier vision, as all who
remember her in the bloom of her days have assured me, could hardly
have been imagined. A form that was fashioned as light as a Fay's; a
complexion of the clearest and lightest olive; eyes deep-set and dazzling
of the finest Italian brown, and a profusion of silken tresses black as the
raven's wing." Unlike most French émigrés, she had a fortune. It came

c

from a brother in Madras. Lord Downshire had got Jean David Charpentier, now Charles Carpenter, a fine appointment in the East India Company. Brother and sister were orphans.

A headlong wooing followed, and according to tradition Scott proposed
in the gorge of the Irthing, in wildly romantic scenery, beside a large
flat stone, hereafter, and probably before, known as the Popping Stone.
By the middle of September Charlotte was writing from Carlisle to ask
the advice of her guardian. This town would not suit. It was much too
dear, and although the Birds had the entrée to the best society, Miss
Nicolson and she could not consider settling there. Meanwhile, during
her three weeks' stay at Gilsland she had "got acquainted with Mr Scott,
a Gentleman of Edinburgh". He had paid his addresses which she had
accepted with the proviso that Lord Downshire should consent and fully
approve. "He is of very good family, his profession that of Advocate,
and with his connections and abilities he must rise; his fortune at present
is moderate, but he has some great expectations . . . I think I can be more
really happy with him than with the most splendid fortune." She asked
that Mr Scott himself might write, explaining his situation, and referring
his lordship to some person who could supply full information concerning
his family and connections.[5]

Seventeen letters from Scott to his fiancée blessedly came to light,
together with three other collections of later date, in 1935, in the desk of
Sir Walter Scott at Abbotsford. They were in time to be included in the
last, twelfth, volume of Sir Herbert Grierson's Centenary edition of
Scott's letters. Lockhart certainly saw ten written by Charlotte at the
same date. When Miss Nicolson and she left Gilsland they took lodgings
with a Mrs Palmer who kept a china-shop on the corner house (Number
83, later 81) of Castle Street and English Street, Carlisle, opposite the old
Crown and Mitre Inn.[6] Scott apparently stayed briefly with the Birds,
who had a country house at Allonby on the Solway, some eight miles
above Cockermouth; his brother picked him up for their return to
Scotland. Charlotte, it seemed, had no idea of preferring the melancholy
solitude of Allonby to the balls and assemblies with which the Carlisle
winter season was about to open. She had told Scott not to attempt to
visit her until they had heard from her guardian. She had even suggested
he had better forget her. He wrote wooingly that if she could form any idea
of the society in Edinburgh, he was sure that the prospect of living there
would not terrify her. Despite her instructions he did appear at Palmer's
lodgings on September 24th before returning to Scotland for the Jedburgh Assizes. He sent for Shortreed to dine with him at Jedburgh. "O ye

never saw a man sae gay and enthusiastic as he was about her. We pledged her health a score o' times, I daresay."

The course of true love did not run smooth. Lord Downshire failed to reply. Still, if he had strong objections, surely he must have hastened to do so. Scott's family, on the other hand, heard with dismay that he had got himself entangled with a French girl at an English watering-place—notorious hunting-ground for persons of dubious character. What was her family and religion? Miss Nicolson fell ill. She foresaw that the young couple meant business and hers would be a case of "Othello's occupation's gone". They had discovered a great link; they were both very unhappy. He was sick of being ordered about by his ailing and ageing father. She was finding Miss Nicolson "took so much upon herself". Very gradually, as it seemed to the lovers, their difficulties sorted themselves out. Lord Downshire did reply. He would be happy to hear from Mr Scott. Charlotte had to warn Walter to write at once as his lordship was leaving for Ireland.

> He is the very best man on earth—his letter is kind and affectionate, and full of advice, much in the style of *your last*. I am to consult *most carefully my heart*. Do you believe I did not do it when I gave you my consent? It is true I don't like to reflect on that subject. I am afraid. It is very awful to think it is for life.[7]

Scott wrote at once and Lord Downshire then wanted to know his income and what provision would be made for Miss Carpenter if she was to be left a widow. "Her good sense and good education are her chief fortune. As children are in general the consequences of a happy union, I should wish to know what may be your thoughts upon that subject." He had for "the estimable young woman" "the highest regard, esteem and respect". Letters flew to and fro. Scott had written to his mother, as his father was in a very poor way after a stroke which had left him partially paralysed and very irritable. Uncle Robert at Rosebank also wanted to be told much more. What had been Miss Carpenter's father's nationality and profession? What was the brother's situation at Madras? This was rather awkward. "My regard for Miss Carpenter herself was so great as to make me utterly careless upon all such matters." And, upon reflection, he did remember what his Charlotte now taxed him with. Miss Nicolson said that when she had offered the information for which he now asked, he had not availed himself of the chance. Miss Nicolson now thought it would be much best for them to wait for Lord Downshire's next letter. He could put his questions to Lord Downshire. (He was not at all likely to do that.)

Charlotte asked how could she possibly give attention to his talk of a house until she had heard from his lordship again? "I believe you are a little out of your senses to imagine that I can be in Edinburgh before the twelfth of next month" (November). She sent respectful compliments to his mother in reply to a message from her. "You don't mention your father." She was expecting every day to hear from her brother. "You may tell your uncle he is Commercial Resident at Salem. He will find the name of Charles Carpenter in his India list." There was another cause for concern which she did not divulge. Her annual remittance from India was over-due; Miss Nicolson's salary had not come from her guardian. Their letters began to cross. By October 25th she was rather pettish.

> Indeed, Mr Scott, I am not at all *pleased* with all this writing. I have told you how much I dislike it, and yet you still persist in asking me to write, and that by return of the post. O, you really are quite out of your senses. I should not have indulged you so soon in that whim of yours had you not given me that hint that my silence gives an air of Mystery. I can have no reason that can detain me in acquainting you that my Father and Mother were French, of the Name of Charpentier; he had a place under Government; their residence was at Lyons, w[h]ere you would find on enquiry that they lived in good repute and on *very good style*. I had the misfortune of losing my Father when very young, before I could know the value of such a parent. After my Father's death we were left to the care of Lord Downshire who had been his very great friend. My Mother went after to reside in Paris, has [*sic*] she had always been very desirous that we should be Educated and even Christen[ed] to the Church of England. We were sent to our Guardian, Ld. D. under whose care we have been left entirely, as I very soon had the affliction of losing my Mother. Our taking the name of Carpenter was on my Brother's going to India, to prevent any little difficulties which might have arisened. Before I conclude this famous Epistle I will give you a little hint, which is not to put quite so many *Must*(s) in your letter, it is *beginning rather too soon*.[8]

She hoped that now he was satisfied; but how could he be? He was rising twenty-seven and had endured a legal training. He can hardly have failed to hear watering-place scandal that the guardian was in fact a closer relation, though this certainly had not dawned upon him when he had proudly told his kin who that guardian was. She said he had been her father's "very great friend", but they were of different generations.

She spoke tenderly of her father but of her mother hardly at all. He saw that the subject pained her and forbore from asking more. "There had been domestic distress and disagreement between Mme. Charpentier and her husband." At least, he told his son-in-law years later, that had been his surmise. For the moment he was all apology. "Do you really think that your Birth, were it the most splendid in Britain, would raise you in my opinion, or would sink you were it otherwise?"

On the very next day after her unsatisfactory "famous letter" she had to write again to acknowledge "the Stranger"—rather a pathetic apparition, the likeness of her lover in uniform by obviously a lesser artist. "He resembles me in gravity, and I believe you may quiz him as much as you please without his offering a word in reply." If she thought he was an intruder she could always throw him into the river Eden. He was getting rather desperate at his father's attitude and thought that if the worst came to the worst he would seek his fortune in the West Indies. She was gracious about the miniature, but huffed at the thought that his friends and family might think that she was not good enough for him. She was reasonable about his father. "If he has an objection on my being French I excuse him with all my heart, as I don't love them myself. As for fortune, it is true that mine is quite uncertain . . . O how all these things plagues me. When will it end—and you to compleat the matter, you talk of going to the West Indies. I am sure your Father and *Uncle* says you are a *hot heady* young man, *quite mad* and I assure you I join with them." If he ever mentioned the West Indies again she would send back his miniature. This evening was the first Carlisle Hunt Ball.[9] (The thought of his Charlotte at a ball aroused dark fears.)

None too soon, the pieces began to fall into place. Old Mr Scott, perhaps bowing to the inevitable, at least withdrew his opposition. Lord Downshire wrote acknowledging Walter's letter. "It was so manly, candid and so full of good sense that I think Miss Carpenter's friends cannot in any way object to the union you propose."[10] His lordship had been out of London, staying at Hertford Castle. His lordship's sister was the famous fox-hunting Marchioness of Salisbury, and he had a long lease of Hertford Castle from his brother-in-law. Charlotte forwarded the order of release, and Walter at once set off for Carlisle, though only to make arrangements for their wedding, as she still did not wish it hurried on. She had taken the opportunity, when writing to her guardian, to explain that she was waiting to hear from India as such an occasion always meant some little expenses. "I should not like to go into his family without having a little of the needful." In fact, it grieved her to have to inform his lordship that "our little stock of money is nearly exhausted". Should they apply to M. Dumergue for Miss Nicolson's next Quarter? Meanwhile, could his lordship have the goodness to advance to her "a triffling sum of money". She would use the greatest economy.

It may as well be said at once that Lord Downshire, her model *grand seigneur*, sent her a wedding gift which relieved all her anxieties and allowed her to write to the Dumergues in Bond Street asking them to execute all her commissions in London. Her "blessed Friend and Protector" sent her further an addition to her trousseau which would ensure that she might shine in Edinburgh society. An India shawl, at this date, was a gift for a queen.[11]

III

Scott arrived in Carlisle on November 8th and took a room at the Crown and Mitre. It was perhaps for the best that he was able to stay only two days, for Miss Nicolson, though recovered from her violent cold, was evidently extremely upset and their quarters were restricted. The best bedroom was accessible only through the dining-parlour. She had always taken her duties as chaperone seriously and could hardly be expected, in November, to pace the streets of Carlisle. Her manner to Charlotte had been so possessive at Gilsland that Scott's Russell cousins had heard that "Miss Carpenter was entirely dependent upon a wealthy relative with whom she resides." "I don't like it," commented Charlotte, "but I cannot very well be surprised at such conjectures." Miss Nicolson laid down the law that the bride would go straight to the furnished house which Scott was taking and not to George Square or any of his Edinburgh relatives. (It must be admitted that Charlotte and all the relatives agreed in this.) Lord Downshire, with surprising lack of tact, had sent a message by Charlotte which provoked a tart reply. "There is not anything she would not do to oblige your Lordship, but when you advise her to marry, she fears you forget that she is neither young, handsome, nor rich."[12] The young lovers treated her with consideration. A beautiful ring, with their initials, was ordered by Scott. But it was not a parting gift. When her lover was gone again, Charlotte believed that she had been poor company—very stupid. Walter told his Aunt Chritty that Charlotte's temper was naturally sweet and cheerful. He had seen it put to the most severe trials. On this last visit before their marriage they were happier than before, but still they had an anxious seven weeks of winter weather to endure apart. They had settled upon the wedding taking place during the legal recess, in Christmas week. The weather might not be good. He might get snow-bound. A hundred miles, he said. When he had ridden away, dreadful melancholy assailed the little French girl. For she had not been quite frank with her lover, and who could blame her? He might be her last, and then she would become a Miss Jane Nicolson. For she was much older than he thought, quite old for anyone from Lyons, nearly twenty-seven— eight months older than her Walter. And she was the child of a broken home.

Her Walter set out for Scotland early, in fine weather, on November 8th, riding fast. *"Dear, dear* Charlotte, how sorry was I to leave Carlisle on Wednesday morning, and how often did I look back upon the towers of its Castle and Abbey till they mixed with the blue sky."[13] He broke his journey at a house in which he was going to spend the happiest years of his life—Ashestiel, which looked down upon Tweed and was owned by his Russell cousins.

Now that the engagement was announced, the tempo of his life quickened. He sent minute details of the temporary home, 50 George Street, which he had taken for the winter months. This was the gay season in Edinburgh, so there had not been many vacant. But if Charlotte did not like it there would be a much wider choice in the spring, when fashionable residents went out of the metropolis. He meant to move in by himself as soon as it was available. His mother was finding them a cook—good at marketing too. Charlotte wrote airily that it was un- fortunate he was such a bad housekeeper, as she was no better. She did not expand on the dismal reason—that she had spent most of her adult life living "in her boxes", after the convent school as a guest of the Dumergues, or hastened from resort to resort by Miss Nicolson. "How often," wrote Walter romantically, "I think upon our fireside *tête à têtes* in your little drawing-room, and how much I long again to tell you how *much*, how *dearly* I love my Charlotte." She was adept at making work- baskets. He pictured her tossing her bright silks in her little basket by their own fireside. His patience was becoming as thin as the flimsiest of her threads. He had been saluted on all hands with jokes and compliments when he entered the Court House and had borne it with tranquillity; but there would be very little peace for him once he had moved into their home. By November 12th his mother had at last composed a letter to the strange little French girl sitting in Carlisle lodgings, whom her beloved Walter was imposing upon them. (Walter had to explain that she had not written on the day he expected as it had been a Presbyterian Fast Day.)

I take with pleasure [announced Mrs Scott] this opportunity of congratulating you upon your approaching marriage with my son. May the Almighty God bless you both with all the happiness this world can Bestow and His Favour which is better than Life and all its enjoyment. Walter has taken a house which he thinks will answer for the present. I hope soon to receive you in it and be assured of a most hearty welcome and that I will do all in my power to make things agreeable. Mr Scott joins Thomas and me in Love to you. Please offer my best Compts. to Miss Nickelson.

Poor Walter had told her that he certainly would expect that his friends would show every attention in their power to "a Woman who forsakes for me prospects much more splendid than what I can offer and who comes into Scotland without a single friend but myself".

He wrote too to his youngest aunt, Miss Chritty, who had been his confidante in the days of Greenmantle. "I may give you a hint," he mentioned after explaining Miss Carpenter's annuity of five hundred pounds from her very affectionate brother, and great obligations to the Marquess of Downshire "that there is no *romance* in her composition, and that tho' born in France, she has the sentiments and manners of an Englishwoman and does not like to be thought otherwise—a very slight tinge in her pronunciation is all that marks the foreigner. She is not a beauty by any means, but her person and face are very engaging—she is a *brunette*—her manners are lively but when necessary she can be very serious."14 He had heard from Charlotte that her annual remittances from her brother had arrived, and with assurances that they might be larger and more regular in the future. Her brother had been very ill. The sum so long looked for totalled about eight hundred and sixty pounds. He had hopes now of his father giving him something towards buying a house. For his own part, he had decided to sell his second horse. Should he sell "Lenore"? He would be loath to do so, as though being in the cavalry was expensive, it also gave him access to a wider circle who might be useful to him in his profession—the Duke of Buccleuch and others. The principal expense he had already incurred—the uniform. "Add to all this, the Service is a little Stylish which I don't think you will dislike it for." Charlotte, wonderfully recovered, replied she was very glad he would not give up the cavalry "as I love anything that is *stylish*". Another link with her brother had been discovered. A Mr Haliburton, during Charles's two first years in India, had been practically in charge of what he described as a most estimable young man. Haliburton was a Scott relation and an

important one, chief of a very old family of that name. "When you go to
the South of Scotland with me, you will see their burying place. It is one
of the most beautiful and romantic scenes you ever saw, among the ruins of
an old Abbey. When I die, Charlotte, you must cause my bones to be laid
there."[15] Her lowness of spirits seemed to have been transferred to him.
"What an idea of yours was that to mention where you wish to have your
bones laid, a very pretty Compliment *before Marriage*." But he was having the
most stupefying headaches. He had sent off the marriage settlement to
Lord Downshire. It left her, as well as what was hers already, whatever her
brother might leave her—"a very slender piece of Justice on my part. Alas!
my love it is all I can at present do for you; but I hope better days will
come, when I shall be able to repay you for your disinterested attachment
to your poor friend, poor indeed in everything but his attachment to you
and your love to him."

He had got into 50 George Street and was gravely instructing little
Robert, their foot-boy, how to lay the table and wait. He had heard from
Mr and Mrs Scott of Harden who did, as he had imagined, know Lord
Downshire in the Great World in which they moved. Uncle Robert had
sent them a true sailor's wedding-gift—a cargo of pickled pork. Walter
would be glad to receive Charlotte's French porcelain tea-service which she
said was on the road by waggon, and her plate which Lord Downshire
thought he could get over for her. Lord Downshire would not be able to
be present at the wedding as he would be in Ireland. He had sent Walter a
typically magnificent gift—a gold watch.

Walter need not say how welcome his lordship would be if he did, as he
held out hopes, visit them in Auld Reekie ("which, as you must know, is the
Scotch name for Edinbro"). He was going to turn Charlotte into a regular
little Scottish woman, partaking of everything national except sheeps-
heads and haggis. He was existing in the most gorgeous bachelor squalor, for
his good mother was housebound with a cold. Charlotte's drawing-room
was a wonderful still-life picture, with a dusty Scots law book with an old
ballad stuck between its leaves, in one corner, and German plays with a
brief as a bookmark in another, a bed and bedding masking the fireplace,
and on them a lawyer's gown and coif, a light dragoon's helmet and sabre.
Young friends dropped in to help him with his bread and cheese and porter
and to play *piquet*. He was seldom alone for supper.

Charlotte was sure that once they were married she would be able to
soothe away all his troubles. She believed that he wrote too much. His sad
letter about being poor made her *triste* again, "for a whole day". "Are you
not ten times richer than I am? Remember that I must depend entirely

on my Brother, and you have only to depend upon yourself and in your profession. I have no doubts but that you will rise very high and be a great rich Man."[16] Her belief in him set him up. "I really do not think I was born to stick in the world."

More letters from Scotland began to descend upon her. Scott seemed to have a great many relations. Lord Downshire, anxious that there should be no hitch, had warned her to tell her fiancé she had three names, Margaret Charlotte Carpenter. Walter feared the document might miss Lord Downshire. Should he send it direct to his lordship's lawyer and co-trustee Mr Slade, and what was his name and address?

Mr Bird sprang into life again, only just in time. Walter's Highland blood had been beginning to boil at his inattention. Mr Bird had needed a pamphlet which had meant a good deal of trouble. Now he wanted an armorial seal engraved. Miss Nicolson was on her high horse—very sorry that Walter had asked the Birds to visit Edinburgh. They were capable of bringing six or seven people with them. He humbly asked to be remembered to Miss Nicolson *kindly and respectfully* and would be more careful in future to limit his invitations. He was sure she would agree with him that it would be best for them to quit Carlisle as soon as possible after the ceremony—the sooner the better, on all accounts. (He was secretly dreading heavy snows.) He hoped she would like Edinburgh. "I am sure she will meet with every civility in the power of my friends here to offer." If it had been summer he would have liked to take Charlotte into "my own Scotland" by a more beautiful road; but in winter the shortest way was the pleasantest. They were going to take it easy—stay a night at Selkirk. Owing to his father's illness, only his brother John would be accompanying him. He was very much obliged to Miss Nicolson for getting the wedding ring.

> I am very awkward upon some occasion; I daresay I shall blunder in putting it on. Have you any furr'd shoes? If not you must allow me to take care of your poor little feet. I intend therefore to bring two pair with me, as I hope Miss Nicolson will do me the honour to accept a pair. All our Scottish Nymphs use them in travelling. Indeed, I wish you to be dressed in fur as much as possible, quite *à la Russe* . . . you are coming to a rougher climate than you have been accustomed to.

In Edinburgh it had begun to snow on November 18th. She answered composedly that she was well provided with furs. (The Dumergues had been shopping in London for her.) Frankly, she wished he would come

alone, and if he had not already engaged his brother, give up the idea. Miss Nicolson said there was no necessity for more than two witnesses at the ceremony. "You must contrive matters so that we may not see anyone, not even of your own family, the evening we get home, we shall be so tired and such figures I should not appear to *advantage*."

On December 14th she heard from the Dumergues that Lord Down-shire had received the document and sent it on to Mr Slade of Doctor's Commons, so it should arrive to her within the week. She would expect Scott on Wednesday, "And on Thursday, 21st, O my dear Scott, on that day I shall be yours *for ever*. Does not that sound very awful ?"

He set out, in the end, on December 20th, and Mr Bird had, as he had promised, got the special licence, but Mr Slade's document was still not in Carlisle on December 23rd and Mr Bird must take services on the 25th. The wedding took place without it on Christmas Eve, in St Mary's Church (the nave of Carlisle cathedral.) The Rev. John Brown, a minor canon, married them. Mrs Bird and Miss Nicolson signed as witnesses.[17] A niece of the Birds who became a Mrs Halton remembered a wedding breakfast and having once taken tea with Mrs Scott and Miss Nicolson in Palmer's lodgings. The skies were ominously dark as bride and bride-groom embarked on the stage-coach for Scotland. With them went Miss Nicolson.[18]

NOTES

1. *Memorials of his time*, Henry (Lord) Cockburn. 1856 edition, 195–6.
2. Lockhart, I, 228.
3. "A Spa that Failed", *Country Life*, 28/4/1955. The Schaws was built about 1700, and originally thatched. It was burnt to the ground in 1859 and the site is now occupied by the Gilsland Convalescent Home.
4. *Centenary Memorial*, which has facts unobtainable elsewhere, mentions the story of the undesirable suitor, and this has been followed by other writers. It is much expanded in an unreliable but colourful article by Robert Chambers ("Chambers's Edinburgh Journal", *The Land of Scott*, July 20th, 1833) hereafter cited as Chambers. Here it is stated that Lord Downshire had asked the Birds to find a permanent cottage in their own neighbourhood for Miss Carpenter and "her governess", but Bird's reply, that he had seen such a thing, but that it would take time to repair, was anticipated by the arrival of the ladies in a post-chaise.
5. Grierson, *Life*, 54–55.
6. *Centenary Memorial*, 21, Letters, I, 65–68. There is a plaque on the house, now 81 Castle Street. The house was of considerable size and had seven windows each

on the second and third floors, and a coach entrance with a lamp above. Illustrations In *Older Carlisle*, Mary Slee, 1917.

7. Lockhart, I, 236 (altered), N.L.S.
8. Ibid., 242 (altered) and Letters, XII, 56–57.
9. Lockhart, I, 243–44 (cut), N.L.S.
10. Letters, XII, 61. Glen MS. N.L.S. Lockhart, I, 244.
11. When the Emperor Napoleon presented an Indian shawl to the Queen of Bavaria in 1806 it was the first she ever possessed and did, as was intended, cement a royal alliance. See also the comments of Nabob Touchwood in *St Ronan's Well* and the saga of Clara Mowbray's fifty-guineas shawl, the only one obtainable in Edinburgh, wheedled from the poor girl by Lady Penelope Penfeather.
12. Grierson, Life, 61.
13. Letters, XII, 64.
14. Ibid., 74–76. Lockhart, I, 239.
15. Letters, I, 83.
16. Letters, XII, 70 and 77 (cut), N.L.S.
17. Letters, XII, 93. In the Register (Page 52, No. 197), Walter Scott, Esquire, bachelor, was described as of the parish of St Andrews in Edinburgh and Margaret Charlotte Carpenter as a single woman of this parish.
18. Letters, I, 88. Scott wrote repeatedly to Patrick Murray of Simprim during the courtship and finally sent an imaginary Extract from a Gazette Extraordinary, headed "Anticipation", announcing his marriage on December 22nd. This set of letters was sold at Sotheby's 29/2/71. Charlotte's letters are almost entirely without punctuation.

V

"Laughing Philosophy"
1798–1799

———————

HE WROTE AS SOON AS HE COULD, WHICH WAS ON DECEMBER 26TH, to explain to Lord Downshire the reasons which had made him and "the *late* Miss Carpenter" leave Carlisle without waiting any longer for the deeds from Mr Slade. The threatened snowstorm had not blocked their road and they had got in last night. "Miss Nicolson and Mrs Scott join in respectful Compliments to your Lordship and in hopes that we may perhaps see you. They are very well, notwithstanding a very fatiguing Journey." He believed Miss Nicolson had already acquainted his lordship of their situation.

Charlotte had at last what she had longed for all her life, a home of her own. At last she saw her Scott's Edinburgh. George Street was a very fine street of new houses, running parallel to Princes Street on the north, and Number 50 was on the south side,[1] but perhaps it was for the best that it was to be their home for only the winter, as it had decided disadvantages. Walter's mother had herself bought their linen, cut it up with her own hands, and set their maid to sewing it. She had made Walter sit with her when this poor creature came to be examined for the post. Cook had been a very long time in service in two very genteel families, and understood marketing as well as how to set down a decent dinner or supper. She was going to be very uncomfortable, for the servants' quarters were, frankly, deplorable. Her bedroom was just off the kitchen; Robert would be roasted like a toad in a hole if the house got on fire. His bed was in a sort of cock-loft attained by a ladder. A young man in love had naturally been attracted by the excellent drawing-room which would be his Charlotte's empire, and by the fact that the furniture was modern and handsome. It had a slip of a room out of it where he would work. This had a glass door with a curtain on one side, and he had ordered a green baize covering for the other side so that all that his Charlotte would hear of his agreeable *tête-à-têtes* with his clerk would be a low murmur.[2] The two bedrooms were small and rather indifferent and, as at Palmer's Lodgings, the best one was only accessible through the dining-parlour. They solved that difficulty by transferring the feast to the drawing-room when they had a large supper party, which soon proved to be very often. Charlotte's gay welcoming cry of "No ceremony" put the most solemn at their ease. She was genuinely interested in her husband's friends, who came largely from two circles, but overlapping, the legal and the Volunteers. There was an agreeable arrangement that the Light Dragoons met weekly in rotation at each other's houses to sup. Nearly every week, too, the young couple stepped out into the glittering northern streets to go to the theatre. James Skene's mother had found room in her coach-house hard by for Lenore and an old chaise for which they could hire post-horses when they wanted to go out of town. Charlotte recognised that she would never really fit in with Scott's family. When she told them, as a funny story, that her land-lady had been shocked that she sat every day in her drawing-room instead of reserving it for best, she found that Walter's mother agreed with the landlady. The sharp eye of love told that stern noble old dame that Walter's wife was maybe not so young as he thought, but also that al-though her manners were of another world, and coquettish, she meant well by him. Old Mr Scott, as soon as he had learned that the "pagodas"[3] ex-pected from a shadowy brother in India had arrived, had been very anxious to see a young lady whose income, though precarious, was at present reassuring. Walter's only surviving sister, Anne, pallid, drooping and with a head full of fantasies, a sort of pre-Raphaelite figure before the advent of the type, was uncritically fascinated by her new relation. With the brothers, John, the regular soldier who had seen her at Gilsland, Thomas, the lawyer of twenty-three, and Daniel, of age but weakish, the runt of the litter, she had no difficulties. And as the poor father was so very ill and his wife and daughter were occupied with him, Walter and his bride did not have to see too much of them. Their relations with George Square were friendly but not close.[4]

II

The spring of 1798 brought changes, all for the better. They moved to a flat, 10 South Castle Street. They also did the fashionable thing—hired a country cottage, just off the main road in the village of Lasswade, on the Esk about six miles south-west of Edinburgh.[5]

In London, Will Erskine had kindly mentioned his friend Scott's German translations to an English author who was enjoying an extraordinary burst of popularity. "Monk" Lewis, Member of Parliament, an ornament of the Foreign Service and the heir to a Jamaica fortune, had said that he would like to see Scott when he next came north. This was Scott's first chance of meeting a successful literary man since his boyhood glimpse of Burns. The Monk appointed a date at his hotel. He had in mind a miscellany, *Tales of Wonder*, in which he wanted to include new and old authors. His popular work *Ambrosio or the Monk* happened to have exactly hit the fancy of a wide public already rendered a little silly by Horace Walpole's *Castle of Otranto* and Mrs Radcliffe's *Mysteries of Udolpho*. Monk was also, in places, rather rude, but the attorney-general had moved for an injunction: he had made deletions. He was younger than Scott by more than four years: he had become famous at twenty. Scott could hardly believe what he saw. The Monk was a mannikin, with protuberant eyes, absurdly affected and overdressed, a torrential talker, and worst of all, seeming to try to increase his consequence by claiming acquaintance with the great. "You could have sworn he had been a *parvenu* of yesterday, yet he had lived all his life in good society." He really had stayed at Dalkeith and Inveraray. Lady Charlotte Campbell, daughter of the legendary Gunning who had married two dukes, was doing the honours of Scotland to "the Lion of Mayfair". Scott met him at a gathering given by this lovely young Edinburgh patroness of the arts. He took the ridiculous-looking little visitor out to Musselburgh sands where the Dragoons were in quarters, and the Monk seemed to like it, and him. It was sad that he repelled four of the plays translated from the German which Scott had eagerly brought for his attention. (Messrs Cadell had been chicken-hearted over the suggestion that they should produce a series of twelve.) But he took away *Götz von Berlichingen of the Iron Hand*, and Messrs Bell promised to bring it out early next year with the name of Walter Scott on the title-page, and pay twenty-five guineas if a second edition was called for.[6]

In July the Scotts moved out to Lasswade and Charlotte explained to

her guardian that but for her fears of worrying him during the late disturbance in Ireland, and her conviction that he would approve their plan,
she would have informed him before that they had taken a cottage. It was
not expensive, thirty pounds a year, and gave them excellent accommodation. It would actually prove an economy. It had been built for Sir
William Clerk whose whim had been to have it thatched. There were two
large fields, and a little garden which would supply them with vegetables.
"We intend next year to be great farmers as we shall have plenty of grass."
They meant to keep a cow and "a couple of horse". At present they had
only one, but next year "I intend to fetch up all my courage, and take to
riding which will be a great convenience to us as we have a great many
neighbours by whom we are much visited."[7] Indeed, they had many
interesting callers—their landlords the Clerks at Penicuik, Henry
Mackenzie, author of *The Man of Feeling*, at Auchindinny, the Tytlers at
Woodhouselee. The heads of two of the most important families with
which Scott was linked in the Volunteers, the Duke of Buccleuch and
Henry Dundas, had castles in the same valley.

The cottage was small, but not at all gimcrack. Its solid walls were of the
local stone and as it was quite new it was in excellent condition. In style,
except for its somewhat startling over-large hat of thatch, it was more like a
small town-house than a rustic abode. It had just what Charlotte needed
for her success as a hostess, one room of good dimensions with an ingle
nook. Her fires were always bright. She made flower arrangements from
her garden, which had a beautiful downhill view. Her occasional outbursts
were April showers, quick to come and quick to go. "I admire of all
things your laughing Philosophy," Scott had written to her during their
courtship, "and shall certainly be your pupil in learning to take a gay
view of human life."[8] They were very gay. He made a dining-table with
his own hands, and was never prouder than when he had fashioned two
willows to form a rustic archway. He turned out with Charlotte to show
her it by moonlight, and they walked backwards and forwards admiring
his handiwork.[9] They were alone. Miss Jane Nicolson had left. She had
promised to come again about the beginning of October.

Miss Jane had no other reasons for leaving me, but that she could not
find any family were [sic] she might have been boarded; her wish
was to have settled near me could she have met with such a situation,
and I should have been most happy if I could have prevailed on her to
have stay'd with me, but her wish was to have a home then she would
come to visit me very often. She says she has wander'd long enough

and wishes now to have a place she might call her home and live quietly. Nothing would make me so happy as to see her well settled and would do all in my power to make her comfortable.

Charlotte was expecting her child in October. Jane Anne Cranstoun wrote enthusiastically from her Styrian castle to congratulate Walter. She had heard from their legal friends that he had got "a sweet little wife". (She had been perhaps his closest woman friend in the Greenmantle days.) She politely wished he could find another Charlotte for her brother George. She had no doubt that his first-born would be a son, and whether he would be philosopher, lawyer, antiquary, poet or hero (and she hoped for a *mélange* of the two last), he would lisp in numbers and kick at *la nourrice*.

Charlotte's child was born in Castle Street on October 14th, and was a boy. In solemn joy and pride Walter wrote off to hold Lord Downshire to his promise to be a godparent. The child died the next day. Charlotte was tiny and about to enter her twenty-ninth year. Miss Nicolson had not come, but Walter's mother, good at need, never left her till she was out of danger. Scott wrote gravely to Lord Downshire on October 23rd, that yesterday had been the ninth day so now they hoped all would go well. He had read aloud his lordship's letter to his wife. When permitted, she wrote in her own fine Italian hand.

> So much kindness, and that from your Lordship, could not but promote my speedy recovery and that of softening the disappointment I felt at the death of the poor Child. I was very ill, and after having suffered so much I thought it hard to lose it, but I must think myself fortunate it was taken before I could have for it that affection that all Mothers must feel. I have been most kindly taken care of by all Scott's family and I was also attended by Dr Rutherford with the utmost attention and kindness. I cannot say enough of their goodness and I believe it is not necessary for me to assure you how affectionate and anxious Scott has been for me and how sensible I am of it.[10]

Eight months later Scott wrote to a bachelor friend that nobody who had not been married could in the slightest degree understand his feelings.[11] He wrote as if the day-old son had been a person.

By the time that they made plans for a trip to London Charlotte appeared, if not in perfect health, most likely to benefit by something agreeable. They set out rather early in the year—the first week in March, and had much bad weather and heavy snow on the road. At Longtown they had an arranged meeting with Miss Jane Nicolson, who sent her best compliments to all in Edinburgh, and at Stilton Scott's youngest brother, Daniel, who was apprenticed in business there, dined with them and they ordered two cheeses for George Square, one a gift from Tom (who was accompanying them) and one for themselves. The Dumergues, "excellent people", had found them a very good lodging—55 Bond Street—just opposite their own house, and at last Scott met Charlotte's guardian who was "very kind". Lord Downshire dined with the Dumergues to meet them. The young Scotts visited the sights together—the Tower and Westminster Abbey. While Walter made enquiries about ballads at Montagu House and from the Keeper of Manuscripts, the British Museum, and the Duke of Roxburghe's librarian at 13 St James's Square, Miss Sophia Dumergue took Charlotte shopping. The appearance of *Götz von Berlichingen* was rather an anti-climax. A few copies had William Scott on the title page, "and though spoken favourably on the whole by the critics did not appear to have attracted the general attention". There was no prospect of the second edition. But Scott had another form of horrific composition at the back of his mind—a Gothick Tragedy. Lewis had introduced him into some literary society; this inevitably touched the fringe of something which always fascinated Scott, the world of the theatre. He was also doing some business for his poor old father. There was a client to be set right with Coutts, "Sir William Forbes's house". While he was still dealing with his father's cares, bad news came from George Square. Tom set off for Scotland at once, but Walter could not consider hurrying Charlotte. It had become gradually clear that she was with child again, indeed must have been so before they came south last month. They might look for a birth in October again, almost on the anniversary of last year's tragedy. At present she was suffering from shock owing to the bad news. Scott had a recurrence of his old nervous headaches. On April 14th they heard that the end had come peacefully, and he wrote a good son's letter to his mother to which Charlotte added a postscript as elegant as it was warm-hearted.[12] Their sympathy took a practical form. Both the widow and her daughter were worn out by looking after a beloved (but much changed) head of the family whose removal could only be regarded as nothing but a relief to all including himself.

Anne and Mrs Scott were asked to stay at the cottage during the four months of the recess of the law courts. They bravely accepted, and a much happier, closer relationship developed. Charlotte was a home-maker. Refusing an invitation to go to Patrick Murray, in June, in Manchester, Scott explained that he intended no long expeditions at present, except perhaps one to Tweedside. But while his wife had his kin to look after her he paid a good number of quiet calls on influential neighbours. He wrote letters—to Mr Riddell of Camieston in Roxburghshire, to Mr Pringle of Haining (influential with Lord Napier of Ettrick, Lord Lieutenant of Selkirkshire). The Lord Advocate had advised him to beat up as many of the gentlemen of that county as possible. These were the days of "interest". He was lobbying for the post of Sheriff of Selkirk-shire. Mr Andrew Plummer, an antiquarian with an enviable library, looked like departing at last. He had not been further than the bottom of his garden for some time. Scott had called upon him in his Liddesdale raid days and hoped he had made a good impression. He longed for the appointment. It would bring him in three hundred pounds per annum and take him often into his darling district—"small, peaceful and pastoral . . . in great part the property of the Duke of Buccleuch".

He had made a very good impression on two ladies whom he had met at Dalkeith and confirmed it when he stayed with the elder one, Lady Douglas, that autumn at Bothwell Castle on the Clyde. She was a sister of the Duke of Buccleuch, and fifty, and nothing to look at, a little round-about brisk body. But even in her check apron, like a hen-wife, you could not mistake her for anything but a *grande-dame*. She took so kindly to the young Scott that she offered him for life a cottage within the precincts of ruined Craignethan Castle. He had to refuse, but the castle became Tillitudlem in *Old Mortality*. He had read aloud some of his old ballads with infective enthusiasm to her and her favourite cousin, Lady Louisa Stuart, who was on her annual holiday to Lanarkshire. She was one of the eleven children of the great but late Lord Bute, and lived in Gloucester Place, Portman Square, which she feared was rather a long journey for the duchess from the Buccleuch London house in Grosvenor Square. She had no carriage. She was seven years younger than Lady Douglas, but had been pretty and still had rare charm and a sharp wit. A love affair in early life had been disapproved of by her parents. She too marked the young Scott down for success and lifelong friendship.[13]

Although it was now the dead season he did have to go in to Edinburgh, and he met there with great pleasure Mr Richard Heber, Member of Parliament for Oxford, Fellow of All Souls, a wealthy bibliomaniac visiting Professor Andrew Dalzel. For his library, pronounced this Macaenas, a gentleman should have three copies of a book, one for show, one for use and one to lend. After a convivial party which sat late, they decided to climb up Arthur's Seat by moonlight and watch the dawn over Edinburgh which a patriotic young Scot no doubt found a sight touching in its majesty. Like Prospero, Heber called down, from the top of a ladder in the back room of Archibald Constable's bookshop in the High Street, one of the most nightmarish figures Scott had ever seen. Heber rightly thought that John Leyden would be able to help him in his ballad search. Leyden was the son of a small Roxburghshire farmer, outsize, uncouth, very opinionated and noisy. "His first appearance," admitted Scott gently, "was somewhat appalling to persons of low animal spirits." He had lived on the traditional oatmeal and water while he won his way through Edinburgh University. It was generally accepted with misgiving that he was studying for the ministry. He could speak eight languages but refused to include English. He thought it would spoil his image. Heber, on his way south, left him with Scott, in the Advocates' Library, looking at an early version of *Sir Tristrem* in the Auchinleck manuscript. It was of the date of Edward III and they both believed that it was by Thomas the Rhymer of Ercildoune, which was the early name for Earlston, close to Smailholm. He soon realised that he had found a treasure and also a scholar of standards far more exacting than his own. An original manuscript was to this fellow sacred. Scott engaged him to send a poem called *The Elf-King* to Lewis, and their friendship prospered rapidly. One day at Lasswade the company, after dinner, were startled by a growing sound "as of the whistling of a tempest through the torn rigging of a ship at sea". It was Leyden chanting in his saw-voice the remaining fragment of an ancient ballad for which Scott had expressed longing two days before. He had walked between forty and fifty miles and back to secure this treasure from the mouth of an elderly person.[14]

After the Jedburgh Assizes Scott went down to stay at Rosebank. The good father's affairs still troubled him. It would take time to clear up the estate. There were many payments from clients which had never been realised. Scott must consult with Uncle Robert about some immediate provision for the widow. She was selling the house in George Square and coming up to a smaller one in the New Town, close to them. After Christmas she would no longer have a son at home. Tom was courting, according to a spinster Russell cousin, a most ordinary girl, not quite young either, Miss Elizabeth MacCulloch. But she was healthy and good-natured, so perhaps quite a match for Tom who was himself something of a "light horseman".

While Scott was at Rosebank, James Ballantyne looked in, ostensibly to beg for some paragraphs on a legal point for his rather dim *Kelso Mail*. When he delivered them at Ballantyne's office Scott showed him some of the verses he had sent to Lewis whose collection was still unpublished. He recited some of the Monk's stanzas, but Ballantyne thought them much inferior to those which Soctt was contributing. Scott smiled and said why did not his old school friend print off a dozen copies or so of them, as many as would make a pamphlet? Ballantyne replied that he had no acquaintances in the Edinburgh trade but he believed he could work cheaper.[15]

On October 24th, 1799, Scott's second child was safely born. She was not precisely the hoped-for replacement, but was to become her father's darling and the ancestress of his line, the only one of his children to resemble him in appearance, his "little Scotch girl". On November 15th she was carried to be baptised by Dr Daniel Sandford of the Episcopal Church of Scotland. Charlotte Sophia's godparents were the Marquess of Downshire, Miss Sophia Dumergue and her Scott grandmother. Her proud young father pretended calm, but notified correspondents who had never set eyes upon her when she was inoculated for the smallpox at twelve months. He said that her mother "had displayed all the perturbation and anxiety proper to the occasion".

In December 1799 Mr Andrew Plummer of Sunderland Hall died. The Duke of Buccleuch and the Right Hon. Robert Dundas set the necessary wheels in motion and Walter Scott, Advocate, found himself Sheriff-Depute of Selkirkshire. Lockhart afterwards remarked delicately that although neither of these noblemen were at all addicted to literature, they had seen Scott frequently under their roofs. His Grace was known to have a partiality for what he recognised as A MAN. The Monk, on a visit to Dalkeith House, had not aroused his admiration.[16]

NOTES

1. Now No. 107.
2. Letters, XII, 79.
3. The "pagoda" of which Charlotte wrote so frequently was at this date equivalent to 7/8d. in English currency.
4. Lockhart, I, 249.
5. Scott's cottage at Lasswade, now The Barony, still exists though much enlarged.
6. Lockhart, I, 253 et seq.
7. In 1825 Scott wrote to Maria Edgeworth that Charlotte had been considered the best lady-whip in Edinburgh twenty-five years ago, and he wished she would take up both riding and driving again as the moderate exercise would do her good. Letters, IX, 43.
8. Grierson, Life, 64–65.
9. Lockhart, I, 251–2.

10. Ibid., II, 21.
11. Letters, I, 88. Grierson, Life, 66.
12. Letters, I, 92–93.
13. Lockhart, I, 265–7. See also *Lady Louisa Stuart*, Susan Buchan, 64.
14. Lockhart, I, 281–4.
15. Ibid., 275–6.
16. Ibid., 255, 276.

VI

The Minstrelsy

1800–1802

I

THE NEW CENTURY OPENED UNDER DARK SKIES. LAST SUMMER THE ebullient Patrick Murray had asked Scott where he thought a Secret Expedition was bound, and Scott had agreed with him that it would be to Holland, but not that victory and peace would follow. The Helder had been the destination of a fine force, including Highland regiments, and the campaign that from which the future Duke of Wellington said that he had learned how one should not be conducted. General Buonaparte, who was one year older than Scott, had followed up his conquests in Italy and Egypt by apparently running away from his plague-stricken army and taking part in a *coup d'état* in Paris from which he had emerged as a sort of Dictator. The classic style was all the rage; he was First Consul. In Britain prices had risen alarmingly and rioters whom Scott knew to be "starving, actually starving", attacked the volunteers who were on duty day and night. Houses and shops were being looted. He was thankful that so far the troops had managed to control the mobs without firing "although much insulted and pelted. My patience began to wax low and I was very near making a fellow who seized my reins leave Brown Adam's pledge—the four fingers of his right hand." He had a "superb" new steed, called after the hero of one of his Border Ballads, "Brown Adam". He wrote to Heber from Jedburgh where he was about to make his first appearance as Sheriff, and broke off dramatically, "But soft! the trumpets call me to swagger in a cocked skyscraper and sword, preceded by a band [of] halberdiers." (Honestly, the halberdiers and their weapons seemed of about equal antiquity and the company of volunteers that followed had not learned to walk in step.)[1] But this was 1800.

He had found a steady inoffensive young man to be his Sheriff-Substitute, Charles Erskine, a Writer from Melrose. The choice had been tricky, as there were two strong candidates, each of whom was supported by people who had backed Scott's own appointment. He resorted to the old diplomatic ruse and chose a third, obnoxious to nobody. Although his duties were not heavy he took them seriously and wrote diligently to Charles about the Selkirk workhouse (much needed), a very cold jail, and inspection of weights and measures used by the tradesmen at Selkirk and Galashiels. At the end of his first year he had found unexpectedly comfortable quarters from which to ride in whenever he was needed in the county town. The little inn Whitebanklee, perched up at a treeless crossroads at Clovenfords on the Edinburgh–Selkirk road, did not look nearly as good as it was. But it was a favourite fishing-station on the Tweed, once a posting-house. In April 1800 he was anxious to get back to Edinburgh as soon as possible, for Charlotte had had a severe attack of influenza. Miss Nicolson (who had taken a great fancy to their little girl) was in command.

His family circle had been recently enlarged by the arrival of a remarkably fine coloured bull-terrier dog, Camp by name. He had always wanted to live in the country and have a dog of his own. There had been a Newfoundland in George Square who had sometimes attended the sermon at Greyfriars in his father's pew, and later "Snap" who had slept on his bed. But his memories of that little animal had been rather painful. He had flown at their house-boy for nearly cracking Snap's skull in an attempt to separate him from a collie. Camp also was pugnacious, but "perfectly manageable" said his master and lovely with children, "gentle as a lamb". His military-sounding name was appropriate, for his sire had been a black-and-tan English terrier, "Doctor", well known to the volunteers as a fighter, on the premises of Mr Storie, the farrier in Rose Street, and his dam a thoroughbred English brindled bull-dog bitch, the property of John Adams, adjutant of the riding-school of the Edinburgh Volunteer Cavalry. Scott knew that although their companionship had not been for long, Camp was now missing him. He was to become "the constant parlour-dog". He was "very gay and droll": he had white forepaws and vest, large chestnut eyes and a gaze of piercing intelligence. He was never

taught tricks, but he invented some. He was the best dog for hares that
Scott had ever known, and excelled as a water-dog. Lockhart heard from
Skene, "he always talked to Camp as if he understood what was said—
and the animal certainly did understand not a little of it". When the
establishment moved out to Tweedside there were two routes by which the
master might come home, and when Camp was alerted with the words
"Coming by the ford!" or "Coming by the hill!" he was off at once by
the right one. When Camp was coming down himself from Edinburgh,
his master always took two seats in the stage-coach. Camp diversified the
journey by accompanying the vehicle for some miles, and when sport
along the roadside palled, came aboard. Nobody objected.[2] But on an
occasion which must be formal and open to criticism, Scott had thought it
more prudent to take no risks, "knowing his tyrannic disposition towards
those of his own species whom he might be quartered with in his travels".
Camp had quite accepted Heber, and any caller wearing bell-bottomed
trousers was now chased, rapturously welcomed and sadly rejected.

As for Scott's literary progress, he said he had heard nothing from
London about *The House of Aspen* (an adaptation from *Der heilige Vehme* of
Weber); but he was already falling out of love with his German translations, and the dilatory ways of actor-managers and other dramatists. There
was a rumour that Sheridan, notoriously unbusinesslike, had the play in his
clutches. Scott's flagging interest revived when Lewis wrote that he
believed Kemble had been persuaded by "the celebrated actress Mrs
Esten"[3] to put it into rehearsal, but this was followed in October by an
apologetic notification from Heber that Kemble had definitively refused it.
By then Scott heard that he had transferred his admiration for Teutonic
drama to the romantic old English style of Miss Joanna Baillie, whose
Plays of the Passions had been warmly received on their publication in 1798.
For Miss Joanna Baillie, the middle-aged daughter of a Glasgow professor, living quietly in Hampstead with her widowed mother and spinster
sister, was a quite unusual literary lady. She was rather plain, kindly,
humorous, and very generous, though severe with her publishers ("I
am not avaricious, but I should not be satisfied with myself if I allowed,
for want of a little firmness, the chief profits of my labour to be filched
from me.") Scott had begun to correspond with her, but did not meet her
for another six years after which they became lifelong friends.

The Gothick seemed to be falling out of fashion. When at last Lewis's
Tales of Wonder (re-named) was produced, it fell flat. Scott had been very
much pleased with the look of his own little collection, cynically entitled
An Apology for Tales of Terror which Ballantyne had struck off at his

request to show Edinburgh literary society what Kelso could do. It contained pieces by himself, Lewis, a Dr John Aiken, who had a Leyden degree but was far more of a poet than a physician, and a friend (as yet) of the doctor, Robert Southey. Scott wrote again, as soon as he got back from Jedburgh, to urge his old school-friend to move to Edinburgh, where he suggested he might find plenty of employment. He said he was resolved to send Ballantyne *Ballads of the Border* which are "in some forwardness". He was taking enormous trouble over *Sir Tristrem* and it now seemed that it would unduly swell the Ballad collection even though that would fill two volumes. Had it not been the work of Thomas the Rhymer? A small separate edition was published by Constable in 1804. Scott had not only edited it, he had added a section (or "fytte") of his own composition.

II

Charlotte had recovered from her influenza and Scott wrote to Heber to ask him to look out for a little low phaeton so that she could drive herself about. It would have to be so tiny, he told her she would look like Titania gliding in her hazel-nut chariot. Charlotte's directions were precise. When he had shown her what he had written she had said he must add two things. "First she is very impatient, and secondly that you must put your glass quite close to your eye when you inspect the state of the wheels. Is she not a saucy Dame?" The phaeton arrived in June and was exactly right, and what was so unexpectedly delightful, only thirty guineas. Tom had heard from London that he would get nothing similar for less than forty. Charlotte bubbled over with pretty French thanks. She was driving herself everywhere attended only by a servant. The exercise was already bringing her benefit. A little cloud no larger than a man's hand had arisen in their sky. Scott was being criticised as a non-resident Sheriff. He set off with his wife to look for a site where he might build a cottage on the Braes of Yarrow. The place would not do for several reasons, and Shortreed beheld with awe and trepidation the progress of the first wheeled vehicle that ever penetrated into Liddesdale. It "coggled" first along one braeside and then down into the dry river bed and up on to the other "for road there was none".

Before they left home Scott had taken an important step. He had written formally to the Duke of Buccleuch to ask for permission to dedicate a small work of old poems to the chieftain of his clan. Duke Henry was the first of his family for four generations to live on his

Scottish estates. James II had granted them to the widowed Duchess of Buccleuch after the execution of her husband, the unfortunate Duke of Monmouth. This indeed was only fair as they were hers from birth. When first the young duke and duchess had arrived in Scotland in 1769, they, and particularly the duchess (who was English and a peeress in her own right), had been watched with more curiosity than cordiality. They had, like other important feudal characters, the custom of running up the flag to show they were at home for the day and neighbours might attend their dinner. When the exiled King of France was entertained at Dalkeith he said that never had he known such perfect comprehension of etiquette, as that shown by his hostess, nor any crowned head so stately. A few close family friends claimed that shyness was a contributary cause of the stiffness of Duchess Elizabeth. Duke Henry could be easier. There were some Haroun al Raschid stories about him. He did not insist on formality. He had chosen to be painted life-size for his family portrait gallery, by Gainsborough, tenderly embracing an enormous sheep-dog.

When the little procession of Mrs Walter Scott in her London-built equipage, her husband finely mounted, their attendant servant and the family dog came in view of Hermitage Castle on a tributary of the Liddell, an inspiring sight met their eyes. This grimly picturesque fortress set in a barren plain of quaking mosses was that in which the wizard Lord Soulis had plotted against the Bruce, and Sir Alexander Ramsay had been starved to death by the Douglas, and—best-loved tale of all—Queen Mary had paid her ill-advised call on the wounded Bothwell, riding from Jedburgh and back in the day, a distance of forty miles. Since its forfeiture by the Hepburns it had been Scott property. It belonged to the Duke of Buccleuch. The towers and skyline around it were on this August day alive with hardy watchful figures. It was made known to the travellers that the Earl of Dalkeith had arranged that pioneers should be ready to receive the orders and guide to safety the editor of *Minstrelsy of the Scottish Border*.[4]

III

Leyden arrived at Lasswade again early in October. He had been in the west on the temporary job, tutoring two German boys, and had returned pro-Ossian. Scott was doing all he could to put work in his way. There was a possibility of a catalogue being required for the manuscripts in the Advocates' Library and it might lead on to one of their whole tremendous possessions. Leyden had a work of his own on the stocks. Constable had taken, on the recommendation of Heber, *The Complaynt of Scotland*, a sixteenth-century manuscript enthusiastically edited with a useful glossary. This was proceeding slowly but in another quarter Leyden was becoming a favourite. Lady Charlotte Campbell insisted on his treading a measure with her. He styled himself her ladyship's dancing bear. The Duchess of Gordon, whose own manners and speech could be those of a fish-wife, found him a new sensation. He was a social success, and gloried in it. At the cottage he passed up his tea-cup to Charlotte peremptorily and repeatedly, never ceasing to declaim.

At Lasswade they had guests nearly every Saturday and Sunday now and when they got back to Edinburgh the "dropping-in" was even worse. But it never seemed to occur to a hard-worked host that between seeing people about books, and writing to more and more about them, he might never find time to produce one.

He always excelled in generosity to fellow authors, old or young. Nothing was too much trouble for him. There was a young lawyer, John Stoddart, who was going to become a leader-writer on *The Times*, who arrived talking of an unusual and he thought memorable little book of poetry, *Lyrical Ballads*, produced by two Lakeland residents, William Wordsworth and Samuel Taylor Coleridge. He meant to call in upon them on his way south, did so, and reported that they would like to meet Scott. Scott was beginning to experience all the inevitable set-backs of the conscientious editor. There was suddenly Mr Robert Jamieson who was also making a collection of Scottish Ballads with a view to publication. He had access to the collection of Mrs Brown of Falkland, some of which sounded good. He had to be asked to Lasswade to dine. He turned out to be only interested in romantic ballads. It was clearly a case for a swop. Scott relinquished some he had intended to print but drew the line at *Brown Adam* or *The Gay Goss Hawk*.

Dr Currie of Liverpool was believed by Heber to have "papers of Robert Burns" and so he had, but had not yet had time to look through them carefully. "The unfortunate bard never arranged his papers." He sent along, after six weeks, amongst others, *O wha' will lace my stays?*, *Young Hunting*, and *There won'd three ladies in a Bower*, and the outstandingly creepy *Lady Mazey* and *Clerk Sanders*.[5] Early in 1801 the venerable Dr Percy, whose *Reliques* had been Scott's joy in his schooldays, answered with old-fashioned courtesy and offered a ballad on the escape of the Earl of Westmorland—not Scottish. The old gentleman's great work had been unkindly rebuked by later critics, notably the waspish Joseph Ritson. Scott had introduced himself as a friend of the Marquess of Downshire, but in September heard with grief that "my excellent and kind friend" had died after a long illness on his estates in County Down. It was the end of a chapter for Charlotte, but she still had one happy link with her unhappy youth, the Dumergues in London.

Quite the best of Heber's efforts to put Scott in correspondence with English literary men was George Ellis, a founder with Canning of "The Anti-Jacobin", a middle-aged retired diplomat, already author of several *belles-lettres* and at present at work on "Specimens of Early English Poets". Ellis, who was a bachelor when Scott began a voluminous series of letters to him, soon married a young lady, suitable in every way except that she was of an age to be his daughter. He read aloud *The House of Aspen* to her on their honeymoon. Ellis's letters promised that he was a delightful character, polished and witty. He was highly intelligent about *Sir Tristrem*. The Scotts were invited on their next trip to London to stay at Sunninghill in Berkshire.

In April Scott wrote that he was back from the wilds of Liddesdale and Ettrick Forest after another search for additional material for his Border Ballads. In May he was in quarters with his volunteer cavalry now joined with the Midlothian Yeomanry, and Ellis was already so much a friend that he reported "a heavy family misfortune". Gentle Anne, his only sister, had died. She was barely thirty. She was buried in Greyfriars churchyard on the last Sunday in May. He regretted that they would not be having an English jaunt this year. Charlotte was again expecting a child in October. She was very well and Camp in his usual state of ferocious activity. Only Leyden was causing exasperation. His *Complaynt of Scotland* was just about to appear and he was tired of his present existence, did not think he would ever get a church and wanted to go to Africa on a voyage of discovery. "Will you have the goodness to beg Heber to write to him seriously on so ridiculous a plan?" Ellis had valuable West Indian connections. Scott tried William Dundas and James Mackintosh, an old member of the Speculative, said to have a prospect of becoming head of a projected college at Calcutta.

"The discoveries of Mungo Park haunted his very slumbers," Leyden said. Mungo Park was the seventh child in a family of fourteen born on a farm on the Buccleuch estates. He had made a successful voyage to Sumatra and afterwards, sponsored by Sir Joseph Banks and the African Association, to explore the source of the Niger. After three years he had reappeared in his native Selkirk, a national hero, married and seemed to be settled with a surgeon's practice. September would bring Leyden to Lasswade, and also "no less a man than Ritson himself, the most rigid of our British Antiquaries". Ellis heard this with some anxiety. Ritson was notoriously difficult. He was an atheist, a Republican and a strict vegetarian; moreover he loathed Scotsmen. In person he was dwarfish and a gift to the cartoonists, particularly Gillray. Ellis knew that if Ritson met his fellow antiquary, the celebrated Francis Douce, they did not bow even if the encounter happened in the reading-room of the Museum.

The visit which was to be for two nights seemed to be going on splendidly when a young visitor from Edinburgh came for the day. Robert Gillies, who afterwards gave Lockhart his recollections, was thought by the biographer to have lapses from accuracy, not surprisingly, as he could not have been more than sixteen at the date; but his memory of Scott at Lasswade was certainly vivid.

The company assembled when he arrived were Mr and Mrs Scott and Mr William Erskine (afterwards Lord Kinneder). Scott, in the lad's opinion, was more like the picture of him, with Camp, painted by Saxon in 1805 and engraved as frontispiece for *The Lady of the Lake*, than to any subsequent portrait. His hair, flaxen as a child, was now brown; in later life it was to revert to lint-white. His complexion was glowing and his features and form were still young. He was tall, slim and extremely active, almost boyish in his gaiety. He wore a comfortable, roomy shooting costume with a coloured handkerchief round his neck— nothing at all of the student or barrister. He welcomed more guests almost torrentially, interrupting himself to show one or another some favourite association object. His delightful programme was lunch, followed by "a long long walk through wood and wold". He said he had just escaped from a weary morning in the Parliament House. Counsellor Erskine said it was his intention to rent a cottage—not here, further out— and after this session never again enter the Parliament House. He was going to grow cabbages, Scott supposed for Mr Ritson. Mr Leyden and Mr Ritson, although staying, did not sit down with them. In the middle of showing his youngest visitor an ancient sword which he said he had got out of the well of Dunnottar Castle, Scott broke off, "But it is time to set out and here is *one friend* (addressing himself to a large dog) who is very impatient to be in the field." They went for a most enjoyable walk, down to Rosslyn. Scott lost his footing as he scrambled towards a cave on the edge of a precipitous bank, but was stopped by a large root of hazel and reached the brink of the river on his back. He was up in a moment, laughing and asking who was going to follow his example. He went up the cliff and was soon raising echoes in the cave. When they

entered the chapel, which contained a pillar of great beauty about which
there was a well-known anecdote, Erskine wanted them to evade the
garrulous crone who showed visitors round, but Scott refused to deprive
her of the pleasure.

They returned to the cottage and Scott enquired for "the learned
cabbage-eater". His lady replied, "Indeed, you may be happy he is not
here; he is so very disagreeable. Mr Leyden, I believe, frightened him
away." She had inadvertently offered Mr Ritson a slice of cold beef and
his refusal had been so outrageous that Leyden had first tried to correct
him by ridicule and then, as he grew more violent, by the threat that if he
did not shut up he would *"thraw his neck"*.

Ritson did return, and Scott saw to it that the quarrel was made up, but
another and final one between him and Leyden happened later, in
London, when Scott was not there to counsel and soothe.[6]

IV

Charlotte gave birth to a son on October 28th, 1801. He received the
family name of Walter, but this caused no difficulty as he was soon
"The Laird of Gilnockie", "The Laird" or simply "Gilnockie".[7] The
birth of the heir took place most inconveniently six weeks before a move
to 39 South Castle Street, another thing long looked for. 39 South Castle
Street was a house of three storeys and an attic, designed as part of a block
in the classic style, half of the façade being occupied by a triple bow
window, facing west across the street—dining-parlour below, drawing-
room above. Both rooms were of good proportions, lofty and spacious.
From the front door, reached by five steps over the area and servants'
quarters, the view was memorable—to the left the tail of the castle on its
rock, and to the right the blue hills of Fife, dazzling on a fine summer's
day, picturesque when snow-clad. It was much more commodious than
anything they had yet inhabited. Scott had a study called "my den",
behind the dining-parlour. It was rather cold and dark; it faced east. It
overlooked a sad little strip of garden, strictly enclosed by massive stone
walls and sloping steeply upwards. It could be best used as a drying-
ground. The staircase of two flights, lit half-way by a round-headed
Venetian window, was also steep.[8]

Scott wrote to Ellis in high spirits on December 8th. Of course the
only way of getting the painters and carpenters out had been to move in,
so he had done that, but he had not yet got his books sorted and the house
was a Tower of Babel. "To augment this confusion my wife has fixed upon

this time to present me with a fine chopping boy, whose pipe, being of the shrillest, is heard amid the storm like a boatswain's whistle in a gale of wind." Leyden had been detached from his dreams of Africa, and had consented to consider the East Indies. But here there was a hitch. The Company could not employ him unless he had degrees as a physician and surgeon. To anyone else this might have sounded like a quietus, but Leyden had said yes, he could do that, and within six months had done so. He had previously attended some lectures. He sailed for Madras at last in the spring of 1803, having made almost as many farewell appearances as a prima donna.[9]

Scott spent Christmas 1801 with the ninth Duke of Hamilton and family. Douglas, eighth duke, fascinating son of the famous Gunning, and possessed of every charm except stability, had left all that he could to his daughter by Mrs Esten. He had been succeeded by an uncle—sixty-two and a widower, who had brought back pictures and furniture belonging to Hamilton Palace. Here Scott met a spinster daughter of the house, Lady Anne Hamilton, who had an appointment which sounded much better than it was. She was lady-in-waiting to the Princess of Wales. He had already been introduced to her by Lady Charlotte Campbell, half-sister of the late duke. He was enthralled by the ruins of Cadzow Castle, ancient home of the Hamiltons, and on his return home sent Lady Anne not the promised poem he had written upon it, to be dedicated to her, but one by a young poet, he was sure a true poet. Thomas Campbell needed help to get his works published. Lady Anne suggested the Duchess of Gordon. He took this advice and was hopeful. "I am no stranger to her Grace's activity when she is pleased to set seriously about such matters." He had met Campbell in a stage-coach and they had beguiled the time in this improbable setting by reciting verses to one another. Campbell had been on the Continent, or at least that part of it left habitable for tourists by Buonaparte, and at Altona when the dreadful battle of Hohenlinden had been fought—"nearly 3000 Men left on the spot". Scott found Campbell's poem "uncommonly sublime" and gravely copied:

> On Linden when the sun was low
> All bloodless lay the untrodden snow,
> And dark as winter was the flow
> Of Iser rolling rapidly.

There were five more verses. "Pray show these energetic lines to Lady Douglas." He had been too much engaged to complete his own impressions

Walter Scott, 1805–6
By James Saxon.
With the dog Camp. Lady Scott's favourite portrait. Engraved for the frontispiece
of the first edition of *The Lady of the Lake,* 1810.
By permission of the Scottish National Portrait Gallery.

of historic Cadzow because at last the two first volumes of *Minstrelsy of the Scottish Border*, elegantly printed by Ballantyne and published by Cadell and Davies, were in the world. In the first week of March he sent off his presentation copies. He need not have been nervous. The ballads were an immediate success. Amongst critics, literary friends and personal friends there was not a dissentient voice. There are lucky authors and unlucky authors. Peace between England and France was announced on March 27th, 1802.

NOTES

1. Letters, XII, 158–64.
2. Letters, XII, 398–9. Lockhart, I, 419. "Sir Walter Scott and his dogs", article by P. R. Stevenson, *Cornhill Magazine*, vol. 47 (December 1919), pp. 584–94. Camp received an honourable mention in *Marmion*, second last stanza of introduction dedicated to Erskine.
3. Joseph Faringdon heard in December 1799 that Mrs Esten was at this date living at Bath with Douglas, eighth Duke of Hamilton, hoping against hope for marriage. Her husband died three months after the duke had succumbed to tuberculosis and alcohol. He left Mrs Esten shares in the Edinburgh Theatre of which he had been a patentee and Scott had correspondence with Robert Dundas about the situation in June 1806. Scott sent "The House of Aspen" as a contribution to *The Keepsake* in 1829 and as he was by then an author of established reputation it was performed in Edinburgh during the next year. Lockhart, I, 259.
4. Lockhart, I, 285–6. *Sir Walter Scott's Friends*, F. MacCunn, 170, 174.
5. Letters, I, 103–8, 110, 118.
6. Lockhart, I, 314–17. In September 1803 Ritson barricaded himself in his chambers in Gray's Inn and set fire to his manuscripts. He was removed to Hoxton where he died.
7. Scott wrote to Leyden in 1806, "Walter has acquired the surname of Gilnockie being large of limb and bone and dauntless in disposition like that noted chieftain." Lockhart, II, 98 (n) explains that he was given the surname in consequence of his admiration for Johnnie Armstrong, hero of a Border Ballad whose ruined tower he had been shown at Gilnockie on the banks of the Esk opposite Netherby.
8. 39 South Castle Street, together with 41, is now the premises of Messrs Murray, Beith and Murray, W.S., incorporated with Messrs Horne and Lyell, W.S.
9. Leyden became expert in the East in Persian, Sanskrit, Hindostani, Pushtu, Maldavian, Macassar and Bugis. The manner of his death in 1811 was characteristic. Although warned, he plunged from Batavian heat into a long-disused library containing fascinating native manuscripts. It struck cold as the tomb and he was dead in three days. Scott commemorated him officially in the Edinburgh Annual Register and tenderly in verse.

VII

Experimental

1802–1803

I

THE AGEING MONARCH GEORGE III HAD PRONOUNCED OF THE PEACE
of Amiens, "I shall call this The Experimental Peace", and he was right.
Buonaparte was merely gaining time. It lasted for one year and sixteen days.
But for Scott it was a very happy year. He was able to get away into
Liddesdale ballad-hunting in April. An enormous number of the inhabitants of Great Britain (including the Duchess of Gordon with marriageable
daughters) had hurried off to see Paris. The Continent was once more
available to a travel-loving people. Scott described his extremely Spartan
Liddesdale quest to Ellis as his Grand Tour. It was his last with Leyden.
He had slept upon peat-stacks and run the risk of sinking in bogs or
breaking his neck over *scaurs*, but he had brought back a rich harvest. The
ballad of *Maitland with his auld berd graie* "copied down from the recitation
of an old shepherd by a country farmer", he reckoned must date from the
days of Blind Harry who chanted of Wallace.[1] In May he addressed
himself to William Laidlaw, Junior, Blackhouse upon Douglas Water,
care of Mr Clarkson, Surgeon, Selkirk, sending him the first two volumes
of *Minstrelsy of the Scottish Border* and adjuring him to look out for more.
Laidlaw owned a very attractive black greyhound-bitch and promised Scott
a brace from her next litter. Percy and Douglas arrived at Lasswade in
1803 not much to the pleasure of Camp, who was, however, a philosopher

and accepted them as members of a lower creation. They were trained by a Laidlaw son and a perfect match. Their appearance at once suggested to a hostess of discernment that hare-soup might be the result of their visit, and Scott took them, but not Camp, when he went to pay his respects to the three old Misses Plummer. These were the sisters of his predecessor as Sheriff, and they guarded the library of the deceased like the three Hesperides and were house-proud about carpets. When Scott moved into the real country his study window was always left open for Percy and Douglas to leap in and out at their pleasure.²

Although this was the first Peace summer Lord Dalkeith organised an impressive turn-out of the Volunteers at the Loch of the Lowes, in July. (To this affair Camp appropriately went.) Scott called at Blackhouse Farm again on his return journey and picked up Willie Laidlaw. They spent the night at another farmhouse, Ramseycleuch, where some cousins of Laidlaw called Bryden lived, and next morning Willie sent a man over the water to fetch another cousin known locally as "Jamie the Poeter" and later as "The Ettrick Shepherd". He had been employed by Laidlaw's father for ten years but was now herding at Ettrick House. He had taught himself to read and write. He was the shepherd who had sent Laidlaw the copy of *Auld Maitland*, but he was not himself old as Scott had told Ellis. He had got the verses from an old uncle. Hogg was ten years older than Laidlaw, but less than a year older than Scott. Both the Laidlaws and Hoggs had peculiarity in their ancestry. The Laidlaws had been rich and powerful, but one of them had married a witch-woman who had put a curse on their descendants. Willie felt this. They were going downhill, do what he would. He had a long, sad Scots face. James Hogg's mother had been a Laidlaw, and her father, who had been shepherd in Phaup in upper Ettrick, was the last man known to have spoken with the fairies. Will o' Phaup had been sitting one evening at the gable-end of his cottage, just like Lady Anne in the fake ballad sent to Scott by Mr Sharpe—when

> Out of the wood cam' three bonnie boys
> As naked as they were born.

They greeted him civilly and asked for "the Silver Key", but when Will asked "In *God's* name where cam' ye frae?" they vanished like a puff of smoke. The Hoggs also boasted more than one wise-woman, of whom the most expert, "Lucky Hogg", had once turned Michael Scott, the warlock, into a hare. Willie and Scott were invited by Jamie into his thatched cottage and his mother recited *Auld Maitland* to them. Margaret Hogg was stern with the Sheriff. "O! na'na', sir, it was never printed i' the world, for my brothers an' me learned it an' many mae frae auld Andrew Moor, and he learned it frae auld Baubie Mettlin, wha was house-keeper to the first laird of Tushielaw! She was said to have been another nor a gude ane." She scolded Scott for spoiling her songs by printing them. "They were made for singin' an' no for readin'; but ye hae broke the charm noo, an' they'll never be sung mair. An' the worst thing of a', they're nouther richt spell'd nor richt setten down." Laidlaw said, "Take ye that, Mr Scott," and when Scott laughed his old hostess gave him a rap on the knee, "Ye'll find, however, that it's a' true that I'm tellin' ye."[3]

II

Gilbert Elliot, Baron Minto of Minto, looked what he was, a Border laird. He had a firm jaw, was a little below middle height, appeared taciturn but was very quick. In 1801 when he arrived in Edinburgh for the winter, after having been Viceroy of Corsica, and Minister Plenipotentiary at Vienna, he was between big jobs. He was a successful Whig politician, but had his own ideas. He had favoured the war with America. The Mintos were charmed with Edinburgh society. There was first-class schooling for their boys, and for their girls of all ages drawing and music and dancing and spelling. The people they met were so cheerful and pleasant. "Even the Scotch pride has its uses by putting the poor on a par with persons of the highest title and rank; their education is equally good, their society the same, their spirit and love of their country possibly much greater." Lady Minto ruthlessly put them much before the English, "too far gone in luxury and dissipation to be agreeable or happy". Soon Lord Minto was hard at work trying to get Mr Thomas Campbell's *Pleasures of Hope* published. When he seemed stuck with that, he asked the young man to stay at Minto House in Roxburghshire indefinitely to meet people who might be useful to him. But it did not really work. The poet's mother even when living in a Glasgow flat styled herself Mrs Campbell of Kirnan, a family mansion now without a roof. Thomas, the eleventh child of the widow, was proud and sensitive, always expecting slights. He was by no means so easy a guest as Walter Scott for whom "his originality, agreeableness and lame leg combined to inspire a *tendresse*". In March 1802 Lord Minto bought "Walter Scott's book and sent it to Pozzo", his eternal Old Man of the Sea, the Count Andrea Carlo Pozzo di Borgo, exiled Corsican patriot, so that Pozzo might see how recently Scotland had resembled Corsica. In August 1800 he had both the coming Scottish poets under his own roof. The house was packed. In the evenings they formed a circle not only of young people, and told hobgoblin stories without candles till supper-time.

> We have had a most capital addition to the Hobgoblinites in Mr Walter Scott, editor of the *Minstrelsy of the Border* who besides an inexhaustible fund of spectres, has a rich store of horrid murders, robberies and other bloody exploits committed by and on our own forefathers, the Elliots. Mr Scott is a particularly pleasing and entertaining man.[4]

III

In May 1803 Scott paid his second visit to London with his wife. Last year had not been possible. His second daughter, Anne, named for his mother, had followed Gilnockie rather close—February 2nd, 1803. There were less than sixteen months between them. He wrote cheerfully to his brother-in-law Charles Carpenter, whom he had never seen.

> Had it proved a boy it was to have been a little Charles. My little Sophia is a thriving little Scotch girl and the boy uncommonly stout healthy and robust, in short quite a model for a little Hercules. My worldly matters jog on very well. Government propose to increase the appointments of the Sheriffs which will put an additional £100 a year into my pocket. Moreover, I have contrived to turn a very slender portion of literary talents to some account by a publication of the poetical antiquities of the Border Counties where the old people have preserved many ballads and ancient songs descriptive of the manners of the country during the wars with England. This *trifling* collection was so well received by the discerning public that after receiving £100 profit for the first edition, which my vanity cannot omit informing you sold off in six months, I sold the copyright for £500 more.[5]

He urged his dear Charles not to put off his retirement too long. Charlotte's idea was that he should arrive home a bachelor and marry in Scotland.

The third volume of the *Minstrelsy* had contained more ballads by modern authors, who had indeed pressed them upon him. Mr Charles Kirkpatrick Sharpe, from Dumfriesshire, collector and caricaturist, had sent him four old ballads, one sham (*Lady Anne*) and two of his own begetting, and Miss Anna Seward from Lichfield *Rich Auld Willie's Farewell* also from her own pen. She could be perfectly absurd and made a *gaffe* in imagining that his next volume was to be published by subscription. She regretted that she had not sooner asked to have her name placed on his list. He answered her very gently. He was to find himself, at the end of a long friendship, her literary executor.

Before he left Edinburgh he had sent off to Ballantyne his list of presentation copies—

James Hogg, Ettrick House, care of Mr Oliver, Hawick—by the
                         carrier—a complete set.
Thomas Scott (my brother)   ditto
Colin Mackenzie Esq. Princess Street, third volume only.
Mrs Scott, George Street,   ditto
Dr Rutherford, York Place,   ditto
Captain Scott, Rosebank,   ditto

Two on "fine" paper were to be sent to the Duchess at Dalkeith, and (by the Inveraray carrier), to Lady Charlotte Campbell.

The address of his letter to Ballantyne of "Abbeyhill, Edinburgh" showed that at last his old school friend had taken the plunge. Ballantyne's new premises were close to Holyrood House, a run-down neighbourhood now enjoying some publicity since the royal exiles of France had been established there.

The Scots had gone first to the Dumergues who had now moved to 15 Piccadilly, on the corner of Whitehorse Street. This time their stay was not interrupted by bad news from home or fears that Charlotte might miscarry, and the visit was such a success that Lockhart believed Scott never stayed anywhere else until he had a child of his own married with a London house. This was not quite correct as Scott soon found the St James's Hotel, 79 Jermyn Street, for short-notice trips to London. But when the Dumergues could have him he went to them.

Their circle included French refugees, often of resounding title but mostly very hard up and inhabiting the district around Marylebone High Street which they seemed to have made their own. Mr Matthew Boulton, engineer and partner of James Watt, who made coins for the British Museum, invited Charlotte to visit him in his own house in Birmingham, the resort of all that was distinguished in the scientific world. The old *beau* was past three score and ten, but still appreciated the gay sallies of an attractive young Frenchwoman.

Sir James Mackintosh, philosopher and political author to whom Scott had been writing about Leyden, welcomed him to town, as did a polished eccentric translator of mediaeval romances, William Stewart Rose, and

Samuel Rogers, connoisseur and banker whose breakfasts were to be better remembered than his verse. That aged recluse the Duke of Rox-burghe had written to congratulate Mr Scott on the Ballads and sent a polite message from Lord Spencer. Scott hastened up the steps of 15 St James's Square to see a collection of manuscripts invaluable for *Sir Tristrem*.

The entertainment provided for him by Monk Lewis was a supper party in Argyle Street where the company (as the Duke said to Lucio in *Measure for Measure*) chanced to be "fairer than honest" in Scott's opinion. The Monk had got Hariette Wilson amongst his guests—the most sought-after "demi-rep" in London. Scott thought her far from beautiful, but "a smart saucy school-girl, with good eyes and dark hair, and the manners of a wild schoolboy". When she brought out her scandalous memoirs some twenty years later he was relieved to find that she had not remembered him. But he had remembered her. "Whore, from the earliest opportunity, I suppose."[6] The Monk was not attempting any more plays. His death on a benevolent cruise to see that the blacks on his West Indian estates were not being maltreated brought out a trait that had always commended him to Scott. Under a veneer of vice and folly his heart was good.

Tom Scott had come south with his brother and sister-in-law as before, but on business, to see Lord Abercorn at Stanmore. They travelled down from London to Sunninghill with Heber and Mr Francis Douce, who had been elected to the Society of Antiquaries when Scott was eight years old. A bear in society, he was much loved by a few understanding friends. To Scott both in criticism of the Ballads and the loan of manuscripts for *Sir Tristrem* he had been princely in his generosity. Later generations were to criticise the Ballads severely, convicting the editor of quite reprehensible omissions and additions. But in 1802 Pinkerton "issued his decree of approbation *ex cathedra*"; Chalmers heartily praised them, and Ritson, who did not like a comma demolished or added had called his copy "the most valuable literary treasure in his possession". And the fact was that Scott had produced thirty-eight ballads never before printed, and people who wanted to read old ballads could read these.

Ellis was "the first converser" Scott had ever met, and although brilliant never monopolised the conversation. He always allowed the other side to come in and bat, a matter in which Scott feared he was himself sometimes negligent. Mrs Ellis was tiny, musical and the daughter of Admiral Sir Peter Parker. Her elderly husband called her "Ladyfair". They asked for a pup from Camp whom the Scotts had brought with them. They took their guests out for an expedition to Windsor Park, and Scott read aloud, under a great oak, the opening stanzas of his new work.

The way was long, the wind was cold,
The Minstrel was infirm and old;
His withr'd cheek, and tresses grey,
Seemed to have known a better day;
The harp, his sole remaining joy,
Was carried by an orphan boy.
The last of all the Bards was he . . .

That was the Introduction. The first canto displayed a complete change of style.

The feast was over in Branksome tower.
And the Ladye had gone to her secret bower;
Her bower that was guarded by word and by spell,
Deadly to hear and deadly to tell—
Jesu Maria, shield us well!

It had occurred to him that as the ballads to which he had only contributed a few items and prose introductions had been so much to the popular taste, his next publication might be a narrative poem all his own composition. Chance had suggested both a new metre and a subject around which to weave his tale of Border chivalry. The intelligent Stoddart who had wanted to put him in touch with the Lakeland poets had repeated to him the opening verses of *Christabel* by Coleridge,[7] something quite new and irregular compared with the stately Augustan style to which the public had so long been accustomed—"a light-horseman sort of stanza". When he had read the opening of *The Lay of the Last Minstrel* to Will Erskine and George Cranstoun, he had concluded them struck dumb with horror and after their departure tossed the sheets into the fire. But it turned out that they had talked about it all the way home, and presently asked eagerly how it was progressing. He tried again when he happened to be laid up for three days, having been kicked by a horse when at Musselburgh with the Volunteers. Then, in December, the beautiful young wife of the heir of Buccleuch, Lady Dalkeith, had suggested to him that he might include in his narrative poem a legendary goblin page, Gilpin Horner, who had appeared and disappeared, near Langholm, in the Buccleuch territory.[8]

After a "paradisical week" with the Ellises, the Scotts went on with Heber to Oxford. Scott sent Miss Seward an account of some further perfect May days in congenial company. "The time, though as much as I could possibly spare, has I find been too short to convey to me separate and distinct ideas of all the varieties of wonders which I saw. My memory at present furnishes a grand but indistinct picture of tower and Chapels and oriels and vaulted halls and libraries and paintings." He had been much flattered by his kind reception by "some of the most distinguished inhabitants of the halls of Isis, which was more than such a truant to the Classic page as myself was entitled to expect".

Heber's half-brother, Reginald, an undergraduate at Brasenose, gave them breakfast in his rooms. He had just heard he had won a University prize for a poem on the subject of Palestine. This, according to custom, he would have to declaim in the majestic Sheldonian Theatre at Encaenia in Commemoration week in June. Scott was given the script and remarked that an important fact in the building of Solomon's temple had not been included—that the labour was accomplished without noise. Young Heber supplied a couplet impromptu.9

IV

On May 2nd, 1803, the First Consul sent for the Governor of Paris and told him to arrest all male British subjects from the age of eighteen to sixty, "This measure must be executed by seven this evening. I am resolved that to-night not an Englishman shall be visible in the obscurest theatre or restaurant in Paris." In vain General Junot pleaded that this action would defy all international courtesies and blemish his master's reputation. The arrests took place and a motley collection went into the bag to become prisoners of war till Waterloo. On May 16th Britain declared war on France again.

The Scotts were in any case "returning to Scotland as soon as possible and by the nearest road", but when their plans had been made this had been upon account of the Assizes. A summer of increased activity was to be expected, and when Scott wrote to Miss Seward from Musselburgh in July, he had to confess he was enjoying the bustle. There was a new raised Corps of Yeomanry likely to be left to practise like so many Harlequins with lath sabres. About thirty thousand patriots were clamorous for arms. His own regiment had got many recruits and was very strong and in good order. While he was writing a letter to Ellis from Lasswade about "the Army of the Reserve, Military, Pikemen and Sharpshooters who were to descend upon Ettrick Forest to the confusion of all invaders", he was startled by "an extraordinary accident, nothing less than a volley of small shot fired through the window at which my wife was five minutes before arranging her flowers". With Camp's assistance (who ran down the assailant's trail like a Liddesdale bloodhound) he caught up with an inept sportsman in search of nothing more than something for the pot. Ellis replied with his usual elegance, "I must begin by congratulating you on Mrs Scott's escape; Camp, if he had had no previous title to immortality, would deserve it for his zeal and address in detecting the stupid marksman who, while he took aim at a bird on a tree, was so near shooting your fair 'bird in bower'." Upon reflection, the ex-diplomatist saw the Government's point in being so slow to issue firearms indifferently to all volunteers.[10] Meanwhile, said Scott, as there was not one regiment of the line left in his country, every individual was just having to do his best. An emergency retreat for Charlotte and her infantry into Ettrick Forest was arranged, and a beacon communicating with the one on Edinburgh Castle was erected outside the cottage, ready to be lit. The invasion was expected from Ostend.

"Friday se'ennight our corps takes the field for ten days—for the second time within three months—which may explain the military turn of my epistle." Ellis had asked, underlined, "*Is Camp married yet?*" and Scott had to add, "Yesterday Charlotte and I had a visit which we owe to Mrs Ellis. A rosy lass, the sister of a bold yeoman in our neighbourhood, entered our cottage, towing in a monstrous form of bulldog emphatically called Cerberus, whom she came on behalf of her brother to beg our acceptance of, understanding we were anxious to have a son of Camp. Cerberus was no sooner loose (a pleasure which I suspect he had rarely enjoyed) than his father (*supposé*) and he engaged in a battle . . ." Scott had interfered with a horse-whip, for the odds had been greatly against the visitor, Percy and Douglas having arrived on the scene. He hoped to send Mrs Ellis a puppy, not Cerberus. A suitable alliance had been arranged for Camp.[11]

It was to this martial atmosphere that the Wordsworths arrived—William and Dorothy—very early, on foot. They had left their hired carriage at Roslin and walked down the lovely valley of the Esk to Mr Scott's cottage *ornée*. They waited rather a long while in a large sitting-room. It was a Saturday morning (September 17th) and the Quartermaster of the Edinburgh Light Horse and his French wife were still abed. The Wordsworths were, quite undistracted by Buonaparte, the Invasion and the Volunteers, pursuing their carefully planned tour of the beauties of Scotland in the fall. Stoddart had promised that if Scott met the Lakeland poets he would have "a rare mental treat", and after an unpropitious start another of Scott's friendships for life was established. He was just off for Selkirk to perform his duties there, and promised to meet Mr and Miss Wordsworth in two days' time at Melrose. He told

them to mention his name at the inn at Clovenfords, and they found this
an Open Sesame in all their travels. He showed them Melrose Abbey, the
Judge's procession, the valley of the Jed, Ferniehurst Castle and William
Laidlaw, who had read one of William's poems in a newspaper. They
parted at Hawick, the unmistakable English dalesman to pursue his
journey home by Eskdale, and the equally typical Borderer to Lasswade.
Wordsworth did not know quite what to make of Scott. His animal
spirits were high. His frank cordiality and lively anecdotal conversation
were attractive. He was so unaffectedly modest and had such cheerful
and benevolent and hopeful views of man and the world. But William
was left with the impression that on the whole Scott "attached less
importance to his literary labours or reputation than to his bodily sports,
exercises and social amusements". He referred to his legal profession as if
he had already given up hope of rising by it. Dorothy, who never had an
unkind thought, wrote down that "his whole heart and soul seem to be
devoted to the Scottish streams . . . He is a man of very sweet manners,
mild, cordial and cheerful." She strode on bravely by the side of her
gaunt, tall, high-nosed brother, as devoted as Camp to Walter. Coleridge
had written of her to Wordsworth as "your exquisite sister", but there
was really nothing beautiful about her except her eyes which saw much.[12]
Her world was quite in ruins, for William had married last year, and they
were only on holiday together now, just like the old times, because Mary
Wordsworth was tied to home by the baby. They had not brought Coleridge with them, and the reason was terrible. He had suddenly left them at
Arrochar, saying he was ill. They were almost sure he was addicted to drugs
—had been for two or three years. Dorothy would have liked to look
after him, but of course he was married too—though unsatisfactorily—
and she would never consider taking a lover. William had hardly any
social sense, so she was the one to suggest that when they stayed at Jedburgh they should order a bottle of wine "that we might not disgrace the
Sheriff". After supper Scott repeated some of his new narrative poem.
"He partly read and partly recited, sometimes in an enthusiastic style of
chant, the first four cantos of *The Lay of the Last Minstrel*; and the novelty
of the manners, the clear picturesque descriptions and the easy glowing
energy of much of the verse greatly delighted me." William sent a typical
letter of thanks from Grasmere. He said Dorothy and he often talked of
the happy days they had spent with Scott. "Such things do not occur often
in life. If we live we shall meet again." He signed himself "Your sincere
friend, for such I will call myself, though slow to use a word of such
solemn meaning to anyone . . ."

V

A few weeks after the visit of the Wordsworths the Volunteers went into quarters again, and this time for over a week. There was a Grand Review of ten thousand troops on Portobello Sands at the end of October. Lord Moira, appointed full General and Commander-in-Chief in Scotland, had arrived to take up his post. He was a very handsome, tall aristocrat, crony of the Prince of Wales, but with a distinguished service record. In the following year he confirmed the good opinion which he had won in Scotland by marrying Flora Campbell, Countess of Loudou, peeress in her own right. Ellis was a little afraid that with so many military engagements Scott might not be able to get on with *Sir Tristrem* as he should. He was more hopeful about *The Lay of the Last Minstrel*. "That, I think, may go on as well in your tent, amidst the clang of trumpets and the dust of the field, as in your quiet cottage." Incredible though it seemed, Scott had just taken on another literary commitment—reviewing. His old co-member of the Speculative, Jeffrey, had succeeded the Rev. Sydney Smith as editor of the *Edinburgh Review*. It was one of Constable's ventures and already had distinguished contributors. Scott had two reviews in the October 1803 issue, both books quite in his line. The translation of *Amadis of Gaul* from the Spanish was by Southey, whom he had not yet met, the other by Stewart Rose was from the French. He dealt gently with James Sibbald's *Chronicle of Scottish Poetry*. The old bookseller-author whose premises were so well known to him had died of a stroke in April. He was able to say that in future all libraries would be imperfect without the glossary which constituted volume four. He went on gladly next year to his friend Ellis's *Specimens of the Early English Poets*, and the works of that pathetic fake-master, little Thomas Chatterton. He showed some signs of the young new reviewer in his piece on William Godwin's *Life of Chaucer*. He was dreadfully funny about the hack work of a dead bore making bricks without straw. Godwin had explained that his biography should have exceeded the two volumes which were all his publishers would accept. "The cold drops", wrote Scott, "stood upon our brow at contemplating the peril we had escaped." (But a worse fate awaited Godwin. He was to become the father-in-law of Shelley.) Not only Ellis was afraid that Scott's Volunteer duties might be absorbing him. Lord Napier of Ettrick was not old, he was forty-five, four years younger than the newly-appointed Lord Moira. But as 1803 wore on, his letters of complaint to the non-resident Sheriff of Selkirkshire grew acid. He had to complain that the incessant drills and musters at Musselburgh and Portobello prevented the Sheriff from being present at the county meetings held in Selkirkshire to organise the trained bands of the Forest. By the end of the year he had come out into the open and suggested that Scott should resign his connection with the Edinburgh Light Horse and fix his summer residence somewhere within the limits of his proper jurisdiction. He went so far as to hint that if this was not done he must, as Lord Lieutenant, report the case to Government. No threat in the world would induce Scott to resign in time of war, with invasion daily expected, from the corps of which he had been a founder-member. But he did begin to consider leaving Lasswade for somewhere in Selkirkshire.

Meanwhile, as Ellis had expected, *The Lay of the Last Minstrel* went well. The introduction to Canto the Sixth was written.

> Breathes there the man, with soul so dead,
> Who never to himself hath said
>   This is my own, my native land!
> Whose heart hath ne'er within him burn'd,
> As home his footsteps he hath turn'd,
>   From wandering on a foreign strand!
> If such there breathe, go, mark him well;
> For him no Minstrel raptures swell;
> High though his titles, proud his name,
> Boundless his wealth as wish can claim;
> Despite these titles, power, and pelf,
> The wretch concentred all in self,
> Living shall forfeit fair renown,
> And, doubly dying, shall go down
> To the vile dust, from whence he sprung,
> Unwept, unhonour'd, and unsung.

VI

A poet of very different cast presented himself at Castle Street just before the last winter month of the resumed war ended. James Hogg who had carefully studied his presentation copies of *Minstrelsy of the Scottish Border* turned up in Edinburgh on business. Laidlaw and his wife were also in town, so Scott invited a little party to dine. After making his best bow on entry, Jamie the Poeter, noticing that Mrs Scott was sitting on a sofa with her feet up, in the style made fashionable by Madame Récamier and other beauties,[13] took possession of another sofa opposite and stretched himself at his full length. "I thought I could never do wrong to copy the lady of the house." His costume was that of a herdsman, his hands bore signs of a recent sheep-shearing. As the evening advanced he enjoyed himself more and more. From "Mr Scott" he advanced to "Sherra", "Scott", "Walter" and "Wattie". Finally, he convulsed the whole party by addressing his hostess as "Charlotte". A kindly host took him to the door and saw him safely down the five steps. He also advised an Ettrick shepherd who had come into town to sell stock, and might have money in his pocket, not to accept any more invitations this evening. It was difficult to say how much Jamie the Poeter took in of this, but his letter of thanks showed that he had been appreciative. It was quite as typical of the man as Wordsworth's had been.

> To Walter Scott, Advocate, Castle Street, Edinburgh.
>   Ettrick House, December 24, 1803.
> Dear Mr Scott,
>   I have been very impatient to hear from you. There is a certain affair of which you and I talked a little in private, and which must now be concluded, that naturally increaseth this.
>   I am afraid I was at least half-seas over the night I was with you, for I cannot, for my life, recollect what passed when it was late . . . If I was in the state which I suspect that I was, I must have spoken a very great deal of nonsense, for which I beg ten thousand pardons. I have the consolation however of remembering that Mrs Scott kept in company all or most of the time, which she certainly could not have done, had I been very rude.

The "certain affair" was a quite outrageous request. He wanted to publish a book of his own songs which, printed as Scott's *Minstrelsy* was, would fill about two hundred pages. Should he have an engraved portrait as frontispiece? (This suggestion showed some native shrewdness, for he had an engaging, open, impudent face.) Would Scott put his name to a little autobiography which he had produced, just putting "he" for "I"? He would like Scott's name to come first as patron to whom he would address a dedication, and after that his choice would be Lady Dalkeith. He presented his kindest compliments to the sweet little lady you call Charlotte, Camp, and young Walter . . . "Believe me Dear Walter, your most devoted servant—James Hogg."

His little collection entitled *The Mountain Bard* was published by Constable in 1807, in consequence of a recommendation from the author of *The Lay of the Last Minstrel, Marmion,* etc., etc., Britain's best-selling poet.

NOTES

1. Letters, XII, 217–18. See Introduction to *Auld Maitland,* edition *Border Minstrelsy,* 306. Margaret Hogg heard the verse from a blind man aged ninety.
2. Letters, I, 227 and 199. *Abbotsford Notanda,* 125–6.
3. Laidlaw and Hogg left differing recollections; Hogg in *Domestic Manners and Private Life of Sir Walter Scott,* 2 vols, and *Abbotsford Notanda,* 113, 120, 128–31. Lockhart, I, 286–7. Laidlaw's memories were collected by Robert Carruthers and printed as *Abbotsford Notanda* at the end of Robert Chambers's *Life of Sir Walter Scott,* 1871. They are reprints from *Chambers's Journal* and the *Gentleman's Magazine.*
4. *Life and Letters of Sir Gilbert Elliot, first Earl of Minto.* 3 vols, 1874, iii, 231, 244, 255. In 1828 Scott wrote sadly, "Lord Minto's father, the first earl, was a man in a thousand. I knew him very intimately in the beginning of the century, and, which was very agreeable, was much at his house on very easy terms. He loved the Muses and worshipped them in secret, and used to read some of his poetry which was but middling." Fate nipped this friendship in the bud. In 1807 Lord Minto sailed for India, appointed Governor-General. He died at an inn on the Great North Road in 1814. "It is very odd", wrote Scott, "that the common people about Minto and the neighbourhood will not believe at this hour that the first Earl is dead." He was said to walk about the woods and craigs at night. Lockhart, IV, 391–2.
5. Letters, I, 1761. Longman and Rees had taken over the publication of *Minstrelsy of the Scottish Border* from Cadell and Davies, and Longman had gone up personally to make the offer for the copyright.
6. Letters, I, 183. Lockhart, I, 325. Journal, I, 41–42.
7. There is really only one line from *Christabel* ("Jesu Maria guard her well"), and one incident, lifted almost exactly by Scott; but the irregular metre and supernatural atmosphere in *The Lay* are obviously derived from Coleridge's unpublished verses and Scott acknowledged it.
8. Lockhart, I, 327.
9. Ibid. Letters, I, 181. The verse from Kings, I.vi.7, to which Scott drew young Heber's attention, was "There was neither hammer nor axe nor any tool of iron heard in the house while it was building." Heber supplied "No workman steel no ponderous axes rung./Like some tall palm the noiseless fabric sprung." When he recited his prize poem there was an outburst of spontaneous applause. It was not printed till 1817.
10. Letters, I, 183, 187–9. Lockhart, I, 344.
11. Letters, I, 205–6.
12. Lockhart, I, 352–6.
13. Lockhart says (I, 357), "Mrs Scott being at the time in a delicate state of health, was reclining on a sofa." At the date when he wrote, this phrase generally indicated a pregnancy. But Charlotte had no child between Anne, February 1803, and Charles, December 1805.

VIII

Ashestiel

1804–1805

I

LORD MOIRA, "OLD HONOUR AND GLORY", WHO WAS A GOOD PUBLIC speaker, had a rousing oration (hardly to be called a recruiting speech as his difficulty was not to find volunteers but equipment), which he repeated with effect to increasingly large audiences.

There had been a mistaken belief that it was impossible for the enemy to invade. In his opinion this had been very dangerous, for it would have been quite feasible for the French to throw ashore some five or six thousand men, probably as close as possible to London, and push for the capital "in the hope of being joined by that profligate rabble to be found in every debauched metropolis, ever ready to seize any opportunity for riot or pillage". Now that Britain was on her guard, that hazard was dispelled. Still, as some attempt would almost certainly be made, it was essential to be prepared to meet it, and not only to be ready to meet it, but to annihilate it. Were Buonaparte now landed in this country with forty thousand men, stores, artillery, etc., etc., Lord Moira would not have a moment's uneasiness as to the result. He passed on to the obvious provision that the gallant force to perform this holocaust must be in a proper state of discipline, trained in the use of their weapons and, at the discretion of their officers, in guerilla warfare.

Buonaparte had abandoned the title of First Consul for Emperor, and

J. M. W. Turner, R.A.   J. Horsburgh

Ashestiel
Engraving by J. Horsburgh from sketch by J. M. W. Turner in the Fitzwilliam Museum. Published in Poetical Works *(1833–34) Vol. VII. Photograph by the Fitzwilliam Museum, Cambridge.*

39 Castle Street, Edinburgh. "The town residence of Sir Walter Scott for upwards of twenty-five years."
Engraving by W. Miller from sketch by J. M. W. Turner, reproduced in Lockhart's Memoirs, *Vol IV (1839). Photograph by Department of Prints and Drawings, British Museum.*

Lady Scott
By James Saxon. Original at Abbotsford.
By permission of Mrs Maxwell-Scott.

had marched a *Grande Armée* to what was now known as the Iron Coast, in sight, in even moderate weather, of the walls of Dover Castle. Scotland had been divided into four military districts, the Northern with Aberdeen as headquarters, the Centre, based on Dundee, the Western on Glasgow, and the Southern on Musselburgh and West Barns. The Southern got an Invasion alarm which was to descend to history on the night of Friday, February 2nd, 1804. The watchman at Home Castle mistook an accidental blaze in Northumberland for the signal-light, and fired his beacon. The signal was repeated through all the valleys on the English Border. If the St Abb's Head had been fired, the alarm would have run north and roused all Scotland; but the watch at that important post used his own judgment and decided that if there had been a descent on the eastern sea-coast, the alarm must have come along the coast, not from the interior of the country.

Scott used the incident fifteen years later in a novel. The elderly hero of *The Antiquary* was comfortably settled with his head wrapped warm in two double nightcaps when he was woken by the screams of a sister, a niece and two maidservants. "Womenkind in my room at this hour of night! Are ye all mad?"

"The beacon, Uncle!" said Miss McIntyre.

"The French coming to murder us!" screamed Miss Griselda.

"The beacon, the beacon! The French, the French!—murder and waur than murder!" cried the two handmaidens, like the chorus of an opera.

Armed with the sword which his father had worn in the Forty-five the Antiquary, attended by a military nephew in uniform but with no weapon, descended into the marketplace of the little town of Fairport, and the final chapter of the novel drew to a close in a fine crowd scene, with bells ringing, yeomanry coming in under the command of invalid local noblemen to the sound of the pipes, drums and fifes beating to arms and bells pealing.

This was comedy, but Scott was proud of the response of the men of Liddesdale, who seized all the horses they could lay hands upon to get them to their rendezvous, and, when they had reached it, turned the intelligent animals loose to find their own ways home. Two members of the Selkirkshire Yeomanry chanced to be sent in Edinburgh on private business. The newly-wedded wife of one and the widowed mother of the other sent their arms, uniforms and chargers so that they might join their companions at Dalkeith. The author was very much struck by the answer made by the old lady when he complimented her on the readiness she had shown in equipping her son with the means of meeting danger when she might have left him a fair excuse for remaining absent.

"Sir," she replied, with the spirit of a Roman matron, "none can know better than you that my son is the only prop by which, since his father's death, our family is supported. But I would rather see him dead on that hearth, than hear that he had been a horse's length behind his companions in the defence of his king and country."

Such an anxious period was not a good time in which to move house, but Scott had definitely decided that he must leave Lasswade. Edinburgh was creeping out and the cot was becoming too small for his family. He seriously considered taking a lease of the old home of his ancestor, Wat of Harden, a deliciously picturesque eagle's nest, a beetling tower above a crook of Borthwick water, but it was in need of extensive repairs and worse situated for Selkirk or Edinburgh. There was a Buccleuch shooting-lodge, Bowhill, set in a splendid situation between the Ettrick and Yarrow, to which he now went often as guest of the young Dalkeiths. With them he rode to Broadmeadows, on the banks of the Yarrow. He used to regard it with longing eyes and his son-in-law eternally regretted that he did not get it. But it had been sold last year when he had not yet decided to move. In the end a death solved his problem. Ashestiel on the southern bank of the Tweed, six miles from Selkirk, fell vacant. He had always liked it, when he had visited his uncle Russell. There was an heir, but he was in India. Scott took a seven-year lease of the house and grounds and a small farm which he would have to sub-let, and wrote to Ellis on May 4th: "You will find me this summer in the centre of the ancient Reged, in a decent farm-house overhanging the Tweed and situated in a wild pastoral country."[1]

It was at this inconvenient moment that he had to find money to send his youngest brother, Daniel, overseas. A woman whom Scott believed to be of unsatisfactory character, the daughter of a Selkirk tradesman, was claiming that Daniel was the father of her illegitimate son, aged four. Scott was so bitterly ashamed of the connection that, when writing to Ellis to ask for an introduction for Daniel in the West Indies, he spoke at first of him merely as "a very near relative". The story of Daniel was one of unrelieved gloom and like all such characters he had the knack of turning up at the worst possible moments.[2]

Another death which took place in June might have upset Scott's plans for moving to Ashestiel. His uncle, Captain Robert Scott, left him, as had always been expected, Rosebank, near Kelso, with about twenty acres of good land. But it was too near Kelso, and although "a beautiful little villa"³ not really as suitable for his family as Ashestiel. He sold it for five thousand pounds. "I shall buy a mountain farm with the purchase money." News had come from India of a wedding which they had always loyally considered desirable, though a bachelor Nabob brother-in-law was obviously more of a financial asset. Charlotte's brother had chosen a Scots bride. Miss Isabella Fraser was a daughter of Colonel Thomas Fraser of Ardachie, and Charlotte, offspring of the Hon. Charles Campbell, third son of Archibald, ninth Earl of Argyll, beheaded in Edinburgh in 1685. She got a beautiful letter of welcome into the family from Walter and complete set of the *Minstrelsy of the Scottish Border*. With the news of the engagement came a further five thousand pounds for Charlotte from her brother, and a dividend of Pagodas realisable at two hundred and eleven pounds.⁴

II

In August 1804 he had to arrange sub-letting the cottage at Lasswade, prepare to sell Rosebank, go into quarters with the cavalry for a fortnight, and superintend "what we call a flitting", the move to Ashestiel. As his new summer home would be larger, he had also to haunt sales and the repositories of dealers in second-hand furniture, some of it much in need of hospital. In his first letter to Ellis from the new home, he admitted the drawbacks in high spirits. "We are seven miles from kirk and market. We rectify the last inconvenience by killing our own mutton and poultry; and as to the former, finding there was some chance of my family turning pagans, I have adapted the goodly practice of reading prayers every Sunday." (Eventually several neighbours came to attend the Sheriff's little service.) Charlotte's poultry-yard was raided by mountain-cats. All manner of wild animals dug up or cropped her seedlings. As soon as the children could sit on a pony, each was provided with transport, but Charlotte was more of a problem. How was Mrs Ellis getting on with her donkey? Charlotte thought she might get one for next summer.

> Our gig can only travel in one direction, being separated from the High road by a deep ford, so that her airings are confined to one line of march. In compensation you may travel over the hills in any direction you please, there being no inclosures: but their steepness would appal a much bolder rider than your little friend . . . Pray, does Donkey require any breaking or do his talents like those of reading and writing come by nature?"

There was, however, an advantage in having the High road so far from the front door. Sitting at his desk, Scott could perceive with delight the carriage of his good friend, neighbour, and fishing crony, Lord Somerville, having safely negotiated the ford, proceeding inexorably in the direction of Ashestiel. There would be plenty of time to order dinner and prepare for a delightful day.

The house, like most of its kind, had a mediaeval nucleus in the shape of an old central tower. To this succeeding occupants added wings. Scott's Russell aunt had added a west wing which had a spacious drawing-room on the ground floor, and above it Charlotte's bedroom also of a good size and known as "The Pavilion-Room". Scott's book- and dressing-room were across a little stair-head. These rooms faced south-east, so waking in the morning on sunny days at Ashestiel was glorious. The house had no less than three staircases and was to have a fourth. At present it was a triangular building set in an angle formed by two remarkably steep banks. There were five outer doors on the ground floor, a pair on either side of the dining-room fireplace and a third, facing west, in Scott's square study alongside. This was the one left permanently open for the greyhounds to come and go at their pleasure.

Behind came old stables and the heathery heights which divided the Tweed from the Yarrow. There was an old-fashioned flower and kitchen garden, with strawberry-beds and apple trees and holly hedges and a sundial dated 1660, and a row of grave-looking Irish yews. The bright berberis and spindle trees had been planted by Mrs Russell. There were hops on the fences of the flower garden and hop arches up behind. The stream came hurrying down the ravine close under the windows on one side of the house, and could be heard at all times. A fine green bank separated Ashestiel from the Tweed. The coach road from Edinburgh to London crossed the Yair bridge only three miles distant, so gear for Ashestiel was dumped there to be met and carried along to the ford. The ford always needed care and in the Lammas floods of 1805 Charlotte's new kitchen range was partially visible for some days sticking up amongst the waters, having fallen off the waggon. It was extracted with difficulty.[5]

The late summer days slipped past almost imperceptibly, and still there was no Invasion. Harvest came, and there was a fine celebration of a "Kirn" at Ashestiel from which a number of revellers had to be removed next dawn by wailing mates, inert on wains and carts, rather as if they had fallen in action at Chevy Chase than into the arms of Bacchus. Scott announced triumphantly to Ellis that *The Lay* was quite finished and in Ballantyne's hands. He would have liked to have had "the appropriate embellishments" for which his friend had suggested that Flaxman should be employed, but he feared Flaxman's genius was too classic for his Gothic warriors. He had considered having illustrations by another fashionable artist, Masquerier, and sent instructions that the Minstrel's plaid must not be a tartan but the "Maud", the Low Country plaid—of the natural colour of the wool with a small black check. This was the design of all the plaids which he himself wore as a Border laird.

Already some of the principal figures who were to form the background of his life at Abbotsford had begun to assemble. He had thought at first of putting in James Hogg to look after his sheep, and the house during the winter. But Hogg had grander ideas. He would like Scott to recommend him as a tenant for a considerable farm on the Duke of Buccleuch's estate. He had no capital and seemed to be proceeding from disaster to disaster. He had actually written a poem, *Farewell to Ettrick*, in prospect of moving to a large farm in Harris which turned out to be disputed property and unavailable. Scott did his best for him. Through Mrs Scott of Harden he tried to get Hogg a job as Bailiff on the West-Country estate of her nephew, Lord Porchester. He tried other Scottish landowners. When the move to Ashestiel took place he had not yet got anyone for himself. Lockhart believed that his first meeting with Tom Purdie, who was to be faithful unto death, was in romantic circumstances. The man had been brought before him, as Sheriff, on a charge of poaching. Purdie had, already, a link with the house. His brother-in-law, Peter Matheson, had been coachman to the Russells and had been asked to stay on.[6]

The newcomer's nearest neighbours were two families of Pringles—at Whytbank and Torwoodlee. Lord Somerville, at the Pavilion, was nearly ten miles down the river. James Skene of Rubislaw came for summer and autumn visits. During his first months in residence Scott had made the acquaintance of Mungo Park, the African explorer whose brother he already knew. He called one day at Foulshiels, the birthplace to which Mungo had returned to settle in medical practice and raise a young family. Hearing in which direction the doctor had gone out, Scott followed down the river. He found his man standing alone on the banks of Yarrow, casting in stones and waiting to see bubbles ascend. Scott presently suggested that such a sport was somewhat idle for one who had seen so much stirring adventure. "Not so idle, perhaps," said Mungo, "as you suppose. This was the manner in which I used to ascertain the depth of a river in Africa before I ventured to cross it—judging whether the attempt would be safe by the time the bubbles of air took to ascend."

At this time there was no local rumour of Mungo going on a second expedition, but Scott at once guessed what was in his mind. He had told Scott that Africa haunted him. He was in the habit of waking suddenly in the night, believing himself to be still the prisoner of the Arab chief, Ali. Scott expressed surprise that he should ever wish to go back to a place from which he had barely escaped with his life, but Mungo darkly answered that Africa with all its horrors attracted him more than wearing out his life in long and toilsome rides over the hills of Scotland as a general practitioner. He came to say farewell before he set out on his last long journey and spent the night at Ashestiel. Scott saw him on his way next morning. It was a dark and boding autumn day, and when they reached Williamhope ridge where the mist was floating heavily down the valley, the troubled and uncertain prospect seemed to Scott an emblem of what the traveller had to encounter. Park had coolly announced that he intended to tell his family that he had business in Edinburgh for a day or two and send his blessing from thence. A small ditch divided the moorland from the road, and in going over it his horse stumbled and almost came down with him. "I am afraid, Mungo," said Scott, "that is a bad omen." The explorer answered with a smile, "Freits [omens] follow those who look to them." He struck the spurs into his horse and Scott never saw him again.[7]

III

The Scott family moved back to Edinburgh, but as 1805 approached could not resist spending the festival at their deep country home. "We are just going to set out for our farm," wrote Scott to Ellis on December 30th, "in the middle of a snowstorm. All that we have to comfort ourselves with is that our march has been ordered with great military talent—a detachment of minced pies and brandies having preceded us. In case we are not buried in a snow-wreath our stay will be short. Should that event happen we must wait for the thaw."

1805 was to be a wonderful year. *The Lay*, published in the first week of January, was a resounding success. The ingenuous author accepted an offer of five hundred pounds from Longmans and Rees for the copyright. Edition followed edition and Scott's fame as a poet was assured. Letters of congratulation poured in from fellow authors and admirers. Gradually it became known at Castle Street that the leaders of both political parties were at one on the subject of Walter Scott. It was to be the year of Trafalgar, and patriotic feeling was running high.

O Caledonia! stern and wild,
Meet nurse for a poetic child!
Land of brown heath and shaggy wood,
Land of the mountain and the flood,
Land of my sires! what mortal hand
Can e'er untie the filial band,
That knits me to thy rugged strand!

Lady Hester Stanhope told William Stewart Rose, who passed it on to Scott, that her uncle had recited at his dinner-table the lines spoken by the old minstrel at the opening of Canto the Third.

And said I that my limbs were old,
And said I that my blood was cold.
And that my kindly fire was fled,
And my poor wither'd heart was dead . . .

"This is the sort of thing," said Mr Pitt, "which I might have expected in painting, but could never have fancied capable of being given in poetry." That inexhaustible fount of honours, the Right Hon. William Dundas, wrote that the Minister had asked about the poet's background. "He can't remain as he is . . . look to it." Mr Pitt, however, was to be removed from the scene within a twelvemonth. "A very kind letter," commented Scott, filing it in 1818. Mr Fox, to be sure, censured his eulogy on Viscount Dundee, but that was purely political. "I am very proud of his approbation in the literary sense."[8]

The Goblin Page was not a favourite with some critics, notably Jeffrey and Miss Seward, and Scott admitted that he was "an excrescence". He had been tacked on to the material after the *toile* had been cut, to please Lady Dalkeith. "I don't know if you ever saw my lovely chieftainess—if you have, you must know that it is impossible for anyone to refuse her request as she has more of the angel in face and temper than anyone alive; so that if she asked me to write a ballad on a broomstick, I must have attempted it." He had sent her a beautiful copper-plate manuscript copy with embellishments at the heads and tails of cantos and a full-page illustration of the Lady of Branksome Tower listening to the minstrel.[9]

His industry at this date was stupendous. The Invasion was increasingly expected, so he had his military preoccupations. He was reviewing for *The Edinburgh* everything from seventeenth-century memoirs and tracts to cookery books, and he had lent Ballantyne five hundred pounds to help him over the move from Kelso. Now James was asking for more. He had transferred his works to larger premises in Foulis Close, Canongate, and was overwhelmed by desirable orders. After some discussion with Will Erskine, Scott offered to become a partner in Ballantyne's, but essentially a sleeping partner, advising only on literary subjects and when necessary on business. The printing plant moved again, to Paul's Work at the back of Canongate. James lived with his widowed mother close by[10] at St John Street. Lockhart believed that almost the whole of the result of selling Uncle Robert's Kelso villa was invested in the expanding business of Scott's Kelso-born partner, of whom he was always critical.

In March 1805 Scott wrote to the Rev. Edward Forster, "Now for the Magnum Opus." This gentleman had been introduced to him by Lord Somerville with a view to getting some of Skene's beautiful foreign drawings published. That venture was postponed, but Scott thought they might pass on together to "A complete edition of British Poets, ancient and modern". He even volunteered to assist Forster on Dryden without his name being mentioned. But the difficulties were many. Forster already had a publisher, William Miller of Albemarle Street, and Ballantyne's estimates for the great series were very large. Miller wanted Scott's name to appear. Forster withdrew with dignity and the edition of Dryden, in eighteen volumes, with introduction and notes by Scott, came forth, printed by Ballantyne and published by Miller in April 1808. It caused Scott much labour and research for nearly three years. He had to decide whether to cut out much that would, at present, give offence to the general reader. But he never hesitated.

> I will not castrate John Dryden. I don't say but that it may be very
> proper to select correct passages for the use of boarding-schools and
> colleges . . . but in making an edition of a man of genius's works, for
> libraries and collections . . . I must give my author as I find him, and
> will not tear out the page, even to get rid of the blot, little as I like
> it.[11]

For the hundred-volume edition of British Poets, Scott tried Archibald Constable whose business was also flourishing. Constable liked the idea very much, but had *Specimens of the British Poets*, by Thomas Campbell, already on his list. Cadell and Davies and others in London had similar plans in mind. Campbell offered to retire. He was asked to collaborate. Both poets wanted to include authors whom Constable would not consider. He was a stout, florid man of eight and twenty, already a little pompous and dictatorial. After a year of dissension, Campbell, who was as difficult an author as could be imagined, found "a very excellent and

gentlemanlike man, albeit a bookseller", John Murray. But after consultation with Constable, Murray said he would not undertake the publication
unless Scott took part, and Scott, by this time, had been convinced that
this was not the hour for it.

When the Courts rose in July, the Scott family set off for Ashestiel.
Their appearance *en route* was remarkable. Charlotte displayed the skill of
Mrs Gilpin in packing herself, a fat maid and three children into the
chaise. Scott, with other lumber, shared the dickie with the driver. Skene
came to stay and they had days coursing with the greyhounds or riding at
random over the hills. They went to St Mary's Loch and the Grey Mare's
Tail. Skene took his sketching outfit and Scott was a most amenable host,
always willing to halt and dismount and sit on the braeside, conning some
ballad while his companion caught the salient features of an interesting
landscape. They stayed for a week with the young Dalkeiths at Langholm
and attended an otter-hunt. At every farmhouse the Sheriff was warmly
welcomed. Lord Somerville and James Hogg came to help them spearing
salmon in the Tweed, in sunlight and by torchlight. "This amusement of
burning the waters as it is called, was not without some hazard, for the
large salmon generally lie in the pools, which it is not easy to estimate with
precision by torchlight." Often, when the sportsman made a determined
thrust at a fish, apparently within reach, his eye had deceived him and he
fell into the pool, having lost his boat, his torch and his spear. Skene
remembered once catching Scott by the skirts of his coat as he plunged
overboard.

Skene noticed with interest that Scott had made an important change
in his distribution of his time. Before the move to Ashestiel he had been
in the habit of working for several hours after bed-time. His doctor had
suggested that this habit brought on the nervous headaches which were his
only complaint. He now rose at 5 a.m. when in the country, lit his own
fire, if it was the season for fires, shaved and dressed carefully. He had a
perfect horror of the bed-gown and slipper tricks attributed to authors.
He generally dressed in a shooting jacket, and was at his desk by 6 a.m.,
all his papers arranged before him, his books of reference ready, and at
least one faithful dog in attendance. By the time the family met for
breakfast between nine and ten he had, in his own words, "broken the
neck of the day's work". After breakfast he attended to his business
of the day and correspondence, and by noon was "his own man". If the
weather was impossible he would work straight on all morning, but there
were few days when he was not out on horseback by one o'clock at the latest.
If an excursion had been planned he was ready to set out directly after

breakfast, but he made a rule that a letter should always be answered the same day. Lockhart found that if a letter had waited several days for reply, it was because he had been obliged to make enquiries or deliberate. He visited his favourite steed regularly, and neither Captain, Lieutenant (given him by Owen Rees, junior partner in Longmans) nor Brown Adam liked food from another hand. Brown Adam used to trot to the mounting stone the moment he was bridled and then stand like Edinburgh Castle.[12]

Last midsummer, Buonaparte had been reported to have murmured as he directed his telescope towards Dover from his pavilion on the heights above Boulogne, "Yes—a favourable wind, and thirty-six hours . . ." One hundred and seventy-five thousand men was a popular estimate of the "Army of England" encamped opposite her shores. But the tremendous flotilla which was to transport these troops was not intended to operate alone. French squadrons must protect it, and make a diversion at the correct moment. "Real sailors—old sailors are what I want," demanded the Emperor.

In London, the Exchequer, Treasury and duplicate books of the Bank of England were prepared for evacuation to Worcester Cathedral, and the contents of Woolwich Arsenal were destined for an inland passage by the Grand Junction Canal. Edinburgh that summer presented the appearance of a camp. As well as a large garrison of regulars nearly ten thousand fencibles and volunteers were almost constantly under arms. "The lawyer wore his uniform under his gown; the shopkeeper weighed out his wares in scarlet." There were sham battles and sieges at Craigmillar, Gilmerton, Braid Hills. The Highlanders became rather restive. They could not understand that they must sometimes consent to be beaten.

An artist presented himself at Castle Street this season. James Clerk of Eldin had sat to him. He painted a likeness of the author of *The Lay* for Mrs Scott. Mr James Saxon came directly from London, but originally from Manchester. He managed to give Scott a cast in his eye, but the likeness of Camp was perfect. Three years later Henry Raeburn engaged by Constable produced a picture very similar in content, but he bestowed chief emphasis on the poet. Camp, except in a good light or in the best reproductions, was not much more than a dark mass on the floor. Scott did not care for this portrait. He sat again, and the greyhound Percy was the chief dog. This picture hung in Castle Street until that home was sold. Skene then housed it and took the opportunity of having a copy made. Eventually the original went to Abbotsford.

Camp was dreadfully ill in the summer of 1805. For two days and nights he was unable to stir, and refused sustenance. His frantic master forced a little milk into his mouth with a teaspoon. He must have picked up something. To the general joy of the family, his recovery, after a crisis, was as complete as his collapse.

Some time during this vacation Scott began a prose narrative which he put in a drawer and forgot after Will Erskine had pronounced unfavourably upon the first seven chapters. "Waverley" was the name of the weakish English hero. (It was just a place-name which he might well have collected when staying with Ellis.) The story was about the Forty-Five and Prince Charles Edward. [13]

The summer days shortened. Charles Erskine had kindly sent a gift of a large cheese to Scott's Ettrick retreat. Charlotte, with Gallic thrift, cut up the cloth in which it came, for frocks for the Infantry. It was at this season, the end of July, almost the exact anniversary of his first visit to Gilsland, in 1797, that he took his wife for a little holiday to the scene of their courtship. They were too late to catch Coleridge in the Lakes, but they found poor Southey, with whom Scott had long been in correspondence, struggling along at Greta Hall, Keswick, "to feed many mouths out of one inkstand". Southey, who had "a mimosa sensibility", had got himself landed not only with an invalid wife and their own family, but the infants of her sister's husband, Coleridge. Southey, doomed to become the victim of ghastly and unmerited afflictions, found in Scott much encouragement. They went boating on Derwent Water.

The Scotts went next to pay their promised call on the Wordsworths at Dove Cottage, Grasmere. Wordsworth took Scott and another guest up Helvellyn. Humphry Davy, who had just been appointed Director of the laboratory at the Royal Institution, was an agreeable young Cornishman who had in his teens attempted poetry. Both Wordsworth and Scott produced poems about a pathetic incident which had occurred on the mountain that spring. It was another story of animal fidelity—a little terrier bitch who had been found after three months, still watching by the side of her master who had fallen over a precipice to his death.

Last season keepers of hotels at resorts had pronounced their business ruined by the Invasion. Although a surprising number of families were still taking holidays, far more were staying at home in the early autumn of 1805. At Gilsland the Scotts were surprised by news that a French force was at last about to land in Scotland. Charlotte, who was expecting another child at Christmas, had been travelling in their carriage, and Scott had been riding alongside. He had to leave her, and set out on a headlong ride of a hundred miles and more. The alarm, like others of its kind, proved groundless, but he was well pleased by the speed with which the yeomen of Ettrick under the guidance of Pringle of Torwoodlee had mustered at the rendezvous. They were quartered along with the Edinburgh troops when he reached Dalkeith and Musselburgh. There were two more invasion alarms to come—in 1807 and in 1811: but the last was only a few weeks before Buonaparte started for Russia; after that there were no more. As soon as he could, Scott rode south again, and Peter Matheson drove Charlotte up to Carlisle to meet him.

Actually, in the autumn of 1805, Buonaparte had already decided to use the *Grand Armée* against Austria. A great part of it had left Boulogne and was on the march to the Rhine. He had postponed the Invasion, but the major naval action necessary before it could be launched was about to take place. In the fogs of early November, Edinburgh learnt that the Battle of Trafalgar had been fought on October 21st.

On Christmas Eve Scott addressed himself to

Miss Nicolson. Lyme Regis. Dorset.

I have the pleasure to acquaint you that Charlotte last night added a little boy to our family, and they are both as well as you could wish—that is as well as possible. In every other respect your Castle Street friends have every reason to be contented and happy.[14]

NOTES

1. Lockhart, I, 386. Letters, I, 220. Reged was a kingdom of the Scottish border visited, Scott fondly imagined, by King Arthur "as conqueror or ally".
2. Ellis did find employment for Daniel Scott in Jamaica, but Mr Blackburn, the owner of the plantation, wrote soon to warn him that though the young man seemed quiet and anxious to please, the climate was the worst possible for an alcoholic. Scott accepted responsibility for the education of the son, William. Daniel was dismissed for failing in courage when ordered to deal with a revolt of negroes, and turned up in Edinburgh again, a broken and discredited man. His mother sheltered him, and he died in 1806, not yet thirty. Scott refused to wear mourning for him or attend the funeral, but afterwards told Lockhart he regretted his severity. He continued to look after William Scott, who ran back to his mother from his first London appointment, and fades from view sailing for Montreal, having been provided by Scott with a letter to the Governor-General, an outfit, and twenty-five pounds to tide him over until he got a job. Letters, XII, 246, 266. Lockhart, I, 329; V, 187. Journal, I, 339.
3. Letters, I, 290.
4. Ibid., I, 225; XII, 265, 268.
5. "Sir Walter Scott's connection with Ashiestiel . . . by Miss Russell of Ashiestiel", *History of the Berwickshire Naturalist's Club*, vol. III, Part 3 (1878), pp. 436 et seq: also Vol. XV (1897), 277 et seq. 2 plates. Lockhart, I, 417.

6. Lockhart, I, 372.

7. Ibid., 373–6. With Mungo went George Scott, son of a tenant on the Buccleuch estate, recommended by Walter Scott and Alexander Anderson, Mungo's brother-in-law. Both perished of dysentery and malaria. The party sailed in January 1805: rumours of Park's death reached the coast in 1806, but nothing certain was known in Scotland till 1809, and hope was not abandoned until September 1815.

   The Niger Explored, E. W. Bovill, 1968, tells the tragic story in detail. Park's death was basically due to two circumstances—the initial delay which lost him most of his men in the rains between the Gambia and the Niger, and his crazy policy of shunning all contact with the natives, thus making enemies of the Moorish chiefs by denying them their customary dues, the river tolls. It was his habit to fire at anyone approaching him. Word was sent down the river from chief to chief, knowing well that they would catch him fifty miles on at the Boussa rapids, from which there would be no escape at that late season, as the rapids would be too narrow to allow the passage of his boat. A fight ensued in which all the party, except one slave boat-man, were killed.

8. Lockhart, I, 394. Letters, I, 253–4.

9. Now at Bowhill.

10. John Buchan (*Sir Walter Scott*, 1932, pp. 75–76) brought to the vexed subject of Scott's relations with Ballantyne's the experience of a professional. He dismissed as "arrant nonsense" the condemnation of Scott's partnership with Ballantyne. "Before the modern development of joint-stock companies one of the commonest ways of investing spare capital was by lending money to some enterprise and receiving in lieu of interest a certain share in the profit . . . Had Scott remained a lawyer and nothing else, I cannot see how his association with the Ballantyne business could be criticised. Criticism arose because he was a writer. The step he took in 1805 was not dishonourable, but it was rash and ill-advised."

11. Letters, I, 265.

12. Skene, 26–40. Lockhart, I, 416–25. Letters, I, 251.

13. Lockhart, 409–10. General Preface to the Waverley Novels, 1829.

14. Letters, I, 270. Charlotte wrote to her brother in 1817 that she heard Miss J. Nicolson had gone abroad. "I am sorry to say she has given up my acquaintance as with the rest of her old friends." Grierson, 65.

IX

"A Little Lion"

1806–1809

ON JANUARY 26TH, 1806 HE SENT A SHORT NOTE TO HIS DEPUTY, Charles Erskine, recommending the County to him in his absence. "A piece of express and important business hurries me to London on a moment's warning." He expected to be away at least a month.

The piece of business was a cake which had been in the oven for some time. A twelvemonth past Lord Dalkeith had written cryptically to say that the duke had seen Lord Melville and thought the affair was in good train though not certain. Scott was lobbying again, this time to get appointed a Clerk of the Court of Session. There was a Mr George Home who ought to retire "as deaf as a post and as capable of discharging his duty as I am of dancing a hornpipe". The trouble was that there was no recognised age or established machinery for retirement. All had seemed to be going well after Scott had proposed to Home that he should perform his duties forthwith, but claim no salary during Home's lifetime. Home had agreed, and the duke had said that a new Commission would name both Home and Scott. Suddenly, Scott heard that by a clerical error Home's name had been dropped from the document. This meant that if the unexpected happened and Scott were the one to go first, Home would get no salary. The Prime Minister had died on January 23rd and a coalition, including Fox, might not favour Scott. It was doubly useless for him to ask support from the Dundas faction. Lord Melville, "the architect of my little fortune", had been hounded out of office on a charge of pecuniary corruption and was likely to be brought to trial. Scott wrote to Ellis, who was at Bath taking a cure. The Clerkship would be a great help to him—eight hundred pounds per annum—and would mean that literature might be his staff, not his crutch. The duty was mainly forenoon attendance during the six months while the Court was in session.

Lord Somerville volunteered to get him an appointment with Lord Spencer at the Home Office. To his surprise and delight this notable Whig behaved in the handsomest manner. Lord Grenville, who had succeeded Pitt, made no objection. Scott did not even approach Fox at the Foreign Office. By February 20th he knew that "I have indeed been rather fortunate, for the gale which has shattered so many goodly argosies has blown my little bark into the creek for which she was bound." His nomination was gazetted on March 6th. He had been extremely nervous that leading northern Whig politicians might have opposed it. Although he had never had anything but civility from Lord Moira, it was common knowledge that the general was at loggerheads with Lord Lauderdale over the patronage of Scotland. Lord Minto was a friendly neighbour, but even Ellis considered that had the office Scott sought been a sinecure at the disposal of Henry Erskine, now Lord Advocate, or the President of the Board of Control (Minto), he might have had strong cause for apprehension. But in this he appeared to be wrong. Minto on this occasion showed signs of being a neighbour first and a local politician second, "infinitely kind and active". Moira remained cordial. Lord Dalkeith wrote in congratulation, "You are now to snap your fingers at the Bar."

Indeed it seemed that Scott was to have the best of both worlds. He had never found the profession of advocate congenial, and although he had not been doing badly he had appreciated hints that young advocates should not flirt with the Muses. Now he would not be giving up the law, only the somewhat visionary possibility of ever proceeding to the Bench. He explained his situation in the Introduction to the 1830 edition of *The Lay*. "My profession and I, therefore, come to stand nearly upon the footing which honest Slender consoled himself on having established with Mistress Anne Page. There was no great love between us at the beginning, and it pleased Heaven to decrease it on farther acquaintance." Lord Dalkeith had said that naturally Lord Spencer, as a professed patron of literature, had done what he ought. "We shall expect much from your leisure. *But* you are not to be idle . . . Go to the Hills and converse with the Spirit of the Fell, or any spirit but the spirit of Party."[1]

It dawned upon Scott rather gradually that his reception in London this year was not quite the same as it had been in 1803. "After all, a literary reputation is of some use here." Three years ago he had looked with almost childlike wonder at "this immense Vanity Fair" in which he knew so few people. Now the author of *The Lay* was invited to that Whig stronghold, Holland House. Mr Canning introduced himself as a friend of Ellis, also Mr Hookham Frere of the Foreign Office, both delightful companions.

He went out to The Priory, Stanmore. It had been a relief to the Scott family firm that, with his third marriage, the domestic affairs of John, ninth Earl and first Marquess of Abercorn, seemed to be approximating to the normal. Walter's father had been the Abercorn's man of business, and now Brother Tom looked after the Scottish estate at Duddingston. But the marquess was an unapproachable figure. One of the handsomest men of his day, with a very dark Spanish cast of countenance, he would unquestionably, in Revolutionary France, have been accorded a place in the first tumbril. He hunted and travelled with all his orders displayed: but he could not keep a wife. His first one had relapsed into invalidism and died; his second, for whom he had obtained the rank of an earl's daughter (as bad a piece of graft, said scandal, as ever was known), had nevertheless gone off with his first wife's brother. He had divorced her with disdain and married a widow, a daughter of Lord Arran, previously wife of an Irish private gentleman of a broken constitution, from whom she had soon separated to enjoy herself on the Continent with a sister. The third Lady Abercorn was forty-three, intelligent and fully alive to the possibilities of her position. She showed Scott a cottage *orné* on the lake at Stanmore, just the haunt for a poet. A house in St James's Square was to be the site of her London *salon*.[2]

He went on an expedition up to Hampstead, to make the acquaintance of a compatriot with whom he had long corresponded. Miss Joanna Baillie had lately removed there on the death of her mother. The famous female playwright was entirely unspoilt. This was the London house to which Scott would send Sophia to stay as soon as she was old enough to attend her parents south. Miss Baillie held out hopes that she might be coming north. She afterwards confided in a friend that at first sight she had been a little disappointed in the author of *The Lay*, having expected something more elegant and refined in feature; but as soon as they began to talk she saw his countenance transformed. And if she had been lost in a crowd, that was the face that she would have chosen to turn to for help amongst a thousand, from its shrewdness and benevolence.

Scott would have liked to go down to Bath to see Ellis, but he was tied

Walter Scott, 1809
By Raeburn. Original at Abbotsford.
An 1808 version is at Bowhill, in the collection of the Duke of Buccleuch, in
which the background is of Hermitage Castle, and the dog Camp is at Scott's
feet. In the Abbotsford version the background is of the Yale of Yarrow and
Camp has for companion one of the greyhounds, Percy and Douglas. This is the
picture housed by Skene when 39 Castle Street was sold.
By permission of Mrs Maxwell-Scott.

to London by the hard fact that Mr Bindley of Somerset House had lent him books essential for his work on Dryden, on the condition that he did not consult them outside the liberties of Westminster.

If he had taken more notice of Lord Dalkeith's warning to keep clear of politics, he would not have gone out to Blackheath to dine at Montagu House with the Princess of Wales—"an honour which I shall very long remember. She is an enchanting princess who dwells in an enchanted palace, and I cannot help thinking that her prince must labour under some malignant spell that he denies himself her society."3

Looking back, his time in London had been spent very gaily, and but for the situation of poor Lord Melville, very happily. But he would be glad to take the early coach home on Sunday morning, March 3rd, "back to wife and bairns".

<h2 style="text-align:center">II</h2>

He wrote to Ellis that his homecoming had been joyous. He now had at Ashestiel two cottages with families in them, and all his other stock, human and animal, were in great good health. Before he left Edinburgh he had taken possession of his new office, and the duty appeared to be very simple, consisting chiefly in signing his name. Luckily his was very short. He had five colleagues, and all their children called the parents of other children aunts and uncles, and they frequently dined together. One of them was Colin Mackenzie, an old schoolfellow. Hector Macdonald Buchanan of Drumakiln had the blood of Clanranald in his veins, and owned a beautiful home, Ross Priory near Dunbarton where Scott became a regular guest.

Every morning a solemn coach picked up the Principal Clerks from their houses and drove them from the New Town to Parliament House in the Old Town where they were seated at their black table in front of the Bench before 10 a.m., when the Judges of the Inner Court arrived and took their seats. The Court sat from May 12th to July 12th and November 12th to March 12th, but never on Mondays or alternate Wednesdays. There was a short Christmas holiday. The Clerks had to draw up a résumé of the oral decisions announced from the Bench. As a body they had a high standard of legal proficiency.4 Scott was by no means always ready when the coach drew up, and had to bolt a last draught of tea before dashing out with half a scone still in his hand.

Lockhart thought that as Scott's literary work and increasing correspondence now had to be done before breakfast or after dinner (provided he had not brought back too much home-work from the Court), he lacked exercise. He still had duty with the Volunteers and went for rides, but on the whole his Edinburgh life was as enclosed and sedentary as his country life was outdoor and active. Skene came to stay at Ashestiel in April. It was to be his last visit before his marriage to a daughter of Sir William Forbes, and his last visit for some years, for the lady proved so delicate that they had to set up house in the south of England—a great disappointment and loss to the Scotts.

When he had no guests at Ashestiel, Dryden was what Scott called the companion of his solitude. He was getting on with the plays, but there was no doubt that his decision not to make cuts was causing him some concern.

Colin Mackenzie handed him a letter from no less a person than Warren Hastings suggesting he should write an epic poem on the career of Lord Nelson. This was not the first suggestion he had received on the subject, and he had made an attempt but knew when he was beaten He managed some very fine stanzas combining Britain's loss of Nelson, Pitt and Fox in the Preface to the third canto of his next narrative poem, but even the subject of that was not yet in his mind.

Lady Abercorn wrote him good letters, opening "My dearest Friend", and he sometimes answered them as gaily as he could, sitting looking very grave in Court.

June 9th 1806

My dear Lady Marchioness,
     Did you ever hear the french parrot's apology for its silence—
"Je pense plus"?

He rambled on telling her of his homecoming to "my little family" whom he had found "at our mountain farm closed in by many a dark hill", and of his many occupations as the head of a family—sheep to be bought, bullocks to be sold, a sick horse, a lame greyhound, salmon to be caught and poachers punished. He pictured her at the Priory which must now be in all the glory of midsummer foliage. He was not quite satisfied with his literary prowess. He hoped his Dryden was going on prosperously. A fourth edition of *The Lay* was coming, and some more of his Ballads. He had a work in view—but so visionary and remote that the distance between Stanmore and Edinburgh was nothing to it—a Highland romance. Mrs Scott was deeply obliged by the message sent to her. "She has a grateful remembrance of her late Protector and friend Lord Downshire which extends to all his friends." He sent to Stanmore his poem, sung loudly by

John Ballantyne at the public dinner given in honour of the acquittal of Lord Melville. It had two rather unfortunate references—"Tallyho to the Fox" gave mortal offence to disciples of the statesman who knew that he was sick to death (particularly Lady Rosslyn, a dear friend of Lady Dalkeith). His toast "Here's to the Princess and long may she live!" was not echoed in well-informed circles.

Before the Courts rose he went out to Melville Castle to dine, and was comforted to find his old patron never better in health or spirits. ("I have seen when the streets of Edinburgh were thought by the inhabitants almost too vulgar for Lord Melville to walk upon.")

Lady Abercorn was so sympathetic, so much interested in his family concerns. He confided to her a grief on which he did not expand to many, "the arrival of my youngest brother from the West Indies with ruined health and blasted prospects: after a tedious struggle he died last week". He was thankful to be out at his farm again, and wished he could transport her on a magic carpet for a day to observe the extraordinary contrast between the scenery there and at the Priory. "Our whole habitation could dance very easily in your great Salon without displacing a single moveable or endangering a mirror. We have no green pastures nor stately trees, but to make amends we have one of the most beautiful streams in the world winding through steep mountains which are now purple with heath blossom." The boast was hardly written when a Scottish tornado broke upon the scene. Charlotte resolved to die in bed like a good Christian. The servants in a body announced that the thunder and lightning heralded the end of the world. At Minto House the inhabitants had to retire to the upper floors as the lower part of the mansion was quite filled by the Teviot in spate. An heroic cook-maid secured a sirloin of beef in her retreat, otherwise the plague of famine would have been added to the distress of the sufferers. Ricks of hay and scores of trees, young and old, even cattle and horses, came swirling past Ashestiel. Scott, although he did think they were all in great danger, "maintained my character for stoicism". Next day he took all hands down to begin repairs to the ford. Skene had always thought it a dangerous one. But Skene had come to the conclusion that Scott liked dangerous fords.

The landscape apparently recovered very speedily, for on August 18th Scott was writing to Heber to urge him to make a push to come up for a stay—not so difficult surely, for a bachelor. "You never saw anything more beautiful than our Border hills in the deep imperial purple of the heather blossom." It was so lovely now that he almost regretted he had not accepted Lord Melville's invitation to the Highlands. The idea of a romance in that direction was growing upon him. But in the end of September Marriott came up "to fish and rhyme", and in November he began another epic poem of the Borders: *Marmion: a tale of Flodden Field*.

Without having seen it, Constable offered him a thousand pounds for it.

III

One of the activities of the new Government, taken over by Lord Eldon, was a project to make radical changes in the Scottish law courts. The present structure must be altered to conform more closely with the English model. Scott held this to be a violation of the Act of Union of 1707. At a debate at the Faculty of Advocates on some of the propositions he made the longest speech he had ever delivered to that assembly, and with a flow of eloquence for which even his friends had been unprepared. Two of the reformers walked home with him. One of them, Jeffrey, began in a jocular manner by complimenting him on his rhetorical powers. But Scott was dreadfully distressed. "No, no! 'tis no laughing matter; little by little, whatever your wishes may be, you will destroy and undermine until nothing of what makes Scotland Scotland shall remain." He turned away, and rested his brow on the wall of the Mound, but not before Jeffrey had perceived that tears were gushing down his face.[5]

Colin Mackenzie had been appointed by the Principal Clerks of Session to fight for compensation if they were to be swept away, but suddenly came news that he was holding on against fearful odds, owing to ill-health, and must be relieved. Scott caught the London stage-coach on March 15th, 1807. It was more than a month later than on his sudden journey last year, but the weather was full winter. He wrote to tell his wife that they had been almost stopped by snow at Morpeth and he had seldom felt colder than during the nights and early mornings.[6] However, he had arrived safely and Miller had got him comfortable lodgings at 5 Bury Street, and he had been greeted by the surprising but most welcome intelligence that his journey might prove unnecessary. The Ministry were in the act of going out. Lord Dalkeith, who was in the secret, told him that all had been settled yesterday. His Majesty had refused to countenance a bill to give commissions in the army to Catholics, and Ministers had agreed to withdraw it, but not to pledge themselves never again to try to rush concessions. "Lord Melville is to be at the head of either the Admiralty or the Treasury,"[7] he wrote to Charlotte. "There's a turn for you—match it in your novels if you can." He was writing to his brother Clerks about the change, which would make the settlement of their matters very easy, and he believed that he would stand very well with the new Ministers as he had stood by them in hard weather. He had even hopes now that they might retire what he called his Old Man of the Sea—George Home. "My being on the spot is inconceivably fortunate." He had seen poor Mackenzie, very thin and his voice altered in a melancholy manner. Doctors said he ought to go abroad.

It turned out that by an Act of Parliament, Home could never be pensioned off. A bill might be introduced to create an additional Clerk; but that would have to wait till next session. Commissioners were to be appointed to draw up a report on the matter, and as two were to be Clerks of Session it was probable he might be one chosen. It was unfortunate that his servant David Ross, whom he had sent by sea with his heavy luggage, had not yet turned up, for he was already receiving many invitations. He had been round to see the Dumergues and put his foot in it by blundering out his joy at the fall of the Government. A great lady present had looked disagreeably. He had discovered that she was Mrs Fitzherbert, said to be the mistress of the Prince of Wales and certainly a devout Catholic. Monsieur Dumergue was going out of town for the Easter holidays. "They pray and keep house so I shall see little of them till these are over." He had arrived to find them all much upset as the Birds' little boy had run away from the Charterhouse School. William Stewart Rose had asked him to dine to meet Canning and Frere, and suggested they should go down together to call upon his father (once Chancellor of the Exchequer) at Cuffnells, in Hampshire, and thence to the Isle of Wight. Scott breakfasted and dined with the Dalkeiths at Montagu House, and called on them almost every day.

David arrived in the nick of time before he went down to spend the long Easter weekend at the Priory. He found a very gay party there including Lady Charlotte Lindsay, one of the wittiest and most agreeable women he had ever seen, young Lord Aberdeen of whose political career hopes were high, and his wife, a reigning beauty, daughter of Lord Abercorn by his first marriage. Kemble and the Duchess of Gordon were expected. Lady Abercorn had been much delighted with the *cadeau* "Mimi" had sent, and was writing. His thoughts were often with home and he never failed to send love to the "monkies" and ask for news of them— The Laird's dancing lessons, he hoped, were not making him forget his other lessons. He expected little Charles was now trotting about. He never failed either to assure a French lady that he was ever hers most truly or "your faithful" W.S. He continued to feel remorse at the thought of the Black Child, Kiki ("Camp"), deserted.

His sixth letter was splendidly headed "On Board His Majesty's Yacht 'Medina', Portsmouth Harbour", and contained descriptions of the dockyard, an expedition in the Port Admiral's barge to see ships of the line at Spithead, and a trip to the Isle of Wight to see Carisbrooke Castle. The return passage to Christchurch was very rough, and Rose had suffered considerably. They had to land at Lymington and take a post-chaise to Rose's marine villa, "Gundimore", near Mudiford. Rose lent him a horse and they rode into the Forest, which was looking absolutely beautiful and quite surpassed Scottish woods in depth and variety, but was lacking in burns and glens.

When he returned to London he found his card-rack quite covered with invitations from Secretaries of State and Cabinet Ministers. He thought this extremely droll. He had also found two welcome letters from "My Dearest girl". His Mimi could be when she chose a good correspondent and told him all he wanted to know. David's wife was doing well, and old Kiki taking his food and regular exercise, his leg no worse. She was going to give a little fête in honour of the change of government. All she asked from London was tea and candles. He urged her not to stint herself and to apply to Ballantyne if she needed more housekeeping money. He enclosed a letter from India. Her brother's wife had apparently had a miscarriage and might have to be sent home.

Not all his news was entirely cheerful. He had thought Ellis looked very ill, but he was pressed to pay a visit to Sunninghill. Another invalid with an even sadder story was poor John Marriott, tutor to Lord Scott, the Dalkeiths' son and heir. He was to have married Mary Scott, and taken a house at Eton in a few weeks' time. "A tendency to a pulmonary complaint" had been diagnosed.[8] It had been truly sad to have to part with him, and Colin Mackenzie, under circumstances which suggested that it might be for ever.

He dined with the Abercorns on the day of his return to London, at their St James's Square house, which was indeed very large. Proofs of *Marmion* had been coming down from Ballantyne: he had corrected some while with Rose and now got Lord Abercorn to frank some more. He showed his host the Introduction to the First Canto, and his lordship suggested a quite reasonable addition to the lines on Fox (though he had been no follower of the statesman.) "The said Marquess has taken prodigiously to my poetry and we are upon a footing of intimacy which, his Lady says, is very unusual with this great man . . ." He had breakfasted twice with the Lady and she admitted him to her boudoir—"There's for you!" But he was beginning to fret to get home to see his boys and girls and their mamma playing a game around his hearthside and the Black Child on the rug. It still all depended on what turn the Bill would take. His list for what he hoped might be his last week was full—Sunday with the Dumergues, Monday with the Wedderburns of Inveresk, a very smart and fashionable young man married to a Minto niece. On Tuesday he was not so lucky. The Wolfe Murrays lived out at Acton, and although the bride was a lively talkative brunette (a favourite type with him), their house, decorated in the latest classical style, was cold; the floors were all marble. Her aunts were a set of old witches, and the only other man was a wordy politician. To complete the horror, a robbery was committed on the road as they drove back into town. He went to the Abercorns again on the Wednesday. Brother Tom had been summoned, and he fancied the marquess was going to read him a lecture. He had his dear Lady Douglas on Thursday, and a rout at the Abercorns for which eight hundred invitation cards had been issued. Friday, he dined with Lord Somerville, and he might go on Saturday to Lady Castlereagh's party after the opera— invited for half past midnight. The First Minister's lady was a good- humoured laughter-loving dame who had been lovely but was now blowsy. (Her laughter was a cloak for much misery.)

Actually he had kept Saturday to go out to Blackheath to see the princess. This duty-visit might prove rather tricky. He had sounded Lady Abercorn on the subject some months past. Was it true that she had been indiscreet? When he got to London he found that the lovers with whom her name had been linked were Admiral Sir Sidney Smith, the Hero of Acre, Captain Manby of the Royal Navy, Thomas Lawrence, the portrait painter, and the Right Hon. George Canning. She seemed to have got into rather bad company. There were a Sir James and Lady Douglas, great new friends. She had stood godmother to their daughter. Lady Douglas was also credited with being a mistress of the Admiral, and there had been a quarrel. The princess, who was allowed to see little of her own child and was very fond of young people, had taken up an unintellectual little boy aged five, called Austin. Lady Douglas said he was an illegitimate child of Her Royal Highness. The prince had seen the Douglases and the king had ordered a "delicate investigation". Of course, to seduce the wife of the heir to the throne was high treason punishable by death. She had been found innocent. Scott had sent her a proof of the Introduction to the Third Canto of *Marmion*, in which he had mentioned the death at the Battle of Jena of her heroic father. Her lady-in-waiting had returned thanks and a silver vase.

Two versions exist of Scott's visit to Blackheath on April 25th, 1807.

In his letter to Charlotte he was careful. Lockhart later heard a little more. She literally received him with open arms, the warmest reception with which he had met in London, although all had been cordial. "She spoke of her situation with her usual frankness." Scott's allusion to her in his poem on Lord Melville's acquittal was known to her. The company at dinner was small and seemed perfectly normal—Sir Vicary Gibbs, old Lord Glenbervie and his wife, a daughter of the late Prime Minister North, Hookham Frere and the lady-in-waiting. Scott thought the princess looked thinner. As soon as she had greeted him she cried, "Come, my dear Walter Scott, and see all my improvements." "Accordingly she whisk'd me through her grotto and pavilion and conservatory, and so forth asking me slily at the same time if I was not afraid to be alone with her." Lockhart's version differed a little. In the course of the evening the princess conducted him alone to admire some flowers in a conservatory, and the place being rather dark, a lame man hesitated for a moment before following her down some steps, which she had taken at a skip. She turned round and cried in mock indignation, "Ah! false and fainthearted troubadour! You will not trust yourself with me for fear of your neck!"9

Next day he set off on the top of the Windsor coach between an old girl who gave the company the history of her three husbands and five apprentices, and an enormous fellow of at least twenty stone who assured him that the peas which they saw in the gardens on their road were not as tall as his, and that there was an uncommonly early and forward crop of ducklings and goslings in the ponds around Brentford. It was a perfect Gillray caricature. He thought what a convenient country this was, where one might dine with the Princess of Wales yesterday, sup with the Prime Minister's lady, and ride on the outside of a coach with a female tallow chandler, without anybody caring a farthing. The fare for himself and his servant came to seven shillings.

It was Sunday morning, and he went to St George's Chapel and saw his king, which had been his reason for going by Windsor and not by the shorter route through Staines. He did not tell Charlotte a word about seeing the king. One glance at that pathetic, vacant-eyed, stone-blind, bearded figure told a loyal subject that Walter Scott had come too late for George III. He had heard rumours that the Prince of Wales was mortally sick—dropsy. If he were to die, his discarded wife, as mother of the heiress to the throne, might yet make her enemies her footstool. After the service, he took a chaise across Windsor Park to Ellis's villa.

Sunninghill was in full beauty, the ground whitened with daises and carpeted with violets. He slipped a sample of violets in his letter, as he knew his Mimi so loved them.

On May 4th he sent a short note to say that his London career of dissipation was over. Parliament was being dissolved, so the Bill could not come on till next session. He was turning homeward tomorrow, after a quiet dinner with Miller. He would go to the inn from which the coach started, for the remainder of the night, as 4 a.m. was the ungodly hour. He was going to Loughborough with Wordsworth who had also been in town, and had been lent a farmhouse at Coleorton by Sir George Beaumont. From there he would wait upon Miss Anna Seward at Lichfield. After the usual shock that the author of *The Lay* did not look like a poet, this verbose but excellent literary success was delighted with him. "Walter Scott came like a sunbeam to my dwelling."

He had to cut out two visits which he had intended to make when he had planned to go home by the western road—those to Robert Boulton at Birmingham and Mr Robert Surtees at Durham, with whom he had been in touch over ballads. He had done what he could for his friends while in London—tried to get the Sheriffdom of Perth for Will Erskine, and pressed Hogg's *Mountain Bard* upon Her Royal Highness, Miss Seward, and the unvisited Surtees.

He exactly hit the election on his homeward road and got no sleep for three nights. If his coach-ride down to Windsor had resembled a caricature by Rowlandson or Gillray, the brush of Hogarth would have been required to do justice to the crowd scenes through which he passed both before and after he joined the Great North Road at York. Post horses were almost unobtainable, and the insides of coaches were packed with voters whom candidates were transporting to the polls, well-fortified with brandy. Fortunately he had sent round by sea a very special and perishable souvenir of Mayfair. Lady Abercorn had called in her husband's fashionable married daughter to help her to choose, out of a great number, a cap for Mrs Walter Scott. It would be the envy of all Edinburgh. It was a replica of one made for Lady Aberdeen.

IV

He had known that as well as editing Dryden, he had this summer what he called a by-job to do for Constable before he had completed *Marmion*—he had hoped for Christmas. It was rather attractive—to produce a biographical introduction and notes for the State Papers of a Tudor diplomat, Sir Ralph Sadler, whose career included having been jailer to Queen Mary at Tutbury. But as soon as the courts rose in July and he got down to Ashestiel, an affliction came upon him. As before, one of the younger brothers was the cause. And this time, though not so utterly hopeless as the disgrace and death of Daniel, it was worse in a way, because this was the one who had taken on their respected father's business, and Tom, though constitutionally lazy, was a good companion. For some years Scott had feared that Tom could not be giving satisfaction to his clients, especially in his handling of the Abercorn estate. The truth so much exceeded his fears that, as he wrote to Lady Abercorn, it gave him a fever for three days, and, if he had had the time, he would have fallen ill with vexation, anxiety and grief. However, as his brother had disappeared and creditors were turning to him for satisfaction, he had to follow his usual recipe and go straight out to meet danger. The affair, at first almost incredible to him, dragged on for about six weeks of high summer. The Marquess (of Carabas, as Scott had sometimes called him in mockery) now displayed all the virtues of his defects. He behaved throughout a very unpleasant affair with the utmost good sense and eventually great liberality. He engaged a Writer to the Signet (a member of the Troop and cousin of Will Erskine) to look into the damage, and Scott had some of the brightest moments of this season when he and Guthrie Wright were held up in the neighbourhood of Dumfries waiting to see Lord Abercorn on his way with his family to Ireland. They visited Sweetheart Abbey, Caerlaverock and other ancient buildings, and Scott thought and talked of *Marmion*. In his darkest hours he had foreseen that to make up to the marquess the loss caused by Tom's mismanagement, he might have to part with all his own savings, his house, furniture and books, and retire from being a Principal Clerk. "Thank God," he wrote to Miss Seward, "everything has turned out better than I ventured to hope." Trouble had descended upon him which had caused him to hang up his harp on a willow tree. At length Tom, when he had found that he was not to be arrested, had returned to the neighbourhood of Edinburgh and found a lodging in Gorgie Park. Taxation was said to be lighter in the Isle of Man where the Duke of Argyll was raising a fencible regiment. He departed with his brood to Douglas, whence he sent to Castle Street and to his old mother in George Street beautiful barrels of red herrings. There had been two alleviating circumstances in his exploits. Guthrie Wright, upon consideration, thought that he had been more slack and incompetent than dishonest, and Tom's poor wife, who had given birth to another child just before he levanted, and who had been thought by the family to be rather an inferior match, showed up in adversity as a pattern wife and mother.

Lady Abercorn, who had been helpful throughout, soothingly said that she could not believe how a brother of his could have acted so ill; there never was, surely, a greater contrast. "I am more angry with him for deceiving you than for anything else."[10] He had reached the fourth canto of *Marmion* before he had to break off, and certain spots at Ashestiel were for ever associated with its composition. There was a knoll on the adjoining farm of the Peel (owned by a Laidlaw known not without reason as "Laird Nippy"). He used to repair there for contemplation, and it was afterwards named Sheriff's Knowe. Another favourite stance was almost on the banks of the Tweed near the *haugh* of Ashestiel. He used to pull reeds from the fen and cast them on the waters to watch them floating down. As he lingered he heard the milkmaid shrilly singing as she descended over rough pastures to the house. He went further afield to Yarrow on horseback. "Oh man!" he told his son-in-law years later, "many a grand gallop I had among those braes when I was thinking of *Marmion*."

At the beginning of September he set off for a little holiday to visit the Douglases at Bothwell Castle. He wanted to show Charlotte the Falls of Clyde. They came home by lonely glens and ran into a storm which brought worse floods than those of last year. The douce little town of Peebles was half under water when they reached it, and in some stretches the road had just disappeared. However, by walking and wading when the coachman could not make out the way, and eventually footing it the whole of the last eight miles, they did arrive at Ashestiel to find that a good part of their crop had been swept away.

In late October the Troop went into quarters again and Skene believed that a whole canto of *Marmion* had been composed on the drill grounds at Portobello Sands around dawn. Scott was often noticed on his black gelding at the very edge of the sea, in complete abstraction. "Now and again you would see him plunge in his spurs and go off at the charge, with the spray dashing about him."[11] Returning from exercises with Skene, in the rear of the squadron, he would recite what he had been composing. It was the Battle of Flodden. He asked Skene to supply some sketches for a copy of the poem to be presented to the Princess of Wales. In fashionable houses guests were not now left to sit with hands across to listen to the prosing of such as could prose, cards, or amateur performances on the pianoforte. Books, he told Miss Seward, were allowed into the drawing-room and no longer respected only for their insides. "The great genius who invented the gilded, inlaid or Japan bookstands, for boudoirs and drawing-rooms, did a great service to the print engraver and bookseller, but I question if literature in general has not suffered from the invention."

V

He wrote to his dear Lady Louisa Stuart in triumph from Edinburgh on January 18th, 1808:

> Marmion is, at this instant, gasping upon Flodden Field, and there I have been obliged to leave him for these few days in the death pangs. I hope I shall find time enough this morning to knock him on the head with two or three thumping stanzas.

Marmion was published on February 23rd, and was even more successful than *The Lay*. It did not escape some criticism. There were Introductions to every canto. These were addressed to friends—William Stewart Rose, John Marriott, William Erskine, James Skene, George Ellis, Richard Heber. He had originally intended them as separate publications and some people objected to them as interruptions to the narrative; but each was a little masterpiece. The whole epic was dedicated to the second Buccleuch son, Henry, Lord Montagu, and in the epistle to Marriott, the boy's tutor, Scott had regretted the prolonged absence from his native land of the little Buccleuch grandson, Lord Scott, a constant playmate.

> No youthful Baron's left to grace
> The Forest-Sheriff's lonely chase,
> And ape in manly step and tone
> The majesty of Oberon.

Eight days after *Marmion* appeared, this promising boy, "my young Chief", died, aged ten, of complications following measles. Scott wrote to offer to cancel the lines in the second edition, but Lady Dalkeith replied with her usual calm dignity that she took pleasure in whatever recalled the memory of her poor boy. She had sent for *Marmion*.

There was another unforeseen minor tragedy. The lines supplied by Lord Abercorn to the eulogy on Fox, added in proof, had not been included in some copies. The *Morning Chronicle* said that this had been deliberate, according to whether the presentation copies had been sent to Whig or Tory. Scott wrote to the press to deny this. Wordsworth's praise was characteristically temperate. "I think your end has been attained." In his personal circle the new poem was as much liked as *The Lay*, although he believed this was not so in the wider world. Ellis wrote that if he had seen *Marmion* without knowing the author, he should have ranked it on the very top shelf of English poetry. The few blemishes noticed by him were not detected by any other reviewer.

A very minor critic, Leigh Hunt, was constitutionally bitter. His *Edinburgh* article was so unhandsome that when Jeffrey saw it in proof in the April number, he sent it along to Castle Street where he was engaged to dine that night, with a note of self-justification and apology. His cruellest cut was an accusation that the author had "throughout neglected Scottish feelings and Scottish characters". Scott assured him that the article had not disturbed his digestion, though he hoped neither his booksellers nor the public would agree with the opinions it expressed. To correspondents he ruefully admitted the review had been "very sharp". Jeffrey presented himself and was received by Scott with his usual cordiality. Charlotte, however, was icy cold and at the guest's departure could not resist a cut. "Well, good night Mr Jeffrey. Dey tell me you have abused Scott in de 'Review' and I hope Mr Constable has paid *you* very well for writing it."

The grand gesture of Constable, "Old Crafty", in offering a thousand pounds for *Marmion* unseen, had created a sensation, not only in the literary world. He also published the *Edinburgh* and Scott was becoming increasingly dissatisfied with it. Jeffrey had attacked both Southey and Wordsworth in its columns, and damagingly. Nevertheless Scott had tried to persuade Southey to become a contributor to the review. It paid well. When Southey refused and said that he was at work on the *Morte Arthur*, Scott, who had long intended to attempt that favourite subject, magnanimously urged him on. But they both had another reason for disliking the *Edinburgh* at present. Trafalgar had, it was true, paralysed the threat of invasion, but the dying Pitt, on hearing the news of the Battle of Austerlitz, was said to have breathed the words "Roll up the map of Europe. It will not be wanted these ten years." Buonaparte had marched from strength to strength upon the Continent. His latest invasion was that of the Peninsula. The Portuguese royal family had fled to Brazil, and he was about to put in his brother Joseph to rule Spain, having completely gulled the decadent Spanish king with an offer to carve up Portugal between France and Spain. Jeffrey and his friends wanted their country to confess itself beat by the greatest conqueror in history, patch up what peace they could, and get on with Reform at home.

Hard on the heels of *Marmion* and bound, Scott hoped, to help the sale of this much more serious work of scholarship, the eighteen-volume edition of Dryden was published. Scott regretted Southey's appropriation of the *Morte Arthur* the less because he had just agreed with Constable, on advantageous terms, for a complete edition of Swift. This, he reckoned, would occupy him for two or three years.

Amongst his current by-jobs were arranging for republication by Miller of thirteen volumes of Tracts collected by Lord Somers, and editing, and writing a final chapter for a mediaeval romance by the late Joseph Strutt, antiquarian and engraver, brought out in four volumes by Murray. Strutt, while retrenching in rural Hertfordshire, at a farmhouse near Tewin, had been struck by the picturesque appearance of a neighbouring manor house, actually built about 1560, and had named his story after it, *Queen Hoo Hall*. Unfortunately he had set his plot in the reign of Henry VI. But for Scott the experience was valuable, as an awful warning of display of antiquarian learning in the guise of fiction. Jeffrey had ridiculed *Marmion* for its mentions of tabard, scutcheon, wimple, etc. *Queen Hoo Hall* far surpassed *Marmion*. This labour, hardly of love, was followed by a reprint of Captain George Carleton's Memoirs and those of Robert Cary, Earl of Monmouth. In vain Lady Abercorn and Lady Louisa Stuart rebuked him for undertaking such distractions. It amused him, he said, to have so many irons in the fire. Ballantyne's, who printed all, naturally needed capital for expansion and he lent them two thousand pounds of which twelve hundred was a loan from his brother Major John Scott. The firm had taken on, two years ago, at a salary of two hundred pounds per annum, John the younger Ballantyne, who had turned up penniless. He had expensive tastes, a poor constitution and an inexhaustible fund of humour.

Joanna Baillie came to stay at Castle Street in March and was the perfect guest. Wordsworth said that if he wished to give a foreigner an impression of a thoroughly well-bred Englishwoman, he would introduce him to Miss Baillie. Scott had never been more lionised in his native city than during this spring. Dryden had enhanced his reputation as a scholar. Of course, as *Marmion* charged on from edition to edition, there were not wanting persons to regret that their poet had not a partner more worthy of him. Miss Baillie, in a company which included Wordsworth, Humphry Davy and Crabb Robinson of *The Times*, struck up staunchly for Madame Mimi. "When I visited her I saw a great deal to like. She seemed to admire and look up to her husband. She was very kind to her guests, her children were well-bred, and the house was in excellent order. And she had some smart roses in her cap, and I did not like her the less for that."

Mrs Siddons was in Edinburgh at the same date to take her farewell of the theatre, or so Scott believed. She was to hang on till 1819. Though he admired her as an actress, her tragedy queen airs in private life contrasted unfavourably with Miss Baillie's cheerful modesty—though she was by no means to be trampled upon. (She put Miss Mary Berry, arbiter of taste, severely in her place for caprice and patronising neglect. "If anything in the simplicity of my appearance has led you to suppose me of an easier and gentler temper than I am, I am sorry for the involuntary deceit.") None of Joanna Baillie's plays had been produced by Kemble for over eight years, and nothing came of her Edinburgh meeting with Mrs Siddons. She fancied that the tragic muse looked a little uncomfortable as she returned her curtsey. Miss Baillie had mistakenly interpreted "Make me more De Montforts" as an order for another drama, and she had written it and it had been coldly rejected.

The early spring had been tragic for the farmer—late frosts, deep snow and rivers overflowing. Poor Hogg lost all his flock. But then came the most beautiful May imaginable. Scott went for a little **sortie** into the Highlands, taking Charlotte and Sophia. They were accompanied by a strange little Welsh lady blue-stocking, wished upon them by Miss Seward, Miss Lydia White. She had her points. She took Charlotte out sketching. Camp liked her; she gave him bits. She put Scott in touch with a clergyman in Ireland who revealed what no one had yet discovered, essential letters from Swift to Vanessa. They parted from her at Loch Katrine and went on for a short stay with Lord Melville, near Crieff.

Another friend for life was looming on the horizon. Lady Louisa had recommended Mr Morritt of Rokeby, an amiable gentleman, a *dilettante* and author of *belles-lettres* who was to become the founder of the Travellers Club. He owned a Palladian mansion at Greta Bridge, Yorkshire. As a young man, on a Grand Tour which had lasted two years, he had explored parts of Greece and Asia Minor unknown to the tourist. Mr and Mrs Morritt arrived in Edinburgh and were expected at Ashestiel in time for the harvest.[12] Scott showed them the capital and the Border with great satisfaction.

Only two things marred the Ashestiel holidays of 1808. The first was irremediable. Camp was failing. The breed was not long-lived. He could no longer follow a man on a horse. Still, the cry of "Coming by the hill" or "Coming by the ford" roused him from his mat to meet his master.

The second cause for anxiety was not domestic. Scott's relations with Constable were increasingly unhappy. Every time he went into their premises in the High Street, Constable's free-spoken, hard-drinking partner Hunter enquired as to the progress of Swift. Scott had liked being asked to edit Swift, and the remuneration offered was handsome, but he was not going to be nagged into pushing aside everything else to concentrate on it. He was also offended by their rudeness to an unusual young German refugee assistant who did good research work for him. Weber, who had a Hanoverian sire, and English mother, and had been born in Russia, came immediately from Jena, where he had been a medical student.

Scott had said that he hoped to get to London again this year, but now he longed to go to Spain. In June a deputation from a Supreme Junta in Madrid had arrived to ask for British aid against Buonaparte. There had been a spontaneous rising and a victory under a Spanish partisan leader, in Andalusia. Scott ardently hoped that Spain had got a Wallace, a Dundee or a Montrose. A British expeditionary force containing famous Scottish regiments landed in the Peninsula and Sir Arthur Wellesley, in whom Scott put faith, won, almost at once, a battle against General Junot's Army of Portugal at Vimeiro. But after that events settled in the bad old pattern. Sir Arthur was summoned home to face a court of enquiry. A humiliating Convention had been entered into at Cintra by which all that Wellesley had won seemed to have been handed back. Both the elderly Commander-in-Chief (of a prominent Scottish family) and his second-in-command were also brought home and the command was given, unwillingly, to Sir John Moore, regarded as a Whig nominee, whose experience of expeditionary forces sent to assist native risings was discouraging. From Salamanca, where he fixed his headquarters for the month of November, he entered into an acrimonious correspondence with Hookham Frere who had been sent to Madrid as Minister Plenipotentiary.

In the October number of the *Edinburgh* an article which Scott attributed to Jeffrey demanded that Britain should cease to attempt to match herself with Buonaparte in support of a stage army of native banditti. Scott cancelled his subscription to the *Review*—published by Constable. It was at this propitious moment that young Mr Murray from Fleet Street, after an arrangement with James Ballantyne at Ferrybridge, accompanied the bookseller north, and presented himself at Ashestiel. Heber happened to be there on one of his flying visits. Murray's first suggestion, that Britain's best-selling poet should enter into a contract with him to edit a large collection of popular novels, was enthusiastically considered by Scott, but eventually came to nothing. The idea of a patriotic Tory magazine to be published in London as a counterblast to the *Edinburgh* engaged Scott's instant support. Murray's list of possible contributors was imposing. Canning himself, though he was somewhat engaged at present, would give his blessing and some information. Scott thought he could count upon Ellis, Rose, both Hebers, Will Erskine, possibly Frere.

The young publisher's background and address could not have been more reassuring. He was the second Murray. His father, who had dropped a Mac on coming south, had been a lieutenant of marines. After young Murray's autumn call, Scott wrote him down as a coming man; he had capital and enterprise, and more real knowledge of what concerned his business than any of his brethren.[13]

It would have been much the best that the new *Quarterly Review* should have begun to appear with a January number, but that was not possible. Its first issue was for March 1809. It sold well in Edinburgh and London sales picked up. On January 14th Scott wrote to Southey, "I have had a high quarrel with Constable and Co." He had offered to resign from the Swift project since they seemed so disappointed with his progress. He offered to buy the portrait of himself by Raeburn which Constable had commissioned. He could not offer to send back the hogshead of claret which had been Constable's gift to him on the publication of his last narrative poem. Dinner-parties at Castle Street had enjoyed many glasses of "Marmion". In the end, the parting was civilly achieved and the inevitable sequel followed closely. Scott had decided to start an Edinburgh publishing firm, John Ballantyne and Co., in opposition to Constable. He was to supply half the capital, and James and John were to find the rest.

Lockhart believed Scott provided James's quarter and John's was borrowed, either from Scott or someone else. They hoped, with the assistance of John Murray in London, "the most enlightened and active of the London trade", to achieve remarkable success. Scott told Morritt that he believed he had "in the celebrated printer Ballantyne, an Edinburgh publisher with a long purse and a sound political creed". John moved to South Hanover Street, James not till 1823 to Heriot Row—new publishers in the New Town.[14]

VI

The winter of 1808–9 was very grim. Before Christmas the news reached Edinburgh that Buonaparte had taken Madrid and that Sir John Moore had been obliged to retire. Until the full story was known, Sir John, who had died a hero's death after fighting an historic retreat, was gloomily supposed to have been "Buonaparte-struck". "What however," wrote Scott to Ellis "can we say of Moore, or how judge of his actions, since the Supreme Junta have shown themselves so miserably incapable?" When what was left of Moore's army had marched down to embark for home after the victory at Corunna, all in tatters, hollow-eyed and heavy with mud and blood, the people of the Spanish port had made the sign of the Cross as they passed. The troops began to arrive in English ports, and on January 25th, 1809, while rain poured down on snow-clogged streets, readers of London newspapers got the first shock. There had been a Black Week, without news except from Paris and the French-controlled Dutch papers. On the last night of January, Scott could not sleep for horror. He had never in his life been so stricken by bad news. As soon as he closed his eyes, he was "harassed with visions of broken ranks, bleeding soldiers, dying horses . . ."

There were two overlapping spectacles in London that winter, the first of which was voted better entertainment than the theatre. It had been whispered for some time that a first-class scandal was blowing up at the Horse Guards. The benevolent but not brilliant Duke of York, Commander-in-Chief, second son of the sovereign, had a mistress. Mrs Mary Anne Clarke, who was extravagant, had been promising commissions in the Army on the receipt of considerable sums. A rival snowstorm—of pamphlets—descended upon the freezing country. Mary Anne, who was witty and pretty, was examined at great length at the bar of the House of Commons. Colonel Wardle's motion brought before the House on January 26th was debated by a council of enquiry until March 20th when the duke was acquitted of having connived at or profited by Mrs Clarke's efforts; but in deference to public opinion he resigned his commission and the lady.

Scott mentioned these affairs only twice in his correspondence. On March 1st he told Southey, "I am as sick as ever dog was of our late parliamentary proceedings. What a melancholy picture of public morals and depravity not only of feeling, but even of taste." To Miller (or Murray if Miller be absent) he supposed he was not immediately likely to be called to London to take up his duties as Secretary to the Commissioners on the Administration of Justice in Scotland, "Mrs Clark [sic] furnishing so much employment to your great folks". The motion for an enquiry into the conduct of the campaign in the Peninsula was defeated on February 19th, but dragged on in the Lords.

Of course some heads had to fall. Amongst them was that of Hookham Frere. Not until April did Canning, a good friend, disgorge Frere's letters to Sir John Moore which produced an explosion of wrath at Whitehall. Moore had not, said Lord Grey, allowed himself to be influenced by the correspondence received by him from "this foolish and presumptuous person".[15] Lord Liverpool believed in Mr Frere's patriotic zeal and purity of motive. Lord Castlereagh claimed that Sir John Moore's march from Salamanca had succeeded brilliantly. When he had found that he had drawn upon himself Buonaparte's whole force, he had no option but to retire. Sir John Moore had saved Spain in spite of herself, said the cynical. Buonaparte had certainly been obliged to abandon his Spanish programme and return hastily to Paris.

On March 3rd Scott wrote to Sharpe of a death which he fondly termed unexpected. Camp, after nearly twelve years' faithful service and a very short illness, had "stretched himself out in his basket and died". Scott excused himself to Macdonald Buchanan with whom he was to have dined "on account of the death of a dear old friend". Camp had been his first dog and his best. He never again had a smooth-hair. Sophia who was nine at the time, long afterwards told her husband that she remembered the whole family standing in tears as Camp was buried, in the little garden behind the house in Castle Street, exactly opposite to the window at which Scott usually sat writing. It was a fine moonlit night and as her father smoothed down the turves his face was sadder than she had ever seen it.[16]

NOTES

1. Letters, I, 273–8; XII, 281. Lockhart, I, 436–46.
2. Farington (iii, 67) wrote on March 7th, 1805, "She went abroad with her sister Lady Elizabeth Gore, then the wife of Mr Monck. Her gallantries while abroad were much spoken of." Scott's summer-house is last mentioned in an account of Bentley Priory in 1881, and does not appear on any large-scale Ordnance map after this period. The Priory is still in the hands of the R.A.F., having been Air Ministry property since 1926. It was the headquarters of No. 11 (Fighter Group) in 1971. The lake has been filled in.
3. Letters, I, 285. Lockhart, I, 251.
4. Letters, I, 284. Lockhart, I, 253.
5. Lockhart, I, 460.
6. A bundle of ten letters from Scott to his wife, covering his London visit of 1807, turned up at Abbotsford in 1935. They mostly open "My dearest Love" or "My dearest Mimi". It appears that Charlotte had a second pet-name, "Lotty". The batch was found in time to be included by Grierson in Volume XII of the Letters.
7. Melville did not obtain either post and never again took office, but he was restored to the privy council and to Scott's great satisfaction Robert Dundas, Melville's eldest son, became President of the Board of Control.
8. Neither Colin Mackenzie nor John Marriott sunk into an early grave as expected by Scott. Mackenzie survived until 1821. Marriott (poet and divine) until 1825. He married in 1808 Mary Anne Harris of Rugby and had issue four sons and a daughter, and he retained a Buccleuch living in Warwickshire though forced to live in Devonshire "through the continued ill-health of his wife". D.N.B. (sic).

9. Letters, XII, 112. Lockhart, I, 451.
10. Letters, I, 367 et seq.
11. Skene, 16. Lockhart, I, 465.
12. Letters, II, 72.
13. Ibid., 100–8, 120–7, 142–3.
14. Ibid., 145, 151–2, 155–65.
15. After his recall from Spain in April 1809, Hookham's public career ended. He refused the offer of the Embassy in St Petersburg, and twice refused a peerage. He settled happily in Malta. After Busaco, Wellington said that he now realised that there never had been a general so ill-used as Moore. Scott in 1809 still believed that Moore had advanced when he should not have done so and retired when he should not have done so. James Moore published his brother's despatches, and they were reviewed in the second number of the *Quarterly*, whereupon he wrote to Scott to scold him for associating himself with such a publication. Scott wrote twice in reply and closed the correspondence by saying that "no man in Scotland could more regret the fate of General Moore".
16. Letters, II, 172, 543; XII, 311. Lockhart, II, 79.

X

Publisher and Poet
1809–1810

I

His family was now complete, "two of each sex" as he told his unknown brother-in-law in India.[1] To any outside observer it was clear at a glance that he had got one Scott and three Charpentiers. Sophia, his only blonde, grown a tall girl, would he believed, be very clever. She was quick. Young Walter, "The Laird", "Gilnockie" was a strapper. But he had his mother's waving raven tresses and flashing eyes. As for Anne, she was his French Mimi in miniature, "a little roundabout girl with large dark eyes as brown as lively and as good humoured as the Mother that bore her". Charles was a black-haired, cherry-cheeked little squire, always in trouble. Already once he had been rescued from a watery end in the Tweed.

> November's sky is chill and drear,
> November's leaf is red and sere:
> Late, gazing down the steepy linn,
> That hems our little garden in,
> Low in its dark and narrow glen,
> You scarce the rivulet might ken,
> So thick the tangled greenwood grew . . .
>   My imps, though hardy, bold and wild,

As best befits the mountain child,
Feel the sad influence of the hour . . .

They came running to him, to ask, saucer-eyed, such innocencies as "Would there ever again be daisies?"—and lambs? and may? and birds singing all day?

He was a devoted father, and his imps were allowed to interrupt him whenever they wished. Like most men, he did not find them of great interest before they could speak, but as soon as they reached the age when they could understand him, he gave tender care to their development. When asked to lay down his pen and tell them a story, he would obediently do so. "He would take them on his knee, repeat a ballad or a legend, kiss them, and set them down again to their marbles or ninepins, and resume his labour as if refreshed by the interruption." He delighted to hear of what they were thinking. They brought him all their little joys and sorrows. From a very early age they dined at table and in company; and to to be allowed to "sit up to supper" was the reward "for very good bairns". The rainiest day was not dull for them if he was at home. On Sundays, after the little services which he took in the house, the whole family set off, dogs included, for a picnic. The ruined tower of Elibank was a favourite site. If the weather was too bad he told them Bible stories. He seemed to have large portions of both Testaments, particularly the Old, by heart.

About the boys' education he did not have to worry. They went in due time, as he had done, daily, to as good a school as could be found in the land—Edinburgh High School. During holidays at Ashestiel he himself taught Gilnockie Latin dutifully, if not cheerfully. The pianoforte and harp were the favourite instruments for young ladies. Sophia played and sang sweetly, and he was not critical of technical execution. Extraordinary though it might seem, after his sufferings while Miss Jane Nicolson held sway, he utterly refused to send his girls to a boarding school. It was generally accepted that at the more fashionable and expensive ones girls learnt only the most superficial and showy accomplishments and a great deal of folly, if not worse things. Evidently he decided that on balance Miss Millar, brown-eyed, gentle and amiable, but no fool, nearer thirty than twenty (who came as soon as Sophia needed a governess and stayed nine years), was the happiest solution.[2]

Like the Persians, said his son-in-law, he held that next to the love of truth came the love of horsemanship. Sophia was the first regular attendant of his mountain rides, and the others followed as soon as they could sit a pony. He taught them to think nothing of tumbles, perilous fords and flooded streams. "Without courage," he gravely impressed upon them, "there cannot be truth; and without truth there can be no other virtue."

II

A letter from the excellent Miss Millar, with enclosures from the children, was awaiting him and Charlotte when they arrived at 6 Half Moon Street, Piccadilly, on Monday, April 10th, 1809. Their journey had been rapid but fatiguing, although they had halted for a night at Mainsforth. At last Scott had made the acquaintance of Robert Surtees, who had supplied him during the past two years with many ballads, including at least two bogus ones written by himself. Surtees had inherited his estate at twenty-four, but he had been an antiquarian since he began to collect coins almost in infancy. *The History of Durham* was his life work, and as he was not so robust as Scott, though eight years younger, he drove about his countryside in a gig. His groom complained he could never get the master past "an auld beelding". He had something of the antiquary in his manner, and was a great talker, but interesting.

Scott had planned to pay another call on his road south, to Lichfield, but had heard with sorrow six days before he left Edinburgh that Miss Seward had died, rather suddenly in the end, though she had written to him of failing health. She had left him as her literary executor. His dates for London had been dictated by the meeting there of the new Commission for the Administration of Justice in Scotland. He attributed his appointment as Secretary, to the Abercorn and Melville interest. The Abercorns were in Ireland, but the indefatigable marchioness had supplied him with a letter to Lord Malmesbury which should get him access to the Dorset Papers.

The Morritts were established in their stately classical London house, 24 Portland Place—the widest street in the capital. They gave several dinner-parties for the author of *Marmion*, who punctiliously asked on arrival if he was expected to roar as a lion this evening. This was generally the case and he always rose to the occasion, though he relapsed with relief when all the guests were gone.

> All this is very flattering and civil and if people are amused with hearing me tell a parcel of old stories or recite a pack of old ballads to lovely young girls and gaping matrons, they are easily pleased, and a man would be very ill-natured who would not give pleasure so easily conferred.

He made a congenial new acquaintance conveniently close to the Dumergues. Mrs Clephane was a widow with three daughters. The eldest, Miss Margaret, had a profile like that of Minerva on a Greek coin. Mrs Clephane was musical, well versed in Scottish lays, the heiress of the Macleans. Miss Baillie's new play was about a feud between that clan and the Campbells. Mrs Clephane supplied him with a drawing of the ancient dress of a Highland lady, and the correct colours of the tartans worn by the protagonists, the Campbells dark green, the Macleans glaring red. He much preferred to drop in for tea at Clarges Street, bringing Miss Baillie's drama, and stay talking till 10 p.m. than to be always on show. "I am so tired of being a teetotum or turnstile in fine rooms, turned round by fine people." Charlotte returned visits while he went down to talk business with John Murray. It gradually appeared that the *Quarterly* had taken root and would thrive, but when he had sent the younger Ballantyne to London to offer another of his fledglings, *The Edinburgh Annual Register*, neither Longmans nor Murray would rise to the bait of a twelfth share. This was rather a tiresome little affair as he had had it in mind since 1800 and Constable considered it his pigeon. The 1809 number appeared in 1810 and proved Murray wise. It was a loser from the start.

There was another musical lady anxious to renew acquaintance. He had met Mrs Hughes, the wife of a canon of St Paul's Cathedral, on his last trip south. Charlotte and he accepted an invitation to Amen Corner. The introduction had come through Miss Hayman, a lady in attendance on the princess. They were soon summoned to her mimic court and found her, as he told Lady Abercorn, "in the highest possible spirits and very witty and entertaining". According to Mr Thomas Grenville, the princess called on him rather unmercifully. She had, rather surprisingly, only just got to know "Monk" Lewis, and he was at every party given by her. "Of course I was only a second rate conjuror but did my best to amuse her." After dinner the party were grouped round the princess's chair, when she abruptly said, "They tell me, Mr Scott, you relate the prettiest Scotch stories in the world; do have the goodness to relate me one." This was making a little of a mountebank of the great bard to be sure, but his deference for royal rank was so great that he merely bowed and said, "Yes, Madam," and began, "In the reign of King such-an-one there lived in the Highlands of Scotland such a laird"—going on with his legend as if he were reading it out of a book. The story was short and neatly told and produced a good effect. "Dear me, Mr Scott, what a clever story!" exclaimed the princess, "pray be so obliging as to tell me another."

"Yes, Madam" said he, and without a moment's hesitation went on with another as a schoolboy would go through his task.[3]

He did not mention in any letter, until he got home, that a new young poet was being rude to him. A young whelp, Lord Byron, had brought out anonymously a satire called *English Bards and Scots Reviewers*. He accused poor Marmion of writing for pelf. The graceless beginner went off from Falmouth for the East six days after Scott turned north, and they did not yet meet.[4]

As soon as the news got around that Marmion was in town, the invitations gathered impetus. It was a minor tragedy that his Scottish man-servant met with an accident and he had to engage a *valet de place* who turned out a rascal. Important letters entrusted to him did not arrive. They only went out of London once on a visit of a few days to Tonbridge. Admiral Sir Samuel Hood and his lady had been in Edinburgh recently, and Lady Hood was a Scotswoman, daughter of Lord Seaforth, and a very brave girl. When her husband had to lose his right arm after a brilliant encounter with a French squadron off Rochefort, and he was brought in to a home port, Lady Hood went out to meet him. She was dropped into stormy waters between the boat and the ship, in total darkness, and sat beside his cot in wet stays all night. Scott was a little unhappy at the thought of her being left alone when Sir Samuel went to sea again as was expected. She seemed so guileless.[5]

While in this neighbourhood, he took the opportunity of seeing the ancestral home of the Sackvilles. He admired the pictures at Knole more than any he had seen in great houses in London, though he had been to one considered unequalled. Charles Kirkpatrick Sharpe had introduced him to Lady Stafford, so he went to Cleveland House where the collection made by her husband's uncle, the last Duke of Bridgewater, included much of that of the late Duke of Orleans.

The Scotts met Mr John Wilson Croker, politician and journalist, the best-informed man in the land about the French Revolution, and Lady Charlotte Lindsay and Rose repeatedly, and Heber and Coleridge. Scott trotted down to St James's Palace to enquire for Lady Charlotte Rawdon, who knew yet another Irish clergyman with news of Swift. He heard with regret that she was gone to Brighton; he had missed her when she came to Half Moon Street. Her brother, Lord Moira, was still a crony of the Prince of Wales and Scott had been told that before he came to town H.R.H. had done him the honour of speaking of him in terms of considerable bitterness; so he jocularly supposed he would not be Poet Laureate in the next reign. "But I can never wish his father's son and the heir of the Crown otherwise than well." It amazed him how people passed on the least fragment of gossip about royalty, which could only annoy.

The Duchess of Gordon had been astonishing audiences, especially Lady Abercorn, by claiming that he had read *Marmion* over to her and she had pointed out many errors. He began to pine for home at the end of his first month in London, and in his heart of hearts thought it (admittedly at a very bad date, when *morale* was low) a fearsome place.

The Scotts set off north on June 15th and paused for the nights of Sunday and Monday, the 18th and 19th, at Rokeby. The Morritts' Yorkshire home, in golden sunshine, almost shook Scott's allegiance to his native land. It was of breathtaking romantic beauty. Only one charm was lacking. By an extraordinary chance, no less than four of the amiable couples by whom they had been fêted in the south were childless—the Morritts, the Surteeses, the Hoods, the Ellises (though this time there had been no question of Sunninghill. Ellis had taken his gout to Bath.)

At Castle Street Scott found "all our little folks well", and a new companion, small, bright and noisy. He had bravely "supplied in some sort the vacancy occasioned by the death of poor old Camp". Wallace, a very sensible terrier puppy "of the old shaggy Celtic breed" and of high pedigree, had been procured for him with difficulty by Miss Dunlop of Dunlop, a descendant of the national hero.[6] The reunited family hastened to Tweedside as soon as the Courts rose. "Ashestiel never looked so enchanting—the ground is quite enamel'd with wild flowers, and all living things in such high spirits as to withdraw one involuntarily from thinking of all warfare and foemen even from Buonaparte down to the Edinburgh Reviewers." He did not go south again for six years.[7]

III

He was so happy, but so busy. Lockhart once asked him, long afterwards, how he had managed to survive amongst such a tumult of engagements. His reply was full of fire.

> Ay, it was enough to tear me to pieces, but there was a wonderful exhilaration about it all: my blood was kept at fever-pitch—I felt as if I could have grappled with anything and everything; then there was hardly one of my schemes that did not afford me the means of serving some poor devil of a brother author. There were always huge piles of material to be arranged, sifted and indexed—volumes of extracts to be transcribed—journeys to be made hither and thither,

for ascertaining little facts and dates—in short I could commonly keep half-a-dozen of the ragged regiment of Parnassus in tolerable case.[8]

He did not only have to help brother authors by finding them employment. He once saved one from the gallows. A bulky packet from the Tolbooth was delivered at Castle Street. Andrew Stewart, a poetical contributor to *The Scots Magazine*, the son of a bookbinder, twenty-three, apprenticed to a tailor who had ill-treated him, married, out of work for nine months, had taken to house-breaking. Scott sent him a pound at once and hurried down to a good-natured old friend, Mr Manners the bookseller, who happened at that time to be one of the bailies of Edinburgh. The dreadful sentence, due to be carried out within the month, was commuted for one of transportation. Andrew had sent Scott his poems, which were "of the humorous cast". They were printed by Manners and Miller and Constable, and appeared soon after the author's departure for Botany Bay, for the benefit of his father, a widower with five children.[9]

Scott's efforts for Southey had occupied many hours of his stay in the south. He really seemed to have tried everyone he knew who might possibly be able to get his poor friend a profitable and settled appointment —Royal Historiographer for England, a Professorship, the Stewardship of the Derwentwater estates . . . The end of his search did not come for four years, but meanwhile Southey was a regular contributor to the *Quarterly*, which paid well.

Miss Seward's Life and posthumous poems was a sacred trust and must be given precedence. This needed diplomatic handling. Constable already had twelve manuscript volumes of her correspondence. They politely gave Scott permission to remove anything he wished from the letters.

The remainder of 1809 saw more of the Somers Tracts in the world, and the last of Sir Ralph Sadler. But Scott had taken on more by-jobs. He was attracted by the memoirs of the Comte de Grammont, a naughty Frenchman at the court of Charles II. Getting on with Swift appeared to be his main occupation that autumn, but he took a beautiful holiday, with Charlotte and Sophia in attendance, to his favourite Highlands. They stayed with the Macdonald Buchanans at Cambusmore and he made the experiment of riding from Loch Vennachar to Stirling Castle on its rock to see if he had got the timing right for FitzJames's exploit in his new Highland poem. He was not exactly mysterious about this, but he mentioned it seldom in letters while it was being composed, though he read aloud stirring passages. Afterwards he explained it had been "a very sudden thought". With the Buchanans from Ross Priory, he explored the islands of Loch Lomond, Arrochar, Loch Sloy. Lady Louisa Stuart and Lady Douglas were visiting the Duke of Montrose at Buchanan House near by. In the ducal drawing-room he noticed Lord Byron's nasty satire. What did a young peer with five thousand pounds a year know of his struggles? The duke provided ten Highland boatmen "all plaided and plumed in their tartan array" to row the whole party for two days amongst the most interesting of the islands.[10]

"A confab. with H. Siddons" had been written down by him as one of the first things he must tackle on his return from London. H. Siddons was Henry, weakish son of the great Sarah, and at the end of seven months of virtuous effort by Scott on his behalf, he produced Miss Baillie's Highland drama at the new theatre in Edinburgh. The patent of the old one had expired. The new one—in Corri's Rooms, Leith Walk—was "bijou" but beautifully constructed and decorated. Scott had bought a share and become a trustee. Charlotte took a party of thirty to a box on the first night. It was such a success that a revival of *De Montfort* followed in April to which both Kemble and Mrs Siddons came north.

There had always been stage-favourites as welcome guests at Ashestiel and Castle Street. Everyone enjoyed them except the Scotts' portly butler John MacBeith, who objected to the late hours his temperate master was obliged to keep, and was huffed by Kemble invoking him as "Cousin Macbeth". Kemble and his sister were now well past fifty and both spoke in private life as if they were still on the boards. This sometimes caused misunderstanding. When Mrs Siddons announced to an expectant drawing-room audience in thrilling tones, "I must have candles!" nobody stirred. She had merely meant she could not see her script. When the Lord Provost apologised at table to her for a joint he feared might have been too highly salted she replied with majesty:

> Beef cannot be
> Too salt for me
> My Lord.

At Ashestiel she startled a page out of his wits:

> You've brought me water, boy!
> I asked for beer.

Amongst junior members of the Edinburgh company was a young actor, Daniel Terry, who performed best as old gentlemen and conceived such an admiration for Scott that he copied his neat, small, legible handwriting, and, not so successfully, his appearance and mannerisms. He had not the height for the part. Both Kemble and Terry had been well educated: the younger man had been apprenticed as an architect to the famous James Wyatt.[11]

Another expeditionary force had been sent out to the Peninsula and to Scott's satisfaction, under Sir Arthur Wellesley. On July 1st he hopefully believed a letter from a friend of Sir Arthur saying that they would be in Madrid in a month. But this was much too sanguine. The Battle of Talavera was won on July 28th, but Buonaparte had turned on Austria and triumphed at Wagram on the 6th. The Treaty of Vienna followed in October, and for Christmas fare he gave Europe news long expected but nevertheless startling. He was divorcing his Empress who was past child-bearing. After Talavera there seemed to be a hitch in the Peninsula, and what was much worse, another expeditionary force was sent to Antwerp, where Buonaparte was building a fleet. It had to be evacuated having lost half its numbers, largely from marsh fever. Another parliamentary investigation was ordered.

Scott was relieved to see Canning's frank on a letter from Ellis on September 26th. Lord Castlereagh (War Office) and Mr Canning (Home Office) had met in duel on Putney Heath and Mr Canning had been wounded. Both ministers had resigned. The Prime Minister resigned. Mr Spencer Perceval, who succeeded the poor over-worked hesitant Duke of Portland, received a deputation from the City of London petitioning that the English force in the Peninsula should be recalled. Mr Perceval threw upon the Commander-in-Chief, now Viscount Wellington of Talavera, the responsibility of making the choice. Lord Wellington chose to stay. Scott longed to have a statesman-hero. Neither Canning nor Castlereagh were very likeable characters. He was "deeply concerned over Canning's wound". "He is one of the few, very few statesmen who unite an ardent spirit of patriotism to the talents necessary to render that living spirit efficient."[12]

He wrote asking the retired duellist to stay, and received a rather unctuous reply hoping to see him in London next spring. It was awkward that at this juncture he needed to ask Lady Castlereagh to give him access to the letters of Swift, which she had inherited from Mrs Howard. Her husband was not on happy terms with Canning—in fact had just shot him in the groin. Scott asked Lady Abercorn if she could forward his request. There was no necessity to mention his *Quarterly* connection with Canning. Lady Abercorn did not at all agree with him about Canning. "I hope you do not defend treachery and arrogance": but she did as he asked. The question of the Henrietta Howard letters hung on. First Lady Castlereagh thought she might publish them herself. Meanwhile Scott had heard they might prove to be only originals of material already used. But Lady Abercorn was not the woman to let a matter rest.

It was sad that Charlotte's effort to send Ashestiel plants for her ladyship's Irish garden seemed to have miscarried. They appeared to have been sent down to Stanmore where the head-gardener had unpacked them. It could only be hoped he had planted them there. *The Lady of the Lake*, which was making considerable progress, was being dedicated to Lord Abercorn. Lady Abercorn had heard a rumour, she hoped true, that her friend was being paid two thousand pounds for it. He replied, "It is true my new ditty is sold but the price is two thousand guineas, not pounds. When I was fond of horses I found from a jockey to sell by guineas and buy by pounds." In the same letter he answered another of her queries. She had staying in the house, a young Miss Owenson (soon to become Lady Morgan), authoress of *The Wild Irish Girl*. "Miss Owenson asked me if you ever had been in love. I told her if I could judge by your way of talking of Mrs Scott I should certainly conclude that you had." He answered:

> Mrs Scott's match and mine was of our own making and proceeded from the most sincere affection on both sides which has rather increased than diminished during twelve years' marriage. But it was something short of love in all its fervour, which I suspect people only feel *once* in their lives. Folks who have been nearly drowned in bathing rarely venturing a second time out of their depth. [13]

IV

The winter of 1809–10 was bitterly cold in Edinburgh. Two bad things were to happen to Scott in that year, and one very good. All were packed into the early spring and summer. The Georgian nursery was always vulnerable. Parents were accustomed to seeing whole families swept off by smallpox, scarlet fever, measles, tuberculosis . . . The Scott nursery was threatened in April 1810. Gilnockie, the heir, was the first to be felled by "an inflammatory fever". For a dreadful fortnight he hung between life and death. All three younger children were in bed at the same time, Anne very ill. Sophia "assisted her mother as a little nurse", until she too went down. Young Walter, after a hard fight for life, was restored to his anxious parents, reduced almost to a skeleton. After what had finally been diagnosed as "some form of influenza" they all developed whooping-cough. In the second week of June Charlotte took Sophia and Gilnockie off to Ashestiel to see if a change of air would relieve them of their obstinate coughs and colds. Scott could not hope to follow for a month.

His second trouble was, not surprisingly, connected with one of his two surviving brothers. He had tried to help Tom, who was living in exile with his good wife and many children in the Isle of Man, by suggesting that he should edit Shadwell's poems, to be published by Miller, and contribute to the *Quarterly*. But Tom was lethargic and nothing from his pen ever appeared, except some quite well done notes on Manx archaeology which would be useful if he wrote a history of the Isle. In 1807, a chance had come to put something in his pocket—a sinecure. It fell to the Clerks of Session to appoint what were called Extractorships in the General Register House of Scotland. Tom got, by means of his brother, a very minor one bringing in an annual income of between two hundred and two hundred and fifty pounds. But he had gone off and remained in the Isle of Man leaving a hireling to perform his duties. Unfortunately, in the winter of 1809 amongst the reforms decided upon by the Judicature Commission was the abolition of all Extractorships. Tom would, however, receive a pension of a hundred and thirty pounds for life.

While Scott was leading his bachelor existence at Castle Street, something happened in the House of Lords which upset him exceedingly. Lord Lauderdale denounced Tom's appointment and pension as a gross and flagrant piece of jobbery. Matters were made worse by Lord Holland adding that much as he esteemed the literary character of Walter Scott, and approved of rewarding literary merit regardless of party, to extend it to the author's brother was indefensible. Mr Thomas Scott had been appointed when his brother already knew the Extractorships were to be abolished, and could not be considered as requiring indemnity for a loss. He was non-resident and held a commission in the militia. These last facts were correct. But Tom's flight from Scotland had not been desired by him, and even in his patriotic effort to join a Fencible regiment raised in the Isle of Man by the Duke of Argyll, he was going to be unlucky. That too was abolished in the spring of 1811.

Scott got wind of what was going to be said in London from Colin Mackenzie, and wrote to his brother in some anxiety to say that Lord Melville and Robert Dundas would help them. It was quite untrue, as asserted by Lord Holland, that as Secretary to the Judicature Commission he had known that the post to which his brother was being appointed was to be abolished. It had been made months before the Commission had come into being.

The Duke of Montrose joined Lord Melville in opposing Lord Lauderdale and the pension bill was passed. Tom's pension was secured, but the end of that story was unhappy.

"Lord Holland," wrote Scott to Tom on August 28th, "has been in Edinburgh, and we met accidentally at a public party. He made up to me, but I remembered his part in your affair, and *cut* him with as little remorse as an old pen." Jeffrey long afterwards told Lockhart that the meeting had taken place at the Friday Club[14] and that in his lifelong knowledge of Scott this was the only occasion on which he had seen him rude. Lord Holland said plaintively, "The bard seems very angry at me, but really I don't know what it is for. It can't be about his brother's business— at least, if it be, he has been misinformed, for what I said was that if the arrangement was about an office, it was a job; but if it was meant as an indirect reward of Walter Scott, my only objection to it was that it was too little."

Nobody present appeared to realise that of all English peers, the amiable Lord Holland was probably the one most touchy about a social cut. The date was that in which the divorced woman was relegated to outer darkness. He could give Lady Holland, who was talented and beautiful (but becoming increasingly sharp-tongued), dog-like devotion, wealth and a *salon* as brilliant as any in Europe, but hardly a woman would attend it. She was cut.[15]

Lockhart was relieved to be able to assert that "in after-days" the wound was healed, and Scott "enjoyed much agreeable intercourse" with Lord Holland and the other Whig gentlemen concerned in the lamentable affair of poor Tom. Tom was rescued from the Isle of Man by two relations of his long-suffering wife. General Ross, a cousin, returned rich from being Governor of Demerara, got him a commission as Paymaster to the 70th Regiment. Robert MacCullough, Mrs Tom's brother, produced one of the thousand pounds, and Walter and his mother, the other required for sureties to the negotiation, and the whole family returned to Scotland where Tom took up his duties at Stirling and Perth. Somehow, another three hundred pounds was raised to pay off his debts in the Isle where he had rented two houses. Walter had discouraged Tom from a despairing solution—that he might perhaps enter the Church. Old Mrs Scott only wished that his new career might have had nothing to do with money.

Henry, third Duke of Buccleuch, and family
By H. P. Danloux. Signed and dated 1798.
The figures from left to right are: Lord Montagu, Lady Caroline, Duke Henry, Duchess Elizabeth, Lady Harriet, Lady Elizabeth, Lord Courtown (son-in-law), Harriet, Countess of Dalkeith (daughter-in-law), Charles, Earl of Dalkeith, afterwards fourth Duke of Buccleuch, Lady Courtown (born Lady Mary Scott).

By permission of His Grace the Duke of Buccleuch, from the collection at Bowhill.

V

The Lady of the Lake appeared in May 1810 while Scott was in the thick of his anxieties over his nursery and Brother Tom's pension. In every way it surpassed the success of its predecessors. The two-guinea quarto edition of over two thousand copies was gone in less than a fortnight. The sales thereafter increased rapidly. By the end of the year Scott reckoned that no less than twenty-five thousand copies had been sold, and Ballantyne was getting such a demand that another edition of three thousand was in preparation. This time no critics carped. Even Jeffrey affected enthusiasm in the *Edinburgh*. Ellis did it proud for the *Quarterly*. There were some strange side-effects. There was a rush of tourists to the Trossachs, and from that date post-horse duty in Scotland rose regularly. An hotel was built at Callander for visitors to Ellen's Isle. The success of *The Lady of the Lake* broke the records for verse, but it was really doubtful whether the poetry was the chief attraction. The story was exciting and romantic. There was a stranger knight, based on James IV who delighted in Haroun al Raschid adventures. Ellen, the daughter of the outlawed Douglas, was beset with three suitors, including the disguised monarch. Under threat of an attack by the royal forces Roderick Dhu, the wild Highland chieftain, summoned the clans. There were two songs which became permanent favourites—"He is gone on the mountains" and the Coronach, "Soldier rest, thy warfare o'er". "The Harp of the North," wrote Heber, "was never before struck or so apostrophised."

The first edition had as frontispiece the Saxon portrait of Scott and the artist now came to Castle Street to paint Mrs Scott (and for good measure Wallace, now the parlour dog). But it could hardly be said that the prophet was honoured in his own family. James Ballantyne asked Sophia how did she like *The Lady of the Lake*? "O!" replied she, "I have not read it. Papa says there is nothing so bad for young people as reading bad poetry." Young Walter returned home from school one day dishevelled. One of the boys had called him "The Lady of the Lake". He thought he was being laughed at as girlish, "and had struck out hard". A constant visitor to Castle Street asked the boy why he thought it was that people regarded his father so much more than his uncles—what was there about him so remarkable? Gilnockie, after thought, brought out, "It's commonly *him* that sees the hare sitting." When Scott had first read the stag hunt to a farmer neighbour, the worthy man had struck his thigh in dismay at the description of the hounds plunging into the lake to follow FitzJames

F

embarking with Ellen. He cried out that the animals must have been totally ruined by being allowed to take the water after such a hard chase.[16]

A copy of the poem reached Captain Adam Ferguson of the 101st regiment at Belem, Headquarters in the Peninsula, and he wrote that he was frequently obliged to go out in the evenings to read it aloud to military audiences. When Lord Wellington retired to the lines of Torres Vedras, Ferguson, kneeling, read the battle scene from Canto Six to his company, ordered to lie prostrate, and they cheered as French shot struck the bank close above them.[17]

VI

If Scott had wanted to create a sensation in the fashionable world while edition after edition of *The Lady of the Lake* was thundering through Ballantyne's presses, he could hardly have done better than disappear for a holiday in the Hebrides. Here he spent the last fortnight of July 1810 in perfect weather and schoolboy spirits. He had always wanted to visit the isles, though he expected what he was to prove. "The scenery is quite different from that on the mainland—dark, savage and horrid, but occasionally magnificent in the highest degree." He longed for Words-worth and Southey to be with him. When Johnson and Boswell had made their tour in 1779, the enterprise had been quite heroic. But the young laird of Staffa, Ranald Macdonald, had tempted him with the assurance that he could provide a stout sloop and eight rowers, himself as pilot and his piper. Staffa (whom Scott loved to call by his *petit titre*) was a brother of Hector Macdonald Buchanan of Ross Priory, "a right and tight Highland chief", and an enthusiastic landlord. The sloop was generally used for transporting kelp. His tenants appeared to love him to distraction.

The party of seven who assembled at Oban consisted of the Sheriff, Charlotte and Sophia and the dog Wallace (brought to enjoy his native land), Sir George Paul, philanthropist and prison reformer, Mackinnon of Mackinnon, born and bred in industrial luxury in England, but never-theless a Highland chief, Miss Hannah Mackenzie, daughter of Henry, and Mrs Apreece, a distant Scott relation, an elegant widow, a Londoner from Berkeley Square, who had been a leading Edinburgh hostess for some seasons. Scott ungallantly suspected her of going to the isles rather to say that she had seen them than to see anything. He may have misinterpreted her unusual desire to examine basaltic formations. She was going to marry

Humphry Davy. Scott offered the females the choice of remaining at Oban or braving the Atlantic, but they all decided to go, and set forth for Mull valiantly, though the spring tide was running with such force that Scott's desire to land on the Lady's Rock to collect a souvenir for Miss Baillie was out of the question. They passed it so close they could almost have touched it. It was the scene of her drama *The Family Legend*. Ruined castles crowded upon their view on every headland, as thickly as on the banks of the Rhine. At one moment Scott could see seven—Duart, Dunstaffnage, Ardtornish . . . "all once the abodes of grim feudal chiefs who warred incessantly with one another".

They landed in the island of Mull very late, after dark, near another old keep called Aros. The wherry following them with their baggage had not been able to keep up with them. Charlotte had lost her shoes and Sophia her precious collection of pebbles, and all the men were separated from their razors. The piper roused a Highland gentleman's house where they were received with profuse kindness and some twenty Mackinnons appeared, as if by magic, to greet their unknown kinsman from the south. Next day they all rode across the isle on Highland ponies to the head of a salt-water loch where Staffa's boats awaited them with colours flying and pipes playing. Ulva House (for Staffa was also the Lord of Ulva's Isle) greeted them with a discharge of musketry. Scott wrote at length to Miss Baillie from the romantic address. The isles of Staffa and Iona were their programme for the next day.

Staffa was one of the most extraordinary places Scott had ever seen. There was not a great deal of it. It was about a mile and a half in circumference, with a perpendicular face rising direct out of the Atlantic towards the south and west, in which direction there was nothing between it and the Americas. The famous cavern of Fingal was over sixty feet high and two hundred long, with a roof supported by black basaltic columns as regular and stately as those in a cathedral. Its pavement was of ruddy marble. He scrambled along to a great stone at the mouth of the cave and sat there awhile alone watching the deep and swelling waves rolling up majestically, and listening to their roar like that of ten thousand giants shouting at once. The boatmen revered his profession and his spunk, and were gratified by his interest in their customs. No one else of the party had ventured so far. They christened the stone on which he sat Clachan-an-Bairdh, the bard's seat, and washed down the toast with a dram, to the cry of the pibroch which roused tremendous echoes. As the complimentary speech made by the head boatman to Scott was in Gaelic, he could only smirk and bow in reply "like a spoilt beauty".

Iona, six miles across the waves, was not so dramatic, but also extraordinary though quite different. Geologically it was the oldest island in Europe. Scott remembered with awe "from this rude and remote island the light of Christianity shone forth on Scotland and Ireland". It seemed half asleep, but they were soon beset by a crowd of well-nigh naked boys and girls begging for alms and offering for sale pebbles blessed by St Columba, and therefore lucky. These were green and rather pretty. Charlotte bought enough to be fashioned into a necklace by an Edinburgh jeweller, and Scott some to be set in silver, in the shape of a harp, for Miss Baillie and the musical Miss Clephane. It was perhaps as well that Mrs Clephane and her daughters were not at home at Torloisk, which was pointed out to Scott, and looked attractive with the sun shining on its face. Young Staffa said the most violent things about the clan Maclean and the non-resident Duke of Argyll, who had certainly let St Columba's holy isle slide into what seemed likely to become a perpetual sleep.

Scott found the church more curious than beautiful, but was fascinated by the numbers of sculptured monuments to priests and warriors in a place so extremely desolate and miserable. He was not allowed to linger there as long as he wished, as a gale was blowing up, "no pleasant prospect in an open boat on the Atlantic". Staffa's hardy boatmen, however, pulled undismayed against wind and tide and occasional torrential squalls for more than five hours "cheered by the pipes and singing all the while to their oars, old ditties of clan-battles and gatherings". All the ladies were sick, particularly Miss Hannah Mackenzie. Sir George looked as if he wished himself rather in the darkest of the dungeons in which so much of his philanthropic life was spent. Even Mackinnon of Mackinnon succumbed. The only survivors of the never-to-be-forgotten expedition to Fingal's Cave and Columba's isle were Staffa himself and the Bard. Scott wrote to Morritt that he had kept himself going on frequent supplies of cold beef and biscuits.

They landed tolerably wet and ready for bed at 10 p.m. and next day two doleful figures were to be perceived setting forth on ponies, looking out for the nearest point in Mull to the mainland. Sir George attended by his English valet had protested that never again would he set foot in a boat until he had discovered the shortest possible passage to *terra firma*. Her father was delighted with the behaviour of Sophia on the holiday. "My eldest little girl accompanied us, and being quite a little doll whom we could fling to sleep in any corner, she was no inconvenience to us, while I hope she attained some taste for the beauties of nature."[18]

VII

He returned to find a minor but not novel horror awaiting him. James Ballantyne, always interested in his health, seemed to be on the edge of a nervous breakdown. He had suffered a disappointment in love—but that was months past. Scott wrote to him in the first week of August to advise him, rather sharply, to eat and drink less and take regular exercise. A short holiday at his old home was to be recommended, provided he could resist the hospitality of his Kelso cronies.[19]

The Lady of the Lake was making such demands upon Ballantyne's presses, which now numbered eleven, that some volumes of Swift for Constable had to be put out to another printer. During the last golden days of September, Scott declared that he spent his days coursing hares and his nights spearing salmon, but he was actually toiling on Swift, and an article on Crabbe for the *Quarterly*.

He had also pulled out and sent to James Ballantyne the chapters of a prose work called *Waverley* which he had put aside five years before. Their publication had been announced in a list of the firm's forthcoming New Works, but without the name of the author. James was polite but not enthusiastic, and Scott returned them to a drawer at Ashestiel and forgot them again.[20]

James, in one of his gloomy moods, said that he would gladly publish all the bairns of Scott's own begetting, but Lord preserve him from the other men's weans Scott fathered. Ballantyne's were faced by 1810 with Dr James Grahame's *British Georgics* which never even be an to sell, and Dr John Jameson's *History* ("of all things", as Scott himself admitted) *Of the Culdees*. Mrs Seward's three volumes of Poetical Works prefaced by a short memoir, were of uninspiring mediocrity and by an authoress recently deceased. Arthur Clifford's *Tixall Poetry* was absolutely James's *bête noire*—(sixteenth- and early seventeenth-century verse) and part of the Sadler Manuscript, was equally fascinating to the antiquary. These last were yet to come, and not until 1815 did death relieve Scott of the profuse works of his German protégé, Henry Weber. It was always so difficult for him to say No to a needy fellow-author. James Hogg had sent him his latest collection, *The Forest Minstrel*, with the request that he should forward a copy to Lady Dalkeith to whom it was dedicated. Scott apologetically feared "the poor fellow has just sufficient talent to spoil him for his own trade without having enough to support him by literature", and the heavenly countess sent him a hundred guineas for the Ettrick Shepherd.

Scott stuck to it that the *Edinburgh Register* must succeed, give it time, but so far it was losing a thousand a year. The brothers naturally wanted him to continue writing verse that got record sales. Scott was fond of both of them. He nicknamed them after two characters in a farce by Henry Carey, poet and musician of the Augustan age, best known as the author of *Sally In Our Alley*. James, who was stout and pompous, was Aldiborontiphoscophornio. John, who was volatile, lean and a mimic, was Rigdumfunnidos. The weather grew grim and Scott wrote from Castle Street to Brother Tom "in confidence" that if Robert Dundas were to be sent out to India as Governor-General and offered him a good post, he would not hesitate "to pitch the Court of Session and the Booksellers to the Devil and try my fortune in another climate". He repeated that this resolution was strictly *entre nous* and that he by no means repined at his present fate.[21]

His present fate was that *The Lady of the Lake* had been turned into a melodrama and was being played to crowded houses in Edinburgh, Covent Garden and Dublin. He avoided seeing any of the scripts. "The Edinburgh piece" had got some clever scenery, "from studies taken at Loch Katrine by Williams, their painter, who is a very good artist and sent there on purpose". When he ventured to witness the Edinburgh piece, he found Mrs Henry Siddons as Ellen "Columbinish" and by no means his idea of a high-born Highland maiden.[22]

All the children were now old enough to be taken to the play, even Charles had come out of frocks and gone into breeches this Christmas holidays. His father thought he looked like a dancing dog. He wrote cheerfully to Lady Abercorn on December 22nd, "We are going to set forward in the middle of a snow-storm I fear to keep an old hereditary engagement of eating our turkey and cheese with my friend and chief, Mr Scott of Harden, on Xmas Day"; and from Mertoun House to Miss Baillie on New Year's Eve: "If there be anything incoherent in this letter pray ascribe it to my writing in the neighbourhood of a ball, for all the little Scotts of Harden with the greater part of my own are dancing the new year in . . ."

NOTES

1. Letters, II, 307. Lockhart, II, 26–28. Lockhart uses the somewhat cryptic phrase "He had now two boys and two girls and he never had more." There is a reference to Charlotte having quite recovered her health, after an unexplained illness, in a letter to Lady Louisa Stuart, March 3rd, 1808.

2. *Letters hitherto unpublished, written by members of Sir Walter Scott's Family to their old Governess*, ed. with an Introduction and Notes by the Warden of Wadham College, Oxford, 1905; hereafter cited as Millar.

3. *England*, J. Fenimore Cooper, vol. II, pp. 124–5. Letters, II, 240.

4. Ibid., 214. Lockhart, II, 82–84.

5. Letters, II, 307–8.

6. Ibid., 215, 442.

7. Lockhart is unreliable about the Scotts' 1809 London visit, and states amongst other errors that they went by sea, took Sophia and stayed a fortnight at Rokeby.

8. Lockhart, II, 13.

9. Ibid., 72–76.

10. Letters, II, 241. Lockhart, II, 82.

11. Lockhart II, 95–97.

12. Letters, II, 251. Lockhart, II, 89.

13. Letters, II, 287.

14. The Friday Club, modelled on Johnson's club which met at the Turk's Head in the City of London was founded in 1803 and met at Fortune's Tavern, Edinburgh Old Town.

15. The letters of Scott and his brother Tom came to light too late to be placed in chronological order. They occupy pp. 393–511 in Volume Seven. The originals are in the Huntington Library.

16. Lockhart, II, 117–24, 130–1.

17. Ibid., 169. It was not surprising that of Scott's old schoolfellows "Linton" was the principal one to go into the regular army. His father, the Reverend Professor, had been chaplain to the Black Watch and charged with his regiment at the Battle of Fontenoy. Adam Ferguson's regiment, the 2nd 58th, was a sickly battalion kept near Lisbon for most of the war. It was stationed in reserve at Torres Vedras, where the 3rd Division was in billets from October until late December 1810. The 58th had black facings.

18. Letters, II, 339, 354, 357–67, 370–84, 398, 401; VII, 320. Lockhart, II, 134–43, 148.

19. Letters, II, 365.

20. Lockhart, II, 251–2.

21. Letters, VII, 452.

22. Ibid., II, 410–11, 415.

XI

The Flitting

1811–1813

I

MANY YEARS AGO, DRIVING ALONG TWEEDSIDE FROM SELKIRK TO
Melrose on business with his apprentice son, Walter Scott, senior, had
suddenly said, "We must get out here, Walter, and see a thing quite in your
line." A stone on the bank, half a mile above the river, marked the site of
the Battle of Melrose, 1526, fought between the Kerrs led by the Earls of
Angus and Home and the Scotts led by Buccleuch. The prize had been the
possession of the boy-king James V, and the spot known as "Turn Again"
was that at which the victorious Scotts had left off chasing the vanquished
Kerrs. The land surrounding it included a farm of a hundred and ten
acres, originally Newarthaugh or Cartley Hole. Lockhart afterwards said
that owing to its messy condition, it had become "Clarty Hole". It was
the property of Dr Robert Douglas, Minister of Galashiels, a character
well known to all Scotts of Harden. He had been one of the New Year's
party at Mertoun House in January 1811. On Thursday, August 29th, of
that year, he dined at Ashestiel with Walter Scott, to shake hands upon
their sale. The reverend gentleman had tussled hard with Charles Erskine
and "Nippy" Laidlaw, negotiators for Scott. In the end they had settled
upon four thousand guineas and vacant possession by Whitsuntide
1812.

The seven years' lease of Ashestiel was out, and though Scott had agreed to carry on for another twelvemonth and become a tenant at will at a much increased rent, he was not inclined to go on improving a property which might at any moment be reclaimed by a kinsman from India. The repairs bill was heavy and he longed for a home of his own. Throughout the spring of 1811 his friends received enthusiastic descriptions of his purchase. The death of his old patron, Lord Melville, had put an end to any dreams of serving in India, but one of his last acts had been to persuade Scott's Old Man Of The Sea, George Home, to retire. At last, after over five years of doing his job without pay, Scott received an addition of thirteen hundred pounds to his annual income.

He told James Ballantyne of his decision to "buy a piece of ground sufficient for a cottage, and a few fields". They were along the Tweed half-way between Melrose and Selkirk, so he would have half a mile of "the beautiful turn of Tweed above Gala-foot". Just below the confluence of the rivers, an old Roman road from the Eildons came down to a shallow ford which must have been used by the abbots of Melrose. He would be perfectly justified in calling his cottage "Abbotsford". To Lady Abercorn he spoke of "a small property delightfully situated by the side of the Tweed, my native river". He had to confess that it was not as beautiful as Ashestiel, as it was very bare, only thirteen of his hundred and ten acres had been cultivated, and the good doctor's principal attempt at afforestation was a singularly sad-looking belt of hardwood and larches which stood up manfully on the skyline against the northern blast, but reminded Scott of nothing but a "redding-comb". There was nothing romantic about the place except the vicinity of the very noble and bold stream. To Morritt he spoke of "a bower", but said he had only fixed two points, one that it should stand in his garden, the other that the little drawing-room should open into a little conservatory in which there should be a fountain. He wanted the stables close to the house, as his boys would be continually in and out of them and he liked to keep an eye on them. He told Miss Baillie that he had bravely determined to plant from sixty to seventy of his acres. At present he intended to have only two spare bedrooms, with dressing-rooms which could at a pinch take a couch bed. Charles Carpenter in India had to be fully informed, and was urged to come home and bring his lady to a house-warming. "We are not a little proud of being greeted as *laird* and *lady* of *Abbotsford*. We will give a grand gala when we take possession of it, and as we are very *clannish* in this corner, all the Scotts in the country, from the Duke to the peasant, shall dance on the green to the bagpipes and drink whisky punch."

Daniel Terry had recommended a Glasgow architect, William Stark, and this expert said that as the local stone was an ugly dark red or blue, it would be much better, though a little more expensive to get beautiful grey-white freestone from Sprouston in Roxburghshire. There was also some fine building-stone available from Melrose Abbey where they were clearing out some later additions from the interior. Stark's sketches and plans began to arrive and were enchanting, but when he envisaged the estimates the author thought he would have to write another best-selling narrative poem. He would probably be wisest to rough it in Cartley Hole farmhouse until he had collected the funds for "my intended mansion".[1]

II

In January 1811 a subscription was set on foot in London in aid of the suffering Portuguese. Scott ruefully explained "Silver and gold have I none", and began work on *The Vision of Don Roderick*, another narrative poem, but much shorter than *The Lay* or *The Lady of the Lake* and in the Spenserian stanza. ("You remember the story of the last Gothic King of Spain descending into an enchanted cavern to know the fate of the Moorish invasion.") It was to be the least read of his poems, but it fulfilled its object and sold well.

Reviewers, with the exception of the *Edinburgh*, were kind and he had never expected a favourable notice from an organ which wished that British troops were not being employed in the Peninsula. Last April, the Emperor Napoleon, successful in everything, had married. On March 20th, 1811, fishermen off Dover heard the guns of the enemy coast speak, and brought in with their catch the news that Boney had got his boy. The dynasty was secure, a King of Rome had been born. Scott's interest in Wellington's campaign became almost feverish. He bought the best available maps and distressed Charlotte by poring over them even in the carriage on the way out to Ashestiel "to fish and rhyme". He spread them out on tables and stuck black and white pins in them.[2] He had confided in Joanna Baillie last year how much he had wished "to take a peep at Lord Wellington and his merry men in Portugal. But I found that the idea gave Mrs Scott more distress than I was entitled to do for the mere gratification of my own curiosity." He had to content himself with a sketch of Buonaparte's tactics for the *Register*.[3]

He had two sad losses of elderly friends this season—Lord President Blair, President of the Court of Session, a man whom every party respected; Lord Melville in the same May week.

The last summer at Ashestiel came. He basked amongst gooseberries and currants. In early August Lord and Lady Dalkeith called in for two nights. Major John Scott, now retired and much concerned with his digestion after a course of Cheltenham waters, came for a month. Old Mrs Scott was kindly invited. "I will send the carriage to meet you at Bankhouse and you may bring Crookshanks or Jessy with you to take care of you like a lady as you are." The usual flood of holiday guests began to arrive. Mr Matthew Weld Hartstonge from Dublin had been indefatigable in his researches for the enlargement and improvement of the edition of Swift. Young Walter was now at the age for sailing a toy boat, and went along with them on an expedition to Cauldshiels loch. The little craft set off bravely, then halted and trembled. She was stuck. Scott waded in. He was forty and had written to tell Leyden, in a letter that would arrive too late, "the outside of my head is waxing grizzled, but I cannot find that the snow has cool'd my brain or my heart". In fact, his hair was returning to the lint-white of his infancy.

Hard on the heels of Hartstonge came the Kembles, "King John" grown very fat, and with asthma. Mr James Ferrier brought his daughter Susan, who had written a book called *Marriage*, not yet published. Daniel Terry and William Stark showed their plans for Abbotsford cottage. Scott was very well satisfied after a November storm, that although the flood water came up to within nine inches of his new dyke, it held out bravely. They were not going to Mertoun House this year as the Harden Scotts would not be at home. Perhaps this was as well for "my kinsman" had got a perfect hobbyhorse at present—a railroad in Berwickshire. Walter could not share his enthusiasm.

That they did not go proved fortunate, for four days before Christmas young Walter developed measles. As soon as he seemed in a fair way of recovery, Scott departed for Ashestiel but was not surprised to hear that all the other children had caught the infection. He had been working hard planting and felling and tidying his shrubbery at Abbotsford though the snow was on the ground. He went back to Edinburgh. In a New Year's letter to Lady Abercorn he told her that if she were to see his two sons again he thought she would desert her original choice of the elder to be her page. "The little fellow, if it please God to spare him, will turn out something uncommon, for he has a manner of thinking and expressing himself altogether original." He had hardly laid down his pen when it appeared likely that Charles was not to be spared. The child had a relapse and became desperately ill. It was not until February 23rd that he was able to tell Southey that at last all his young people were on foot again. He knew that several of his infant brothers were said to have died of measles, and what some of his friends had sustained in this winter's epidemic made him tremble at its very name.4

The death of the Duke of Buccleuch in this hard season was not unexpected. Scott, when he had seen him last, about a month before, had thought that "the hand of fate was upon him". There was not a dry eye at a funeral of extreme simplicity. Only about forty persons, nearly all kinsmen, were present. This absence of parade had been at the duke's own request. "He is truly a great loss to Scotland and will be long missed and lamented, though the successor to his rank is heir also to his generous spirit and social affections." His successor was an intimate friend of Scott since earliest days and far more decisive.

The spring of 1812 was slow in coming to Tweedside. In mid-April hill and vale were still doing penance in a sheet of snow of very respectable depth. It had lain for a fortnight. Fieldmice ate all the Irish acorns which Hartstonge had sent. Scott and Charlotte planted a second batch with their own fair hands. On May 7th it snowed all day again. "All of a sudden" next morning they woke to absolute summer "greatly to the refreshment of the young lambs and grass and corn, not forgetting my young trees and shrubs at Abbotsford". He had acorns also from Lady Stafford (Sutherland Bower) and Rokeby (Morritt Grove). Ellis, Joanna Baillie, Lords Clarendon and Glenbervie, and of course Lady Abercorn, all contributed. Lord Fife sent seed of Norway pine and Lord Montagu lime-seed. Scott knew the soil here was good for trees. He sent orders to Laidlaw to be passed on to Purdie, "the happiest and most consequential person in the world", not to stint. He wanted oaks, chestnuts, red beech, elms, birch. On the bank above the house there must be privet, holly, sweetbriar, honeysuckle, wild rose, white convolvulus and blackthorn. He learned that the tree with a leaf shaped like a saddle was the tulip tree.

He sent off to James Ballantyne the first canto of *Rokeby*, his English narrative poem which was going to pay for all this. No poem had ever so vexed him. That autumn, when he was straining to be finished, he tore up and burnt a whole canto. On the very day of his flitting from Ashestiel he replied to Mr Blackwood, bookseller, of 64 South Bridge, saying that he could not resist some items in his interesting and curious catalogue. "I am here ruining myself with planting and building, so that adding to my library is in fact burning the candle at both ends." But he was comforted by the fact that the value of the volumes he already possessed had so much increased that they would fetch nearly double what he had given for them. He proudly signed that letter "Yours very faithfully, Walter Scott, Abbotsford, May 21st 1812."

Hogg had asked him, "Are you not sorry at leaving *auld Ashestiel for gude an' 'a?"* Joanna Baillie said that if she was ever happy enough to be at Abbotsford she would like to revisit Ashestiel. "I have a kind of tenderness for it, as one has for a man's first wife, when you hear he has married a second." Lockhart heard that for many a poor neighbour the disappearance of the Scotts had been grievous. They had been "very generous protectors". "Mrs Scott in particular has made it so much her business to visit the sick in their scattered cottages and bestow on them the contents of her medicine-chest as well as of the larder and cellar with such unwearied kindness, that her name is never mentioned there to this day without some expression of tenderness." Nobody ever heard a word of complaint from Charlotte at having to leave her Ashestiel garden, in which she had laboured so effectively. With Gallic common-sense she foresaw that she was moving to improved circumstances. The garden of the lady of Abbotsford had already a wall sheltering three-quarters of an acre of fertile soil. She would also be able to go for drives in more than one direction.

Her only regret was that during the months before the move Scott would keep on buying more association-objects for Abbotsford—targes and claymores, a Spanish weapon with Rob Roy's initials, a sword presented by Charles I to the great Marquess of Montrose . . . The flitting was picturesquely described by him to old Lady Alvanley whom he had met with the Ellises.

> The neighbours have been much delighted with the procession of my furniture, in which old swords, targets and lances, made a very conspicuous show. A family of turkeys was accommodated within the helmet of some *preux chevalier* of ancient Border fame, and the very cows, for aught I know, were hearing banners and muskets. I assure your ladyship that this caravan, attended by a dozen of ragged rosy children, carrying fishing rods and spears, and leading poneys, greyhounds and spaniels, would, as it crossed the Tweed, have furnished no bad subject for the pencil, and really reminded me of one of the gypsey groupes of Callot upon their march.

To Terry who had gone south to appear with success as Lord Ogleby at the Haymarket, he said that the flitting baffled all description "We had twenty-four cartloads of the veriest trash in nature, besides dogs, ponies, pigs, poultry, cows, calves, bare-headed wenches and bare-breeched boys." He was going to get some more dogs. Poor old Percy died in time to find a grave at Abbotsford. Wallace followed soon. But the Ellises had sent the children, last summer, the most beautiful black greyhound bitch, Lady Juliana Berners (after the famous hunting Abbess of Sopwell, St Albans).

That spring Wellington began to move. On May 5th, while snow was still falling on Tweedside, Masséna was defeated at Fuentes d'Onoro; Soult was vanquished in the very bloody battle of Albuera on the 16th, and two months later Wellington, wrote Scott jubilantly, "had almost entirely destroyed Marshal Marmont's fine army". He celebrated the news of the Battle of Salamanca with a bonfire and whisky punch, and assembled, amongst others, between forty and fifty of the masons and workmen of Messrs Anderson and Paterson of Galashiels who were employed in building Abbotsford. "The banks of the Tweed looked very merry on this glorious occasion."

Buonaparte's marshals were faring ill in Spain, but the Emperor had lost interest in a campaign which he called "a running sore". On the very day of the Shirra's flitting, Boney had set his *Grande Armée* on the march from Dresden. He was going to attack Russia.

III

The little farmhouse called Cartley Hole was frowned down upon by a barn erected by Dr Douglas. Inside it was totally inadequate for the family of an author with a wife, four growing children and a governess. A tutor, with a wooden leg, Mr George Thomson, son of the minister, was walking up from Melrose daily to instruct young Walter in the classics, so there was one chore farmed out, but of course in wet weather they needed a study, and that was a thing which even the laird of Abbotsford did not at present possess. Scott wrote *Rokeby* in the window of a room about twelve foot square—the parlour, which was also the dining-room. An old bed-curtain was nailed up across the recess, close behind his chair. There were, in all, four rooms available and a kitchen. The children had cribs, fine fun, in one of the upstairs rooms, subdivided as if they were on board ship. By September Scott told Lady Abercorn they were all "screwed in" and he had "resumed the pen in my old Cossack manner".[5] While the Court was sitting he had gone to Edinburgh, very reluctantly, every Monday morning early. "Abbotsford is looking charming." The plantations were coming up splendidly, oak trees nearly as tall as Miss Baillie's knitting needle, he told her. Only at first had he found the noise of the building of Abbotsford distracting. "As for the house and the poem there are twelve masons hammering at the one and one poor noddle at the other, so they are both in progress."

It was not to be imagined that he had given up his letter-writing. He had recently added three new literary correspondents—two very solemn, the Rev. George Crabbe and Mr John Galt, and one the pink of fashion. John Murray had found it plainly ridiculous that Walter Scott and Lord Byron should not appreciate one another because of a little misunderstanding. So the publisher of *Childe Harold* reported Lord Byron's account of his conversation with the Prince of Wales, who had declared Walter Scott his favourite poet and recurred to his name and writings incessantly in a conversation lasting for more than half an hour, and Scott in reply had sent a few lines of gratitude to the young lord hoping he would not consider it intrusive in a veteran author to pay his debt for the high pleasure he had received from *Childe Harold*. He also took the opportunity of explaining that he had indeed produced *Marmion* at top speed, which he regretted, but not upon contract for a sum of money. His haste had been "to extricate himself from some unexpected misfortunes of a very near relation" (Brother Dan's speculations). The young lord replied most handsomely that his satire (*English Bards and Scots Reviewers*) had been written "when I was very young and very angry, and fully bent on displaying my wrath and my wit", and thereafter all went merry as a marriage bell, with an invitation from Scott for Lord Byron to visit his native land and stay with Lord Somerville if Abbotsford was not quite comfortable. They were not, however, to meet for another three years.[6]

Scott took his only holiday this year with part of the family, on business and pleasure. They arrived to visit the Morritts at Rokeby for the second time in golden early autumn weather. Charlotte rode in her carriage, driven by Peter Matheson, and beside her sometimes Sophia and sometimes young Walter. Scott rode, and Gilnockie (so much improved in health that he again deserved the nickname) rode on his pony beside his father for a distance of twenty-five miles most days. When he had had enough, Sophia relieved him.[7] They set off on Thursday, September 24th. They slept at Edgerston. At Flodden Scott showed his children the battlefield and next day they crossed the Border to Hexham, Corbridge and Bishop Auckland. While seeing over the castle at the last place, Scott was recognised (from his portrait now frequently engraved) by an aged cleric who turned out to be Shute Barrington, Bishop of Durham. He was seventy-nine. He insisted on showing the family party the picture gallery, and after they had attended service in the chapel gave them breakfast, sent for a splendid steed, and put them ten miles on their road to Greta Bridge. They arrived at Rokeby in time for Sunday dinner.

Lady Louisa Stuart was staying there, as they had hoped, and both she and Morritt applauded Scott's reading of the first canto of *Rokeby*. He read them also part of a poem, only half the length of *Rokeby* which he meant to publish about the same time, as a lark. He hoped that Jeffrey in the *Edinburgh* would attribute it to Will Erskine. Will was in the plot and made no objection to being supposed the author of *The Bridal of Triermain*.

They had to hurry home because an election was looming. In May Spencer Perceval, most diminutive and gentle of Tory Prime Ministers, had been assassinated by a fanatic, actually in the House of Commons. The news had been received with horrible rejoicing by starved workers who were rioting and smashing machinery in the north of England. As Sheriff of Selkirkshire, a district with factories, Scott was deeply concerned by the prevailing industrial unrest. However, the principal rogue who had been stirring up trouble in Galashiels, although he had not been captured, had made himself scarce. The last of *Rokeby* went off to Ballantyne on December 31st and Scott said in his accompanying letter to James, "There is something odd and melancholy in concluding a poem with the year."

He had a personal reason for grief and anxiety. For nearly two months, until December 8th, 1812, absolutely no news of the *Grande Armée* had reached Britain from Russia. It was as if it had simply vanished. But three days after Buonaparte began his retreat from Moscow, Wellington was also retreating from a fiasco—the siege of Burgos. In that affair Adam Ferguson had been captured. He was a prisoner of war. It was impossible to think of the ebullient "Linton" in such a situation, and to add to his chagrin must be the fact that affairs in the Peninsula offered now a great chance for a bold fellow. Scott did all he could. By February 1813 he had heard from Patrick Murray of Simprim, convalescing at 14, The Crescent, Bath, that the best hope for Linton seemed an exchange with a French officer of equal rank. Such a business would be slow and very doubtful. Scott sent a book to the prisoner—a dove from the ark. It gradually appeared that the best hope was the cessation of hostilities. This was so. Linton was released in 1814.

IV

Rokeby was published on January 10th, 1813, and seemed at first to be likely to satisfy all the author's hopes and needs. John Murray received a typical letter from Byron, "Send me 'Rokeby'. Who the devil is he? No

The Abbotsford family
By Wilkie.

"Mr. Wilkie, the painter, has made a capital picture of the whole family which he intends to finish in London for the Exhibition. We are all drawn in character. Anne and I are two milkmaids with pails on our heads, papa sitting, and Captain Ferguson standing looking for all the world like an old poacher who understands his trade." Letter from Sophia Scott to her governess Miss Millar, November 25th, 1817.

Sir Walter wrote to Sir Adam, March 7th, 1827 (Letters, X, 168) that the remaining characters were an octogenarian shepherd, and his own two sons, little Charles and tall Walter, behind Sir Adam, left and right respectively. The dogs were Maida and Ourisk.

By permission of the Scottish National Portrait Gallery.

John Gibson Lockhart (1794–1854)
By H. Pickersgill.
Private collection.

matter. He has good connexions and will be well introduced." A young student at Oxford University, John Gibson Lockhart, never forgot how the booksellers' shops were besieged by his contemporaries. They followed to his rooms any friend lucky enough to have secured a copy. They were as eager to read *Rokeby* as to see the finish of a race at Newmarket. Indeed, the race for popularity between Scott and Byron was made the subject of bets. All seemed to be going well. Morritt liked the poem, which was most important, Miss Baillie found it noble, His Royal Highness, now Regent, signified that whenever he came to town Mr Scott was to have access to his library, and was to be introduced. Only one fellow author was rude. Tom Moore in his *Twopenny Postbag*, said that Scott had left the Border and meant "to do all the gentlemen's seats on the way" to London.

The *Bridal of Triermain* followed after eight weeks, and took in every one except the one person Scott had intended. Jeffrey had gone on a trip to America. But gradually it became obvious that Scott's narrative poem with an English setting was by no means going to sell as astonishingly as the Scottish predecessors. Scott looked the problem fairly in the face. Round-heads, perhaps, were not found attractive by the poetry-reading public. There were three lyrics well up to his previous standard—"O Brignal banks are wild and fair", "A weary lot is thine, fair maid", and "O Lady, twine no wreath for me". There was a rollicking banditti catch, "Allen-a-Dale". The heroine, in his own opinion at least, surpassed Margaret and Ellen. Matilda was drawn "from the existing person and character of a lady who is no more".[8] Greenmantle, his first love, had died on December 10th, 1810, in Edinburgh. No published Scott letter mentions a fact which he must soon have heard. (It was shortly before the Christmas when he had listened to his children and the little Scotts of Harden dancing in the New Year.) *Rokeby* had a more difficult plot than any of his previous poems—almost fit for an historical novel. He finally decided that *Childe Harold* had won the poetry world. This was serious as already, before the publication of *Rokeby*, James Ballantyne had told him that their ship was going fast on the rocks and they would have to go cap in hand to Constable. Scott, counting on success as before with a poem, had been much against "taking a stroke so fatal to our reputation as striking sail to Constable in our own harbours". It was unfortunate that the fabulous library of the Duke of Roxburghe had come on the market last year. Both Heber and Terry had secured for him some items which would appreciate in value. Terry had also bought him some desirable armour. The *Gazette* was full of unnerving bankruptcies. The weather in Edinburgh in April seemed an aftertaste of that which had wrecked the *Grande Armée* on its retreat from

Moscow. "One day . . . it blew such a tempest of wind and snow that I could not go along Princes Street to get to the Register House." By May he had decided that the publishing firm of Ballantyne would have to be wound up. He still hardly recognised that the brothers really never had been publishers by training or experience. Hunter, the difficult partner in Constable's, had died and had been succeeded by a writer to the Signet, called Robert Cathcart, and his brother-in-law, Robert Cadell. Constable was approached and began to study Ballantyne's books. That summer again Scott took only a brief business-and-pleasure holiday. The season was bedevilled by "these damned affairs". The late Duke of Buccleuch had inherited in 1810 the estates and title of the Duke of Queensberry, and thus acquired Drumlanrig Castle in Nithsdale. When Mr and Mrs Walter Scott approached the formidable pile they were greeted by the young duke and duchess waving handkerchiefs from the battlements.

At Longtown the Scotts found the inn (considered very good) where they were to meet the Abercorns, in an absolute turmoil. The marquess, wearing the Garter and accompanying a *cortège* of four carriages, had been preceded the day before by a fifth equipage containing his major-domo and *chef*.

The Scotts had a day at Keswick with Southey, but Morritt had to put them off. His wife was ill. At both Drumlanrig and Penrith, Scott received urgent notes from John Ballantyne demanding large sums for unexpected expenses. By August, Constable agreed to taking over the copyright and publication of some of Ballantyne's list. He refused to touch the *Edinburgh Annual Register*. There was a haggle over the copyright of a quarter of *Rokeby*, and Scott suggested five thousand pounds as a suitable advance for his next poem, not yet written. Cadell gloomily envisaged what would be their situation if Scott were suddenly "summoned to the other world, and not a sheet at Press". Scott thought that he might have the poem ready by November. He mentioned the possibility of applying to Longman or Murray. Constable, who knew now much more about the state of Ballantyne's than Scott, enquired if the poet could not get the support of some of his wealthy London friends in guaranteeing a London account and an overdraft. The printing concern was bringing in about eighteen hundred pounds annually, but an immediate advance of four thousand was needed and it would not be possible to dispose of stock and copyrights in haste. Scott wrote to the Duke of Buccleuch and had a hideous week of waiting for a reply. But "my princely chief" had responded the moment he got Scott's letter, which had merely missed him.[9] Almost at the same date came another reason for a letter to the duke. The Prince Regent was offering Walter Scott the post of Poet Laureate. Under Henry Pye the office had fallen somewhat into disrepute. Scott mistakenly believed that it carried a salary of four hundred pounds per annum. The duke's reply to this question was equally unhesitating, and Scott wrote to Southey to say that he had given his most influential London friend, John Wilson Croker, a hint to approach him. It turned out to be only a hundred and fifty pounds, but Southey accepted and performed diligently. He was let off the mockery of a Birthday Ode to His Majesty. The monarch was blind and senile.

Amongst Scott's anxieties, and the calls upon his purse at this moment, was that Tom's regiment had been ordered to Canada, and Mrs Tom, who was pregnant again, needed support and advice before she decided whether she and the children should follow him.

A summer more beautiful and serene than any Scott remembered was drawing to its close. Some unusual guests came to dine at Abbotsford in the 1813 holiday season. A hundred and ninety French officers, who had been prisoners of war since the Battle of Fuentes d'Onoro in May 1811, were moved up to Selkirk. Amongst them was an agreeable young man, Adelbert Jacques Doisy de Villargennes. His reminiscences were published in Cincinnati in 1884. He had been a vice-consul there for many years. He had dined with Walter Scott several times. Mr Henderson, the agent appointed by the Transport Board, turned a blind eye to the fact that on certain evenings a closed carriage arrived at the boundary stone on the Melrose road and picked up a party of three or four. Doisy never saw Abbotsford by daylight, and his memories were rather more magnificent than can have been the case at the date. Its rooms were described by him as spacious and well-lighted. Mrs Scott, he astonishingly wrote down as having been married to her husband in Berlin. She never dined when her compatriots came. Mr Scott showed great interest in anecdotes about the Emperor Napoleon. A good many local gentry followed Scott's example, and gradually some of the French prisoners on parole became expert fishermen. No Scottish host was more affable and gay than the Sheriff of Selkirkshire.[10]

Scott heard that his old mother was coming to stay quite close, with the Scotts of Raeburn at Lessudden. Abbotsford could offer her a room, as Sophia and Anne would be away for a few days. Peter Matheson would fetch her and return her anywhere she chose. She came in the second week of September, and Scott reported to Brother Tom's wife that she seemed in better health than for several years. She was eighty-one, but her faculties seemed unimpaired and she sent a careful message to know if Tom had received, before he sailed, a letter from her with some medical advice.

Old Mrs Scott was followed by a legal friend from the south, a little parliamentary solicitor, John Richardson, a keen fisherman. Although some of the children had to be sent elsewhere while such a valued guest as their grandmother was entertained, Scott had a room attained by a ladder in one of the outbuildings—Peter Matheson's premises—where a not too exacting bachelor, chiefly bent on sport, could be accommodated. Looking into an old desk which had been stored since the flitting from Ashestiel, in search of some fishing tackle for Richardson, Scott came upon the fragment of *Waverley* which had been put aside twice and forgotten. He carried it downstairs and after looking through it, decided to finish it.[11]

NOTES

1. Lockhart states that Major John Scott lent two thousand pounds for the purchase of Abbotsford and Ballantyne's advanced the other half for *Rokeby*. Letters, II, 492, 500, 508, 527, 535, 538. Lockhart, II, 174–80, 195.

2. Lockhart, II, 159–60.

3. Letters, III, 44, 51–56, 69.

4. Ibid., 122, 128.

5. Ibid., 154, 156. Lockhart, II, 224, 226. George Thomson, who continued at Abbotsford for many years, was accepted by Lockhart as the prototype of Domine Samson in *Guy Mannering*.

6. Letters, III, 134–41. Lockhart, II, 211–17. Scott had written to Miss Baillie on the publication of *Childe Harold*, "I think it a very clever poem but gives no good symptom of the writer's heart or morals", and had agreed with Morritt that there was something provoking and insulting, both to morality and to feeling, in the young lord's misanthropical *ennui*. Nevertheless, he told both correspondents that there was much merit in the production and that it was a poem of most extraordinary power.

7. Lockhart, II, 229, says that both the eldest boy and girl rode on their ponies, but Scott (Letters, III, 173) wrote to Miss Baillie, "My boy on his little pony rode about twenty-five miles a day with me without being fatigued and was sometimes relieved by his sister."

8. Letters, V, 145. Letter to Miss Maria Edgeworth, May 1816. With feminine intuition she had discerned that this heroine must have been drawn from life.

9. Grierson inserted in an Appendix to Volume I of *Letters of Sir Walter Scott* a collection of letters to the Ballantynes covering the years 1807–18 which occupies 120 pages. They were inscribed in the handwriting of John Ballantyne "OPEN NOT READ NOT", and discovered accidentally in the office of a W. S. Grierson, *Sir Walter Scott*, Bart, pp. 108–9, deals with the 1812–13 Ballantyne crisis. See also Lockhart, II, 267–88.

No adequate study of the Ballantyne–Scott relationship has yet been published.

10. Doisy's reminiscences were also published in France in 1894, and translated selections in 1912, in Hawick and Selkirk. They were the subject of an article by Sir Charles Oman in Volume 225 of *Blackwood's Magazine*, January 1929.

11. Letters, III, 354: General Preface to 1st Ed. *Waverley*, Chap. 72, 1814, and General Preface, 1829. Lockhart, II, 300.

XII

The Author of Waverley
1814–1815

I

ON THE NIGHT OF AUGUST IST, 1814, WHEN HE WAS NEARLY BECALMED off the little town of Fraserburgh, after watching a noble sunset and the moon rising, Walter Scott wrote down in his diary, "We are now out of sight of land", and ceased to worry. He was on one of the most enjoyable holidays of his life, business-and-pleasure, and—except for having had to bring a quantity of whisky on board—at no expense. Will Erskine, now Sheriff of Orkney and Zetland, had got him an invitation to go in the lighthouse yacht "to Nova Zembla and the Lord knows where". They were a party of seven—three Commissioners of the Northern Lights (the Sheriffs of Lanarkshire, Forfarshire and Orkney and Zetland), a young son of the Provost of Edinburgh, David Marjoribanks (soon "Marchie" to all) who had brought his fowling piece, Mr Turnbull, the Minister of Ting-wall needing a passage to Zetland, and the chief of the expedition, Mr Robert Stevenson, Engineer-Surveyor to the Board, very well known in the scientific world and liked by all for his good sense and manners. Captain Wilson had under his command, in his stout cutter, ten men and six guns —for privateers were to be expected. There were no wives and daughters or Mayfair widows on this holiday. It was going to be tough. Indeed, it had already proved so, but Walter Scott had shown his mettle from the first. Disdaining the offer of a chair from the yard-arm in which to be swung aloft, he had gone up a rope ladder, thirty feet above boiling seas, to breakfast in the Bell Rock lighthouse, fifteen miles off Arbroath. He approved very much of the interior of his first lighthouse—gleaming brasses, solid oak. It was two years old, and Mr Stevenson's own design, accepted after fierce struggles. Erskine said he must write "something more than Walter Scott" in the album produced on departure. He looked out of a window for a few moments and then spoke for the lighthouse—

> Far in the bosom of the deep,
> O'er these wild shelves my watch I keep, etc. etc.

They had landed at Arbroath to collect Mr Duff, Sheriff for Kincardine-shire and Forfarshire. This was the countryside through which Scott had travelled with a too fast-beating heart to woo Greenmantle. He had first walked with her in the aisles of the abbey, which he again revisited—giving advice as to repairs. The snows of four winters lay on her grave. "Alas!" he wrote sadly in the first of the five little notebooks which he had brought along in order to jot down notes on what he headed as—VACATION 1814.

He was the author of Waverley and nobody knew it except Morritt and Erskine, and of course his publishers. He was out of sight and out of mind, rocked on the bosom of the deep. He was going to circumnavigate his native land—go round the top and come in through the western isles.

His winter had been rather trying. His poor painstaking German amanuensis, Weber, had suddenly gone mad—in the study one evening at dusk, offering him the choice of a pair of pistols. Scott had told him calmly that they must not alarm Mrs Scott and the children, and put both weapons in a drawer. They had dined en famille, but when a friend, summoned by an urgent message, had made his appearance, the poor demented man had rushed from the house. He was now confined in a home for mental cases in York.

Stark, who had presented fantastically beautiful designs for Abbotsford, had died. Anyway, unless Waverley proved a miracle they would never have been able to afford them. They would just have to enlarge the cottage. One of Scott's lame dogs seemed to have hobbled unaided over a stile at last. James Hogg's Queen's Wake had delighted Lord Byron, as indeed it might; the Ettrick Shepherd's heroine seemed to have stepped straight out of a Cluny tapestry . . . The Buccleuchs had given a splendid Twelfth Night party at Dalkeith House and asked Sophia and young Walter, who had thought themselves in the world of the Arabian Nights. There had been three hundred guests. February had been more than usually unpleasant. At one moment there had been four posts due from London—roads blocked in every direction. Sophia had a new pet-name now, "Fia", and was sensible enough to be sent directions as to illuminating Castle Street. "You must get the little tin things to hold the candles. We shall need a great many—as many as there are panes in front of the House." It was April 14th and Edinburgh knew that the Allies had entered Paris. By the end of the month they heard that Buonaparte had abdicated and was going to be sent to Elba.

By-jobs still fascinated Scott. On July 1st, Constable had published nineteen volumes of Jonathan Swift, edited by Walter Scott, and on July 7th *Waverley* anonymously. John Ballantyne had copied Scott's manuscript so that typesetters should not recognise a familiar hand.

On July 29th Scott had sailed on his holiday.[1]

II

Aberdeen, Old and New, from the sea was quite beautiful. The lighthouse yacht proceeded slowly along the coast and some of her passengers took her boat to view the celebrated Buller of Buchan, a huge cauldron into which the waves rushed through a natural arch of rock. They had a hard pull back to the yacht.

After leaving Fraserburgh they saw no land for two days and guessed correctly that they had missed the Fair Isle. At Lerwick the harbour was crowded with drunken sailors, crews of nine Greenlanders—whalers. Will would have to try them and put them in prison. An intelligent officer of the garrison showed Scott his first Pictish fort—only scattered remains. The Zetlanders struck him as a strong, clear-complexioned, handsome race, and the women were very pretty. The main street was flagged and the narrow lanes descended by steps. There were no carriages or even wheeled carts. The sheep on the rocky, treeless hills were of every colour, even sky-blue, and the farmhouses wretched. They seemed a very superstitious people. They had a horrible belief that if you saved a man from drowning, he would live to do you an injury.

Scott began an epistle in rhyme to the Duke and Duchess of Buccleuch. Stevenson had gone off with the yacht for a week, surveying the northern isles. The party were visited by the notables of the island, and Scott went with old Mr Mowat, a friend of his father, and Adam Duff, to inspect another Pictish castle. Its arrangements confirmed his impression that Picts had been undersize. Lerwick was decidedly not Paradise, but Scott was enjoying himself. He hired a six-oared whaler-built boat and set out with Duff and Dr Edmonstone, author of a history of Shetland, to see the Cradle of Noss; the scene, after they had rounded the most northerly of the four capes and turned into the open sea, was tremendously sublime. These huge precipices abounded in caverns haunted by vociferous sea-fowl. The party landed on Bressay and walked three miles across the isle to dine with young Dr Mowat at his seat, Gardie House. They got wet through, but saw interesting Zetland methods of ploughing. The plough, drawn by four young oxen and as many ponies, might have been that invented by Triptolemus.

On Sunday Scott rode with Duff and Erskine to Tingwall to hear Parson Turnbull, who had come up with them in the yacht, doing his best with great patience and judgment to set a good example to his flock. He was from Jedburgh, and gave an excellent discourse. After church they visited another castle—Scalloway. They dined with a Mr Scott and two young ladies, both Mrs Scotts, having married brothers. One was a widow. She had lost her husband last year in the wreck of the *Doris* merchantman, off Rattray Head. They were very agreeable women and gave Scott information about a sea-monster, visible for a fortnight off Scalloway, two winters past, and a sort of sword-dance still practised in the island of Papa.

Just as they were going in to dinner at Lerwick next day, having paid their farewell calls, the yacht appeared and they went aboard. But they had to go ashore very early the next morning to see another Pictish fortress, probably the most entire in the world—Mousa. In form it resembled a dice-box. Mr Stevenson measured it. The top gallery was so narrow and low that Scott had to creep.

They had contrary winds and rough weather off Sunburgh Head, the extreme south-eastern point of Zetland, where there was a frightful tide caused by the union of the Atlantic and German oceans. They made three frustrated efforts to enter a bay between Sunburgh and another headland, and in the end had to run into a roadstead called Quendal Bay on the south-east, and anchor. Next morning only Scott ascended Fitful Head to enjoy the view. Stevenson had gone off to inspect a possible site for another lighthouse, and Marchie to get rabbits. The night of August 9th made history in the Diary of Vacation, 1814. Everything possible on board was smashed and nobody got a wink of sleep, "all the landsmen sicker than the sick". Scott had succumbed before—off Arbroath— but had recovered quickly. For the first time now he got up with a head-ache. He would have to give his servant, John MacBeith, notice. Evidently loathing and fearing the yacht and all its works, he had scarcely been sober since they sailed. His appearance was that of a demented and half-drowned baboon.

The natives of Fair Isle, who came out to hail them in a crazy-looking craft, wore extraordinary costumes—striped worsted caps on long elf-locks, and raw-hide footwear. Their dexterity in boats without a single whole plank was a thing of wonder. The visitors went three miles round the coast to look at the inhabited part of the isle. The tacksman, Mr Strong, who lived in solitary state like Robinson Crusoe, made them welcome to his cottage, but they took their own food. There had been an American Commodore off the Isle last year; the clergyman from Zetland came once a year to marry and baptise a people living in unappetising squalor . . . The women were great knitters and exchanged wares with any merchant vessels which came in sight. Mr Strong's dwelling was that in-habited by the Duke of Medina-Sidonia, Commander-in-Chief of the invincible Spanish Armada. This grandee had spent several winter weeks there after losing his vessel to the eastward of the isle, and before getting off for Norway. Scott received from Mr Strong the gift of a curious old chair for Abbotsford.

They were escorted by two very sportive whales on the first stage of their passage to the Orkneys. They landed in Kirkwall Bay two days later and Scott found the capital city somewhat depressing at close view. Only the cathedral of St. Magnus, the bishop's palace, the castle and some houses above the harbour were handsome and picturesque. Marchie went off in search of a pointer. Their lodgings were comfortable, but it was dis-appointing to find no letters from home.

The soil of Orkney was better and its air more genial than that of Zetland, and grouse abounded. But he found it less interesting than Zet-land—not so wild and peculiar. After two days in Kirkwall he was not sorry to round the mainland (romantically called Pomona)[2] and get into the Sound of Holm, on the right of which a deep bay called Scapa Flow indented right up to within two miles of Kirkwall. The breeze was too fresh for them to land at Skerries and an attempt to stand over for Thurso was also frustrated. The Pentland Firth, so celebrated for the strength and fury of its tide, lived up to its reputation. They passed John o' Groats' house or rather the storehouse now so called, and were told nobody had ever seen him. Next day they succeeded, with the aid of a pilot boat, in landing on the Skerries and anchored with dawn in Stromness Bay. Two miles on ponies brought them to one of the sights of Pomona—the Standing Stones of Stennes, excelled by Stonehenge but otherwise unparalleled in Britain. In a lofty cabin at Stromness a dreadful-looking old hag called Bessie Miller, upwards of ninety she told them, and dried up like a mummy, sold them for sixpence "a fair wind". This lasted through the Mouth of Hoy and into the Atlantic, but deserted them before they had doubled Cape Wrath, justly so named. Duff and Scott continued on deck, like two great bears, wrapped in watch cloaks, the sea flying over them now and then. After a sound buffeting they stood away for Loch Eriboll. This was Lord Reay's country, and one of his lordship's tacksmen asked them to breakfast at his house at Rispan and offered fresh herring, haddocks, eggs and butter, barley bannocks, oat-cakes, tea, coffee and whisky. Thus fortified they went off to see something Scott would not for the world have missed—the famous Cave of Smoo or Smowe. They clambered through the first immense cavern, which was incrusted with stalactites, and took a local boat, a light skiff, into the third chamber which was subterranean. Here they passed from dubious twilight to pitch darkness. Coming back, Will Erskine turned giddy and Scott had to shout for a rope to assist the Counsellor. Mr Stevenson said the stalactites were inferior to those they would see in Macalister's cave in Skye. An old man, recently dead, in the little harbour of Scalpa called Donald Macleod had been host here to the unfortunate Prince Charles Edward during his wanderings in 1746, and could not until his dying day mention the Young Adventurer without tears.

They sailed early in the morning of August 22nd to cross the Minch, but a contrary breeze kept them creeping along the Harris shore.

They woke under the Castle of Dunvegan in the Isle of Skye next morning, and the Laird of Macleod arrived with his piper before they were dressed to carry them off to see his castle, some of which was so old even tradition knew no date for it. Mrs Macleod and her daughter were pretty and accomplished women—a thing the party had not seen since they left Edinburgh. Scott seized the opportunity to write a letter home and instructed Charlotte to tell the children he had just slept in a haunted chamber. The Lady had asked him if he would like to sleep in it. It had antique-looking furniture, tapestries on enormously thick walls and a stupendous view lit by moonlight. As Scott had had a long day at sea and an excellent claret with his dinner, he got into his bed and knew no more till his servant called him in the morning. The only thing he found uncomfortable was that, in Scandinavian style, the feather-bed or *duvet* was the top article on the bed. Dunvegan also possessed a fairy flag, valuable in battle, spread on the nuptial couch, and to bring herring into the loch. He was again disappointed to find no letters. Unless they had cross-winds, now they should be at Greenock within a fortnight.

Looking back on his cruise he decided that the agreeables had far surpassed the disagreeables. He was a good sailor and would like to repeat the experience some day. "We had constant exertion, a succession of wild and uncommon scenery; good humour on board, and objects of animation and interest when we went ashore." There had, to be sure, been a good many hours when they were reduced by the weather to songs, ballads, recitations, backgammon and picquet, but a rather oddly assorted little party had never had the slightest difference of opinion, though so closely packed for six weeks.

Macleod had promised them they should find "a fine romantic loch" under the western termination of the high peaks of the Cuillins, which they had admired from Dunvegan. Loch Corriskin, dark and inscrutable, veiled in drifting mist, or sudden showers giving place to silvery sunlight, was the most dramatic scene on which he had yet set eyes on the cruise. Will Erskine noticed with awe that Scott seemed quite overwhelmed by the savage majesty of their surroundings. He went off by himself and when recalled to join the departing party by a sailor, the man said, "Strange! he did not seem to know me."

Macalister's cave in Loch Slapin was superior to Smoo in that it was the most elegant white inside as if made of marble, and had a pool which from the depth and purity of its waters might have been the bathing grotto of a naiad. In Fingal's Cave, which Scott revisited after two attempts to land on Staffa, "Would you believe it," he wrote to Morritt, "my poor Willie sat down and wept." They had now seen the three grandest caves in Scotland. Smoo won for terror, Scott decided, Macalister's for its whiteness and graceful dignity, but Staffa could only be called sublime.

At Torloisk Mrs Clephane and her three Graces begged him and Will to stay several days, and it was ludicrous that after expressing their urgency to get on board their yacht they lay without a wind in full view of the house until evening fell.

September came in with glorious sunshine and they decided at Oban, where Scott thought trade was dull, to run over in weather so clear and serene to take a look at an Irish monument, the celebrated Giant's Causeway. The heat, for the first time since they had left Leith, was almost too much. They spread a handsome awning on deck "to save our complexions God wot". He had already warned Charlotte from Dunvegan that his hands were the colour of York tan.[3]

The happiness of his holiday ended abruptly at the dinner table of Dr Richardson in the little fishing-village of Portrush. Here he heard, just as the latest gossip from Scotland, of a death which caused him inexpressible surprise and distress. The Duchess of Buccleuch, "my lovely chieftainess", as good as she was beautiful, had passed away suddenly four days after the birth of a daughter. "God grant comfort to the afflicted survivor!" He now only longed to go home.

III

He wrote to ask advice of the duke's younger brother (a thing he was to do increasingly). Lord Montagu thought it would be a help to the family if dear Scott visited them as often as possible. So he was continually at Bowhill that autumn.

Meanwhile, *Waverley* was proving the most successful anonymous novel ever published. By the end of the year five thousand copies had been sold and the profits exceeded two thousand one hundred pounds. James Ballantyne replied for the unknown author to an effusive letter from Maria Edgeworth. She had been deeply touched that she had been mentioned on the last page as a model with her "admirable Irish portraits".

The *Quarterly* thought *Waverley* "a Scotch *Castle Rackrent*" but much better. The *Monthly*, the *British Review* and the *Edinburgh* all praised it, and the two last reviewers, one of them Jeffrey, hinted that Walter Scott must have performed this miracle. There were other good and bad guesses. Will Erskine, one of the few people in the secret, was a popular candidate, so were Brother Tom Scott, now in Canada, and even Mrs Tom. Henry Mackenzie seemed past it, otherwise he might have qualified. Scott refused to come out into the open. He confided in Morritt. "I am not sure it would be considered quite decorous for me as a Clerk of Session to write novels."

His unexceptionable edition of Swift had come out, with thirty poems hitherto unknown, and twenty-eight letters to Vanessa. He had had *The Lord of the Isles* in the back of his mind now for four years. In spite of by-jobs, he had written three cantos by November. He produced a preface and notes for *Memories of the Somervilles*, a labour of love for a neighbour now in failing health in London. One of his reasons for bringing out *Waverley* anonymously had been that he did not want to damage his reputation as a poet. He knew now he could lay aside that fear. He had struck a gold mine. He began to write *Guy Mannering*.

Constable was not at present in funds to take over any of Ballantyne's well-nigh unsaleable stock, even at the mention of a successor to *Waverley*. He was staggering under the burden of the *Encyclopaedia Britannica*. In mid-October James Ballantyne made one of his typical *gaffes*. While he was away at Kelso, a distraint for debt was served on him in Edinburgh. His brother John came forward with suggestions, all of which Scott thought wretched and damaging to Constable. "I will never give Constable, or any one, room to say I have broke my word to him in the slightest degree." Longmans, "the Leviathan of Paternoster Row", were offered *Guy Mannering* to be brought out before or soon after "Mr Scott's new poem". Constable was to be allotted the Scottish sale.

While Scott had been in the Hebrides, Lord Byron had sent him "a high-spirited Turkish fragment", *The Giaour*, with an inscription, "To the Monarch of Parnassus, from one of his subjects". Scott said to James Ballantyne, "Byron hits the mark where I don't even pretend to fledge my arrow." He was going to cease attempting to appear as a poet; yet he still had minor works to come.

He was working at Abbotsford for Christmas, when a son of his fellow Clerk in Session, James Ferrier, died suddenly; he had to take over his old friend's duties. Perhaps it was for the best that he had not been able to take his own treasured first-born out for a hard day's shooting wild-duck in mid-winter weather, for it was gradually borne in upon him that Gilnockie was at death's door. Apparently, and in spite of previous inoculation and vaccination, the boy had the dreaded smallpox. Despite his other involvements, every correspondent had to be told by Scott of the horror hanging over Castle Street. Morritt, Ellis, Lady Abercorn were all advised. Young Walter was "the talk of the town". It would seem that not until this dark hour had Scott realised how he had pinned his hopes upon this promising sprig. There was nothing for it but to stay in Edinburgh, and watch and wait and work. The mists parted from his memories of Galloway in his expedition of 1793, and with terrible anxiety resolutely pushed aside, he sat, hour after hour, doing the only useful thing possible —getting on with his second novel.

IV

1815 opened badly. Gilnockie made a recovery almost as spectacular as his collapse, but when *The Lord of the Isles*, published on January 8th, had been in the world for a week, Scott had to ask James Ballantyne outright what were people saying? James hesitated so long that Scott had to give him a lead. "I see how it is: the result is given in one word— *Disappointment* . . . Well, well, James, so be it—but you know we must not droop, for we can't afford to give over. Since one line has failed, we must just stick to something else."

Actually, after a slow start, the first edition sold well. Lockhart eventually considered that the poem was about as popular as *Rokeby*, but never touched the heights of *The Lay*, *Marmion* or *The Lady of the Lake*. Scott could not afford to give over because he was building at Abbotsford again. He still said that he could not afford Stark's plan, but there was a new small bedroom, and an enlargement of the parlour-dining-room made out of the laundry. And, excited by the success of *Waverley*, he had promised to spend a spare hundred or two taking Charlotte and Sophia to London, when the Courts rose. He told his wife that if she would consent to go by sea, instead of by that vile North Road, they might use the money saved, on hiring a carriage in London, and be free of the necessity of paying hugely for distasteful hackney-cabs. *Guy Mannering*, "that old little tale", the work of six weeks at Christmastide, appeared on February 24th and although not all reviewers were courteous, the reading public greeted it with rapture.

The Scotts sailed from Leith on March 21st. The winds were their enemies: a collier-brig almost sank them in darkness, and they lay hammering on a rock for two hours until floated off by the rising tide; but they arrived at last, safe and sound, at the Dumergues' on the corner of White Horse Street and Piccadilly, on Saturday morning, April 8th, 1815.

Napoleon Buonaparte, having escaped from Elba and landed at Cannes, had reached Paris on March 20th. The Hundred Days had begun. He had been carried into the Tuileries, shoulder-high, by a rejoicing mob. Louis XVIII, unwieldy and gouty, had left the palace hurriedly on the preceding night, for Ghent. For England to go to war again with France would be unpopular in many quarters. The country was wild for peace after twenty years of almost uninterrupted war. The armed forces had been cut down to the bone, and everything French welcomed back with almost uncritical enthusiasm in the English capital. The French fashions which greeted the eyes of the party from Edinburgh seemed to the pater-familias monstrous. A French female singer who performed at Arlington House on one of Lady Salisbury's Sunday evenings, with extravagant gesture, seemed to him quite awful. He had been warned that the Prince Regent expected him at Carlton House where the lavish redecoration ordered by an heir to the throne in Britain's hour of need was causing deep concern amongst the serious-minded. "Let me know when he comes," said the prince, "and I'll get up a snug little dinner that will suit him."

The company with which Scott sat down on a spring night in Aladdin's cave consisted of the Duke of York, his host's military brother, the

Marquess of Huntly, heir of the Duke of Gordon, the Earl of Fife, Sir William Adam, soon to be appointed Lord Chief-Commissioner of the Jury Court in Scotland, Lord Melville, John Wilson Croker, and the Vice-Chamberlain, Lord Yarmouth, son of the Regent's elderly mistress, the Marchioness of Hertford. The entertainment was first-class. "The prince and Scott," explained Croker, "were the two most brilliant story-tellers, in their several ways, that I have ever happened to meet; they were both aware of their *forte* and they both exerted themselves that evening with delightful effect." The prince, amongst other accomplishments, had an acute ear, and an eye for the ridiculous; he was an expert mimic. In appearance now he was, like his palace, rather overwhelming. Scott, in letters to discreet correspondents, often alluded to "our fat friend". He was a very bad fifty-three, but he still had the wrecks of the looks and manners which had made him the Prince Charming of Europe. Towards midnight he called for a bumper "To the Author of *Waverley*", looking significantly at Scott, who appeared puzzled for a moment but then produced a polished sentence inferring that he had no claims to this high compliment, but would see that it did reach the ears of the author. Before they could sit again, the prince ordered "Another of the same, if you please, to the Author of *Marmion*." Afterwards James Ballantyne enquired of Scott if it was true that the prince had asked him direct if he was the author of *Waverley* and that he had given a distinct and solemn denial. Scott replied that the prince was far too well-bred a man ever to have put such a question. He had found him "certainly the first *English* gentleman of his day".[4] Before he left town he dined again at Carlton House and he availed himself of permission to visit the library. Here he met rather an unctuous person, the Rev. James Clarke, Librarian and Domestic Chaplain, himself an author, and a most deplorable editor. At present he was at work on a life of James II from the Stuart Papers. This collection had come from the late Cardinal York, brother of Prince Charles Edward. The Crown had acquired it, together with other valuable relics of the ruined and exiled house of Stuart. Scott had a long audience with the prince in the library, and Baron Adam who was present said he could not decide which was the greater Jacobite—the Regent or "Walter", as the prince had at once begun to call him.[5]

He had, of course, attended a *levée* before he entered on this succession of royal hospitalities, and he saw himself as rather a comical figure as, still attired in bag-wig, dress-coat and sword, he sat down to write to Miss Margaret Clephane to tell her what trouble he was taking over her affairs. In 1813 Morritt had sent to Ashestiel a letter of introduction for

The Daughters. Sophia (left) and Anne Scott, 1818
By William Nicholson. Originals at Abbotsford.
By permission of Mrs Maxwell-Scott.

two young Englishmen, Mr Pemberton and Lord Compton, who were making a Scottish tour. Scott had passed them on to Mrs Maclean-Clephane at Torloisk and the result had been that Lord Compton had fallen passionately in love with a Lady of the Lake, the eldest daughter of the house. One of Scott's jobs in London was to draw up, together with the bridegroom's family, a marriage settlement. At first all seemed charming. Lord Northampton, at his house in Brook Street, appeared the very model of a good-humoured old peer; he was a widower. Lady Frances (sister) expressed her highest pleasure in the proposed alliance. It was from Mr Boodle, family solicitor, that Scott began to hear of unexpected difficulties. So that there should be no fear of Boodle "turning my flank", he took the precaution of calling in John Richardson, also a solicitor, practising in London, and finally David Douglas, Lord Reston, a friend since Edinburgh High School days. He positively wore out his shoes running between Brook Street, Portland Place and Fludyer Street, Westminster. For suddenly Mr Boodle transmitted a "cruel" letter from the marquess, which turned out to be because the charming old noble-man's estates were heavily encumbered. Another blow came from Mull. Mrs Maclean-Clephane had to disclose that her late husband's family had never been friendly to her. Margaret was the heiress of Torloisk, but there were two younger sisters, Williamina and Anna Jane. That difficulty was overcome by Mrs Douglas Clephane (grandmother), convinced of the desirability of the match, coming forward with the offer of settling the estate of Kirkness on the bride. An old lady whom Scott had once visited and thought odd, was making a virtue of necessity. Gradually the affair was sorted out, principally because both the young people were deter-mined to marry and live happily ever after. Miss Clephane, whose profile was classical, heard without alarm of the dreadfully narrow provision originally proposed for her, should she be left widowed as countess or marchioness, without an heir, or perhaps worst still, with many children. The young earl was an amiable youth, also with a classic profile, who sketched delightfully. He was so much in love that once, emerging from a long and painful discussion with Scott during which a thunderstorm, complete with thunder and lightning had shaken the house, he was utterly surprised to find the streets flooded. Scott had a pocket chart of London and it was very necessary, for Romeo was so busy talking of Miss Clephane that he took them by every wrong turning.[6]

One of the friends whom Scott had most looked forward to meeting was George Ellis. He heard with a great sense of loss that this most conversable man had died on April 10th two days after his own arrival in

London. He was, however, going to overlap with Wordsworth and he was going to meet Lord Byron.

This historic occasion took place at last in the new premises of John Murray between three and four o'clock on an April afternoon. Number 50 Albemarle Street had recently been made over to the carpenters, painters and decorators on the courageous move of the firm from its old, noisy, bustling Fleet Street birthplace. It looked as if it had been a gentleman's residence, not a place of business. It stood just off Piccadilly, in a shortish street, running north and south, facing east, at the south end. With its ascent of several steps to a comely entrance and two flights of stairs lit by a Venetian window leading to the first floor, it bore a decided resemblance to home—39 Castle Street. The only notable differences were that the view from the doorstep was not Princes Street and the tail end of Edinburgh Castle, but Piccadilly and, downhill, the front of St James's Palace. The London house had fine carved banisters and the ascent aided by them was not quite so steep as in Castle Street. "Mr Murray's literary lounge", which was going to become the centre of friendship and communication between gentlemen of the pen in the West End, consisted of two lofty and well-proportioned rooms, opening out of one another, not very large, but capable of swallowing a surprising number of articulate authors. The family lived above, and John Murray III, aged seven, was on the look-out. He remembered that Lord Byron's deformity in his foot was very evident, especially as he went downstairs. He carried a stick. After Mr Scott and he had ended in the drawing-room, it was a curious sight to see the two greatest poets of the age—both lame— stumping out, side by side. They were, of course, also both Scots.

John Murray II noted that Scott arrived first, but Byron was on time. He made his introduction and they embraced each other in the most affectionate manner and entered into a conversation which lasted nearly two hours. Droppers-in came and went—James Boswell (son of the biographer), William Sotheby, poet and dilettante, Richard Heber . . .

Byron was at the height of his looks and powers. He had made what should have been an advantageous marriage four months past, and there were, amongst well-wishers, hopes that he had ceased to be a rebel against society. Scott, who had been prepared to meet a difficult young man of peculiar habits, was "most agreeably disappointed. I found Lord Byron in the highest degree courteous and even kind." He was also, surprisingly, rather snobbish and not very well read. When he fell silent and looked gloomy, Scott just waited until that passed off. Byron had accepted an appointment as a Director of Drury Lane and told Scott to let loose upon him any good playwrights. Except as to religion and politics they agreed upon most things. Scott did not believe that Byron had given careful thought to either problem. "I suppose," said Byron rather sharply, "you are one of those who prophesy that I shall turn Methodist." "No," said Scott, "I don't expect your conversion to be of such an ordinary kind. I rather look to see you retreat upon the Catholic faith and distinguish yourself by the austerity of your penances." Byron seemed rather taken with that idea. "Like the old heroes of Homer", the bards exchanged gifts. Scott sent Byron, by Murray, a beautiful dagger once the property of Elphi Bey; Byron responded with a large silver sepulchral vase, suitably inscribed, full of dead men's bones found within the long walls of Athens in February 1811. They met thereafter for an hour or two, almost daily, at Murray's as well as at evening parties elsewhere.[7]

When the visitors from Scotland had been in London for a month, and Sophia had been taken to see all the suitable sights, she was driven up to stay with the Baillies at Hampstead. Joanna's drama, *The Family Legend* had been produced at the Lane, and Lord Byron had accompanied the Scotts and the authoress to a performance. Scott and Charlotte were enchanted by a new actress at Covent Garden. Miss O'Neill was the sweetest Juliet Scott had ever seen.[8]

On June 5th Scott found himself engaged to attend no less than "three grand déjeuners". "Make up your mind," Joanna Baillie had warned him, "to be stared at only a little less than the Czar of Muscovy or old Blücher." She was alluding to the portraits of these heroes, now the principal attraction at the Royal Academy summer exhibition. The news that the author of *Marmion*, etc., and perhaps also of *Waverley*, was in town had meant an increasing rush of invitations. He had not done so badly. He had seen Terry, who was now married, quite often, and Heber and Morritt and Humphry Davy. He had met Mrs Amelia Opie, the novelist, and much interesting artistic company at the house of Sir George Beaumont. He had revisited Lady Stafford at Cleveland House, and Samuel Rogers whose breakfasts were now famous. But he was perfectly ready to leave a capital which he thought was getting more absurd than ever, and it was with relief that he was at last able to tell Miss Clephane that he had finished her business. If she was left a widowed countess she should be assured of about six thousand pounds per annum. If her father-in-law predeceased her husband, the income of their estate would exceed eighteen thousand pounds, "no bad prospect for our young lady". News from the Continent was meagre and exceedingly unreliable. In the third week of May

Parliament was still debating Peace or War. There was considerable hope, actually founded on fact, that Buonaparte was making secret overtures for peace. But the Congress sitting in Vienna had no doubt of his eventual intentions. The Duke of Wellington, appointed Commander-in-Chief of the Allied forces, had arrived in Brussels on April 4th and complained much of the quality of the troops sent to him. On June 1st Buonaparte held a monster meeting on the Champ de Mai. It was not called a review, and he wore a theatrical civilian costume, but on June 12th he left Paris at the head of an army.

Scott was back at his desk in Castle Street by June 15th and writing to the Rev. Charles Maturin about efforts to interest Lord Byron in his dramas. It was not until June 24th that *The Caledonian Mercury* announced:

> An express is this moment arrived forwarded by our worthy Provost, for the gratification of the inhabitants of this city, communicating the glorious intelligence of a complete overthrow of Buonaparte by the Duke of Wellington. Annexed is a copy of the communication received by Mr Kerr of the Post Office, which has thrown the city into a greater state of ecstasy than we ever remember to have witnessed.

The astute Murray had already sent an account to Blackwood, his Edinburgh agent, who carried it off to show Scott before noon on the 24th. "The whole town is in an uproar, and all the bells have been set a-ringing.'⁹

V

Walter Scott, who had reached Edinburgh on June 10th, left it again on July 28th. He was going to quit his native land for the first time in his life. Nothing could have been more inconvenient for him than another absence from home, but a letter sent round by a distinguished legal neighbour, George Bell, whose brother Sir Charles was on the medical staff in Brussels, absolutely determined him that he must set out to see the battlefield of Waterloo and the victorious army, as soon as possible. He could not desert Miss Clephane, whose wedding was to take place on July 24th. ("Do you know, through it all, who has been father, brother, everything to me? Mr Scott!") He duly saw his *protégée* become the Countess Compton: Dr Daniel Sandford, the episcopal clergyman who had baptized Sophia performed the ceremony. He was now the Right Rev. Lord Bishop of Edinburgh.

Scott had picked up three neighbours, John Scott of Gala, Alexander Pringle of Whytbank, and a young advocate, Robert Bruce, son of George Bruce of Langlee. Every member of the bachelor party, except Pringle, was going to keep a diary, and Walter Scott was going to pay his expenses by publishing an account of his experiences in the form of letters. He envisaged half-profits on a first edition should bring him in four hundred and fifty pounds, and told Ballantyne to print it and offer the remaining half-profit to Constable, Murray and Longman. *Paul's Letters to his Kinsfolk* would be sheer journalism to meet a popular demand. It ought to be published in the second week of September. The letters, of which there were eventually sixteen, were written to an imaginary military man (his brother Major John), a sister (actually Miss Chrittie, his favourite aunt), Paul's Laird (Lord Somerville, long President of the Board of Agriculture), Paul's cousin Peter (recipient of social and political news, Will Erskine), and a Minister of the Gospel (Dr Douglas of Galashiels). The major got the lion's share.[10]

The party from Tweedside left at 5 a.m. in the Wellington coach and did some sightseeing on their route. They attended Sunday service in York Minster, heard at Hull that they must go on to Harwich, saw Lincoln Cathedral by moonlight; heard service again at Peterborough and at Cambridge, where both Gala and Pringle had been students. They stayed a night at the Sun in Cambridge so that they could see Trinity and St John's colleges. Scott was much impressed by King's College chapel. They fitted in Bury St Edmunds Abbey and reached Harwich, by Ipswich, late on the night of August 2nd. While the Custom House officers were searching his luggage (Scott had taken firearms), he dashed off a line to Charlotte. The packet had sailed, but they had got a passage in a nice little cutter where they should be very snug. "I hope to be in Holland tomorrow, so My Native Land Goodnight.' His optimism was misplaced. They landed at Helvoetsluys two days later, very washed out.

The first of Paul's letters, naturally, went to the Major, as this character had taken part in the Duke of York's unfortunate campaign of 1799. Bergen op Zoom appeared a very strongly fortified town. They had a fine hot Sunday for visiting the splendid churches of Antwerp, but the French seemed to have taken away almost all the famous pictures. They travelled towards Brussels in a long, black, queer-looking hearse of a thing, open at the sides, but with curtains which could be closed if it rained. It was drawn by three horses and their coachman shrieked at them like a Highland drover pushing on his bullocks. Scott found no difficulty at all in making himself understood. Gala came on fast, Pringle improved, but young Bruce was a cause of amusement. The inns on their road over-charged them abominably for lodging, but their fare was delicious—"a capital French dinner of two courses and a dessert of mulberries, cherries, capital greengage plums, peaches, nectarines etc. and as much Burgundy as you pleased for not quite five shillings a piece".

They arrived at the Hotel de Flandres, Place Royale, Brussels, on August 7th. Scott was fortune in his introductions. The Duchess of Richmond, who was a daughter of the late Duchess of Gordon, had already written on his behalf to the Duke of Wellington, now established in Paris. Sir Frederick Adam, the Major-General left in Brussels in charge of the garrison, was a son of his old friend Lord Chief Commissioner Adam. The general had been wounded and still could not ride, but he sent an aide-de-camp, Captain Campbell, and a French officer with the party which set out two days later to view the scene of Britain's glory. They started well by breakfasting in the very room where Wellington had slept the night before the battle. They were also accompanied by a half-pay Scottish major, Pryse Lockhart Gordon, domiciled in Brussels, like the Richmonds, for reasons of economy; and they picked up what Scott wrote down as "honest John de Costar, the Flemish peasant whom Buonaparte had made immortal by pressing into his service as a guide". Later, Pryse Gordon said that this character was a charlatan. A blacksmith at the inn of La Belle Alliance deposed in his presence that they had hidden together ten miles from Waterloo on the day of the battle and Monsieur D'Accosta could not deny this. However, he could soon afford to give this inconvenient witness sufficient hush-money, and continued to escort parties round the battlefield at increasing cost until 1824. So Scott heard with edification how Buonaparte had ridden a dappled horse, and worn a grey *surtout* over a green uniform, and a violet waistcoat and pantaloons, and much more circumstantial detail.

Wednesday, August 9th, was a very hot day, nevertheless Scott spent upwards of two hours prowling around the ridges of St Jean and the Belle Alliance, the ruins of the "sweet little château of Hougoumont" and the farm of La Haye Sainte where the conflict had been fiercest. As the slaughter had been great and the bodies of men and horses had been disposed of as quickly as possible by fire, or rather shallow interment, the stench was awful. But Pryse Gordon, having heard they were now plough-ing on the battlefield, had taken the precaution of sending out a couple of saddle-horses and the author of *Waverley*—who made no secret of the fact that the notes he was taking were for publication—was well pleased with the manners of the steed provided for him. Needless to say relics from the battlefield were pressed upon the party in every hamlet by flocks of natives who had long since removed most that was interesting or valuable. All that was left now were bones of horses, a great number of hats, rags and scraps of leather and uniforms, account books, prayer books and papers. Later, Pryse Gordon got Scott "a French soldier's book, well stained with blood, and containing some songs popular in the French army". One of his party picked up at a spot where the Scottish regiments had been engaged, a copy of Allan Ramsay's *Gentle Shepherd*. Scott bought a Cross of the Legion of Honour for forty francs, and an ordinary cuirass for Abbotsford for about six, and, to send to the Duke of Buccleuch, a very handsome inlaid one belonging to an officer of distinction. But he got that in Brussels and at a high price, and he forbore, on the battlefield, from imitating the many visitors who were collecting stones of peaches, filberts, etc. so that a corner of a British garden should come from Waterloo.

He lingered at the spot where the Life Guards coming up in the rear of the Rifle Brigade had called out to them, "Bravo, ninety-fifth, do you lather them and we'll shave them." He was thrilled to hear that when the Scots Greys performed their historic charge through the ranks of the Gordons "all joined in a triumphal shout of 'Scotland for ever!'"

The travellers set out by Mons on August 11th to cross the border at Quiverain for France.

VI

On the night of August 16th, finding himself a little early for a dinner engagement, he strolled out to enjoy the pure and delicious air of a summer's evening in Paris. He was elegantly lodged in the Hotel de Bourbon, Rue de la Paix, and he soon arrived in the Place Louis Quinze where he halted spellbound by the beauty and nobility of the scene. He could hardly believe that he was, at last, in a city he had so long wished to visit and under what extraordinary circumstances. The lights glimmering through the trees amongst the alleys and parterres of the Champs Elysées were the watch fires of an English camp. The illuminations and music which came from a great house on the corner of the nearest street were those ordered in honour of a visit from the allied sovereigns to the Duke of Wellington. He listened as if in a dream to a distant roll of drums, English airs, the pipes . . .

Paul's two letters to his sister from the French capital had to tell her of first impressions likely to interest a female. Whatever its faults of frippery and affectation he could not deny that of all capitals that of France offered the greatest number of objects of curiosity accessible in the easiest manner. The quarter around the royal palaces was superb, but only the Rue de l'Empereur (now promoted Rue de la Paix) had two gutters. In all other streets there was a single drain running down the middle, and even in the Rue de la Paix you took your life in your hands. There were no pavements in Paris, and many strangers might be run down at any moment by a member of the English Four-in-hand Club, a German nobleman, or a Russian drosky-driver with a beard down to his girdle. The houses of the old aristocracy stood back in their own courtyards, and the streets surrounding them were often narrow, dark, perilous and odorous. In one respect, however, Paris completely beat London. As the inhabitants burnt only wood and charcoal, in stoves, the air was of a crystalline clarity. The Seine was small compared to the Thames, but a great many of the sights of Paris were free. The *Jardin des Plantes* had a zoo as well as fine botanical specimens. The Central Museum of the Arts (Palace of the Louvre) had splendid exhibits, not all looted and due for return to other capitals. He could not sufficiently praise the Apollo Belvedere. He asked a Highland sergeant whom he found earnestly regarding the Venus de Medicis, "How do you like her, countryman?" "God bless us! Is your honour from Inverness?" The kilted troops were very popular in Paris, as they had been in Brussels, where the Black Watch and Gordons had lain in garrison all the preceding winter. They had become so domesticated in Flemish households that it was nothing unusual to find a Highland soldier minding the children or behind the counter in his host's shop. Paul heard one *Parisienne* explaining to another, *"Aussi, j'ai vu les sauvages Americains."* The visitors from Tweedside met two artists from England —Sir William Beechey and Mr Hoppner. The variety of countenances and uniforms to be seen was bewildering. Scott went to a review of Russians only, and it took two hours to pass, but he could not honestly claim to have seen it all, for towards the end the dust rose in clouds. As usual at Paris shows there were far more performers than spectators and very few natives, and those of the lowest sort. The men looked down, sulkily, and as for the women, you had only to ask them a question for them to burst out a-crying. The people of France had been very badly treated by their monarchs, and called the one they had got now, "Louis l'Inevitable". Buonaparte had brought them terrible casualties, but there had been glory.

The Russian infantry were firm, steady-looking men, in green uniforms, rather stocky. Their principal light cavalry were not much seen in Paris. Their Hetman, Count Platoff, resided there but only occasionally summoned his children of the desert. They were very handsome, with high features, and wore long blue coats, sheepskin cloaks, and arms and accoutrements often richly decorated with silver. Paul saw one who had come with his tribe from near the Great Wall of China. His only complaint—for he was in hospital—was sore feet.

There was an alarm of a project to upset the Government one night, and Paul, walking home to his hotel, was challenged six times, and in a new language at every post. The word ENGLISH was a sufficient answer. The Austrian Emperor's troops and particularly his Hungarian guards were the most disliked of the allies, though, in their white and green uniforms, they were much the most impressive. The Prussians were the most destructive, their rank and file the biggest eaters, and their officers bullies, and the principal customers of the most expensive restaurants.

Paul told his Laird of husbandry upon Flemish and French farms, and the lack of arrangements in plantations. There were hardly any fine châteaux to be seen in the country between Mons and Paris—only ruins. He told his cousin Peter about the leading political figures. People at home, he believed, had been surprised at the Duke of Wellington and Lord Castlereagh acquiescing in the appointment of Fouché as Minister of Police under the reinstated monarchy. This man had voted for the death of Louis XVI, been an agent of Robespierre, and ruled the police of Buonaparte. But he seemed to have come back to stay. The same could not be said of Talleyrand.

Paul's letter to a Scottish Minister of the Gospel was his shortest. There really was not much to be said about religion in France at present. The churches were almost empty except of elderly men and women. In Flanders, services had been well attended, but in both countries the clergy were uninspiring and their vestments antiquated and tawdry. It seemed curious that in a country which had so recently, under the Revolution, abolished Sunday and Christian marriage, more vice than crime seemed to be the result. Murders and robberies with violence, which were the mainstay of the English sensational press, were little known in Paris. There were few street quarrels, and drunkenness was rarely seen. The French crowds that milled through the rich apartments of the palace of Versailles appeared to Paul to behave much better than an English mob. Naturally, he had to mention the Palais Royal "in whose saloons and Porticos Vice has established a public and open school for gambling and licentiousness". The *Salon des Etrangers*, the most celebrated room, an immense hall, was decent and silent to a degree of solemnity. The profits made must be very large, for refreshments were distributed to the players gratis till three in the morning. "This is Vice with her fairest Vizar; but the same unhallowed precincts contain many a secret cell for the most hideous and unheard-of debaucheries . . . the whole mixed with a Vanity Fair of shops for jewels, trinkets and baubles, that bashfulness may not lack a decent pretext for adventuring into the haunts of infamy." As to the future of France, Paul could only remember with hope, "the present Royal Family have been bred in the school of adversity". He had not availed himself of an opportunity to be presented to the restored monarch. He had seen Louis XVIII tottering into his coach, with a hand-kerchief to his eyes, after an affecting interview with Madame de Labé-doyère, now widow of the first Buonapartist martyr—or traitor. Paul believed he had heard the sound of the fatal firing-squad from the Champ de Mars; he wondered if Ney should be the next victim, or Masséna. He had been to all the best restaurants—Vérys, Tortonis, Beauvilliers, and to the Opéra, the Comédie, the Variétés, and Théâtre Français, and seen Talma, Vestris, and Mlles Georges, and Mars, and High Mass at Nôtre Dame, and the Panthéon and the Palaces of the Luxembourg, and St Cloud, and poor Josephine's Malmaison, and the poor Duc d'Enghien's Vincennes, and the site of Marie Antoinette's cell in the awful Temple prison (demolished 1805). He had been in company with Canova, the great sculptor, and with the most villainous-looking fellow he had ever in his life set eyes upon—David, Buonaparte's first painter.

It was August 12th and he had written to Bowhill, "I imagine your Grace to be about this time tolerably well fagged with a hard day on the moors." By the time he had composed enough letters from Paul to fill his intended volume, it was September 6th, and in his last pages a kindly author did not forget to mention obliquely other publications on the same subject, particularly those of two young advocates, Archibald Allison and Patrick Fraser Tytler, and Mr S(impson) of Edinburgh.

Of course Walter Scott had enjoyed a good deal of private hospitality that Paul could not mention. Afterwards, John Ballantyne was surprised to hear that Scott had ever felt awed. It had been when he stood before the greatest soldier and statesman in the world. John had asked whether the duke had not realised he was in the presence of a great poet and novelist; but Scott had no opinion at all of a man of letters as compared to a man of action. "What would the Duke of Wellington think of *a few bits of novels*?" The duke had sent for him to sit next to him, at a supper in his own palace (the Hôtel de la Reynière, once the property of Marshal Junot). The Order of the Bath was being bestowed on Blücher and other foreign potentates that evening. Scott had asked the Saviour of Europe if he had ever seen Buonaparte, and the duke had replied, "No, but at one time, from the repeated shouts of 'Vive l'Empereur', I thought he must be near."

He had asked him plenty of questions, about his campaigns, and got very direct replies. He wrote home to Charlotte, "He is the most down-right person you ever knew." The first of Paul had gone off together with a last letter to Castle Street. He supposed they must travel with all the diplomatic secrets of Europe for they had gone in Lord Castlereagh's bag. All the young Englishmen in Paris piqued themselves on imitating the duke in nonchalance and coolness of manner, wandering about the streets with their hands in the pockets of their long waistcoats, staring and whistling as if they owned the place, or tearing about on Cossack ponies. Lord Cathcart had presented Mr Walter Scott to the Czar who had asked him in French in what engagement he had been wounded. This was rather awkward but Scott had passed it off by explaining that his lameness was a natural infirmity, and when pressed as to the actions in which he had taken part had called to mind two very slight ones, "the Battle of the Cross Causeway and the affair of Moredun Mill". He was also introduced to "Old Platoff" and the next day the Cossack leader, careering along the Rue de la Paix, sprang from his steed and kissed him on both cheeks. Lady Castlereagh had asked him to all her parties, great and small, and had taken him with her *suite* to see the waterworks at Versailles specially turned on for the English. Seated in the British Embassy with Lord Castlereagh, his host had told him a very strange story. Lord Castlereagh had seen, in a desolate Irish country house, the famous apparition of the Radiant Boy. The scene in which the ambassador, a man apparently of much sense and steadiness of nerve, had recounted his tale of horror could hardly have been less appropriate. The British Embassy had been the palace of Princess Pauline Borghese, Buonaparte's favourite sister, and was decorated and furnished in the height of fashionable luxury.

Scott had escorted an old acquaintance, Lady Alvanley, the amiable widow of a Lord Chief Justice, with poetical tastes, to many entertainments, together with her daughters. Towards the end of his stay two much closer friends had arrived—Miss Dumergue and Miss Sarah Nicolson. He had been assiduous in waiting on them although they were in quite another part of the town—in the Rue des petits Garreaux, very cheap but excellent . . . He gave a farewell dinner to "our Piccadilly friends" and the two young Slades, at Doyen's, "and I can assure you I have bespoken one of the handsomest dinners he can give us, as I know it will give them pleasure to be treated smartly". He had been shocked to notice, quite unmistakably, that at least one returned French aristo family, to whom the royal dentist's sister and housekeeper had been truly charitable in the days of their London exile, had not called on them in Paris.

There was only one prominent character whom he had failed to meet. Marshal Macdonald, Duke of Tarentum, was with the army of the Loire, trying to reorganise it for the service of Louis XVIII. Marshal Macdonald's father had been Niel MacEachainn (Niel son of Hector) Macdonald, and had sailed for Skye with Miss Flora Macdonald and Prince Charles Edward and followed the prince to France, "after our affair (I love the delicate expression) of 1745".

Upon reflection, the author of *Waverley* decided that Mrs Arbuthnot, the Duke of Wellington's great friend, was more beautiful than any *Parisienne*.

VII

Pringle and Bruce went on to Switzerland on September 7th, Scott and Gala to Dieppe, two days later. In the Palais Royal on September 8th Scott met Gala also buying souvenirs. Lady Alvanley was going to smuggle a lace shawl for Charlotte. Scott bought silk shawls for his mother and Miss Millar and "necklaces and other little trinkets for the party at Abb". At a tobacconist's in the Passage Vivienne, he found just the gift for Tom Purdie, a snuff-box representing the cross-cut of a small tree, in which the veins and knots were carefully imitated. He had ventured into the Salle des Etrangers and staked three Napoleons and got back six or seven. He never would forget his hours in the libraries of Paris—the Royal Library, now the National, and particularly that of Ste Geneviève, from which the venerable M. Chevalier, librarian and astronomer, had called repeatedly to take him and Gala round places and collections of interest, including those of Baron Denon (Egyptian and Phoenician antiquities). He had bought some rare books from M. Debure, royal bookseller, in the Rue Serpente.

Their homeward journey was full of incident. They walked on the famous terrace at St Germain, home of the exiled Stuarts. At Louviers, the inn was a fearsome-looking place, just the setting for a murder, and in the middle of the night they were woken by people trying to break down their door. Forgetting where he was, Scott called out in English that he would shoot the first man who attempted to enter. The noise ceased. The trouble-makers turned out to be English travellers who had mistaken their room. The landlady cheated them, charging them for delicacies they had never ordered, but they had to pay up. At Rouen there was a service going on in the cathedral, but they managed to see the tombs of Richard I and

John, Duke of Bedford, the Palais de Justice and a statue of Joan of Arc. Their passage from Dieppe was tedious. They were at sea from Sunday evening till Tuesday morning, "with nothing to eat the whole time but a few oysters and a crust of bread". They "slept rough" as the sailors say, without taking off their clothes. They landed at Brighton, and at once things began to look up. On the beach, Sir Edward Antrobus, a partner of Coutts, asked them to dine. Next morning before they set off, rather late, for London, Scott packed "my firearms", his pistols, having arrived in a country where they would not be needed. He had never used them in France but had often been glad they were in his pocket. He booked a room at Long's Hotel in Bond Street, and hearing that he was going round to Piccadilly Terrace to try to collect Lord Byron to dine, Gala decided not to press on north alone. At the little party which followed, Scott thought Byron was at his best, "playful as a kitten" Gala found him bitter and somewhat contradictory, but was much impressed by Byron's beautiful pale face—"like a spirit's—good or evil. How I did stare". Byron's dress was plain, but very *recherché*. Two popular actors, dear Daniel Terry, and old Charles Mathews, who claimed to have been dandled by Garrick, made up their party, and next morning Mathews, who had an engagement in Leamington, embarked with Scott and Gala on the coach which left London at 6 p.m.

A programme of sightseeing much after Scott's heart, followed. They saw Warwick and Kenilworth castles, Haddon Hall, the famous caves in the Peak District, Speedwell lead mine, Ripon Minster, Middleham, Barnard and Brough castles and Fountains Abbey. Mrs Morritt was too ill for guests, so they pressed on to Carlisle. ("I was married here, and never spent happier days than when I used to take excursions in the neighbourhood.")

They arrived at Abbotsford on the night of September 24th and Gala was easily persuaded to stay a few days. One more guest could not make much difference as they already had Mr Skene of Rubislaw and Mr James Ballantyne with a budget of bills, booksellers' letters and proofs, burning to hear about Waterloo. There was a comic incident connected with the homecoming. During Scott's absence, Charlotte and the girls had prepared a beautiful surprise for him. The little parlour of the cottage had been fitted up with fresh and fashionable chintz covers and curtains. He failed to notice anything, until Charlotte could bear it no longer and burst forth in indignation. After that, during the evening, he kept on recurring unctuously to the beauty of his surroundings. Next morning, the strangely-named Daisy, "a gallant grey", the last of "my chargers", was brought round and would have none of his old master. "When I put my foot in the stirrup he reared bolt upright and I fell to the ground rather awkwardly." After this had happened once or twice, it struck Scott that Daisy might not know him in strange clothes, so one of the old white hats and green jackets which always descended to Tom Purdie was sent for, but the result was the same. John Ballantyne fell heir to Daisy and drove him about Edinburgh in a gig in high spirits. Scott decided to stick to a good sober cob.[11]

VIII

A wonderfully happy autumn stretched before him. As far as could be seen his financial anxieties were at an end. Every favourite spot and soul must be greeted. He wrote to Morritt on October 2nd:

> The contrast of this quiet bird's nest of a place with the late scene of confusion and military splendour which I have witnessed, is something of a stunning nature—and for the first five or six days I have been content to fold my hands and saunter up and down in a sort of indolent and stupefied tranquillity, my only attempt at occupation having gone no further than pruning a young tree now and then. Yesterday, however, and today, I began from necessity to prune verses, and have been correcting proofs of my little attempt at a poem on Waterloo.

The profits of the first edition of this were to be given towards the fund for the relief of the widows and orphans of those slain in the battle, so it behoved him to hurry. He explained in an introductory note:

> It may be some apology for the imperfections of this poem, that it was composed hastily, and during a short tour upon the Continent, when the Author's labours were liable to frequent interruption; but its best apology is that it was written for the purpose of assisting the Waterloo Subscription.

Its twenty-three regular stanzas opened rather charmingly:

> Fair Brussels, thou art far behind,
> Though lingering on the morning wind,
>   We yet may hear the hour
> Peal'd over orchard and canal,
> With voice prolong'd and measured fall,
>   From proud St Michael's tower . . .

It was published about October 21st, and went into a third edition before the year was out. Critics were not enthusiastic and, next year, Byron had visited Brussels, and famous lines in the third canto of *Childe Harold*, wiped Scott's topical effort from the public mind. He had not, however, quite done with poetry. There was an offshoot of *The Field of Waterloo*, "an odd wild sort of thing" which he called *The Dance of Death*, and there was *Harold the Dauntless* (the son of a Viking, converted to Christianity by St Cuthbert), already conceived before his lighthouse yacht cruise.

In November, Charlotte, accompanied by Sophia, went into town for the musical festival. Scott was spared, and wrote cheerfully to tell her the great news that he had succeeded in adding a long-coveted farm to their property. He signed himself in a letter to Joanna Baillie "Abbotsford and Kaeside". His purchase more than doubled his domains and he had got it cheap. It included Turn-Again hill, and ran to within a quarter of a mile of Cauldshiels Loch, reputed haunt of the water-bull where young Walter as a little boy had almost lost his toy boat.

Young Walter was now as tall as his father, and "a bold horseman and a fine shot . . . I assure you, I was prouder of the first black-cock he killed than I have been of anything whatever since I first killed one myself, and that is twenty years ago." On December 4th, the heir of Abbotsford and Kaeside was indeed a sight to make a parent's heart glad. A football match had been got up under the auspices of the Duke of Buccleuch, between the men of the Dale of Yarrow and the Burghers of Selkirk. The proceedings opened with little Lady Anne Scott delivering to Walter Scott, junior, "the ancient banner of the Buccleuch family, a curious and venerable relique emblazoned with armorial bearings".[12] The remarkably handsome dark boy, finely mounted, "dressed in forest green and buff" with an eagle's feather in his bonnet and a large gold chain with a medal round his neck, rode about the field of Carterhaugh displaying the standard, while the pipes played. There were about two thousand spectators. The Selkirk party, headed by the Earl of Home, the duke's brother-in-law, to whom the Ettrick Shepherd acted as aide-de-camp, wore slips of fir as their mark of distinction and the Yarrow men, sprigs of heather. The Scotts had a song composed for the occasion by the author of *Marmion* and the Homes one by the Ettrick Shepherd. The *Edinburgh Journal's* tactful account represented the result of the contest of three hours terminated only by darkness as a draw, followed by a challenge to a further meeting. But when Mr Washington Irving from New York visited Abbotsford two years later his host told him that "the old feuds and local interests and revelries and animosities of the Scotch still slept in their ashes, and might easily be roused; it was not always safe to have even the game of football between villages; the old clannish spirit was too apt to break out". Nobody had been allowed to sell ale or spirits on the field; refreshments had been distributed from a booth by staff from Bowhill. Nevertheless, after darkness had fallen there were fisticuffs and duckings in the river. "The fascination of Gow's violin and band" detained the duke's guests in the dancing-room of his shooting-seat till dawn of the winter morning. At the banquet which preceded the ball Hogg tried to seat himself at the table reserved for the children and when Scott led him away—to an honourable place between himself and Scott of Harden—complained, "I am convinced he was sore afraid of my getting to be too great a favourite with the young ladies of Buccleuch." He had been particularly absurd some months before when being as usual in financial straits he had tried to collect works from brother poets to appear in a collection to be edited by himself for his own benefit, *The Poetic Mirror*. Naturally all the brother bards—including Scott and Byron—had either declined the proposition or failed to reply. Lockhart was not sure whether it was on this or some other occasion that the shepherd sent a letter to Scott opening, "Damned Sir" and ending "Believe me, Sir, yours with disgust". By February he had repented. Scott, hearing that he was dangerously ill, had sent John Grieve from Cacra-up-Ettrick, a benevolent and cultivated man, to enquire as to his situation and managed to secure the best medical attendance without the knowledge of the touchy sufferer. On his recovery Hogg decided to end a quarrel he had himself begun. "Mr Scott, I think it is great nonsense for two men who are friends at heart," etc. etc.

NOTES

1. Lockhart, II, 331.
2. The Orkney mainland was named Pomona in the belief that it was the island of the apple-trees guarded by the Hesperides. The mistake was due to a mis-reading of C. Julius Solinus, author of a geographical compendium largely based on the Natural History of Pliny, dated about A.D. 238.
3. There are four principal sources for Scott's Vacation, 1814. Lockhart, II, 337–447 prints in Chapters XXVIII–XXXII the Diary kept by Scott; Scott wrote to his wife, Letters, XII, 117–34; and to Morritt, Constable, Miss Clephane, Ballantyne, Letters, III, 470–90. See also: in *Poetical Works*, Appendix and Notes to *The Lord of the Isles*; and Introduction and Notes to *The Pirate*.

4. Lockhart, II, 519–23.

5. Letters, IV, 42 et seq.

6. A somewhat unrewarding anonymous article in *Blackwood's Magazine*, Vol. 184, p. 620 et seq., is entitled "Some letters of Sir Walter Scott from Lord Northampton's MSS".

7. Lockhart, II, 514–18. *A publisher and his friends, Memoir and correspondence of the late John Murray*, 2 vols, Samuel Smiles, 1891. I, 266–7, hereafter cited as Smiles.

8. Eliza O'Neill (1791–1872), daughter of an actor-manager at the Drogheda theatre, was hailed on her first appearance at Covent Garden, where Mathews had secured an engagement for her, as "a younger and better Mrs Siddons". She retired in 1819 to marry Mr (afterwards Sir William) Becher, Bart., an Irish M.P., and had numerous issue.

9. *The Edinburgh Evening Courant* and *The Caledonian Mercury* published on June 24th the news of the victory curiously described as "in the neighbourhood of Charleroi", and *The Edinburgh Advertiser* on June 27th Wellington's Despatch received at Downing St, June 22nd. Smiles, I, 269.

10. There are six main sources for Scott's Waterloo trip—his letters to his wife, Letters, XII, 134–54, and to other correspondents, IV, 78–96; his publication, *Paul's Letters to his Kinsfolk*, which is excellent reading, provided that the student bears in mind that Scott was writing too close to the event to be perfectly accurate. Scott of Gala's *Journal of a Tour to Waterloo, and Paris, etc. in 1815*, a charming little volume, was published after his death in 1842. His dates do not always agree with Scott's. Robert Bruce's Journal is in the National Library of Scotland in manuscript. See also *Personal Memoirs etc.*, Pryse Lockhart Gordon, Vol. II, Chapters IX–XI; and for other visitors to the scene, *Waterloo Days* by an Englishwoman, 3rd Edit., 1888. Miss Charlotte Anne Waldie, afterwards Mrs Eaton, visited the battlefield on Saturday, July 15th. Lockhart, III, Chapter XXV, adds little.

11. Lockhart, III, 26, 29.

12. A banner similar to that carried by the young Walter Scott at the Carterhaugh football match, showing the Buccleuch armorial bearings, and the war-cry "Bellenden", is still flown from the tower when the duke is in residence at Drumlanrig.

XIII

"Conundrum Castle"
1816–1819

———————

I

1815 HAD BEEN CROWDED WITH EVENTS OF THE FIRST IMPORTANCE.
1816 was comparatively quiet. *Paul* came out in January and was well
received as indeed it should have been, as a capital piece of journalism;
later, most unjustly, it came to be regarded as hack-work. He worked
hard on his third novel. *The Antiquary*, his favourite, appeared in May
and was a wonderful success.

Early in that month Major John Scott died, rather suddenly at last.
Scott summoned from Abbotsford over icy roads, in darkness, arrived at
George Street too late. This brother had never been a great friend. Since
his retirement he had lived a narrow life, lodging with their aged mother,
his chief occupation being games of whist with brother officers at
Fortune's tavern. He left six thousand pounds to be divided between
Walter and Tom out in Canada, hardly anything else of any value except
a gold watch, a gift from his deceased sister Anne. That he had directed
should go to Walter's eldest son. Walter wrote to Tom that Gilnockie
should receive it on the condition that Tom's little Walter should accept a
duplicate. There were fears for the old mother, all alone now. But she
bore the shock with great firmness. (The major had been remarkably
fretful towards the end.)

It was a dreadful spring in Scotland. Looking out from Castle Street on May 16th Scott could still see the Pentlands and Arthur's Seat white as a wedding cake. Some characteristic occupations continued. He wrote many letters, some recommending lame dogs on whom he had never set eyes; others for old friends. There was a Dublin clergyman, the Rev. Charles Robert Maturin, who had written a high-flown tragedy.[1] Lord Byron, who was on the committee for production at Drury Lane, got it accepted by Kean, but was not able to find a post for the brother of the late Mungo Park, ruined by one of the bank failures prevalent at this date. Scott persevered and got the man an appointment in the Customs. William Scott of Maxpoffle wanted the Collectorship of Taxes for Roxburghshire. His unlikeable father had always been incredibly mean. Adam Ferguson, quartered in Ireland, was likely to retire on half-pay. It was delightful to be able to ask such a good companion to set up house with his spinster sisters at a nominal rent on a second addition to the Abbotsford estate—just bought from neighbour John Usher.

Scott helped Terry to concoct a stage version of *Guy Mannering*. The result of their "Terrification" was performed to admiration at Covent Garden. It seemed difficult, in view of his contributions to this, over which he made no secret, that he persisted in denying that he was the author of *Waverley*: but he did, except to Terry. He held that if people were so unfair as to ask him the direct question he was justified in disclaiming his children. Even Lady Abercorn, since Scott solemnly told her he did not think either Henry Mackenzie or young Harry Mackenzie was responsible, fell back on a popular theory that Tom Scott, the brother in Canada, was the genius. Lady Louisa Stuart (now in the secret) did not believe that Mrs Tom had owned four novels as hers, "with some help from her husband and brother-in-law".

Terry had married a talented young woman, a daughter of the landscape painter Alexander Nasmyth. James Ballantyne took the plunge at last—a bride twenty years his junior. Both were to present Scott with godchildren.

By-jobs continued. He wrote the history of 1814 and 1815 for the *Edinburgh Annual Register*. He wrote two reviews for the *Quarterly*, the first on "The Culloden Papers", the second on a novel by a fair unknown. "Could you dash off something on *Emma*?" enquired Murray. Scott did much more, and gladly—sixteen pages, double column.

> The author is already known to the public by the two novels announced in her title-page, and both, the last especially, attracted with justice an attention from the public far superior to what is

granted to the ephemeral productions which supply the regular demand of watering-places and circulating libraries.

He told the stories of the two previous novels, *Sense and Sensibility* and *Pride and Prejudice*. He admitted that Miss Edgeworth laid her scenes in higher life and offered more romantic incident. *Emma*, it must be acknowledged, had even less story than either of her predecessors. But Miss Jane Austen (whose name he did not mention, though it was an open secret) stood almost alone in the new style of novel. Nowhere else had he found sketches of such spirit and originality. He commended the peculiar tact with which she presented characters that the reader could not fail to recognise. Miss Austen's anonymity apparently shrouded a situation so unspectacular that it was hardly to be believed. She was one of the spinster daughters of a deceased clergyman of limited means, domiciled in Hampshire. He admired her knowledge of the world with a tinge of sadness. "We are aware that there are few instances of first attachment being brought to happy conclusion." When he heard of her death, from a decline, he commented sadly, "What a pity such a gifted creature died so young." But although her genius had received little recognition during her short life, the Prince Regent and Walter Scott had always been her devotees.

He had written to ask Lord Byron to be kind to Miss Clephane, now Lady Compton, if he came across her in the high society in which she must now move. His request showed how utterly out of touch he was with sinister London gossip. Lord Byron had shaken the dust of his native land from his feet for ever. Within a month of the birth of their daughter, he had cruelly asked his wife to leave their home. Miss Baillie wanted Scott to plead for a good allowance for the innocent lady. "There is nobody whose good opinion he is more anxious to preserve than your own." But Scott said, "How can I meddle in such matters?"

He had a new source of amusement in making up suitable verses for his chapter headings and labelling them "Old Play" or "Old Ballad". The idea had come quite by accident when John Ballantyne, searching against time to complete a proof with a quotation from a Beaumont and Fletcher drama, had to confess himself beat. Scott had also invented an editor for his next series of novels, "Jedediah Cleishbotham, school-master and parish-clerk at Gandercleugh". The set was to be called *Tales of my Landlord*. James was sent off to offer Blackwood, Murray's agent in Scotland, a work of fiction, un-named and by an anonymous author, a dead secret except, of course, from Mr Murray. "It must be Scott," said

Murray on hearing the extraordinary conditions, "no one else would think of burdening us with such trash as John B's wretched stock." They agreed to all the suggestions of the Great Unknown who would not even let them publish the forthcoming works as "by the author of *Waverley*".

The first offered were *The Black Dwarf* and *Old Mortality*. When Blackwood had read the first hundred and ninety-two pages of *The Black Dwarf* he could not sleep for excitement. As he received later chapters he was disappointed. He intimated that he would like major alterations both in plot and conclusion. "My respects to the Booksellers," replied the Great Unknown, "and I belong to the Deaths-head Hussars of literature, who neither *take* nor *give* criticism." Blackwood gave way. The second novel in the first series was *Old Mortality*, adjudged one of Scott's best. He said he wrote the last half of the last volume in four rainy days. The climate suited the grim noble tale of the old Covenanter and Bonnie Dundee.

He had not forgotten Constable. John was told to offer in this quarter a child's *History of Scotland*. Constable in return was to take over the *Edinburgh Annual Register*. Blackwood heard of this contract with fury. He said he had always thought John no better than a swindler, but he had hitherto put some faith in James. "Constable is the proper person for them. Set a thief to catch a thief."

James had now set up house in style in St John Street with his young wife, and by misadventure, in October, when he was away from home and his brother John, with whom he had left money in cash, was also absent, a bill was presented and dishonoured, apparently a debt of James Ballantyne and Company about which Scott had never known. A storm in a tea-cup was forgiven, but not perhaps entirely forgotten.

John had always been the brother with expensive tastes. He had a charming villa on the Firth of Forth, "Harmony Hall", where he gave banquets with French cookery, and whoever of note happened to be visiting Edinburgh in the musical or theatrical world was sure to be invited. He went racing regularly and even when auctioning his own books sometimes appeared in the uniform of a sporting club. He eventually played off Scott's publishers against one another so successfully that he got Constable "to clear the Augean stable"—remove all the remainder of unsaleable Ballantyne stock in his cellars, two-thirds of which proved a dead loss. Constable paid £5,270 for it. But he got the second series of *Tales of my Landlord* and *Rob Roy*.

Scott's only recorded failure as a host took place in the late summer of 1816. He had always been anxious to repay as far as was in his power the debt he owed to "our Piccadilly friends", the Dumergue family who had behaved with such unbounded generosity to himself and his wife. He had much better have refrained from the effort. Miss Dumergue and Miss Sarah Nicolson arrived at the house in Castle Street in July. The Courts had risen, so everyone who could manage it was hurrying out of Edinburgh. He therefore planned their first ten days for a tour of Loch Katrine and Loch Lomond, returning by the Falls of Clyde. It rained. It was a relief to reach dear Abbotsford. They had three August weeks there and it rained and blew nearly every single day. The poor Piccadilly ladies had a strong taste for gossip, and no company upon which to exercise it. The children and visits to cottages were their chief solace. Scott even took to cards to amuse them. He wrote to Morritt, now a widower:

> You will pity both hosts and guests. I walked them to death, I talked them to death. I showed them landscapes which the driving rain hardly permitted them to see, and told them of feuds about which they cared as little as I do about their next door news in Piccadilly . . . Yesterday they left us, deeply impressed with the conviction, which I can hardly blame, that the sun never shone in Scotland . . . In you I expect a guest of a different calibre; and I think (barring downright rain) I can promise you some sport or other.[3]

The premises of Abbotsford were still rather small, and the animals were increasing in number and size. "Maida" had arrived at Castle Street in March. He was the gift of Alexander Macdonell of Glengarry, of deer-, or Spanish wolfhound origin, the most magnificent creature ever seen for height and strength—six feet long from nose-tip to tail. He sat beside Scott at meals, the picture of dignity, "his head as high as the back of my chair", but was terrified of Mr Hinze of Hinzefeld, the brindled tomcat, when he encountered that deity on the stairs. He whispered, he wailed and shook, but dared not pass. Maida's name came from the plain in Calabria where Alexander Macdonell's brother, Major James, had led the 78th Regiment to victory, under the command of Sir John Stuart, against General Regnier, on July 4th, 1806. Maida was to be the second most important dog in Scott's life and appear in many paintings, and with his master on the Scott Memorial.[4]

II

The triumphant end of the war had left the Allies masters of sea and land, but the inevitable economic distress followed. The National Debt trebled. Farmers who had become accustomed to high prices found themselves suddenly faced by the competition presented by the opening of continental grain ports. Government contracts for a Navy and Army which had ceased to expand, fell steeply. As the church bells of Perth rang out to greet the peace, George Williamson, a great Aberdeenshire breeder and dealer, passing south with a big drove, heard them with dismay. "It was a sorrowful peace for me, for it cost me four thousand pounds."[5]

Scott was glad that he would be able to provide labour on his estate. Mr Edward Blore, "a very fine young man, modest, simple and unaffected in his manners as well as a most capital artist", appeared at Abbotsford in November and was a sympathetic listener.[6] Scott envisaged a dining-parlour overlooking the Tweed through a lofty bay window. The window on the opposite wall was to be Gothic and filled with stained glass. Terry's artist wife could provide the armorial shields for the boudoir, which would also contain a superb cabinet pedestal for a bust of Shakespeare, the gift of Mr George Bullock, antiquarian furniture dealer and interior decorator who had accompanied Blore. This ingenious fellow had by November fashioned several casts of grotesques from Melrose Abbey which would make perfect cornices. The old Tolbooth in Edinburgh had recently shared the fate of the sinister Temple prison in Paris, and Scott had been promised several niches and carved stones from this source.

The Black Dwarf and *Old Mortality* were published on December 1st. In spite of the silence on the title page and the change of publisher, they were greeted in London with immediate enthusiasm. Murray wrote archly:

> Dear Sir,
>   Although I dare not address you as the author of certain "Tales" (which must however be written by Walter Scott or the Devil) yet nothing can restrain me from thinking it is to your influence with the author that I am indebted for the honour of being one of their publishers!

He had to report "the most complete success. Lord Holland said, when I asked his opinion—'Opinion! we did not one of us go to bed last night—nothing slept but my gout.' Frere, Hallam, Boswell, Lord Glenbervie, William Lamb, all agree that it surpasses all the other novels."

Scott reviewed the books for the *Quarterly*—incorporating some passages provided by Will Erskine. He told Murray that he now had about

seven hundred acres, thanks to the booksellers and the discerning public.
Although the winter had set in early, he made a pilgrimage of two miles
through the snow to fetch a new addition to his menagerie—a greyhound
pup, a present from Terry, who had christened him "Marmion". The
author, however, changed the name of the most beautiful prince of darkness to "Hamlet". He looked forward to a Christmas dinner at Bowhill.
The duke had been at Bath for his cough but would be home again, and
Scott believed the Chief Baron, Robert Dundas of Arniston, would also
be under that hospitable roof. He was in good fettle but had asked the
duke now to add to many past kindnesses by furthering his request to be
considered for a Barony of the Exchequer when the next vacancy occurred.
It would mean retiring as Clerk of Session and Sheriff of Selkirkshire,
and there would be an addition of only four hundred pounds a year to his
earnings, but there would be a valuable difference in rank and in leisure.
He believed he stood well at Carlton House, and he ought to have the
support of the Scottish members of the Cabinet. He was entirely surprised that the duke, in reply, disclosed that he was by no means as
omnipotent as his old friend believed. He was smarting from "the
rebuff I got about the situation of Lord Registrar—a rebuff which I
forgive but can never forget". What he most dreaded was a virtual refusal
covered up by some verbiage "about a promise to the Lord knows whom
for the reversion of the office". Scott might depend upon his best
endeavours.

III

In January 1817 he sent off copies of *Harold the Dauntless* by Walter
Scott, published by Constable, to all his best cronies. In the last number
of the *Quarterly* he had reviewed Canto III of *Childe Harold*. He told
Murray that if he thought what he had written would give offence either
to Byron or the public, to put the sheets in the fire. They were generous,
discerning and full of praise. Murray printed them, and Byron was
deeply touched. Some of Lady Byron's friends were annoyed.

There was another consideration which Scott had not mentioned when
writing to the duke. As the winter drew on he had been afflicted by
stomach cramps. During the Christmas holidays at Abbotsford he had
persisted in his usual routine of early rising and writing and violent
exercise in very cold weather. He had three astonishingly bad nights
before he got back to Castle Street. He did subconsciously realise that he
had been in mortal pain, but he disregarded it. After a night when he had

actually fainted, he arose and went to Court. It would pass off. It grew worse during the next few weeks, and he wrote for advice to Joanna Baillie's doctor brother. On March 4th, before he could get a reply from London, he was due to dine with the duke at Dalkeith. He honoured his engagement but to Charlotte's relief he did not, as usual, stay the night there. The carriage drove up in the cold darkness and the master of the house disembarked, apparently none the worse. At midnight he terrified her by another violent attack. He spent the day in bed, a thing he had not done for thirty years, but arose and dressed to attend a merry party in his own house. His sister-in-law was returning to Canada the next day and they had asked James Ballantyne, Mrs Henry Siddons, and Hogg. Suddenly, as they sat at table Scott uttered an involuntary yell of agony and staggered from the room. He sent down a message that he hoped they would proceed with the feast. It would do him good to hear Mrs Siddons sing. But the party was a shambles. The enormous Maida put the finishing touch by ominous clamour. The guests slipped away; the doctors came. As James Ballantyne and Hogg walked down the street James said he had often seen their friend look jaded recently. He was now afraid "it was serious". Hogg told him to shut up or he would knock him down. "Ye daur to speak as if Scott was on his death-bed. It cannot be! It *must* not be! I will not suffer you to speak that gaite."[7]

IV

Scott's agonies were diagnosed as being the result of gall-stones.[8] He did not die, but for almost exactly three years, from 1817 to 1820, he was never free from fears of another seizure, and he very nearly did die twice. He was bled and blistered and purged and dieted. He loathed opium and laudanum which relieved his pain, but made him stupid. When unable to write he dictated. The greater part of *Rob Roy*, *The Heart of Midlothian*, *The Bride of Lammermoor*, *A Legend of Montrose* and *Ivanhoe* were produced during this period. James Ballantyne said that while Scott remembered afterwards the main outline of the eerie and tragic story on which *The Bride of Lammermoor* was founded, he discovered, when he came to read his own novel, that he had absolutely forgotten it. He read it as something unknown to him.

His courage was indomitable. Kemble was about to take leave of the stage and Scott had written a farewell address for him to speak in the character of Macbeth. The date was less than a month since his last and most incapacitating seizure. He told Morritt that what he hopefully believed to be his recovery was being slow and tedious. He was almost too weak to move, and giddy when he tried; he could not read for the dazzling in his eyes nor listen for the whizzing sound in his ears, nor even think clearly. But he was there on March 29th, "very totterish", to attend an old friend on an affecting occasion.

When he got back to Abbotsford in a cold April, a move about which Charlotte was naturally anxious, fate sent him a good companion for his daily stint of authorship and much else. Amongst the victims of the prevalent agricultural depression was William Laidlaw. He was invited to come with his wife and young family to occupy a cottage on Scott's property at Kaeside "till some good thing casts up". Laidlaw, like William of Deloraine, "good at need", accepted gladly.

Another architect visited Tweedside, Mr William Atkinson of St John's Wood, famous for his patent cement. He was going to make a new library for the duke at Bowhill. His plan for improving Scott's home included the conservatory for which Charlotte longed. The fountain had to be dismissed, and an aviary. Hinze of Hinzefeld would soon clear that of inmates.

Adam Ferguson and three sisters were definitely coming to settle in the much larger new house at Toftfield which was to be renamed, on their suggestion, Huntly Burn. (Scott believed that the glen was the very one in which Thomas the Rhymer had met the queen of the fairies.) An artist found Abbotsford at midsummer 1817 so full of guests that he despaired of getting Mr Scott to sit. David Wilkie was celebrated for his genre pictures of Scottish life and character. Sir George Beaumont had bought his "Blind Fiddler". Dr Baillie had once saved his life. Adam Ferguson, whose sense of fun was chronic, suggested that the extraordinarily solemn, cadaverous artist should represent Mr Scott in humble life, as a Lowland farmer, surrounded by his family. Originally it was intended that the painting should be performed out of doors, but eventually the figures sat separately in shelter. Scott was the only one who sat literally. Lockhart thought all the likenesses, except that of Ferguson, very poor.[9]

The masons had begun on the new buildings "practising on a piggery". Although he had not been free from pain and had noticed warning spasms in May when Constable had come down, Scott felt well enough to venture on a little peaceful holiday in July. Ferguson, Charlotte and Sophia went with him to Loch Lomond and on to Drumlanrig. He had a severe attack the day before they were due to set off, but stuck to his plans. Anne, whom he nicknamed after Shakespeare's Beatrice, already showed signs of being a critical hostess, and in August Lord Byron's wronged lady was coming. He asked Lord Somerville and Laidlaw to dine to meet her. Laidlaw wrote down that she was a beautiful little fair woman with large blue eyes who seldom smiled. Her mouth indicated obstinacy.

Mr Washington Irving arrived while the family were breakfasting on Saturday, August 30th. He brought an introduction from Tom Campbell, and was most welcome. His father had been born in the Orkneys and his mother in Falmouth, but he was quite a novelty, a successful American author. He had good easy manners, and obliged posterity by writing down everything about his four days' visit to Abbotsford. His comical *History of New York* by Dierdich Knickerbocker had long been a favourite with both Scott and his wife. After breakfast Scott said he had household affairs to attend to, but Charles, aged eleven, could take the guest to see the ruins of Melrose Abbey. On their return Scott joined them for a ramble with the dogs. There were a great many dogs, a huge staghound, a black greyhound, a silky-haired setter, a terrier with glassy eyes, and a flurry of smaller animals. Miss Sophia and Miss Anne Scott were a pretty sight as they came bounding lightly along the hillside like young fawns, their dresses fluttering in the pure summer breeze. Their morning studies completed, they were off to pick flowers. He thought that, of the four children, Miss Scott and little Charles seemed to have most of their father in them. Irving was unwise enough to express himself a little disappointed with the views he was shown. "A mere succession of grey waving hills", and the Tweed, "a naked stream . . . without a tree or thicket on its banks." Scott said that, for his part, when he had been among the rich scenery about Edinburgh for some time, which is like an ornamented garden, he began to wish himself back again amongst his own honest grey hills. He thumped his staff on the ground and said, "If I did not see the heather at least once a year, *I think I should die.*" He was dressed in an old green shooting coat, brown pantaloons and a worn white hat. For dinner he appeared in a black suit, and the daughters of the house had twined heather wreaths in their hair. The Laidlaws and a widowed lady came to dine. After dinner, they adjoined to the drawing-room; Scott read aloud from Malory's *Morte D'Arthur*, and Sophia accompanied Scottish songs on the harp. Scott had not yet got a study of his own, but the new house was high in its scaffolding.[10]

The excellent Miss Millar had now left to embark upon a succession of situations, none of which ever surpassed that of Sir Walter Scott's family in her lofty reminiscences. Sophia wrote to her this month sending all the latest news likely to interest her.

Perhaps you have heard that Lady Hood is married. She married a very pleasant clever man, Mr Stewart of Glaserton, who has a very good fortune; so she has dropped her ladyship, and is now plain Mrs Stewart Mackenzie: she sent us gloves, cake and favours. The new house is coming on very fast; they are building the last storey, and it looks beautiful. We spend most of our time in airing ourselves upon the top, and I think it will be wonderful if it is finished without any of us breaking our necks.[11]

V

At 4 p.m. on the hazy evening of Wednesday, March 4th, 1818, large crowds waiting on Castle Hill, Edinburgh, broke into loud applause on seeing the royal standard run up above the castle. The Regalia of Scotland had been found. The search for this hidden treasure had been proposed by Scott to the Regent as long ago as 1815. The prince was interested and had given orders for a commission to be set up, with the Duke of Buccleuch at its head, to investigate a mystery. The story was romantic. In 1707 amongst the provisions of the Act of Union had been one that the ancient Honours of Scotland should never be removed from their kingdom. Some fifteen or twenty years ago the Crown Room as it was called in Edinburgh Castle had been opened, and it was reported that a chest had been identified but not opened. In spite of the fact that records of 1707 described a pompous ceremony of locking up the Regalia, rumours had long been current that it had been sent south. Scott reminded Morritt that they had together seen at the Jewel Office in London an antique crown said to be that of Scotland. All the investigators had affirmed was that the chest had the dust of a hundred years, "about six inches thick", upon it, and on the floor around, so they had concluded that if it had been violated, it must have been soon after the Union.

The company who assembled on March 4th numbered about a dozen, and included the Lord Chief Commissioner of the Jury Court, the Right Hon. William Adam, the Solicitor-General, the Lord Provost, the Major-General commanding the Forces in Scotland and Walter Scott Esq., one of the Principal Clerks of Session.[12] Nothing could have been more awe-inspiring than the procedure. There were massive doors of oak and iron to be unlocked before they entered a chamber dimly illuminated by a barred window where dust indeed lay thickly. Workmen were summoned to attack a chest for which no keys had been found. "It sounded very hollow when they worked on it with their tools, and I began," wrote Scott to Croker at the Admiralty, "to lean to your faction of Little Faiths. It would be very difficult to describe the intense interest with which we watched the rising of the lid." But it was with satisfaction that he worked up to his climax. "I have the pleasure to assure you that the Regalia of Scotland were this day found in perfect preservation." There they lay, wrapped in folds of old linen—the crown, dating basically perhaps from the days of Bruce, of pale gold, set with uneven stones, the Sword of State, a gift from Pope Julius II to James IV ("the scabbard richly decorated with filagree work of silver, double gilded, representing oak leaves and acorns"), the sceptre of James V, with a large beryl as finial; the silver mace of the Treasurer of Scotland.

Next morning he took Sophia up to see them. Several Commissioners' families were coming. She had been told how these beautiful relics had once in the history of her country been hidden for safety and at great cost by loyal royalists. They had been lodged, according to his privilege, in Dunnottar Castle, the seat of the Earl Marischal, and in 1652 sent out of the fortress in a bag of lint on a woman's back. They had been buried under a pulpit in a kirk, and when Dunnottar had been captured, the defender and his wife had been threatened with torture and even death if they were not produced. The governor had said they had been sent away without his knowledge; his lady had said she had entrusted them to a son of the Earl Marischal who had taken them to France. The couple were not executed but they suffered long imprisonment.

Sophia's feelings had been worked up to such a pitch that when the heavy lid was slowly lifted she nearly fainted. She drew away from the circle. As she was retiring, she heard her father's voice, in a tone something between anger and despair, exclaiming "By God, no!" One of the gentlemen present seemed about to place the crown on the head of one of the young ladies. It was an embarrassing moment. The frivolous gentleman laid down the ancient diadem. Scott whispered, "Pray forgive me," and turning perceived his daughter deadly pale and leaning by the door. As soon as she had recovered a little, he walked with her across the Mound down to Castle Street. "He never spoke all the way home, but every now and then I felt his arm tremble; and from that time I fancied he began to treat me more like a woman than a child. I thought he liked me better too, than he had ever done before."

The finding of the Regalia had aroused interest in Scotland, and since the Crown Room was now likely to be a tourist attraction it was obvious that its custody must be vested in some responsible quarter. Scott was doing all in his power to secure the post of Keeper for Adam Ferguson, whose qualifications seemed ideal. Even a small admission fee to view one of the established Lions of the city should supply a revenue to remunerate responsible guardianship. A salary of three hundred pounds a year was suggested and two rooms in the castle. Three months passed. He wrote to William Dundas, brother of the Chief Baron. He asked the duke to jog the memory of Lord Melville. He went to see Chief Commissioner Adam in George Street. There were difficulties about the appointment. Ferguson was a good nominee but Scott knew that his kinsman and friend, Keith of Ravelston, claimed the privilege as descendant of the Earls Marischal. And then he had heard privately that His Royal Highness had intimated that Walter Scott should be given the post, without emoluments, but with the rank of a baronet. He had written to Lord Melville to say that should His Royal Highness be disposed to give the Keepership to others, he would consider the rank suggested for him an honour.

Adam told him that Keith had withdrawn and Ferguson was accepted and would be knighted. "But yours must be more permanent than knighthood." Scott said that his fortune was now sufficient for him to support the rank of baronet with decency, and it would be "of very great consequence to my son".[13]

VI

He was now in a tantalising position. He reckoned that if he continued turning out Waverley Novels at his present rate he should be making ten thousand pounds a year regularly. His new Abbotsford would be ready for him to move into, at least by Easter, and he would then have ample room for house-guests. But he could not from day to day be sure that he might not be prostrated by increasing agonies. He warded them off with laudanum, but it disagreed with him and made him melancholy.

He had a new secretary, Mr George Huntley Gordon, the gentle deaf son of the retired officer with whom he had ridden over the field of Waterloo. He was, he admitted to John Richardson, coining gold. His attacks had seemed to be establishing a pattern, coming at five- or six-week intervals; but in March 1818 he had two in a fortnight. Sophia was his little housekeeper when he went out to Abbotsford. The weather was too severe for Mrs Scott, he wrote to Southey, "till the sun comes over the hill". She was beginning to suffer from asthma. But they had good company and good news. Scott had been elected a member of "The Club", the famous Literary Club of Johnson, Burke, Goldsmith and

Garrick. He could dine with it at the Thatched House in St James's Street on his next London trip. Adam Ferguson came, and Captain Basil Hall of the Royal Navy, who had visited the Emperor Napoleon at St Helena. Charlotte arrived in April, and on the night of the 28th they were woken by "a violent noise, like drawing heavy boards, along the new part of the house". It was about two in the morning, and Scott did not worry as he concluded that something had fallen down. The workmen were dreadfully careless. But when the same thing occurred the next morning at the same witching hour, he arose, armed himself with the sword of his great-grandsire "Beardie", and made a reconnaissance. He could not find anything out of place. He returned to his timorous partner cursing "Tenterden Street and all its works". This was the site of Bullock of Hanover Square's factory from which doors and windows were said to have been despatched a fortnight since. Will Erskine happened to be breakfasting with Terry when Scott's letter describing his nocturnal experiences arrived, and it gave them rather a turn. Bullock had died suddenly on the night, and as far as they could discover, at the very hour when Scott was roused by his second "mysterious disturbance". Scott wrote it down as no more than an extraordinary coincidence, but said that "Poor George" would be greatly missed at Abbotsford especially by little Charles who had been fascinated by him at work and followed him round. "He had taken an uncommon and most friendly interest in furnishing our little castle, designing doors and windows and getting some of them executed in London under his own inspection . . . Our present new building occupies the space betwixt the old cottage which we still inhabit and the courtyard wall."

He left Abbotsford for the summer session with regret. It was the middle of May, and the leaves were just coming out. But in Edinburgh the saga of Bullock was by no means ended. He had taken the measurements for chimneypieces and grates, and also for beds, dining-room chairs and tables. There were to have been couch beds for dressing-rooms, "the drapery hanging from a hook over it, as in France". Scott thought that if the orders had not been set in hand they could manage for the bedrooms, but for the parlour, armoury, etc., they would have to look to London. Terry replied that Mr William Atkinson was dealing with orders at Hanover Square. Bullock's business was closing. The doors and windows which arrived without explanation at Leith, if they had been intended for the greenhouse (for which Mrs Scott was growing impatient), were all a foot short.[14]

However, by the time he returned in the end of July to what he now called "Conundrum Castle", affairs had begun to look up. They had taken possession of their own bedroom in the new wing and were "snugger than snug". All the upper storey was convenient and perfectly habitable and he had his study at last, "my own room, as charming a den as you ever saw". When it got a fireplace it would be perfection. Luckily at present Scotland was as hot and serene as Italy. The chairs and stools for the armoury must match the marble's *green moiré*, those for the dining room *red*.

A familiar figure for many years, so often dismissed, so often pardoned, had at last departed from his life. But he was most unhappy about poor MacBeith whose family had behaved cruelly to him after his accident, which providentially had happened before Scott left Castle Street. He was demonstrably insane. All that could be done was to get him into the asylum and take care he had better comforts than ordinary. William Dalgleish, his successor as a permanency and in many respects as unusual, was not to come for nearly four years.

After a week at Drumlanrig covering August 12th, 1818, Scott really felt much better. The only shadow was that the duke shot very little and only ambled about on a pony, taking absolutely no fatiguing exercise. This was quite unlike him.

Scott went on to Rokeby and consulted his host there about carriage-horses. In Edinburgh, they asked a hundred and forty pounds a pair, one being usually a brute. He did not care for chestnuts, or greys, or bright bays. Black or brown would be his choice. Both his visits were blessed by superb weather. His little summer cruise ended with two days at Melville Castle, after which guests began to arrive at Abbotsford. He wrote to Lady Abercorn in mid-September, "Since my return, I have been busy with my farming matters and with receiving visitors, mostly travellers who come to see Melrose." She had lost her rather terrible marquess and he sent tactful lines of comfort. "My own life is positively a blank, but a very agreeable one . . . I have given up all country sports to my son who is a very tall and handsome young man. His bent is towards the army and I shall not contradict him because it is the line of life I myself would have chosen but for my lameness."

Not all his visitors came principally to see Melrose Abbey. John Gibson Lockhart had now finished with Balliol College and would have liked to have gone as a chaplain to the Peninsula. His father had persuaded him that the war would be over before he could take Orders; he had much better aim at the law. On a hot night of this summer he had happened to dine with a friend, William Menzies, whose family house

Cornet Scott of the 18th Hussars
By William Allan. Original at Abbotsford.
By permission of Mrs Maxwell-Scott.

was in George Street at right angles to Castle Street. A young party, mostly intending advocates, continued enjoying themselves after they had left the dining-room for the library, which looked out on the backs of the houses in Castle Street, over their little strips of gardens. Presently, Menzies had to ask Lockhart to change places with him. There was a confounded *hand* working in a Castle Street window which never stopped. Night after night, it completed page after page and threw it on a pile. When candles were brought in, and curtains were drawn, it was worse, for it was silhouetted on the blind, like the writing at Belshazzar's feast. One of the party suggested, "Some stupid endorsing dogged clerk, probably." But Menzies knew better. "No, boys! It is Walter Scott."[15]

VII

The autumn guests included one more from America, Edward Everett, Professor of Greek at Harvard, Mrs Hamilton, an amusing sister of the dismal Duchess of Wellington, and her husband, "travelling esquires and bankers, and I don't know whom beside". On October 8th came Mr John Gibson Lockhart, very shy, dangerously handsome, kindly invited with his friend Mr John Wilson, so that two bright beginners should meet Lord Melville. Nobody would have guessed that the very day before, their host had recognised familiar symptoms generally preceding an attack. "We found him walking in his plantations, at no great distance from the house, with five or six young people, and his friends Lord Melville and Captain Ferguson." After introducing the new arrivals Scott fell back a little with them, to give them a word of warning. He said that he trusted they had had enough pranks with the editor of the newly established *Blackwood's Magazine*, and if so, Lord Melville would have too much sense to remember them. They were decidedly notorious in their journalistic capacity as "The Scorpion" and "The Leopard". They had sent a challenge to an anonymous critic, who, however, had failed to take it up. They sat down to dinner at least fourteen, and the meal which was excellent opened with *Potage à la Meg Merrilees*, from a recipe invented by the Duke of Buccleuch's famous cook, Monsieur Florence, when he had heard that Mr Walter Scott was coming to Bowhill. A stalwart piper stalked up and down outside. John o'Skye, in his professional capacity, was a capital hedger and ditcher. After dinner younger members of the party ascended the western turret to enjoy a moonlight view of the valleys of the Tweed and Gala. Lockhart thought nothing could be more romantic.

H

The evening ended with their dancing reels to the sound of the pipes in the new dining-hall.[16]

Brief though his visit was Lockhart noticed that Mrs Scott for all her overflowing good nature was a sharp observer. She gave their marching orders to two "rich specimens" rigged out in new jackets and trousers of the Macgregor tartan (though apparently one was a lawyer and the other a Unitarian preacher from New England). At first she and her daughters had shown them Abbotsford, in the absence of the master, with their usual politeness, and said that he would be back for dinner. But Mrs Scott's suspicions had been aroused when one of them had produced a notebook and asked for the date of birth of the owner of the house, and even her own. They turned out to have no letters of introduction from anybody and did not get their dinner. Scott was a little sorry for them.[17]

Lord and Lady Compton came at the same time as John Richardson, Mrs Terry and her father at the very moment when the whole troop of Forest Yeomanry arrived to dine. It was young Walter's birthday party. He was seventeen and very pleased with his uniform as a cornet. "I assure you," wrote Scott to Morritt, "the scene was very gay and even grand, with glittering sabres, waving standards and screaming bagpipers." Lady Compton had changed. She was now the mother of two infants, both boys, and she was jolly, "but otherwise has improved on her travels". He had a long chat with her and she told him that she was very happy and contented, and her father in law, Lord Northampton, was kind to them. It was of course not ideal to have to go abroad to economise, but Florence had been a good choice. Lord Compton sent, with her letter of thanks, one of his accomplished sketches of "Conundrum Castle" from the gardens. Lady Compton ended, "I feel considerable regret that this will probably be amongst my last letters to you addressed to the hands of Walter Scott, a name to which no title can add dignity however much it may increase trouble and care." He had heard from Lord Sidmouth, Home Secretary, that he was not to wait until the next batch of baronets was dubbed; his affair could be separately arranged next time he came to London, which would probably be next spring.

His anxiety about the duke darkened the winter months. He wrote to Lord Montagu repeatedly to report and ask for advice. The duke was behaving so unlike himself. He was markedly changed even from what he had been at Drumlanrig in August. Ought Scott to attempt to press him to seek a warmer clime? Bowhill was kept so overheated. After much resistance he had consented to see Dr Dick, lately of the East India

Company, a military surgeon retired to live in Darnick. The fatal words "disorder of the lungs" were at last breathed. His Grace had much liked Captain Ferguson when he had come to Drumlanrig. This gentleman was the easiest companion in the world, and though his appointment as Keeper of the Regalia had been gazetted, there had as yet been no other announcement, and he lacked employment. After many weeks, a solution was worked out and the duke, attended by Captain Ferguson (who had so recently served in the Peninsula) and by a personal medical attendant, and M. Florence, would try Lisbon, where the Duke of Wellington had offered quarters in a palace given him by the Portuguese.

On Friday, December 12th, Sophia addressed one of her neat letters to Miss Millar.

I wrote this to let you know that we have just heard of the death of Mama's brother, Mr Carpenter; he died upon the 4th of March, after an illness of about a week. You will be glad to hear that he has left the *whole* of his fortune to be equally divided between us four; that is to say we are to get full possession of it after Mrs Carpenter's death, as she is to have the interest of it in her lifetime. He has not even left a farthing to Mama, or any other person. We do not know exactly how much the fortune is, and I believe there is as much or more in India. Papa is talking of going abroad in September, and taking Mama and us four as far as Geneva, there to leave us to join some party, and proceed homeward by Paris, while himself and Walter will proceed to Italy and from thence over to Greece . . . Our uncle dying has made quite a noise in the town: all the old women in the town torment Papa with questions about poor Mr Carpenter's will. Papa wishes he could write the whole story over the door, I hope that you will write to me very soon and let me know how you like your new situation.[18]

Scott wrote proudly to Morritt that the first thought of all his children when they heard the terms of their uncle's will was to give up all to their mother. He had explained to them that it was out of the question, but they might, if they liked, when they came into possession of the property, make an annual allowance to her. "She will not need it but it is pleasant to see them grateful and affectionate." For himself, he was neither richer nor poorer than before, but fortunes of ten thousand pounds would ensure his girls "the choice of marrying suitably or of an honourable independence as single women . . ." He was glad that he would now be able to help his brother Tom's family, and expand his plantings and policies with a clear conscience. But he grieved for Charlotte, who had been looking forward to her brother's return from India. She had absolutely no living relative. An uncle, the Chevalier de la Volère, captain in a Russian regiment, had been missing, believed dead, since the Russian campaign. Scott wrote letters, full of hope, on January 1st, 1819, quite undisturbed, as he sat at his desk, by the sound of the piper singing gaelic songs to his staff in the hall.

VIII

He told Morritt of his coming baronetcy, and also Joanna Baillie. The duke had been to see Dr Baillie before sailing for Portugal. Letters from the duke and from Ferguson arrived at Abbotsford. While they were still in London, waiting to embark, the duke sent an urgent message that one of the Barons of the Exchequer at Edinburgh was going to retire; but Scott could not think of renewing his application. Sir William Rae was a very old friend and also had claims. He wrote cheerfully to suggest that he might perhaps be coming to join the exiles in Portugal and Spain and France, in the spring. A last letter from the duke came while they were windbound at Portsmouth. He wanted Scott to sit for Raeburn, perhaps attended by "my friend Maida", for "a picture to be hung above the chimney piece of the library of the new wing at Bowhill". Scott would rather have sat for Allan, to help him on, but fate was to make the duke's request a command that must be obeyed.

Scott had planned to go to London in April to receive his baronetcy and introduce young Walter to useful company. But "my old enemy" returned in March. He lay "in absolute agony" hating the laudanum which was all they could give him to dull his pain, and presently jaundice was added to his miseries. John Gibson Lockhart was a constant caller. He was courting Miss Scott of Abbotsford and produced a little sketch of her playing the harp, seen with the eye of love.[19] She excelled as a ministering angel, and when her father was stricken in the country and her mother was not present, showed calm managing qualities remarkable at the age of nineteen. Despite his parlous condition the author never gave up hope. American guests still came to be entertained—Professor George Ticknor from Harvard, Joseph Cogswell going to occupy a chair of Geology at the same stately abode.

On April 16th Scott wrote to Ferguson that he had crawled out on his cob, Sibyl Grey, the very picture of Death on the Pale Horse in the Book of Revelation. He sat lantern-jawed and stooping, as if he meant to eat the animal's ears. "London is out of the question." He could hardly go at more than a footpace and needed Purdie to lift him into the saddle. Before this letter reached Lisbon the duke had died of "a consumption, in his forty-seventh year". Scott got the news on May 5th, and though it was not entirely unexpected, he realised with a shock that it closed a chapter in his life. On his last expedition to Yarrow, his horse had turned by habit up Bowhill avenue. The surviving second son who would become the fifth duke was a boy of thirteen left to the care of the formal old, Dowager, his grandmother, and his uncle, Lord Montagu who lived at Ditton on the Thames. The whole family had moved down to England.

He performed all the necessary sad duties—wrote at length and repeatedly to Lord Montagu whose letter telling him of the event had just been outstripped by one from Lord Melville, and overnight by an Edinburgh rumour. He offered his services in anything possible in the local scene, political, or with regard to the rebuilding in progress at Bowhill. He wrote an obituary for the next issue of the *Edinburgh Weekly Journal*.[20]

It would be many years before there were balls at Bowhill or Dalkeith again, and the delicious flurry of getting Mama and the girls, and Gilnockie (and recently even Charles), all off with the Shirra to stay the night with his Chief, kindly provided with instructions to arrive early, before dusk.

Not surprisingly, Scott had a relapse. For over a week, at the end of the month, he was bedridden again and in extreme pain. It may have been that his sense of humour helped him to turn the corner. He had said farewell to his children. At a critical moment, he heard sounds of a dispute in his outer chambers in Castle Street. The knocker had been tied up, and Peter Matheson had strict orders for No Visitors. It turned out that David Erskine, eleventh Earl of Buchan, aged seventy-seven and always renowned for his oddity, had caused the disturbance. He had pushed aside Peter, and when Sophia appeared, patted her head as if she were a child. He had even laid a hand on the knob of the sick-chamber. But Sophia was no longer a child, and Peter, commanded to see his lordship out, employed such a shove that he nearly sent the old totterer flying. Scott, who had James Ballantyne with him, sent him off in haste to enquire if there had been any particular reason for the call. There had indeed. The earl had come to embrace Walter Scott for the last time and set his mind at rest over arrangements for his funeral in Dryburgh Abbey at which his lordship was going to recite an *éloge* over the grave after the fashion of French

Academicians at Père Lachaise. He angrily showed the publisher the plan he had drawn up for the procession.[21]

IX

As 1819 progressed Scott wrote, "This is a woeful year to me." Lord Somerville, another regular companion for happy country days, died at Vevey and Will Erskine's wife on a tour of the Lakes. Will seemed to be able to rally, but this loss was to have dreadful repercussions. In July, young Walter set off alone for Cork and his regiment, via London, "a *tall* copy, not quite as well lettered, as the collectors of books would say, as the old original edition". Cornet Scott's looks proclaimed that his mother had come from Lyons. Scott did all that a father could, perhaps more than he should, for a very handsome young man leaving home for the first time. He gave him letters of introduction in London to the Dumergues, Lord Sidmouth, John Murray, John Richardson and John Ballantyne, and in Ireland to Miss Edgeworth and Hartstonge. Ballantyne had taken trouble over getting "his rattletraps" which had been abominably expensive. Gilnockie failed to make contact with Richardson, who was an astute man, and the proud father had to send an apology. "He had a world of trinkums to get, for you know there goes as much to the man-millinery of a young officer of hussars as to that of an heiress on her bridal day." His plume swept the rafters, his sabre trailed on the floor. "His complete equipage, horses not included, cost about three hundred and sixty pounds and if you add a couple of blood-horses, it will be two hundred more." This was without the price of his commission, another seven hundred and fifty pounds. Scott got an introduction to his son's colonel from Lady Shelley, whom he had met in Paris—much admired by the Duke of Wellington. She was a beautiful little blonde; her husband was a regular Newmarket type. Lieutenant-Colonel the Honourable George Murray, a brother of Lord Mansfield, sounded a sensible officer. He thought that with an allowance of two hundred and fifty pounds in addition to his pay, and a good servant, the young man should find himself comfortable. Sophia wrote to Miss Millar that the 18th Light Dragoons (now Hussars) was amongst the most dashing regiments in the service. One of its attractions, apparently, was that it was not likely to be ordered to India. "He is too happy and the only thing that is to be feared is his dying of pride and conceit before he joins."

Scott's letters to his soldier son, as well as containing much advice, gave a running commentary on doings at Abbotsford, from the moment the boy had left, when "Anne had hysterics which lasted some time." St Boswell's Fair, a most popular annual event, had been miserably wet. Mama was quite well and so was Papa, though he still took the calomel prescribed by Dr Dick, late of the East India service.[22] He reminded his son to be attentive to his colonel and the colonel's lady. He repeated warnings against buying a gig, forming sudden intimacies with brother officers, and drinking too much. "I believe the poor Duke of Buccleuch laid the foundation of that disease which occasioned his decease in the excesses of Villar's regiment."

In September came a visitor of royal blood. Prince Leopold of Saxe-Coburg, the widower of Princess Charlotte, had wanted to see Mr Scott in his own home. He proved a most appreciative guest, with modest un-affected manners and a touching expression of melancholy. He admired the armour. Mama had managed to serve up at shortest notice fresh salmon, black-cock, partridges, cold lamb, plums and pears, and Papa had added some fine old hock. As the year faded, Abbotsford was described as "jogging on here in the old fashion". On October 14th "Mama and the girls went to the Melrose hop."[23]

The family moved up to Edinburgh, where, if they had accepted all the invitations they got, the young ladies might have revelled in two or three places a night. Anne had grown very handsome, wrote Sophia, and was much admired. Mr Pole said that if she would but practise she would be one of the best players of the harp in town. Anne, like Sophia, had admirers now.

But 1819 was to be an outstandingly unlucky year to the very end. Scott had made his plans for London around Christmas. On Sunday, December 12th, the girls drank tea with their grandmother who was in unusually good spirits, recalling old stories with all her usual alertness and vivacity. Next day she was paralysed on one side and had lost the power of speech. On Wednesday morning, 14th, as her half-brother Dr Daniel Rutherford waited for his carriage to come round for him to visit the invalid, he dropped dead. His sister Miss Chrittie, Scott's favourite aunt, never heard of the family tragedies as she herself died suddenly on the following Saturday. Scott thought that Dr Rutherford had never recovered from the shock of losing a beloved eldest son on a passage to India. He suspected that the doctor had already had a slight stroke. Miss Chrittie had been unwell for a long while but had enjoyed a summer stay at Abbotsford. His mother was eighty-seven and he could not wish her to linger inert, though he was devoted to her and said that whatever success had come to him in life was due to her early encouragement. She died peacefully on Christmas Eve.[24]

Of course there could be no question of his going to London in deep
mourning to become Sir Walter. There seemed to be a fate against this
expedition. It must be postponed again, probably till Easter. In the midst
of these distresses *Ivanhoe* was given to the world on December 16th, his
first English novel. When John Ballantyne called at 39 Castle Street on
Christmas Day, they knew already that in spite of the universal wail of
high prices and hard times, ten thousand copies at thirty shillings had
been sold. This seemed fortunate, for Brother Tom had written from
Canada to ask for eight hundred pounds, and as his daughter Jessie was
making what appeared to be an advantageous marriage with a Major
Huxley of the 70th Regiment, Scott added a hundred pounds for a
wedding gown. His own gallant son and heir let three weeks pass without
writing home, and when he did the script looked as if it might have been
performed by Mr Hinze, the Abbotsford cat. Scott told him that he did
not intend to keep him in the cavalry as promotion to the Staff could
only come through the line and it was therefore important that he wrote
legibly. He was pleasantly amazed when Gilnockie refused a draft of
fifty pounds on Coutts, saying he did not need it at present, but within
the month he did need it, having bought a second charger for a hundred
and twenty pounds on the advice of his colonel, whom, he added, did not
in his opinion know much about horseflesh.

Meanwhile, Scott was in the world of volunteers again.

> Amidst all this family distress we have enough to do with the public
> bustle. The Yeomanry are come back from Glasgow where all is
> quiet but the temper of the populace execrable . . . Scott of Gala and
> I have offered a body of 300 or more which, if accepted, may be
> very useful about Carlisle. All Roxburghshire is very loyal.

This force—eventually amounting to a thousand—was never called
upon. Before the winter was out Scott had gathered from Lord Montagu
that the Government had no notion of giving financial support. And it
was as well, for the winter was remarkable for its severity, and the
volunteers were "chiefly shepherds".

Looking out of his window in Castle Street, he reported to Laidlaw,
"deep deep snow here", and trembled for the lambing. "The little bodies
will be half buried in snow drift." He sent a cheque for sixty pounds.
He wanted ten pounds distributed amongst the poorer neighbours. "I
mean not only the actually indigent, but those who are in our phrase
ill aff."

NOTES

1. The disasters which befell the Rev. Charles Robert Maturin were spectacular. He was the descendant of a Huguenot family which had settled in Ireland on the revocation of the Edict of Nantes. He had a brilliant career at Trinity College and married at the age of twenty. His father, who held an important post in government service, was then dismissed with ignominy, though afterwards this was discovered to be a mistake. Maturin, now a curate, tried keeping a school and writing a novel. He had to abandon both his curacy and house having imprudently become security for a friend who turned out to be a crook. Scott, who had got in touch with him over a review, sent him fifty pounds and forwarded *Bertram*, first to Kemble, then to Byron. It was a fashionable success and he was lionised in London where he was found very naïve. He continued to write less acceptable drama, reverted to novels, and, unlucky to the last, died at the age of forty-two, apparently from taking a wrong medicine.

2. Scott's review of *Emma* appeared in the January issue of the *Quarterly* for 1816, vol. 28. He noted in his diary on March 12th, 1826, that he had been re-reading "for the third time at least" *Pride and Prejudice*. "That young lady had a talent for describing the involvements and feelings and characters of ordinary life, which is to me the most wonderful I ever met with. The Big Bow Wow strain I can do myself, like any now going; but the exquisite touch . . . is denied to me."

3. Letters, IV, 283. Lockhart, II, 174.

4. Letters, IV, 180. Lockhart, III, 56.

5. *The Drove Roads of Scotland*, A. R. B. Haldane, Edinburgh, 1952.

6. Edward Blore (1787–1879) came from Derby, son of an author of *The History of Rutland*. He illustrated this, and also *The History and Antiquities of Durham*, for Scott's friend Robert Surtees. He was employed together with Turner on Scott's *Provincial Antiquities and Picturesque Scenery of Scotland* (1819–26). But he did not plan Abbotsford.

7. Lockhart, III, 99.

8. William Cheselden (1688–1752) performed at St Thomas's Hospital on March 27th, 1727 "a lateral operation for the stone", to witness which surgeons from Paris and other places came over. It was virtually a new invention and made his name a landmark in the history of surgery. Scott's advisers evidently considered his case was not one for operation and event justified them. The word gall-stones had entered the English language in 1758.

9. This famous oil-sketch is now in the Scottish National Portrait Gallery. Sophia sent a full account to Miss Millar (Millar, 44–45) and Scott to Sir Adam Ferguson. Letters, X, 168. The original is surprisingly small, 10 inches by 14.

10. Lockhart, III, 131–7. *Life and Letters of Washington Irving*, Vol. I, 285 et seq.

11. Millar, 42. Lady Hood's second marriage was fruitful. She had inherited the Seaforth estates and the name of Mackenzie.

12. Lockhart, III, 151–8. Letters, V, 53–55, 74, 77, 87. Andrew Geddes (1783–1844), who had a studio in York Place, produced a picture "The discovery of the Regalia of Scotland 1818", exhibited at the Royal Academy 1841. It contained full-length portraits of all the Commissioners, but was afterwards ruined by neglect and only heads were preserved. That of Scott is in the National Portrait Gallery of Scotland.

13. Letters, V, 81–87. Lockhart applied to Adam, who gave him this account, in 1837. See also "Sir Walter Scott's baronetcy", *Review of English Studies* (October 1946), and "Some New Letters", *T.L.S.* (October 25th, 1946), both by Professor Aspinall.

14. Letters, V, 133–47, 164, 171, 396–401, 435–6.

15. Lockhart, II, 332. Lockhart dates this anecdote 1814, but Menzies was sure that his father had not moved to George Street before 1818.

16. Lockhart, II, 332; II, 216 et seq.

17. Ibid., 229.

18. Millar, 49–51.

19. Lockhart's sketch of Sophia playing the harp is reproduced in Andrew Lang's biography of Lockhart, I, 288.

20. This obituary was afterwards included in *Miscellaneous Prose Works* (1827), Vol. IV.

21. Lockhart, II, 296–7.

22. Dr Dick, who apparently advised Dr Ebenezer Clarkson, Scott's Selkirk physician, from Tullymet, near Dunkeld, said that unless the liver was afterwards fatally affected he did not know of a case which did not respond to the calomel treatment. He advised that it could be safely discontinued from August 1819, but repeated if further symptoms returned. He was a Scott novel enthusiast. Scott appears to have been cured by 1820. Letters, V, 48, 90, 127.

23. Letters, V, 505. Lockhart, III, 308–12, 323.

24. Lockhart, III, 347, et seq.

XIV

Crest of the Wave

1820–1822

I

WHILE THE FAMILY WERE AT ABBOTSFORD FOR CHRISTMAS, SOPHIA received a letter which caused her the mingled bliss and anguish usual on such occasions. Lockhart had offered. She carried it to her father, and he listened with great understanding and they agreed that she should say nothing to her mother, her sister or her brother, and that it was essential that she and her suitor should consider whether their different tempers and dispositions would give them reasonable prospect of happiness. So she replied somewhat confusedly that although she was Sophia Scott, she was afraid that Mr Lockhart probably expected that she was much more talented and well informed than she was, and

> Mr Lockhart, for God's sake, if you love me do not be so unhappy; it makes me quite wretched to think that you are so, and to feel that I, who would do anything for your peace of mind, am the cause. Do not answer this, as I know that any further correspondence of this kind, unknown to Papa, would be very wrong.

No clandestine correspondence was necessary. Lockhart was asked to wait upon Mrs Scott, and Mama, carefully prepared, joined with Papa in allowing an engagement. Scott reported to Gilnockie, on January 17th, "I think Mama would have liked a little more *stile*, but she has no sort of objections to the affair." Scott did his future son-in-law proud in his explanation to Lady Abercorn. "He is highly accomplished, a beautiful poet, and what is better, of a most honourable and gentlemanlike disposition. He is handsome . . . They have enough to live upon and the world for the winning." "He comes of a good Lanarkshire family and is very well connected. His father is a clergyman."[1]

Sophia wrote to Miss Millar.

> I wish to be the first to tell you that I have at last made up my mind to marry Mr Lockhart. Anything that I may say to prepossess you in his favour in the present state of my feelings might appear to you overdrawn, but Papa has the highest opinion of him, and his opinion is worth all the world to me. That I might have made a much higher marriage in point of rank and wealth I have little doubt, but I am not the one who can be persuaded that happiness can depend upon those two alone.

The wedding was fixed for Castle Street during the Easter recess—at the end of April, for May, a traditionally unlucky month, must be avoided. On February 3rd, 1820, Lockhart formed part of a family group standing in the windows above Constable's shop in the High Street to watch King George IV proclaimed at the Cross in Edinburgh. The longest reign in English history had ended. George III, blind and imbecile, had died peacefully at Windsor. The morning in Edinburgh was a beautiful one of brilliant winter sunshine. There was one figure in the window who was not a member of the Scott family, and seemed to behold the moving and pompous scene with a watery eye. Prince Gustavus Vasa of Sweden who was travelling with a Swiss baron, a tutor, under the pseudonym of Count Itterbourg, was the son and heir of the deposed Swedish royal family. Marshal Bernadotte now occupied the throne which many in Edinburgh believed should be returned to the exile. He had been wished upon Scott by Lord Melville, and the proclamation had appeared at first sight an admirable entertainment to which to invite a foreign royalty. Scott withdrew to another window and said to Lockhart, "Poor lad! poor lad! God help him." He was thinking of Bonnie Prince Charlie.

For a few days it seemed possible that George IV was going to follow his father with record speed. He had been too unwell to attend the funeral. He went to Brighton and did not die. On the morning of March 17th, Scott set out for London. Gilnockie had got leave and was going to meet him there. In view of his recent illness, Scott altered his usual routine. He put up for the night at three places on the road, and in London he hired a carriage. He could afford it. *The Monastery* had appeared early in the month, and although he did not himself think it very thrilling, there seemed no doubt it would sell. He had agreed with Constable that he would produce another "English" novel, introducing the character of Queen Elizabeth. But first he decided on a sequel to help along *The Monastery—The Abbot*.

Just before he set out, he wrote to his old friend William Stewart Rose that he had a saddish feeling in turning his face southwards, he had so few friends left in London. But although it was true he had neither of "my sheet anchors", poor Ellis or Morritt, this time his fears of loneliness were entirely illusory. Gilnockie was a beautiful surprise—improved in every way and handsomer than ever, "the very true cut of a soldier". Scott introduced his son and heir to the Duke of York, Commander-in-Chief, who lacked the grace of his brother, now His Majesty. Charles Arbuthnot asked them to dine quietly to meet the Duke of Wellington who expanded on Waterloo and said that the most distinct writer on military affairs he had ever read was James II in his Memoirs. The only drawback in being guests of the Dumergues on the corner of Whitehorse Street was that as there was an election in progress on account of the change of sovereign, a noisy mob swept past Number 96 twice a day.

There was a new lion at evening parties, which were as tiresome as ever, but an experience for a young officer. Giovanni Battista Belzoni was said to have overawed the Arabs by his great strength, height and energy. He was the handsomest man in the giant class that Scott had ever seen. He had excavated the second pyramid of Gizeh, and published an account of his Egyptian operations and discoveries. Scott took the first opportunity of waiting upon his early patroness, Lady Abercorn, and found her now a much aged and alarmingly correct dowager staying with the Bishop of London at Fulham Palace. She spoke of going abroad and wanted Scott to sit for a portrait by an Edinburgh artist of her choosing, John Watson. (As this progressed, Scott had to write to warn her that she might think he looked a little sleepy. He was having to give the man of colours sittings between six and seven in the morning.)

Lord Sidmouth said that the baronetcy would be gazetted on Saturday, April 1st, and the king would be back in London before the end of the month. Sir George Naylor, at the Herald's office, confirmed the designs and fees for the escutcheon, etc. (When Tom Purdie at Abbotsford heard the news he spent a day marking all the sheep S.W.S. for Sir Walter Scott.)[2] Lord Melville's guests drank a bumper to the new baronet, and Lady Huntley sang and played Scotch tunes like a Highland angel. The

Dumergues gave a stately banquet with carefully chosen company—Sir Alexander Boswell, son of Johnson's Boswell, Washington Irving, who brought the artist Charles Leslie. The architect who designed the whole of Abbotsford, William Atkinson, invited to meet Scott the artist whose out-size "Christ Entering Jerusalem" was drawing crowds to the Egyptian Hall. Scott arrived there so early that the Guest Room was not yet open, and the attendant found him sitting patiently on the stairs, his lame leg stretched in front of him. Scott advised a highly neurotic artist that he might find it well worth his while to exhibit the picture in Edinburgh. Allan Cunningham was a countryman, who in his early days, when earning his bread as a stonemason in Nithsdale, had walked into Edinburgh and back for the sole purpose of seeing the author of *Marmion* as he passed along the street. He was now Clerk of the Works to Chantrey, the famous sculptor, and came on behalf of his employer to beg Sir Walter to sit. It was about 9 a.m. when he sent in his card at 96 Piccadilly.

> It had not been gone a minute when I heard a quick heavy step coming, and in he came, holding out both hands, as was his custom, and saying, "Allan Cunningham, I am glad to see you." He had the power, I had almost called it the art, but art it was not, of winning one's heart and restoring one's confidence beyond any man I ever met.

Scott duly appeared at Eccleston Street the next morning, and found Richard Heber at the breakfast to which he was invited on the following day. A character called Fuller, Member for Surrey and the standing jester of the House of Commons, joined them, and after watching Scott's face Chantrey told Cunningham that he would have to alter the perfectly serene expression he had intended to give his sitter. "I must try his conversational look, take him when about to break out into some sly funny old story." Scott's own opinion of the finished result, a year later, was "Chantrey's bust is one of the finest things he ever did." But with characteristic modesty he was surprised to hear that it was quite the fashion to go to see it.

As on previous London trips he found that once the news he was in town got about he could have dined out three times a day, but after his appearance at the *levée* to kiss hands he was only anxious to get home. The First Gentleman of Europe had a fine speech ready. "I shall always reflect with pleasure on Sir Walter Scott's having been the first creation of my reign."[3] His Majesty would hardly permit a lame man to kneel, and shook hands with him "repeatedly". Scott told Hector Macdonald

Buchanan, "The fun was, that the folk in waiting who I suppose had not augured any mighty things of my exterior, seeing me so well received, made me about five hundred scrapes and *congées* as I retired in all the grandeur of a favour'd courtier."[4]

He had two peaceful and enjoyable Sundays—one with Joanna Baillie and John Richardson at Hampstead, and the other at Lord Montagu's at Ditton, from where he went on to Eton to pay his respects to his young chief, the Duke of Buccleuch. He had a very late night when Croker saw to it that Gilnockie and he should go to Woolwich in the Admiralty barge to witness an after-dark display of Congreve rockets. He saw the end of the trial of Thistlewood, the leader of the Cato Street conspiracy who had planned to murder the Cabinet and carry off the heads of Lords Sidmouth and Castlereagh in bags. His last Saturday breakfast was alone with Lord Melville. Lockhart wanted him to say a word in favour of John Wilson, who aspired to the chair of Moral Philosophy in Edinburgh University.

He set out for home with Gilnockie on Monday, April 24th, and travelling fast reached Edinburgh on the night of Thursday. He had in his luggage some splendid presents for Sophia—a veil of Flanders lace, from her godmother Miss Sophia Dumergue, a most beautiful necklace from Lady Compton, and indeed so many gifts of jewellery that he thought his daughter would resemble an Indian princess, and promised her as his own contribution a simple cheque, "for pocket money".

The wedding took place, "Scottish fashion" explained Lockhart, in the drawing-room at 39 Castle Street on the evening of Saturday, April 29th, and the happy couple set off for a honeymoon to explore the "lions" of Perthshire where Lockhart had engaged good quarters for his bride. "The country," he instructed her, "is beautiful in the highest degree." They had taken a house in Edinburgh, in Great King Street, and Scott was making additions to a cottage for them not two miles from Abbotsford.

After nearly all the guests had departed, Scott noticed the dispossessed Swedish prince ("How very odd that he should have been in my house on such an occasion"), and began himself to feel a little melancholy. Gilnockie was leaving in four days' time, "Charles must go to school somewhere and I suppose by-and-by some kind suitor will carry off my black-eyed maid, and then the old folks will be lonely enough." But he wrote to Morritt, "To me, as it seems neither of my sons have a strong literary turn, the society of a son-in-law possessed of learning and talent must be a very great acquisition."[5]

II

The remainder of 1820 was as fortunate as the three preceding years had been miserable, and indeed with Sir Walter Scott, happily settled in his new-built (but not yet completed) baronial hall, and turning out regularly (though still anonymously) works acclaimed as masterpieces, the pattern seemed set for many happy years. Within a few weeks of his return in May he had to refuse offers of honorary degrees from the universities of Oxford and Cambridge. He could not face making "that most tiresome of all journeys" again for ceremonies in June. He must get on with *The Abbot*, and he was expecting many friends. John Gibson Lockhart noted all down. The guests this summer and autumn (some harmoniously overlapping) included William Rose, Richard Heber, Morritt, Henry Mackenzie, "The Man of Feeling", Patriarch of Scottish *belles-lettres*, Dr Wollaston and Sir Humphry Davy from the Royal Society, Lord and Lady Compton and nursery, Charles Young (of Covent Garden), Mrs Clephane and the Misses Anna Jane and Williamina-Marianne, Joanna Baillie and her sister, Constable and his son David, and the brilliant young heirs of Lords Morpeth and Shaftesbury, both from Christ Church and expected to take Firsts. (Scott wrote down Lord Ashley, the future philanthropist, as "an original".) Prince Gustavus came to take his leave charmingly before quitting Edinburgh, and Scott who had heard that the reigning Bernadotte, Crown Prince Oscar, was said to be coming to Scotland thought he would have to sit firm in his saddle.[6]

Lockhart told William Allan, the artist, when the house-party mustered before the porch early on a dazzling September day, "A faithful sketch of what you this morning see would be more interesting a hundred years hence than the grandest so-called historical picture." All was set for anglers, and a coursing match near Newark Castle. Every available greyhound from Darnick, Melrose and Abbotsford was present, and Sir Walter, mounted on Sibyl Grey, was marshalling the procession attended by the huge Maida gambolling like a pup. At the last moment Miss Anne Scott ran up. "Papa, papa, I know you would never think of going without your pet." A favourite small black pigling frisking about Sir Walter's steed was removed. The sportsmen met to feast amongst the mossy rocks overlooking the Yarrow. Lady Scott had gone ahead, in her sociable, with her elder daughter, the picnic baskets, the venerable Mackenzie and his negro page.

Harriet, wife of Charles, Earl of Dalkeith, afterwards fourth Duke of Buccleuch
Artist Unknown.
"My fair chieftainess" to whom Scott dedicated *The Lay of the Last Ministrel*, 1805. Died 1814.
By permission of His Grace the Duke of Buccleuch, from the collection at Bowhill.

Sir Walter Scott. A study for "The Finding of the Scottish Regalia", 1818
By Andrew Geddes.
By permission of the Scottish National Portrait Gallery.

G. 1823

Two annual events henceforward took place at Abbotsford—"The Abbotsford Hunt", a coursing match, around October 28th, the birthday of Sir Walter's heir, and the party to sit down at Abbotsford afterwards for a gargantuan feast with songs and speeches sometimes swelled to forty. This was generally held on the moors above Cauldeshiels Loch. "The Boldside Meeting, a solemn bout of salmon-fishing", ended with an alfresco repast beneath a grand old ash adjoining Charles Purdie's cottage on the northern bank of the Tweed, about a mile above Abbotsford. This sometimes lasted until the harvest moon had risen and Lockhart thought the various groups might have made a fit subject for Watteau.

Lockhart noticed that whoever might be staying, Tom Purdie always appeared at his master's elbow at the close of Sunday dinner and was given a quaigh of whisky or a tumbler of wine to drink the health of the Laird and Lady and all the good company. Scott conversed with his staff, both outdoor and indoor, with a freedom which his son-in-law had seen practised by hardly any other gentleman. He talked with his coachman if he sat by him, as he often did, on the box, and with his footman if he happened to be in the rumble. He was particular that when a very young lad was engaged, his work should be arranged so that he had time for his studies. Such beginners had to bring their copy-books to the library once a week. When Tom Hutson, the head keeper from Bowhill, came over with a gift of four brace of moorfowl, he talked to Scott for an hour without interruption. Scott had a satisfactory new link with the absent ducal family, Hay Donaldson, a solicitor recommended by him to Lord Montagu. The last grand entertainment of the year was always The Kirn, or Harvest-Home for the peasantry on the estate. Young and old danced in the great barn from sunset to sunrise, to the sound of the bagpipes and occasionally an itinerant violin.

The invaluable Lockhart solved the problem of Charles, who was, said Sophia, "very clever and very idle". He had got quite beyond his poor lame Dominie Thomson, and cared for nothing but days with his rod, his gun and his pony. Lord Bathurst, whom Scott did not know, had unexpectedly offered a writership in the East India Company for one of Sir Walter Scott's sons. If a lad went out, aged eighteen, after two years at the Company's college, Hertford Castle, he would get five hundred pounds a year and be able to retire with a fortune before he was forty. But Charles was still only thirteen. The offer was obviously too valuable to be refused outright, but Charles must get some more discipline and education. There was a seminary in Switzerland, Ferden, near Berne. Two of the Fraser-Tytlers had done well there. Scott wrote to Canada to ask if

Brother Tom would consider sending his only son, Walter, to India. He thought now he might be able to get a cadetship for the boy, who would be very welcome at Castle Street and Abbotsford. Lockhart, meanwhile, had bethought him of the Rev. John Williams, vicar at Lampeter in Cardiganshire and master of the grammar school there. He had been at Balliol with Lockhart, and for four years second master at Winchester. He came of an irreproachable scholastic family. A brother, David, a fellow of Wadham College, had been honoured by Lockhart last year with the dedication of *Peter's Letters to his Kinsfolk*—sketches of leading dignitaries of Edinburgh, something in the satirical vein. Alternatively, Lockhart had approached Professor Jardine at Glasgow University who had volunteered to take Sir Walter Scott's son under his own roof. But Lockhart was sinister about the possibilities of dissipation for Charles at Glasgow even if he lived with the Professor of Logic. At Lampeter, on the contrary, he would find few opportunities. The inhabitants spoke Welsh "almost entirely". Charles went off in a hurry, in the end, in October. His brother-in-law saw him board the coach at Selkirk, with a guinea in his pocket. Mr Robert Cadell, of Constable's, travelling south, had most humanely offered to take the boy absolutely to Mr Williams's door—five days' journey. Charles had a talent for playing truant. He went off somewhat tactlessly, "in high spirits".[7] "Poor fellow," said his tender-hearted father, "he will think of this house often before he sees it again." Nobody liked leaving "Abb". When the carriage had come round, Lady Scott's spaniel, Fifi, had resolutely refused to embark for Edinburgh and had carried the day. Animal life at Castle Street was reduced to a small Kintail terrior, Ourisk.

1820 closed full of hope. Scott wrote to tell Gilnockie that they had called in upon Sophia who seemed as complete and serene a little housewife as if she had been one for five years. "She is preparing in due time to make you an uncle and me (God help me) a grandfather. The prospect is still at some distance however."

February 1821 found him at his desk in a London hotel—a good one in Numbers 85–86 Jermyn Street, renamed "The Waterloo". The Dumergues were away, but it was convenient to be under the same roof as the Lord Advocate of Scotland, for he had come south on business, legal and family. His fellow Clerks of the Court of Session had asked him to accompany Sir William Rae to see a bill which affected them closely safely through Parliament. His family business was also pressing— Charlotte's widowed sister-in-law, Mrs Carpenter, had arrived from Madras.

London was fearsome. At 10 a.m. he was still having to write by candlelight and could not see across the road for fog. There were no animals at The Waterloo, he told Sophia, except a tolerably conversable cat who had soon learned that the gentleman from Scotland would provide a dish of cream at breakfast time. There had been no question of Charlotte accompanying him. Sophia's child was not expected for another month, but almost from the first she had been what the village calls "carrying badly", and the affair in January of Mr John Scott (no relation) had certainly happened most unfortunately. Lockhart, whom Scott had always realised was fiery, had got into a foolish scrape with a blackguard who had attacked him in a publication named *Baldwin's London Magazine* on account of articles in *Blackwood's*. Lockhart had charged down to London and, on Croker's advice, sent his antagonist a note in which he said that he considered him a scoundrel and a liar. As he had received no reply after repeating his note and waiting some days, he had charged back home believing that he had called a coward's bluff. But Sir Walter, arriving on February 11th, soon found that in addition to his own two pieces of business in town, he must involve himself closely in the alarming repercussions of Lockhart's paper war. For an innocent Mr Christie, a Balliol friend who had carried Lockhart's notes, had himself been challenged. He met "Scoundrel Scott" on February 16th at Chalk Farm by moonlight and fired his first shot in the air, but with his second wounded Scott in the stomach. The villain had lingered eleven days, during which time Sir Walter had been obliged to make inconspicuous calls at an address in Woburn Place at which Christie had gone to ground and from which he had fled to France as soon as he heard that his aim had been fatal. Then Sir Walter had to find out and comfort Mrs Christie, who was expecting again, and write to Christie's father—a clergyman in Aberdeenshire.[8]

It was with as much relief as he remembered in his whole life that he got a line from Lockhart to say that Sophia had been taken with premature labour, and given birth to a beautiful son on St Valentine's Day. He was just off to the brilliant beauty of Ditton Park for the weekend, and the whole Montagu and Scott family drank the health of mother and child. The young duke and his brother Lord John came up from Eton to see him.

Charlotte's sister-in-law was a dire disappointment, the poorest-spirited creature you ever saw, and she had with her, to encourage her in every doubt and fear, a companion, a cousin, called Miss Hooke, "a little howdy-dowdy ugly thing". Moreover, as soon as the lawyers had seen the legal papers from India which she tremblingly produced, it appeared that the fortune left to the Scott children was going to prove about half what had been expected. She was entitled to sixteen thousand pounds in property by her marriage articles. Scott had to warn Lockhart that Sophia would be five thousand pounds less wealthy than they had calculated when they had drawn up her settlement. He did not believe either of them would care, but he must beg Lockhart in future to be more careful, and if possible to retire from *Blackwood's*. His unfavourable comments on Mrs Carpenter went to Gilnockie and Lockhart. In his frequent letters to the young mother he recounted nothing but what could encourage and amuse. "You are now my dearest girl beginning a new course of pleasures, anxieties and duties, and the best I can wish for you is that your little boy may prove the same dutiful and affectionate child which you have always been to me . . . Pray be extremely careful of yourself for some time."

He sent his carriage to take out Mrs Carpenter and her companion for drives. He got them a permit to visit the royal apartments at Carlton House. He accompanied them to Chantrey's studio and The Institution. Not even a dashing picture of Belshazzar's Feast seemed to arouse a spark of interest. She was most miserably thin and could neither eat, nor drink, nor sleep. He told "My dearest Love" that he was inclined to like Mrs Carpenter very much. She seemed thoroughly good-humoured though much depressed both by circumstances and recollections, "Her great wish is to see Mama." (Later, when she had removed Sir Walter from the post of leading Bogey in her world of fears, she replaced him by Charlotte who might not take the reduced expectations of their children so philosophically.) A land journey for Mrs Carpenter was out of the question. "You never saw a creature so exhausted."

Both she and Lady Compton, who was herself expecting another infant any day, had been much pleased when he called to tell them his splendid news. "Spencer Scott", a third Compton son arrived, and he was godfather. "I have a gay time of it." He meant to fill in the days as his bill progressed through Parliament and Mrs Carpenter regained health, by a trip down to Bath with Lord Montagu, and if possible a call on Charles in Wales. He sent the bantling Lockhart "a kiss extraordinary from Grandpapa". He was amused when he heard that the child had dark hair and black eyes—Daddy's boy!

> My kind love to Lockhart and to Pickanini but don't kiss it too much for fear it melt away like one of (the) lumps of barley-sugar you were so fond of. I expect by your description quite a cherubim . . . though not I hope representing in voice those whom we are told in the prayer-book continually do cry.

East wind had driven away the fog. When the wind dropped snow fell, and lay an inch thick upon the streets. But he was still sitting to Mr Lawrence for a full-length portrait ordered by His Majesty for his gallery at Windsor, between 6 and 7 a.m.—an hour also favoured by the Iron Duke. Scott wanted Maida included, "so that there may be one handsome fellow in the party". Now that town was filling, he had so many invitations that he made two capital blunders about where he was asked to dine. Only an accident recalled to his mind that he had forgotten the Foreign Secretary. "Were I to tell this in a stage-coach, or in company, what a conceited puppy I would seem; yet the thing is literally true—as well as my receiving three blue ribbands and a marchioness in my hotel the same day." The consequences of that had been awkward. The proprietor of The Waterloo had asked him to procure a renewal of a Crown lease; and the man that hired horses expected him to be able to get a permit to keep hackney coaches, and "who knows what other vain expectations my state of favour has excited".

Kenilworth was such a success, said Mrs Hughes, that tourists were crowding down to the little village of Cumnor, where the parish clerk was making a fortune by showing the site of the old mansion which Lord Abingdon was attacked for having demolished! Every village child could point out the staircase down which poor Amy Robsart had fallen. Finally, the publican had changed the name of his house from The Jolly Ringers to The Black Bear. Such was fame!

Scott had thought of a title for his next novel, *The Buccaneer*. But he still would not admit, even to Mrs Hughes, that he was the author of *Waverley*. He asked Sophia to let him know what article of dress, or for the new house, or the cottage, he could bring "to show I have been in London, and am a loving papa". There was a dark period during which he began to think he would have to summon Charlotte, perhaps attended by Anne, to help him with Mrs Carpenter. "I cannot think of this poor creature being in a state so utterly desolate as she is at present." But presently one of Mrs Carpenter's two distinguished military brothers took some responsibility. General Fraser was in London and she was persuaded to invite a second opinion—Dr Baillie.

Sir Walter struggled into court dress, in which he had agreed with Allan Cunningham that he did not look quite canny, and had a warm reception from George IV. His king greeted him like an old friend, "and shook hands with me, before the whole circle, which I am told is unusual". The new sovereign had indeed reason to treat him as a friend. One of the immediate results of the succession had been that Queen

Caroline (although her husband refused her the title and was trying to divorce her) had arrived in England. On his last London trip, Scott had been surprised by an urgent messenger on behalf of the Privy Council to ask for guidance. The Duke of Hamilton was hereditary Keeper of Holyrood House, and it was well known that His Grace's sister had been a devoted lady-in-waiting, although she had not gone abroad with Queen Caroline. How far did His Grace's authority extend? Her Majesty had signified her intention of setting up a Court there. Mr Scott had suggested sending an express to Edinburgh with orders to put in fifty or sixty workmen to repair the palace, paint some rooms, and take up the floors of others. This had been done and the impatient queen had not come.

Dr Baillie's diagnosis, although most politely wrapped up, was that there was absolutely nothing the matter with Mrs Carpenter, at least, at present, nothing physical. He recommended that she should not go to Scotland till May, and should take a small house in Kensington.[9] "So now my mission is ended and in a great measure, my anxiety. I will see the Court of Session Bill through till the 26th and then set sail for the North." He was perfectly weary of driving through streets in a carriage, and feasting on turbot and plover's eggs and champagne, with pretty hostesses who asked him to very late parties. (He still thought Mrs Arbuthnot the most beautiful one in London.) In the end he did not get away quite so early. The Duke of York gave him an appointment at which he understood that Gilnockie need only ask Colonel Murray to forward his application to be admitted to the military academy at Sandhurst. He then chose the west road, quicker than "the tiresome North district", and arrived in Edinburgh on April 10th. The city looked ten times more stately after his stay in London, where there was far more smoke and dirt and much less fine architecture.

III

He thought the business that awaited him at home was remarkable in its variety. Before he could cry "Hey! for Tweedside!" he must attend a funeral, the baptism of a grandchild, and a wedding. The first ceremony was that of old Colonel Swinton, a relative. As he had been warned, the infant to be baptised was "a most exquisite specimen". Sophia's little maid, Cathy, was relieved to see it safely christened; she thought that otherwise the fairies would steal it. The young parents had thought of Mungo, but to Scott's relief, John Hugh was eventually chosen, John for the father, Hugh for Scott of Harden, who was present as a sponsor.

They had inconveniently already called their dog Mungo. Their cottage on the Abbotsford estate was not yet quite ready. Messrs Smith of Darnick were afraid that if they put down the new floors now, the planks would shrink. A six-week heat-wave obliged them, and Lockhart did not remember a happier time in his life than this summer and autumn, and those which immediately followed them. Originally it had been, somewhat prosaically, called Burnfoot. But Sir Walter had bought more land around it and it was sheltered by a belt of firs on the Duke of Buccleuch's estate. "Chiefswood will be one of the snuggest and most beautiful cottages that has ever been seen." The main road leading south from Darnick had been diverted to the east. Sophia would have a brook running in front of her cabin in the green glen, and a spreading ash under which to sit above its banks. (Actually this became her father's favourite seat when he arrived early, to wait happily surrounded by dogs until the young people got moving.) A specialist, "John-Cock-a-Pistol", was planting shrubs from Abbotsford. Sophia would have a fruit garden and a flower garden. Her father quoted Samuel Rogers' *Wish*:

> Mine be a cot beside the hill,
> A bee-hive's hum shall soothe my ear

But instead of

> And Lucy at her wheel shall sing,
> In russet gown and apron blue,

he threatened

> But if Bluestockings here you bring
> The Great Unknown won't dine with you.[10]

"Linton" Ferguson's match was a surprise. When Charlotte had heard of the engagement she had burst forth in Gallic scorn. Why a man of fifty with three single women to look after him should wish to add a fourth was beyond her understanding. Scott, always kind, although he had early nicknamed the Misses Ferguson the Three Witches, wrote to Lord Montagu that Miss Margaret, the eldest, was the very picture of an old maid, but had not a grain of bad humour or spleen. She was Mrs Lockhart's best friend. Miss Mary was known by the local children as "the daft lady". She was slightly deformed and rose early to wander over the Abbotsford estate wearing a number of coloured handkerchiefs on her head, assisting her steps by a stick twice her height and attended by two of the noisiest dogs Scott had ever known. Miss Bell would be recognised by all at Ditton as a sister of Ferguson, for she bore the most remarkable likeness to the captain. She commonly wore a small brown wig. After a honeymoon at Harrogate and Bath, the happy couple and Miss Margaret were going to stay with the Montagus who never forgot the essential services performed by Captain Adam Ferguson for the late duke.

"Linton" advanced to the sacrifice, on the appointed day, with a jaunty military step and "a kind of leer on his face that seemed to quiz the whole affair". The bride appeared to Scott a good-humoured, purpose-like body of no particular age. They had taken Gattonside House for the present year. She had been presented to the neighbourhood as a Mrs Lyon, a widow, daughter of the late John Stewart of Stenton, but the wedding announcement in *The Scots Magazine* said that George Lyon had been of Bucklersbury—evidently a merchant. She had a good jointure and savings, and a good idea of looking after them. When she had left, Lord Montagu told Scott that she seemed to have travelled all over the world, to the great mortification of her bridegroom, for he could not begin one of his celebrated anecdotes but she had been to the place. However, she had been very good-humoured and joined cordially in a good deal of laughing. Charlotte came to recognise her worth.

The spring was late that year but when sunshine came it stayed. By midsummer they were praying for rain. Scott had some annoyances. He had utterly failed in an attempt to win a local election for his kinsman Scott of Maxpoffle—the Collectorship of Roxburghshire. Lady Louisa Stuart wrote to ask if it was true that Abbotsford had been attacked because of his failure to illuminate his house when the Government dropped the bill against the queen. It was quite untrue, but he had received threatening letters. Lockhart was gone to Inverness to try some smugglers, so Sophia wrote to ask if it was true that Gilnockie's regiment was going to be sent to India in disgrace for seditious toasts supporting the queen. This scandal was painful and partially founded on fact. Letters to Ireland flew from the author's pen. Sir Walter did not intend that his son should go to India. "The ass wishes to go, himself, and talks of being absent five or six years when I will be bound not one of them sees British land again till their beards are grey." Gilnockie complained of the Commander-in-Chief in Ireland, Sir David Baird, and that Sir Walter listened to the lawyers and gossips of Edinburgh. Sir Walter replied stormily that his son's military politeness handsomely classed such persons together when writing to a lawyer. Gilnockie ought to know that he had to stand discipline. "I am aware that Sir David is considered a severe and ill-tempered man and I remember a story that when report came to Europe that Tippoo's prisoners (of whom Baird was one) were chained together two and two, his mother said 'God pity the poor lad that's chained to our Davie'." He was horrified and disgusted to hear from his son that amongst the irregularities acknowledged was that a young brute of an officer had introduced a common prostitute into the mess of the 18th. Gilnockie said jauntily that the man had been drunk of course but the mess had voted a fine of a dozen of claret upon anyone who repeated his offence. He said he had himself exceeded only on guest nights whan a man could not well refuse toasts, and once to avoid giving evidence. It was true that he never had shown a taste for drink, but he had already in the past eighteen months alarmed his family by complaints of dysentery and jaundice. His handwriting was a disgrace.

The Edinburgh press noticed an affray near Waterford where the magistrates had been obliged to call upon the military to separate peasants fighting about a cutting of turves for peat. About half-a-dozen Irish had been killed. Gilnockie had been the officer in charge of a sergeant and twelve dragoons. He appeared to have acted well, but Sir Walter Scott did not intend that his heir should perish in a squalid unmemorable Irish riot. Nor did he intend that he should show marked attention to a young lady. (She turned out to be a fair maid of Cork, but the regiment was now in Dublin which would be much gayer.)[11]

The two sons seemed like the two figures in a Swiss weather clock to replace one another regularly in sunshine or darkness. For while Gilnockie could not do right, Mr Williams's reports of Charles were encouraging. He was reading Tacitus with some relish. He had made a suitable friend in a nephew of Lady Eldon, a classical scholar, Villiers Surtees by name, and emulated him in painstaking effort. Charles was invited to bring this paragon to stay at Abbotsford, and they came in June and were both very cocky; but Villiers showed good taste in falling a hopeless victim to the charms of Mrs Lockhart. Charles wrote much the best hand of the family. The trouble was that he seldom wrote.[12] A much better mannered boy of the same age had also just arrived from Canada—nephew Walter, son of Brother Tom. He had evidently been impressed by his stalwart and much-tried mother with the necessity for behaving well for the good of his family. He was grave for his age, but he did not seem to have a fault except a slight inclination to sarcasm. Sir Walter, while in London, had seen Lord Sidmouth and the boy was accepted as a cadet for the cavalry of the East India Company. Meanwhile he was receiving his education in Edinburgh at the High School, at the expense of his uncle who had also paid for his passage and outfit. After he had found his way to Mrs Lockhart's cot he became "gay as a lark".

Sir Walter had received with some misgiving the offer of the Presidency of the Royal Society in his native city. He did not consider he had claims as a scientist. But it was represented to him that the society embraced a section for literature. He accepted with pleasure, and his gentle skill as chairman was found most effective. He had also become President of the Celtic Society, "to encourage ancient Highland manners and customs, especially the Garb of old Gaul". In January 1821 he first presided over a "superb" gathering, "all plaided and plumed in their tartan array".[13] He answered at great length suggestions from a son of Lord Clarendon for the foundation under the patronage of His Majesty of a Royal Society of Literature. He did not get it quite right. His impression was that its principal aim was to support neglected authors by stipends of a hundred pounds per annum, "solid puddings and pensions to men of genius". He foresaw great difficulty in selecting for membership distinguished authors of varying politics. Lord Sidmouth agreed with his strictures and asked permission to show them to His Majesty, who was much taken with the scheme. Morritt believed that when the Society did come into being, its programme had been radically altered in accordance with Scott's criticism.[14]

Mrs Carpenter was on her way to Scotland at last. Dr Baillie's advice seemed to have worked wonders. She was taking regular exercise and was much improved in health, longing to meet her sister-in-law. She caused high alarm by failing to turn up on her appointed date but this was a blessing in disguise. John Ballantyne died, very suddenly in the end, on June 16th, of a consumption of the lungs. Lockhart, who had no instinctive admiration for the brothers Ballantyne was surprised to find Scott so upset at the funeral.

> While they were smoothing the turf over John's remains in the Canongate churchyard, the heavens which had been dark and slaty, cleared up suddenly and the midsummer sun shone forth in his strength. Scott, ever awake to the "skiey influences", cast his eye along the overhanging line of the Calton Hill, with its gleaming walls and towers, and then turning to the grave again, "I feel," he whispered in my ear, "I feel as if there would be less sunshine for me from this day forth."[15]

John had left Scott in his will two thousand pounds to build a library, charged upon his estate, but that turned out to be bankrupt and his widow long outlived his patron.

Mrs Carpenter arrived on July 2nd. She had been taken ill in London just as she was due to leave. This did not sound very promising, but she fell effortlessly into the Abbotsford routine like the valued member of the family that she must be. She had already sent, by Scott, wonderful gifts from India for the womenkind—splendid cashmere shawls, fans and card-cases. She brought more with her and seemed pleased with her welcome. Her own room was to be kept for her. The weather was heavenly. But she was not, perhaps, quite the person for frequent visits to a hilly country. When she had been under his roof a fortnight, her host left for London.

He could not resist the coronation. It was going to be magnificent. He had inspected the new steamship *City of Edinburgh* which did the journey in sixty hours. He would be staying in Old Palace Yard with William Stewart Rose, who would accompany him north after a flying visit. It was a little unlucky that he had been so withering about the idea of pensions for poverty-stricken geniuses, for James Hogg would have been an ideal object for such charity. He had taken passages in the steamship for himself and Hogg, whose affairs were again in a bad way, in hopes that the Ettrick Shepherd might produce something about the coronation, perhaps a popular ode. He wrote to Lord Montagu, on behalf of their countryman. Lord Sidmouth said that places had been reserved for Sir Walter and the Ettrick Shepherd in the Abbey and at the banquet in Westminster Hall. Scott had never thought such a thing possible, but Hogg was haughtily not available for a coronation on July 19th. It would mean missing St Boswell's Fair. "The fair carried it."[16]

IV

Scott's eyewitness account of the coronation was published anonymously by Ballantyne in *The Edinburgh Weekly Journal*, and was an excellent piece of journalism. It told Scottish readers exactly what they wanted to hear, and did not evade difficulties. It was, for instance, not ideal that the hero of the whole admittedly vastly expensive pageant was a very bad sixty, twenty stone, and in such poor health that well-informed persons doubted whether he would ever get through an exacting programme in warm weather clad in many yards of velvet and ermine. There were doubts, which he shared, as to his reception, and he was very nervous. He knew that his queen meant to make an attempt to create a disturbance. Scott disposed of this early in his narrative. "You must have heard a full account of the only disagreeable event of the day." "The misguided lady" of

course had attempted to intrude herself. "It seems singular that being
determined to be present at all hazards, this unfortunate personage should
not have produced a Peer's ticket, which I presume would have insured
her admittance. I willingly pass to pleasanter matters." She had, in fact,
made little more than a token protest—driven up to a side door of the
Abbey at about 6.30 a.m. attended only by the veteran Lord Hood and
an unidentified "lady or two", and when she had been refused admission
had gone quietly. He told Ballantyne by letter, "She retired amidst groans
and cries of 'Shame, Shame' and 'Home, Home'." A few people had
exclaimed, "That's it, Caroline" and "Go it, my girl", but they were
ragamuffins of the lowest description. Scott really believed that "the
Bedlam Bitch" was mad.

George IV had determined that the greatest event in his career, for
which he had waited so long, should be worthily celebrated. Officials had
been at work for months establishing historical precedents. This had not
been cheerful work. Fire had broken out at the coronation of the Conqueror. That of James I had been almost private, because of the plague.
Richard III had used up the properties ordered for his murdered nephew.
So many monarchs had ascended the throne as bachelors or spinsters, but
never yet one who had a living but neglected queen. James II was the best
example for splendour, and he had lost his throne. However, there existed
in the late king's library a copy of a book which his Stewart predecessor
had caused to be made—an illustrated record by Francis Sandford,
Lancaster Herald. George IV ordered that his procession should open
with the hereditary royal herbwoman, leading her six maids, carrying
baskets of two bushels of show blooms and sweet herbs, to strew before
him. They advanced slowly and gracefully. After this the proceedings
moved as it were by clockwork, without a hitch, or perhaps, as it was all
accompanied by splendid music, like a classical opera. Considering that
there is but one step between the sublime and the ridiculous, Scott found
it surprising that with so many people in unaccustomed costumes playing
parts in antiquated ceremonial, the whole passed off without the slightest
circumstance which could derange the general tone of solemn feeling.

"The scene in the Abbey was beyond measure magnificent." (He had
got a seat with a very good view.) He admired the cross-gallery occupied
by Westminster schoolboys in white surplices, waiting to greet and
acknowledge their sovereign. "The spectacle on the floor" was fascinating
for many reasons—the altar surrounded by the Fathers of the Church and
the king by his nobility and counsellors. (An ardent Tory handsomely
rejoiced to see the Duke of Devonshire and many of the Whig peers

prominently assembled.) There were hardened warriors and learned counsellors, and seldom had he seen so many elegant and beautiful girls seated amongst the noble matronage of the land. The foreign ambassadors' box was perfectly ablaze with diamonds. Prince Esterhazy glittered like a galaxy. "Beside him sat a good-humoured lass who seemed all eyes and ears (his daughter-in-law I believe) who wore as many diamonds as if they had been Bristol stones." It was particularly delightful to see the royal brothers led, by the Duke of York, performing homage. The king seemed much affected. However, throughout the long service he acquitted himself with his usual grace, and seemed to gain in confidence as it was accomplished. He was smiling as he passed to the banquet, under a golden canopy wearing his regalia. On their arrival both he and Lord Londonderry must have heard a few cries of "Queen! Queen!", but now he was acclaimed vociferously. If the author were asked who appeared to him most impressive, he had no hesitation in saying Lord Londonderry in his Garter robes (lately Lord Castlereagh—he had recently succeeded his father), and the Duke of Wellington with his baton. Lord Anglesey, who had left a leg on the battlefield of Waterloo, showed superb horsemanship. "I never saw so fine a bridle-hand in my life." Another of the hereditary participants, the King's Champion, managed his steed well when he had to ride into the hall and throw down his gauntlet. He looked a maiden knight—a fine youth. Henry Dymoke was representing his father, the Rector of Scrivelsby, who deemed the office incompatible with the functions of a clergyman. His armour was in good taste, but Sir Walter Scott was scandalised by his shield—a round Highland target, a defensive weapon, instead of three-cornered and slung round the neck. The fancy dress of the Privy Counsellors had slightly horrified him when he had seen them individually. Many of them were elderly or ill-made men and they had been attired in Elizabethan costume, trunk hose, and mantles of blue and white satin. But massed together they were effective, none more so than the Lord Justice Clerk of Scotland.

The pages at the banquet were almost entirely young gentlemen of the very first condition, who had taken these menial characters in order to see an unforgettable show. They looked quite beautiful in *Henri Quatre* coats of scarlet cloth, gold-laced, with blue sashes, white silk hose and rosettes. It must be owned that they showed very indifferent skill in dispersing the good cheer and were adept in securing themselves from starvation. There was a tremendous supply of delicacies available, but the peers got only a cold collation while the Aldermen feasted on venison and turtle.

Scott got away from the banquet between two and three in the morning and could not find his carriage. Somewhere near Whitehall he and a young friend got locked in the crowd. A sergeant of the Scots Greys to whom Sir Walter addressed himself, asking to be allowed to cross, answered shortly that his orders were strict: the thing was impossible. While they were trying to persuade the sergeant to relent, the crowd gave a heave. His young companion called out, "Take care, Sir Walter Scott! Take care!" The stalwart dragoon said, "What! Sir Walter Scott? He shall get through anyway. Make room, men, for Sir Walter Scott, our illustrious countryman." The men answered, "Sir Walter Scott! God bless him!" In a moment he was safe.[17]

V

In view of extraordinary exertions this year, he had added a new member to his staff, the ideal butler-valet. He thought he knew all about William Dalgleish, who had waited upon him at a solitary dinner one day fifteen years ago at Selkirk, when he had been up there for a trial. The neighbour to whom he had invited himself at short notice was engaged, but had left him a comfortable meal and Dalgleish. The man was not too young—rising sixty by the time he came to Abbotsford, but he had been nine years in his last situation, and was known to the Russells at Ashestiel. He was strictly honest. When he had made himself invaluable Sir Walter discovered that Dalgleish could not function without fairly frequent doses of what he engagingly described as "a drope of the cratur". He had some rows with Charlotte, but he became so much a family institution that when Gilnockie needed a new charger he wrote to the butler to ask him to break the news to Sir Walter. After that had been settled, the young hopeful did not write again to his parent for a month. He had been ill.[18]

Sir Walter returned from London to a serene and beautiful autumn and a windy but not severe winter. He rode or walked for two or three hours every day about his property. He had brought back for Charlotte from his first trip to London this year "a delightful plan for the addition at Abb. which I think will make it quite complete and furnish me with a handsome library and you with a drawing-room and better bedroom for company, etc. It will cost me a little hard work to meet the expence, but I have been a good while idle." The rustic porch of the old cottage, original nucleus of the house, was still in existence, almost hidden by roses and jessamine. He could hardly bear to sign its death warrant, and made an excursion from Edinburgh on purpose to witness its demolition. He saved as many as possible of the creepers to adorn a porch of somewhat similar design at Chiefswood.

The Buccaneer, now *The Pirate*, was published early in December. He had finished writing it in peace in a dressing-room at Chiefswood. Lockhart never forgot the day when *The Fortunes of Nigel* was begun. It was that of the Abbotsford Hunt, October 21st. He had ridden over, and while he was chatting with Terry and master-mason John Smith, Scott had come out of the house with a bunch of manuscript in his hand. "Well lads, I've laid the keel of a new lugger this morning—here it is." He had readmitted James Ballantyne to partnership, and before he went to Edinburgh in November concluded a new negotiation with Constable— agreed to give him the remaining copyright of his last four novels: *Ivanhoe*, *The Monastery*, *The Abbot* and *Kenilworth* in consideration of a pay- ment of five thousand guineas. He still refused to have his name revealed. Lockhart, writing with hindsight, believed that the novels that had followed *Ivanhoe* had not sold quite so well, and that hints had been dropped that the Great Unknown might call a temporary halt, but that Scott, backed by Ballantyne, thought that his best work was that thrown off easily, and Constable considered that if the books sold less well that might be counterpoised by a greater rate of production. Scott had not ceased to undertake "by-jobs". *Halidon Hill*, a two-act drama, composed for an anthology, to oblige Joanna Baillie, turned out to be too long. Cadell gave him a thousand pounds for it, to appear individually. He had completed the Life of Smollett for John Ballantyne's Novelists Library and edited *Franck's Northern Memoir*.

Lord Byron, who had now been abroad six years, had asked Murray to send Scott an advance copy of *Cain* and enquire if he would accept the dedication. Scott replied that he would be proud to prefix his name to "this very grand and tremendous drama in which Byron has certainly matched Milton on his own ground". Byron himself wrote in January 1822 one of his witty letters, opening, "Since I left England (and that is not far off the usual term of transportation) . . ." He said he had found the idea a hundred times in his head of writing to Scott "and always in my heart". Scott answered at length and approached with delicacy "the painful circumstances" of Byron's exile. "I would have done a great deal— had anything been in my power—to prevent the unhappy family mis- understanding." He told an exile with an appreciation of tragedy of an incident which had shaken Edinburgh. "Our violent party disputes here have just occasioned a melancholy catastrophe in the fate of Sir Alexander Boswell (the son of Johnson's Bozzy) who is as I learn by this day's post,

mortally wounded by a Mr Stewart, a high Whig." Later, when the full
story was known, Lockhart, much shaken, realised that the poor young
Boswell when he had been the life and soul of a Castle Street dinner
party must already have made all arrangements for his fatal encounter.
He had lampooned his assailant in *The Sentinel* which had followed *The
Beacon*.[19] Scott realised grimly that this fellow was "the party who had
attempted to inveigle me into a correspondence last year. But I cut him
short". Lockhart had learnt his lesson. He was now writing a novel about
a Roman soldier who fell in love with a British maiden. The whole Boswell
incident went into *St Ronan's Well*.

> I think [continued Scott gently to Byron] you would like my son-
> in-law Lockhart who is bold very clever and a little inconsiderate
> with the kindest and warmest feelings . . . My eldest son is a soldier,
> Lieut. in the 15 Hussars, but now on half pay. I have sent him to
> Berlin for a year or eighteen months. He is said to be a very active
> officer . . . I saw him shoot a black-cock with a single ball at upwards
> of eighty yards. He is besides a true-hearted honest fellow that never
> gives me any vexation . . . The younger brother whose character is
> literary is to go to Oxford soon and I think will do well . . . I ought
> to tell you of the precocious talents of my grandchild, but magnani-
> mously resist the temptation—enough that he brays for the ass,
> smokes for grandpapa—and thrusts out his tongue for the large
> wolfhound which licks his face, and all this—hear it ye Gods! at
> only twelve months.

He was being a little brave about Gilnockie who was costing him a
great deal of money. It was not the boy's fault that, on a reduction of
forces, the 18th had been disbanded. The anxious parent had seen the
Duke of York when in London, and another of the royal brothers, the
Duke of Cambridge, had consented to take the boy into his own regiment,
the 15th, the King's Hussars. That meant a complete new outfit. Before
he had left home his father had engaged Allan to paint him full-length
for the new library at Abbotsford. Scott was very pleased with the portrait
which he thought was almost worthy of Van Dyck. (Allan was really a
painter of historical pictures telling a story.) Scott was thankful to have
reclaimed his son from his outpost command at Cappoquin on the Black-
water. When Dominie Thomson had heard of his pupil's prowess, he had
gone off prancing with joy and making extravagantly ferocious actions
with his staff. But Scott had written to warn the young officer that
peasants in Ireland were not like peasants in Scotland, and now that he had

Abbotsford, 1837

By Thomas Allom (1804–72), engraved by Thomas Prior (1809–80) for Vol. I of Scotland *by William Beattie (1838).*

been the means of killing six or seven, he must not go out on long solitary expeditions shooting or fishing, as he was accustomed to do at home. William Rose's brother, Sir George, was British Minister at Berlin, and by February Sir Walter heard that the lieutenant was moving in the best society, had been invited to a boar hunt by Prince Radziwill and several military reviews. He was studying French and German from lodgings in Unter den Linden.

Mr Williams, who had himself lost relatives in India, wished that Charles should go on to a University, not Hertford East India College. Scott began to think of his younger son for the Law—the Scottish Bar.

The only member of the family to cause concern this season was Mrs Carpenter. She had left Scotland after a prolonged stay much improved in health, in fact, too well. She was thinking of remarriage and going to Bath. If she married, her fortune would pass instanter to her new husband. It appeared that this *beau* was considerably younger than herself. It was obvious that she had few vestiges of beauty left and believed herself in failing health. Scott applied himself to the problem calmly, and decided that what she really needed was not a young mate but a competent accountant. She said herself that she needed someone to help her with her money. Her brother-in-law did not wish to deprive her of a chance of happiness, but must face the possibility that she might find herself destitute. As the Dumergue family had been out of London when she had arrived from India, it had fallen to a member of the younger generation to look after her.

Mr Stephen Barber (of the house of Perrins, Barber and Co., 72 Cornhill), was the husband of Catherine Nicolson, and his firm had been the late Charles Carpenter's agents. He had not, in Scott's opinion, shown great intelligence in placing her up in Harley Street where she had been miserable, but he seemed businesslike and prepared to accept responsibility. He said that if Mrs Carpenter would not execute a proper Deed of Trust before her remarriage, the Scott children should be made Wards in Chancery. He said he suffered from the disability that the lady herself had never mentioned the idea of remarriage to him. All he heard came from his Aunt Jane. It was evidently enough. He was appointed Trustee for Mrs Carpenter, and John Richardson for the Scott children. It was pointed out to "the poor helpless lady" who was "extremely reasonable", that every man of honour was not only willing but desirous that such arrangements should be made before marriage as would protect her property and independence, should his own prospects be overtaken by some unforeseen calamity. Finding her so well looked after, the young *beau* faded from the scene, and although warmly invited to do so, Mrs Carpenter did not come to occupy her room at Abbotsford next summer.[20]

But this was as well, for as early as March Scott had confirmation of a report current when he was last in London that "our Fat Friend" intended to inspect his northern kingdom. A visit to Ireland last year had been a success, though it had been awkward that before he landed he had heard of the death of his wife. He had remained invisible for five days, then fulfilled his programme. He was said to have been rather unwilling to go to Scotland where domestic morality was strict. (Scott accepted that his monarch was having a sad time of it between the jealousies of his two Sultanas—Lady Hertford displaced by Lady Conyngham.) But the Government told His Majesty it would make a bad impression if he spent a great deal on a continental tour. He ordered a kilt—two kilts.

VI

The *Royal George* anchored in Leith roads at 2 p.m. on Wednesday, August 14th, and the Right Hon. Robert Peel went on board. When he returned to the quayside, an officer went with him who announced that in view of the weather His Majesty had decided to put off his landing till twelve noon tomorrow. The next craft to come alongside the royal yacht was the barge of the Admiral on the station, Sir John Beresford, bringing "several distinguished persons". "What?" said the king, "Sir Walter Scott? The man in Scotland I most wish to see. Let him come up." Sir Walter had a duty to perform. He had been entrusted by the ladies of Edinburgh with a silver badge set with river-pearls and cairngorms in the shape of a St Andrew's Cross. The Gaelic inscription meant "Long Life to the King of Scotland". Rain was coming down in torrents. Sir Walter struck just the right note with one of his comical broad Scottish imitations of a West Highland innkeeper who had once greeted him with the words "Gude guide us, Sir Walter! I cannot think how it comes to rain this way just as you, of all men in the world, should come to see us! I can only say for my part I'm just ashamed of the weather." The king called for a bottle of Highland whisky. He gladly agreed that Sir Walter might take away as a memento the glass out of which his sovereign had toasted him. Scott was wearing his uncomfortable Windsor uniform. He stowed the glass away "in what he conceived to be the safest portion of his dress".

An awning had been rigged up on the quarter-deck, and as a great many boats had come out, despite the swell and downpour, the king graciously walked up and down and returned greetings. A good number of his subjects were able to see that he was a fine figure of a man, wearing a blue coat lined with yellow, and over it a blue military *surtout*, with a large flowing cape, blue pantaloons and boots, and on his head a travelling cap with an oilskin cover. He was to need it.

At dinner Sir Walter Scott sat on his right hand. The next guest to be announced was Mr Peel again. An express from the Prime Minister had brought him the news that Lord Londonderry, Foreign Secretary, had committed suicide. The king was much shocked but not entirely surprised. At his last interview with Lord Londonderry, he had begged him to see a doctor. His manner had been extraordinary. Scott remembered that in Paris, he had told a full audience at his supper table at the British Embassy how he had seen the awful vision of the Radiant Boy.

Sir Walter could tell nobody that he himself had received a far worse shock that morning. His greatest friend, Will Erskine, promoted to the Bench only six months before as Lord Kinnedder, had died at dawn, done to death like Shakespeare's Hero by slanderous tongues. The king retired with the Home Secretary, and Scott made his way in wet dusk towards his home which for the past three weeks had been no home for an honest man—just a pageant-master's headquarters. Will Erskine had always seemed to Lockhart an incomprehensible person to have been his father-in-law's most intimate friend. He was terrified of so many things. He shuddered if he saw a party setting off for coursing; he found a cool meditative angler abominable. He would dismount at the slightest provocation, and weep at the sight of a magnificent landscape, or the sound of a fine strain of music. He had gradually sunk into melancholy after his wife's death, and the realisation that he was being slandered by an unknown enemy had acted like slow poison. "One of the most sensitive and tender-hearted of God's creatures", he had simply turned his face to the wall and died.[21] An apothecary called Burt, married to a woman of higher rank, had been the object of jealousy by a business rival. This fellow had started a whispering campaign that Lord Kinnedder had seduced Mrs Burt and that a divorce was pending.

It gave Scott particular pain that Erskine had been sinking at a time when he was absolutely unable to be with him as much as he would have wished. The whole business of the royal visit seemed to have descended upon him. He considered that it was probably for the best that they had received such short notice in the end. There was less time for absurdities. He was getting sixty callers a day. Their eventual official notice had been so uncomprehending, so English—"about the

Twelfth of August". "Though scarce with the purpose of going to the moors, I should think," wrote Sir Walter to Morritt.

Lockhart saw that—

> The local magistrates threw themselves on him for advice and direction about the merest trifles and he had to arrange everything, from the ordering of a procession to the cut of a button and the embroidering of a cross. Ere the greenroom in Castle Street had dismissed provosts and bailies and deacon-conveyors of the trades of Edinburgh, it was sure to be besieged by swelling chieftains, who could not agree on the relative positions their clans had occupied at Bannockburn, which they considered as constituting the authentic precedent for determining their own places, each at the head of his little theatrical *tail*, in the line of the King's escort . . . It required all Scott's unwearied good humour and imperturbable power of face to hear in becoming gravity, the sputtering controversies of such fiery rivals . . .

He had, however, the first essential of a successful organiser—he could depute. He had a small committee of assistants and advisers, the Lord Provost of Ravelston, James Skene, and for the services, a figure of unassailable authority, General David Stewart of Garth, author of *The History of the Highland Regiments*, a veteran of the campaigns in Egypt and the Peninsula, now commanding officer of the civilian Celtic Society.

When Scott had last been in London, Murray had introduced him to the Reverend Thomas Crabbe, descriptive poet ("Though Nature's sternest poet yet the best," wrote Byron). They had corresponded since 1812: Crabbe was intending a northern tour and Scott had invited him to Edinburgh and Tweedside, mentioning dates when he might not be available and concluding that his elderly guest would wish to avoid the royal visit. But he had come a week ago. When Scott got back to Castle Street, this evening, sad, weary and wet, he found Mr Crabbe. "The royal gift was forgotten—the ample skirt of the coat within which it had been packed, and which he had hitherto held cautiously in front of his person, slipped back to its more usual position." He dropped down beside Crabbe and uttered a yell. His wife imagined he must have alighted upon a pair of scissors. But very little harm had been done except to the valued memento—crushed to atoms.

Scott was only once able to take Crabbe out himself—for a scramble up to Muscat's Cairn and St Anthony's chapel. He had to call in Lockhart, who decided that no Englishman in modern times had ever arrived in

Scotland with a scantier store of information about the country. But the venerable parson was delighted with everything, and without understanding much, marvelled at the machinery Scott had set in motion. This was indeed remarkable. A letter to Macleod of Macleod was a fair specimen of his methods.

> The King is coming after all. Arms and men are the best thing we have to show him. Do come, and bring half a dozen or half a score of clansmen, so as to look like an Island Chief as you are. Highlanders are what he will like best to see, and the masquerade of the Celtic Society will not do without some of the real stuff, to bear it it out. Pray do come and do not forget to bring the Bodyguard for the credit of Old Scotland and your own old house.

The chieftains had responded competitively, and their followers made Sir Walter Scott's Edinburgh house their rendezvous. About three hundred Highlanders paraded in front of it with pibroch and banner. On August 10th, he had arrayed himself in the "Garb of old Gaul"—his tartan was Campbell in honour of a great-grandmother. He was going to review the Celtic Society in Queen Street Gardens and give them a set of colours. A number of members, in full costume, had been invited to breakfast. When he entered the dining-parlour he had surprised a capital scene. Mr Crabbe, dressed in the highest style of professional neatness as a clergyman of the Church of England, was attempting to explain himself to a party of kilted chieftains in French which he understood to be the universal language! They had all been talking to one another in Gaelic. They, for their part, had decided the polite old man must be some French abbé. They could not take orders from anyone except their own leader and Sir Walter, and in spite of all the efforts of the committee Glengarry had a row with the Celtic Society. ("I was in hopes they would have fought it out with sword and target and stop'd at the first blood drawn, which would have cool'd their spirits without doing any great harm".) It had been about a piper.

Lockhart was on duty on the great day of the king's landing, in the character of a volunteer cavalryman. He could not afterwards remember if it was on this grand occasion or another that he beheld his father-in-law seated in an open carriage and four, dressed in Highland costume, with General Garth seated beside him and Peter Matheson on the box wearing a cocked hat and flaxen wig, which were never again seen after the royal fortnight.

The morning of Thursday 15th was that typical in Scottish late summer after a day of storm—quite idyllic. When His Majesty was seated in an open landau drawn by eight bays, Glengarry, whose sense of drama was strong, forcing his way through every obstacle, advanced close to the carriage crying, "Your Majesty is welcome to Scotland!" All the way to Holyrood House there was a continued roar from the populace thronging the streets, packing the stands and even perched on roofs. It was said that a hundred guineas was asked and given for windows in a good flat over-looking the route. The king, who was looking at everything with fixed attention, was observed to be overcome by emotion when he came to the Tollhouse where the banner read—"Descendant of the immortal Bruce, thrice welcome". The Lord Provost got through, without a hitch, the business of offering and receiving back again the keys of the capital. On reaching Princes Street and beholding the dramatic panorama of the junction of the New and Old Towns, "How superb!" cried the king. He entered his palace to the sound of shouts of triumph, a royal salute and bands playing "God Save the King". He moved upstairs with a firm step. The scene in the presence chamber was very grand. His Majesty sat on a throne (imported from London) and received the Regalia, the Lord Provost and Magistrates (with an address), the Judges, and the Captain-General and Council of the Royal Company of Archers, his bodyguard.

It had been arranged that he should hold ceremonies at Holyrood House, but be the guest of the Duke of Buccleuch at Dalkeith House six miles out of town. His Grace would be sixteen in November. His uncle and family had all come north with him and the house was staffed by many of the late duke's household. Mr Florence, the arch-cook, was here. Two of the young Ladies Montagu Scott would be going to the drawing-room. There was a dinner party at Dalkeith that night, and the king was in excellent health and spirits. On Friday he was not visible—but Saturday saw great things. For the *levée* he appeared in Highland cos-tume. (On coming out of his dressing-room at Dalkeith his comment had been "I cannot help smiling at myself".) He said he believed he had received no less than two thousand gentlemen, and an Archer who had counted said they had passed through at the rate of fifteen a minute. Sir Walter Scott was down to present Captain Adam Ferguson, one Pro-fessor ("Christopher North"—a triumph), two doctors (Hamilton and Ross, highly thought of by the Lockharts), one advocate (his son-in-law), one country neighbour, two chieftains and one artist, David Wilkie, R.A. After this ordeal came a Privy Council but lasting only half-an-hour.

On Sunday the king was allowed off-duty again. Scott wrote to Gilnockie that His Majesty had never gone out, but the press said he had, once in the park at Dalkeith to try a horse. Monday was very solemn—a court and closet audience. The reception of the General Assembly of the Church of Scotland, and the Universities of the Kingdom, was from the throne in the presence chamber. For the Episcopal clergy the monarch retired to the closet. The Highland Society followed, and that night there was another dinner-party at Dalkeith at which the Duke of Argyll, President of the Society, was chief guest. Tuesday was the drawing-room. Sir Walter had been told by fluttered compatriots that he knew all about courts, from his London experiences. He said it was a case of the purblind leading the blind. But Mr Mash of the Lord Chamberlain's Office had been sent south as long ago as May for a tour of inspection, and had come again to settle on July 26th, none too soon. Sir Walter had crossed swords with him once and forever. The official had begun by talking continually about what had been done in Ireland last year. "I beg, Mr Mash, to hear no more of Ireland. Ireland is a Lordship; when His Majesty comes amongst us he comes to his ancient kingdom of Scotland, and must be received according to her ancient usages. If you persist in bringing in English customs, we turn about, one and all, and leave you. You take the responsibility on yourself." After this Mr Mash was quiet, but over the drawing-room he was in his element. There were five hundred ladies wanting to attend, and press reports were fascinating: *Countess of Elgin*—a rich white French satin dress, trimmed with a double flounce of magnificent Brussels point, looped and intermixed with *blanc de hout*, and laburnum, over which an elegant French lilac silk train, trimmed with a handsome garniture of satin tulle. A superb headdress of feathers and diamonds . . .

The Honourable Mrs George Forbes, presented by the Duchess of Atholl. A white net dress richly embroidered in appliqué and elegantly trimmed in festoons of blush roses. *Corsage à la vierge. Manteau*, white satin, trimmed to correspond. Headdress, feathers and profusion of diamonds. *This dress was quite unique.*

The costumes and arrangements of the Scott family had evidently been the result of much conference. Lady Scott was presented by the wife of the head of Sir Walter's ostensible profession—Lady Melville. She wore gold brocade, ornamented in a novel fashion with a gold rose and thistle, and presented her daughters and two of Lockhart's sisters. They all wore white and silver, and pink trains. "Linton" Ferguson's elderly bride was presented by Lady Montagu, who extended her kindness to a débutante niece of Mrs Ferguson, Miss Jane Jobson of Lochore, a very pretty girl and an heiress. Nobody tripped or fell flat.

Scott wrote to William Laidlaw, "Mama, Sophia and Anne were dreadfully frightened of course, and afterwards they could hardly remember anything." However, the king had actually spoken to them and they were all kissed in due form.

There was another dinner-party at Dalkeith the next day, and Sir Walter was much struck by a *gaffe* of his young chieftain. The king had the Duke of Buccleuch on his right hand and kept on sending him to ask the names of tunes played by Gow's famous band. "What are they playing now? Come Buccleuch, you are the youngest man in the company and must make yourself useful." To the horror of Sir Walter, the boy came back with the answer that it was "the old song, 'My wife is come back again'." "Oh then!" said the king, "I'm off." He went to see Gow and said, "From my earliest years I have always been fond of Scottish music and have often listened to it with pleasure, but have never had so great a treat as this evening." Before retiring at midnight he sent the band a copious supply of Atholbrose, but when somebody offered his young host a glass of liqueur he interposed majestically, "No! no! it is too strong for His Grace!" The young duke, to Scott's delight, was showing promising signs of taking his responsibilities seriously. He did think that he ought to lead in contributing to the restoration of Melrose Abbey.

Sir Walter had taken immense trouble over the stately procession of the monarch, preceded by the Regalia, from Holyrood House to the castle. He had written in hot haste to Terry to ask him to get the historic sword of the Marquess of Montrose out of the firm who were making a scabbard, and if that was not possible, anyway to send up the sword by mail-coach. It was to be carried by his kinsman, the Knight Marischal, Sir Alexander Keith. There had been disputes about who should carry the crown and the sceptre. In the end the king had come down on the side of the Duke of Hamilton for the crown, but a committee was to sit to judge between his claims and those of Lord Douglas. As to the sceptre, a son acting for the Countess of Sutherland had performed until yesterday morning, when he had sailed for Dunrobin Castle, and a younger son of the Earl of Moray had been called in.

When His Majesty in his carriage and six reached the Netherbow, "six beautiful girls, clad in white, with blue sashes over their shoulders, from which depended a St Andrew's cross, and their heads adorned with wreaths", went before him scattering flowers. Scott had been on the scene early. Mr Peel had said that it was impossible that he should get through the crowds without being recognised and proved right. He noticed Sir

Walter was greeted everywhere with enthusiasm. Again there was the rolling cheer. The king was in Highland dress again; everything was perfect with one exception. "The weather was peculiarly unpropitious." The windows of the coach had to be closed, but he bravely alighted at the barrier-gate of the castle to receive the keys, and again at the top platform above the half-moon battery. Attendants reminded him that he was getting very wet. "Oh! never mind! I must cheer the people." He waved his hat repeatedly, and said "This is wonderful!" and "What a sight!" (It was regretted that the thick fog which brooded over the landscape deprived him of a famous view.) He drove straight back to Dalkeith from Holyrood House in his wet clothes. He had brought north with him Sir William Knighton, a court physician generally believed to advise him on more than his health. (When this character departed, he had come to an agreement that Sir Walter Scott was to write to him privately about Scottish affairs, particularly political.)

It was noticed that His Majesty was remarkably abstemious both as to food and drink, though Atholbrose was his favourite beverage. When he paid afternoon visits to two prominent subjects with country houses—Lord Melville and Lord Lothian—although a superb collation had been set out, he did not partake.

As before, a very wet day was followed by one of uncommon beauty. The Cavalry Review on Portobello sands, "the grandest military spectacle ever witnessed in Scotland in modern times", was blessed by unbroken sunshine. On the Saturday night the Lord Provost, Magistrates and Town Council offered a banquet in the Parliament House where three hundred sat down and the arrangements were said by Sir Walter to be far superior to those at the Coronation. Two of his family, his son Charles and nephew Walter from Canada, were pages, in suits of scarlet and white satin. There was much drinking of toasts, the first being a bumper in honour of the Lord Provost, who arose Sir William Arbuthnot, Baronet. Next the king gave "All the chieftains and all the clans of Scotland and may God bless the Land of Cakes". Later Lord Errol gave "Sir Walter Scott, and thanks to him for the share he had in bringing us together", and Sir Walter said he really wanted power to express his feelings—he had merely thrown out a few hints to Magistrates who were ready to command and had to deal with a people equally willing to obey.

His Majesty's behaviour at a service at St Giles's on the second Sunday of his stay aroused approbation, and for his part he was struck by the utter reverential silence of the enormous crowds through which he passed. They simply uncovered.

He had attended a ball at the Assembly Rooms in George Street and asked for Scottish airs and dances—reels and strathspeys. He was to go to another, offered by the Caledonian Hunt. The royal fortnight was drawing to a close, and he spent what would be his last day at Holyrood House being shown over the palace privately. He had asked that the apartments used by his royal ancestors should be left undisturbed. He lifted a blanket on Queen Mary's bed and remarked how well it had worn. Suddenly, the visit had to be extended for a day. His Majesty would very much like to go to the theatre. Sir Walter Scott saw Mr William Henry Murray, Manager, and it was arranged that *Rob Roy* should be put on. This was agreed to be one of the most popular of the great occasions. It was also the only one at which the loyal crowd got out of hand—a wet night. The king had not appeared that afternoon at another wholly open-air ceremony—"the laying of a foundation stone on the Calton Hill of a monument upon the model of the Pantheon, in testimony of the nation's gratitude for successes in the late war".

There was a final dinner-party at Dalkeith at which His Majesty told Sir Walter that he hoped to return to Scotland frequently, and Sir Walter gave the toast, "The Chief of the Clans, the King". Next morning the rain continued to come down relentlessly. It could only be represented as his northern kingdom weeping for the departure of her good king. This took place from Hopetoun House on the Firth of Forth. The owner was Captain-General of the Royal Company of Archers, and they lined the many steps of the palatial entrance as the king drove up in a plain travelling carriage, escorted by Royal Scots Greys. Under the colonnades which connected the two wings of the house, ranges of tables had been set up, covered with the richest and most substantial viands. A multitude of tenants, farmers' wives and daughters dressed in their Sunday best had stood on the roofs of the colonnades and wings of the building, bidding defiance to the pelting of the storm, for several hours. An elegant *déjeuner à la fourchette* was waiting and during it the sons of the house were intro-duced—ten boys and an infant daughter. "Good God, is it possible!" exclaimed the king to his beautiful and youthful-looking hostess, and to the youngest son, "Is that a new frock, my little man?" Afterwards, in the saloon, the names of Captain Adam Ferguson, Deputy Keeper of the Regalia, and Mr Henry Raeburn, the famous portrait-painter, having been called, both received the honour of knighthood. The king drove off at 3.15 for Port Edgar, and the *Royal George* passed through Leith Roads at 5 and stood over to the coast of Fife.

Sir Walter had made two requests—for the return of the historic cannon

Mons Meg from the Tower of London to Edinburgh Castle, and for the restoration of the Scottish peerages forfeited in the "affairs" of 1715 and 1745. Both were duly granted. Sophia wrote to Miss Millar that it had been lovely to see the old halls at Holyrood lighted up again after so many years, and His Majesty had said to her father, "Never king was better received by his people and never king felt it so."

When the king landed at Greenwich, Croker was waiting to receive him, and he at once began talking "all about our friend Scott". Some silly or malicious person had said that there had been some coolness between them, but it was utterly false and he was "in every respect pleased and gratified and *grateful* for the devoted attention paid him". Croker passed it all on at once as was intended. Of course there had been some jealousy of Scott's leading rôle, and a good many people, including Lockhart—a Lowlander—thought that the king must have received the impression that they were a nation of Highlanders. "The bagpipe and the tartan are the order of the day."[22] Sophia ended her letter to Miss Millar with the news that "Abbotsford is now finished up to the top storey and really is quite a palace." The foundation stone had been laid in February.

Scott had been exhausted by his efforts and anxieties, and had come out in an exasperating body-rash. He gathered that if this had not happened he might have been very ill. He departed to Abbotsford "to live the life of a cow".[23]

NOTES

1. Lockhart's father was the second son of William Lockhart, Laird of Birkhill and Wicketshaw, Lanarkshire. John Gibson Lockhart was his eldest son by his second wife, a granddaughter of Henry Erskine, third Baron Cardross, and niece of David Erskine, fourth Baron Cardross, who also succeeded his kinsman as ninth Earl of Buchan. William Lockhart, half-brother of John Gibson Lockhart, purchased, in 1819. the property of Milton Lockhart. His maternal grandmother, Violet Inglis, had been heiress of Corehouse. Letters, VI, 151.
2. Lockhart, V, 61 n.
3. Ibid., III, 373-6.
4. Letters, VI, 173.
5. Ibid., 173.
6. Count Itterburg, the Young Pretender, was said to have devoted his time in Scotland to the study of military matters, and "roughing it" on dark and stormy nights, making his way across country. Such preparations were traditionally those made by Prince Charles Edward Stewart, before setting off for Scotland. But the Bernadotte prince

Oscar, who adopted a liberal policy, was perfectly acceptable to Sweden. Prince Gustavus became a Field Marshal in the Austrian army and died at Pillnitz in 1877 leaving a daughter who became Queen of Saxony. Journal, I, 385–6.

7. The Rev. John Williams (1792–1858), Archdeacon of Cardigan, became the first Rector of Edinburgh Academy.

8. Letters, VI, 341–86. Lockhart had to be dissuaded from coming south when Christie returned from France to stand trial in April 1821. He was acquitted, as "Scoundrel" Scott had sent the challenge, and Christie had fired his first shot in the air, so the fatal shot was considered accidental. But although the Duke of Wellington, Croker and many more thoroughly supported Lockhart, the fallen man had sympathisers, including Byron. It was objected that Lockhart had not answered the accusations (three of them absurd) of his assailant, and although not the proprietor of Blackwood's, he was a regular contributor who wrote provocatively. Doubts of his courage gradually faded. This affair helped to kill The Beacon, a Tory magazine published only from January to September 1821, to the foundation of which Sir Walter Scott had donated a hundred pounds. Scott did not contribute any articles but was mistakenly identified as having written a violent one involving a leading Scottish Whig, named Gibson, who threatened him with a duel.

9. Mrs Carpenter outlived Scott and all his children, dying in 1862. Lockhart and Grierson mistakenly place some of the letters about her in 1820 not 1821.

10. Letters, VI, 209, 345, 452–4; Lockhart, III, 387, 501. "John Cock-a-Pistol" was so named because he lived on the site where the Battle of Melrose (1526) had begun.

11. Letters, VI, 387–91, 423–44, 450–3, 482–4, 490–2.

12. Villiers Surtees became one of the Judges of the Supreme Court in Mauritius.

13. Letters, VI, 338. Lockhart, III, 433–5.

14. Letters, VI, 397–405, 417–19, George IV, Joanna Richardson (1966), 211–212.

15. Letters, VI, 479. Lockhart, III, 460.

16. Letters, VI, 488. Lockhart, III, 468.

17. Letters, VI, 488.

18. "Memoirs of William Dalgleish, butler to Sir Walter Scott", Cornhill Magazine, N.S. LXX and LXXI. Mr Mitton, the editor, discovered them in the offices of Messrs. Black, publishers.

19. Letters, VII, 116–121. Lockhart, III, 528.

20. Letters, VII, 32, 47, 53, 72, 181.

21. Scott made searching enquires which satisfied him that the accusation against Kinnedder was entirely slanderous. Letters, VII, 221–2, Lockhart, III, 504–6, IV, 47–48, 66.

22. An attractive octavo leather-bound volume of 338 pages, Historical Account of His Majesty's VISIT TO SCOTLAND by Robert Mudie, was printed and published by Messrs Oliver and Boyd of Edinburgh High Street in the year of the visit and quickly ran into four editions. It was dedicated by permission to George IV and included eyewitnesses' descriptions of every ceremony, four panoramic line engravings (very long, folded in) and, largest of all, "A Plan of the Grand Banquet in Parliament House", with the tables set for the first course, and menus. See also Letters, VII, 193, 212–32, 241–3, 259, 262–3. Lockhart, IV, Chapter LVI. Tom Moore was told by Crabbe on August 19th, 1824, that the king had disliked Scott "pushing himself forward so officiously", but this was denied by the king.

23. Dr James Corson, who has made a detailed study of the architectural drawings and original drawings, assures the author that the whole of Abbotsford was planned by William Atkinson. Statements which have appeared in many books claiming that the first part of Abbotsford was designed by Edward Blore are entirely without foundation.

XV

Happy Days

1823–1825

I

PEVERIL OF THE PEAK WAS PUBLISHED IN EARLY JANUARY 1823. IT HAD been held up by what Scott described as "the Royal Row". But he had attacked it again when he got back to Abbotsford, and as soon as that was done had gone on to a novel staged in mediaeval France—the adventures of a Scottish archer—Quentin Durward. He had written to Joanna Baillie wishing her "Many merry New Years. Ours will be rather a sad one."

There had been minor set-backs, such as the death of Hay Donaldson, the agent whom he had recommended so successfully to Lord Montagu; but a Mr John Gibson, highly qualified, stepped into that big job. Scott had given up for the second time the idea of a spring trip to the Continent, perhaps taking Mama and Anne and Charles. Charles was going to Brasenose College, Oxford, and Charlotte had asthma. Nor could he think of going off on a foreign tour alone with his handsome soldier son, leaving Charlotte to the care of Anne. He never ceased to miss "Sophia's constant good-humour and good sense".

He was delighted with the preparations he had made for adding association objects to his new wing at Abbotsford—a bed once the property of Queen Mary, two chairs from the Villa Borghese, Rome (sent by Constable), "the most splendid China wall-paper"—enough for the drawing-room and two bedrooms, gift of Captain Hugh Scott, a younger son of Raeburn, late of the East India Company's Marine Service. He supposed now that the drawing-room curtains would have to be silk damask. For the library he was going to have superfine crimson cloth from Galashiels "made out of mine own wool".[1]

Only to his old friend Mistress Baillie could he pour out what had made him miserable since November. "My brother, the only relative left me out of a large family . . . is dying in Canada, under the dreadful circumstances of debt and an unprovided family." He had received a visit at Abbotsford from an officer of the 70th Regiment, Major Huxley. This was the very satisfactory husband of Brother Tom's daughter Jessie. Poor Mrs Tom had said when she wrote to congratulate on the baronetcy that it was a pleasure to be able to write on such an occasion. She feared her communications were generally those of a Raven—prophesying doom. Now Tom was in trouble again. It sounded very serious. He needed £1,440 to put his regimental accounts right. A year later Sir Walter was still fearing he might be called upon for another sum, of a thousand pounds, "kept hanging over my head as security for my unfortunate brother", and the present moment was inopportune, for he would have to produce as much for Gilnockie's new commission. He asked first for a clear statement of the worst. He told Mrs Tom, meanwhile, that if they were in want she could draw upon him for a hundred pounds, and there was plenty of room at Abbotsford for her and her nymphs. The only bright spots in that family seemed Jessie Huxley and her nursery, and Young Walter who had gone off for Addiscombe Military Academy, Croydon, through snow-drifts twelve feet high. The saga of poor Tom was solved on February 14th, 1823. He died, worn out mentally and physically. Sir Walter refused to lay claim to any of their late mother's property left to both sons; it must go to the girls. He wrote personally to Lord Palmerston about a widow's pension. It was, at any rate, a relief to hear that the complaint about irregularities in Tom's accounts dated apparently back to his Irish period—nothing since he had been in Canada.[2]

But there were also some amusing episodes this New Year. Sir Walter was the first President of the Bannatyne Club—devoted to printing rare Scottish books in private editions, on the lines of the London Roxburghe. That famous institution waggishly invited the Author of *Waverley* to dine.

Having "packed off Quentin Durward" he began a Scottish modern novel—about a little local watering-place. Laidlaw had put the idea into his head during a ride one day on the Eildon hills, above Melrose. When he had finished it, to his chagrin, Ballantyne could not allow a heroine who was a young lady of county family to have been seduced. Manners were changing. Old Mrs Keith of Ravelston had asked Sir Walter if he had ever seen the novels of Mrs Aphra Behn, a best-selling authoress of the days of Charles II. He admitted he did think he could get her a sight of some; but he did not advise it. However, to hear was to obey; so he sent off a packet sealed and labelled "Private and Confidential". Next time he saw her, she gave him back Aphra, neatly sealed again. "Take back your bonny Mrs Behn; and if you will take my advice, put her in the fire; for I found it impossible to get through the very first novel. But is it not a very odd thing that I, an old woman of eighty and upwards, sitting alone, feel myself ashamed to read a book which, sixty years ago, I have heard read aloud for the amusement of large circles, consisting of the first and most creditable society in London?"[3]

Gilnockie arrived in May and went to bed with influenza. Everyone got it, but Scott only slightly. Sophia's darling infant caught it and was very ill. Charles and Villiers Surtees were coming again, and amongst the literary lions expected to a house in which masons and carpenters were still in evidence, Miss Maria Edgeworth.

II

The Great Maria had corresponded with him for years and there had been more than one cancelled project. Suddenly, she was coming. He wrote joyfully to say he would be ready as guide and host for meals in Edinburgh. Castle Street could not accommodate three Miss Edgeworths. At Abbotsford there would be no difficulty.

The ladies arrived at Castle Street after 10 o'clock on the fine night of June 6th. A letter from Sir Walter had said he would call for them at Gibbs Hotel, 32 Abercromby Place, about 12 noon on Saturday (tomorrow). A postscript said the Scott family coach was licensed to take six, and a second postscript that his wife insisted that they should come round now. "No dressing to be thought of." The Laird of Staffa, a Highland chieftain, had promised to look in, bringing one of his clansmen to sing boat songs. There were three Miss Edgeworths—the Great Maria, bird-like, with a Duke of Wellington's nose, tiny, fifty-six, but quite as agile as her two half-sisters. Harriet was twenty-two, pretty, very clever; Sophy, twenty, musical, curly-headed, very pretty. Sophy had cried, "My dear! it's too late." But Maria had said it was best to accept a cordial invitation from *Walter Scott*. She had never been one for dress. She could not wait to see Walter Scott. A hackney-coach was called and they were struck by the beauty and magnificence of Edinburgh streets. At number 39 the hall was lighted, and the moment the door was opened they heard happy songs. "Three servants in livery. 'The Miss Edgeworths' sounded from hall to landing place . . . I heard the first sound of Walter Scott's kind voice . . . The Miss Edgeworths COME." The room was lighted only by one globe lamp. A circle were singing loud and beating time. "Miss Edgeworth, this is so kind of you." All stopped in an instant.

Her first impression was that he was neither so large nor so heavy as she had been led to expect. He was more lame, but not unwieldy. His countenance was benevolent and full of genius, but his expression perfectly natural as if he thought of nothing but making others happy. He introduced his wife, Staffa, his daughter, son-in-law, Mr Clarke and Mr Sharpe, old friends. Maria politely desired that they should go on with what her entry had interrupted, and they were soon off again, the boatman uttering astonishing roars in Gaelic, and the company stamping time, repeating the chorus, and waving the silk handkerchiefs by which they were linked. All seemed delighted except Lady Scott, a French-woman, much dressed—with a cockatoo of scarlet feathers on one side of a scarlet turban. She said, in broken English, "Scott, we had better have done with this now. I was just saying that if anybody from the street had looked in upon us they must have thought us all mad—I am sure."

Lady Scott was so exactly like descriptions of her that Maria felt she had met her before. "She must have been very handsome—French, dark, large eyes—civil and good-natured."

They had a family supper at a round table.

> The impression left on my mind that night was that Walter Scott is one of the best bred men I ever saw—with all the exquisite politeness he knows so well how to describe—which is of no particular school or country . . . As I sat beside him at supper I could not believe he was a stranger and forgot he was a great man.

The son-in-law, Mr Lockhart, was very handsome, very silent. Scott said he was a devoted husband and father but reserved, and unaccustomed to ladies' company. He seemed to be deaf which must be inconvenient for a rising advocate, but Harriet had heard that he was not rising as he spent his time writing novels. He had eyed them all very sharply, and had a bewildered look when addressed. Next morning it all seemed like a happy dream, but at noon Lady Scott appeared, resplendent in rouge and flowers and veil, and they called for Scott who came out of the Courts with a joyous face, and gave them an unforgettable day of sightseeing accompanied by informed anecdote.

Among the Northern Lights whom he displayed to them was Sir Henry Raeburn, who had at the moment in his studio two portraits of him, one for Lord Montagu, the other for the artist to keep. Scott had in past years been inclined to be critical of Raeburn, but he knew now a sad and sufficient reason for the old man having a reputation for pot-boiling and hardfistedness. He had been overtaken by financial disaster in 1808 following the failure of his son's West Indian business. He was now in easier circumstances and had seemed in good health and spirits at the recent Blair Adam meeting. When he heard that Raeburn had died suddenly, Scott wrote at once to London, trying to interest Knighton, Lord Melville and Peel into candidature of his great friend Charles Kirkpatrick Sharpe, "an amateur but a gentleman". He was too late: Wilkie succeeded Raeburn as King's Painter for Scotland.4

III

The Miss Edgeworths went on for their Highland tour and Maria and Susan were both taken ill, but the Scottish hotels were so good and so reasonable. Those at Callander and Loch Katrine had been "raised by the genius of Scott almost as quickly and as surely as the slave of the lamp raises the palace of Aladdin". They drew near to Abbotsford very weary, on the last Sunday in July. Lockhart remembered it as having been one of the most brilliant he had ever known. But it was half past nine and nearly dark when the Irish ladies were roused to hope by seeing an immense dog, and soon after, three gentlemen with burning cigars in their mouths, walking along. Their carriage turned in at a gate and down an avenue. It drew up in front of a pile of buildings which looked enormous in the dim light; they heard Sir Walter's kind voice. "Everything about you," said Maria, dismounting and looking around, "is exactly what one ought to have had wit enough to dream!"

They had come for a week but they stayed twelve days; everything was so delightful. Of the three men puffing cigars, the tallest turned out to be Lieutenant Scott, the son and heir. (Sir Walter had thought, when he arrived back from the Continent, that Gilnockie had acquired easy manners, but Maria found him, though alert, excessively shy.) The other two were a nephew from Canada and Addiscombe, and a friend of the younger son. In the house Harriet found Charles Scott much smaller than

Villiers Surtees; he was still a schoolboy while Surtees was already at Oxford. Charles looked rather cross, but he had now the Foreign Service in the back of his mind as a career and was surprisingly suave and attentive. There was a sad-looking Mr Campbell, and finally Mr Constable, the bookseller, very fat, very clean-shaven, rather sleeky and silky. He presently told the authoress confidentially that he had manuscripts of forty-five Scott novels in his possession.

Their bedrooms were small but comfortable, and Sophy's was beautifully furnished. Next morning the fun began. They set off soon after breakfast, five of them in the sociable, which was a very nice one lined with blue calico. Sophy rode Miss Anne Scott's bright bay pony with a white tail. It had been called "Queen Mab" like that which Willoughby had given Marianne Dashwood in *Sense and Sensibility*. Sophy had as escort Surtees and a rather nice young Pringle, a neighbour, who was at the Hertford Castle training college for the East India Civil Service. Some of his ancestors were buried in Melrose Abbey which was their first call, and after they had sufficiently admired that, they were joined by Lieutenant Scott on his famous black charger. They were being given dinner by the Lockharts at Chiefswood. Harriet was enchanted by this example of love in a cottage. Both Soph, as her family called Mrs Lockhart, and John were so nice in their own home, and the little boy "Donihue" John-Hugh, went so winningly from his mother's lap to his father's knee. On the ground floor, beside nursery and kitchen, there were only two rooms, but so elegantly furnished. The harp stood so picturesquely in the corner of the parlour where the windows looked out upon a green and wooded glen, with a bubbling stream running through it. There were roses and honeysuckle over the porch. The company asked to meet them were Sir Adam Ferguson and lady, and a quite horrible Miss Wells, companion to Mrs Jobson, sister of Lady Ferguson. John had drawn a caricature of Miss Wells fastening her garter. Sir Adam had a wine-red face and kept up a running battle of badinage with his wife. He had wooed her for five years and gone off to the Peninsula when she refused him, he thought finally. The Ettrick Shepherd had been asked, but failed. Maria was most disappointed. Perhaps, like John, he was not wild to meet a literary lioness. But John was completely *bon enfant* as a host, and today nobody noticed any deafness. Sir Walter had promised that his daughter's veal pies were the best in the world, but for this occasion she had ordered two hens which she asked her father to carve. The dish on which they had been served fell to pieces the moment he stuck knife and fork into one of the birds, and all the parsley butter joined them in flooding the table.

Lady Scott buzzed fuss and advice, but the master and mistress laughed so nicely.

Gradually the Edgeworths made all the necessary visits and met the Scotts' circle—Miss Pringles, Miss Fergusons, Laidlaws, Shortreeds, Mr Scott of Harden, Chief of the Family. At Mertoun they were asked to dine and stay all night, but though the house was old and large, it was cold—nothing to Abbotsford. Mrs Scott was very well-bred and fashion-able looking, with an English voice. The Chief was a little fat man with clarety cheeks, and gentlemanlike but with an expression of helpless though good-natured indolence. There were two young Scotts of Harden, Francis and George, very dark, very handsome, absolute bears. There were three young ladies dressed in blue and white, one little and black, and one tall and pale, and they thought the third must be another sister until she repaired to the pianoforte after dinner and began to yell. Mrs Scott of Harden said, "Of course she is a professional." She was a Miss Schetky, a sort of singing mistress.[5] Next morning on the way home in the landau, Sir Walter said "Miss Schetky ought to be assassinated", to which everyone cordially agreed.

They stopped in the village of Darnick to see the old oak panelling from Dunfermline Palace being got ready for the hall at Abbotsford. There was a green *calèche* with the leathern curtain up in front of the house when they came through the gates, and a servant had a letter of introduction for two foreign guests, a Prussian prince and a Swiss baron. They could stay only half an hour. The Edgeworths were told that when the shooting season opened, Abbotsford was never without a carriageful of unexpected strangers once or twice a week, introduced by some particular friend. Sir Walter divided guests into light and heavy birds—birds of passage who only flew in, and those who settled, like geese.

Blue days succeeded one another. They made a party to Dryburgh Abbey and picked up Sir Adam Ferguson at Gattonside and dined with Lord Buchan. He was an extraordinary old man and kept on talking while Maria tried to tell him she had once had the pleasure of meeting him in Edinburgh twenty years ago. After dinner they went to see the Abbey which Harriet thought a pretty but not very wonderful ruin, and a naughty son of Lord Buchan showed her his father's grave, all ready, with a cast of his face on it. They saw many scenes immortalised in the poems. There was a day fishing in Cauldshields Loch with dinner on the heathy bank, and another picnic by Thomas the Rhymer's waterfall in the Fairy Glen. The stone on which Maria sat was ever afterwards called "Edgeworth stone". Further afield they were shown all the upper scenery of the Yarrow, not Newark Castle only. The baskets were unpacked about sunset, beside the ruined chapel overlooking St Mary's Loch. Their kindly host scrambled to gather bluebells and heather which the young ladies must twine in their hair, and they sang and recited until it was time to go home under the softest of harvest moons.

Maria had some days in bed, slightly indisposed, and entirely revised her opinion of her hostess. Mrs Dugald Stewart, sister of Lord Corehouse, had told her at Kinneil House, before they got to Edinburgh, that Lady Scott was said to be a daughter of the late Lord Downshire, and drank. From Edinburgh, Maria had sent to Ireland rather an unflattering description.

> Lady Scott is very civil and always crowned with large full-blown roses—and the oddest, dressed-out, French, large black-eyed, brown-skinned and rouged figure I ever saw. Her hands are ever in motion picking at some imaginary pin in her sash or touching herself here and there, as if she was picking off hairs, and getting out her broken French–English sentences all the while making a prodigious number of faces with as much difficulty as if she had not landed from France above a week. But peace to her follies. She is only a fool, and does no body any harm—give her finery enough and she is happy.

From Abbotsford she took this all back.

> This Lady Scott has been in my opinion much belied and misrepresented. As to that of which she has been accused I can only say I have never seen the least symptom of it. But she has, I confess, so odd a manner, and speaks in such broken English Language and has such a quantity of BOTHER in all she attempts to say, that I do not wonder at SLANDERS having established the report, working upon the credulity of the foolish and the envy of the malicious. She and Sir Walter must excite a prodigious quantity of envy by their rise, prosperity, wealth-Castle-possessions style of living, and above all by his genius, and I must add Tory party principles.[6]

None of the Edgeworths had taken much to Anne, who was tart, but even she, thought Maria, improved on acquaintance. For Mrs Lockhart she had absolute adoration, and even Lockhart, "with his Spanish hidalgo look", could be very clever. Lockhart, for his part, had sent his impressions in a letter to Professor Wilson.

Miss Edgeworth is at Abbotsford and has been for some time; a little dark, bearded, sharp, withered, active, laughing, talking, impudent, fearless, outspoken, honest, Whiggish, unchristian, good-tempered, kindly, ultra-Irish body. I like her one day and damn her to perdition the next. She, Sir Adam, and the Great Unknown, are too much for any company.

Her father who was writing to Walter at Sandhurst presently let Anne slip in a note. "Did you hear of the scene when the Edgeworths went away? They wept for two days before they went and the great Miss E. ended by going into fits in my room. Harriet and Sophy do nothing but write to me—what an amiable family we *must be.*"

IV

After the Edgeworths had gone, birds of passage and geese continued to arrive all autumn. There was a happy day, quite like old times, when a party came over from Bowhill, the young duke, grown taller and stronger-looking, "really a most delightful young Man", wrote Anne to Miss Millar, and Lady Isabella and her intended, a cross-looking younger son of Lord Brownlow. Lady Anne had grown quite a beauty. She was the contemporary of Miss Anne Scott, who in childhood days had been heard to say plaintively she wished she was called Lady Anne. "It sounds so much prettier." The wedding took place in October and Lord Montagu wrote that they had toasted Lady Isabella Cust under Raeburn's portrait of Sir Walter, just hung—the last sitter Raeburn ever had.

The Robert Dundases came, and Rose for a month, and Davy, and Heber's young don from Oxford, Mr Adolphus, who had published a brochure proving that no one could have written the Waverley novels but Sir Walter Scott. They had to keep off the subject. Anne found him "more plain than pleasant", but he left behind in his Memoranda of his Abbotsford visit a charming little picture of his host.

At this period he used to be a good deal on horseback, and a pleasant sight it was to see the gallant old gentleman in his sealskin cap and short green jacket lounging along a field-side on his mare, Sibyl Grey, and pausing now and then to talk, with a serio-comic look, to a labouring man or woman, and rejoice them with some quaint saying in broad Scotch.

Mr Constable came again, with his wife, and Violet Lockhart, always welcome . . .

Lockhart's half-brother, who had inherited the Germiston estate from his mother, had married a Bath belle in a hurry, a complete Lydia Languish. Her mother, Lady Palliser, had died, and the young lady chose to shut herself up in a black room and behave like a passionate fool, to the distress of her good honest husband. Something quite the reverse had just happened at Abbotsford—gas-light! Anne was enchanted with it, and Sir Walter was proud, but Lockhart had just better not say what he thought. It made everyone look corpse-like, it smelt, it ran out, it broke down, and this house was remote. He could not think it was good for the old gentleman to sit hour after hour working just under this burning glare. The lamp above his writing-table hung, as it were, in the air. It was in the shape of a star. He loved it.

Sir William and Lady Rae came, and Sir Alexander Wood and lady, and the Skenes, with their daughters. Smith of Darnick had promised to put down a new floor so that they could have a dance at Christmas. The Lockharts would not be able to come this year. Sophia was expecting again. Her father was anxious. "Lockhart is perfectly and indeed exclusively, as far as his pleasures are concerned the husband and father, and *one* baby not very strong though lively and clever is a frail chance on which to stake happiness." He wished they would have Dr Clarkson senior, of Selkirk, who never lost a mother, but they preferred young Dr Hamilton "who is an ass and a theorist". In November he sent off *St Ronan's Well* to Ballantyne:

> Dear James,
>
> I was pretty well aware that the enclosed was either a hit or a miss. I am glad you think it is the former.

He had never himself cared for it, but although intellectual critics, with the exception of Sydney Smith, held somewhat aloof, next summer Innerleithen sprouted smart new hotels and became a proper tourist centre. Some people said that Melrose and Peebles should be allowed a share of the takings. A St Ronan's Border Games was advertised, with the Ettrick Shepherd as Captain of the bowmen in Lincoln green amongst whom Sir Walter was enrolled. A stage version of the novel, brought on at the Royal Theatre in Edinburgh, was packed out. Mr Murray was great as Touchwood.

Mrs Tom Scott from Canada had arrived with her daughters, Anne (named for the old grandmother) and Eliza. The poor exhausted mother fell ill; Eliza seemed to have some liver complaint. She was only thirteen, but Anne was out of her teens and had refused several officers; a good sensible lass. They had gone first to MacCulloch relations in Ayr, but had been briefly to Abbotsford and were coming again for Christmas, which would make it a little sad. Sir Walter was still being asked for very large sums to settle poor Tom's troubles, and had not yet succeeded in getting the widow's pension. Cadet Walter had said he had better stay and work at Addiscombe, but Hussar Scott would be with them.

The meeting of the Bannatyne Club on November 25th was truly convivial. Sir Walter admitted that he had stumbled getting into his carriage. Lord Eldin had a very bad fall on the stairs which gave rise to a very good legal joke. To match *Coke Upon Littleton*, they now had *Eldin upon Stair*.

Christmas passed off better than expected. The library with its fine cedar-wood shelving was so far finished that they were able to dance in it, and on New Year's Eve they heard a howl outside and it was about two hundred brats dressed up fantastically with wooden swords and white shirts come for their Hogmanay dole of an oaten cake and a penny. "You never saw so many happy little faces."

V

Anne had to write to thank Miss Millar for the little cap for Sophia's baby. She had a daughter, easily, on the last Saturday of January 1824, who lived only till the Monday. She had gone her full time and it was a beautiful child. She had suffered much since but was being brave. Her father rallied her tenderly—watched, he said, her face which had been the size of a sixpenny piece, becoming a shilling. He waited for it to regain its usual circumference—half a crown. In the spring, if Lockhart had to go to London, they would take her to Abbotsford where she would become as fat as a Norroway seal. He did not himself think of London this year. He only spent money there and he had too much to do at home. He was having to read all the applications for the post of Rector at the projected Academy in Edinburgh New Town. By what seemed incredible luck, Colin Mackenzie's letter to the inspiring Rev. John Williams of Lampeter, asking if he had any recommendations, brought the answer that he would himself like to offer for the post. It was October before Sir Walter triumphantly attended the opening ceremony. Williams had been a Tory, and was said to have a bad temper and no manners. A letter to the just-retired Dr Gabell of Winchester College followed by a personal interview, settled that.

Scott had not seen *Redgauntlet* through the press when the news of the death of Lord Byron at Missolonghi, on April 19th, reached Edinburgh. He went straight down from the Court of Session to dictate to Ballantyne an article for that week's *Journal*.[7] He had thought some of Byron's poetry bore the stamp of genius, and he had loved him as a man.

It was now the season when young men's fancies should lightly turn to thoughts of love. It was rather fortunate that the Fergusons said they could not have their niece to stay till August 12th (a most inconvenient date for Abbotsford), for the spring in Tweedside that year was very late. Sir Adam, most probably egged on by his lady, had thought what a good thing it would be if their heiress niece married the heir of Abbotsford. She had been brought to dine and "seemed a very sweet pleasant young woman with none of the conceit of an heiress about her". Sir Walter wrote to Sandhurst. For some reason known only to himself he adopted, in presenting the project to his quite unliterary young hussar, pseudonyms from *The Merry Wives of Windsor*. Miss Jane Jobson was sweet Anne Page and Gilnockie Master Slender. Gilnockie bent his brows over the problem and wanted to know, before he committed himself to anything, would he be expected to give up the army and his name and what was the fortune? Sir Walter was entirely against his son having to retire to become Mr Scott-Jobson, and Sir Adam was sure the young lady would never wish either thing. He thought she might easily be persuaded to sell her estate in Fife and settle where her husband chose. The fact was that it had not been long in the family. Her father had been in trade (pickled herrings, but that was not mentioned), and had bought it in 1814. It was absolutely in her hands. Sir Walter had not been able to pin down Sir Adam to mention its probable extent, but no harm could be done if Gilnockie came this autumn on an exploratory expedition. If he was not satisfied as to the young lady's principles, temper and manners, he need not pursue the acquaintance. Her mother was a Tartar but very proud of her descent from Robert II. As far as birth went, the Scotts of Abbotsford were cadets of Raeburn who were cadets of Harden, so lesser gentry. If the match took place it would almost certainly ensure his son's rise in his profession. Sir Adam thought he had a very good chance. In his third letter on the subject Sir Walter was able to say that their joint income would be up to two thousand pounds a year. Lochore might realise fifty thousand pounds, and there was large personal property including cash

in the funds—say another twenty thousand pounds, burdened only
by the widowed mother's jointure of eight hundred pounds. But he
had better make up his mind at once whether he was coming or not,
and if he was not, should send his father a letter proper to be shown
to Sir Adam saying he was too much in love with his profession to
wish to marry yet. His son's fear of discreditable connections was quite
unfounded.

Mrs Carpenter was thinking of Abbotsford again. If they arranged to
travel together Sir Walter hoped she would not keep Gilnockie waiting in
London as long as she had his father. Long before August a reason for
haste presented itself. The Fergusons had only rented Gattonside—a
dog of a Banker, Mr George Bainbridge of Liverpool, had bought the
place. (According to Lockhart, Abbotsford soon resumed friendly relations
with Gattonside.)[8] Scott began *Tales of the Crusaders*. The first guests this
season were upon him in May, much too early, and Dr Hughes, Canon of
St Paul's, was convalescent and very deaf. Mrs Hughes was voluble. But
their first stay at Abbotsford was a complete success, and was repeated in
1828 by a couple who were no fair-weather friends.[9]

There was a rush of artists. A nephew of the celebrated Bewick of
Newcastle had come to make a copy of the picture by Amias Cawood of
Queen Mary's severed head on a silver salver, sent to Sir Walter by a
foreign admirer. He did a sketch of Abbotsford and presented it to a
fellow bird of passage, the Baron D'Este, an agreeable young Saxon who
was an enthusiast over Scottish landscapes, played the Spanish guitar,
and loved his mother. Maida was getting very old and had seen too many
artists. At the mere sight of an easel being set up now he slunk off silently
to the stables. He died quietly in his straw that October, and his master
had him buried outside the front door under an effigy. Scott's Latin
inscription on the monument which was to be the "louping-on" stone,
was translated by him—"Beneath the sculptured form which late you
wore, Sleep soundly, Maida, at your master's door." Dalgleish would have
had him stuffed. Mrs Hughes said Abbotsford was a paradise for dogs.
Scott said Landseer painted every dog in the house, and ended up with
the owner.

An American, Gilbert Stuart Newton, who was staying at Chiefswood,
produced a portrait of her father for presentation to Sophia. When endur-
ing Charles Leslie, who had come up from Murray bringing a Lord
Byron mourning ring, the sitter suddenly rose. A thunderstorm was
coming on. "I must go to Lady Scott, she is always frightened when it
thunders." But she seemed better, and before Sophia's arrival had

actually walked the whole way to Chiefswood to satisfy herself that all was in apple-pie order.

Beside the artists there was a curious mixture of guests, Rose and Terry, and Mrs Coutts, who had been Harriet Mellon the actress and had married old Coutts a fortnight after he became a widower. She could not be refused. She was a relation by marriage—quite distant. Coutts had been a cousin of Scott's Haliburton grandmother. She travelled as if she was a royalty, with seven carriages. She turned up at the same time as Lady Alvanley and daughters, and Mrs Clephane and daughters, and afterwards told Newton that she had left prematurely as the other women staying were horrible. Sir Walter had been very kind and done all in his power. He had, in fact, taken Lady Compton apart and begged her to use her influence to prevent the females from giving the poor, rich, impossible old woman the cold shoulder.

After the Abbotsford Hunt came Wilkie, commanded to put Scott's figure in his grandiose crowd picture of the arrival of George IV at Holyrood, and Sir John Malcolm, diplomatist, who wore a ribbon and star which fascinated John-Hugh, and Lord Minto (politically a lion lying down with the lamb). His servant, instead of waiting behind his master's chair, placed himself behind that of Sir Walter to enjoy his conversation. William Dalgleish, who fancied he had himself considerable literary ability, noted this with professional disapproval. As a rule, after dinner, conversation and reading aloud (at which Mr Adolphus thought Scott was unrivalled) was the only entertainment. When somebody had once suggested cards, Scott had absently believed there was a pair somewhere. But a French ventriloquist was among the attractions of autumn 1824. He was not so brilliant, in the opinion of Dalgleish, as Mr Mathews, a gentleman from London. Scott could make his hearers' flesh creep but he could also show comical common-sense. Basil Hall heard him tell a very good tale of arriving late at a country inn and being told there was no bed for him. "'No place to lie down at all?' 'None except one in a room in which there is a corpse lying.' 'Did he die of anything contagious? Well then let me have the other bed.' So, I laid me down and never had a better night's sleep in my life."

He had been to the usual meeting of the Blair Adam Club and there met, as if by accident, the Fergusons and their niece. Contrary to what he had been led to believe, he thought the scenery of the adjacent estate of Lochore very lovely. His son and heir had come and gone, and had met Miss Jobson at Gattonside, but apparently nothing had resulted. He was coming again at Christmas, and so was she. Abbotsford was at last finished. On January 7th, 1825, a ball took place. Lockhart considered that night "one of the very proudest and happiest in Scott's existence". Captain Basil Hall wrote a Journal about his visit which occupied the lion's share of a whole chapter in Lockhart's *Memoir*. Captain Hall noticed everything. Like many present he imagined the occasion was a sort of house-warming. But it was to celebrate the acceptance of the heir by Miss Jane Jobson. "It was," remembered Lockhart pontifically, "the first regular ball given at Abbotsford, and the last . . . I myself never again saw the whole range of apartments thrown open for the reception of company except once— on the day of Sir Walter Scott's funeral."

VI

The wedding took place in the drawing-room of Mrs Jobson's fine Edinburgh house, 6 Shandwick Place, on the evening of February 3rd. The course of true love had not run smooth. She had ordered her sister and brother-in-law out of this very apartment when she had heard of the encouragement they had led her daughter into giving to young Scott. For, of course, there could be no question of a marriage between her beloved Jane and a hussar officer, heir to a baronetcy, but a very new creation, whose father had made his fortune as an author. Authors were notoriously immoral. There was an unhappy period while Sir Walter considered agreeing with the Fergusons' suggestion that the wedding should take place from Gattonside. He was in a sea of troubles. Terry needed instant financial support. He and a fellow actor, Yates, wanted to become proprietors of the Adelphi Theatre. Scott offered to be a guarantor for £1,250. Lady Alvanley had died suddenly at the British Hotel after two excruciating operations and her daughters were quite useless, "in a state of absolute distress and desolation". He was their only intimate friend in Edinburgh. At this most unsuitable moment he had to take upon himself all the business of the funeral and informing relatives. But he managed a superb letter to Sir Adam Ferguson to be shown to Mrs Jobson. Far from being a dissolute officer, he could assure his dear Adam that Walter's moral character had been uninterruptedly blameless—even amongst the notorious dissipations of foreign courts. He could produce evidence from the British Minister under whose roof the boy had stayed. He sent a letter of introduction with which Mrs Scott of Harden had supplied his son when he was ordered to Cork. It was to a lady of distinction, and all who knew Mrs Scott of Harden would realise that she was a severe judge of character and the last person to patronise a *roué* or even a coxcomb. She had known Walter all his life. The Duke of York had shown him repeated marks of patronage. Sir Walter was ready to apply direct to his Royal Highness for a confirmation of his favourable opinion. He suggested that Mrs Jobson should condescend to know Walter a little. He sketched a brief statement of his own financial situation. He introduced some discerning praise of Jane. If he thought his son capable of ingratitude towards her he would rather wish him dead at his feet than married to her. "I am sure the sight of his dead body would not give me so much pain as his degeneracy."

But in the end it was the little heiress herself who settled the matter by her calm and resolution. Like many only children of possessive and volcanic mothers, she had mastered the art of getting her own way quietly. For it would appear that her affections were deeply engaged, and the young couple had met when she had first been introduced into Edinburgh society more than two years past, and they had "looked and liked . . .". She was romantically determined to have her Black Hussar, the very picture of a Waverley Novel hero. So Sir Walter was able to write to the duke, and Lord Montagu, and Lady Abercorn, and Mrs Clephane and Lady Compton, and Mrs Hughes and Morritt and John Richardson and little Charles, presenting the acquaintance as being of quite long-standing. The wedding had to be at once because Walter was ordered to Cork and was going on to Dublin with his new regiment, the King's 15th Hussars. Sir Walter had settled Abbotsford upon his son, which made the young couple's fortunes tolerably square though hers was established and Walter's only an expectancy. He was perfectly delighted with his daughter-in-law and sent her a first letter, opening, "My dearest Child", to greet her on their arrival at Abbotsford. As an antiquary, he hoped his son had remembered the old custom of carrying his bride into her future home. After a week they were to go south, picking up their new emblazoned travelling carriage and much else in London. Jane had given her mother a benefaction which would cover the cost of a new carriage for her too, and presented Charlotte with a pony and a pony carriage. It was a welcome and thoughtful gift. Already Scott had noticed that she had tact. She had written from London that the Dumergues had all been most kind, especially Miss Nickie. Jane might not be a beauty or exceedingly talented, but she had a pretty, pensive little face, and if her manners were diffident almost to awkwardness, good society would soon cure that. He had been generous too. Jewellery for the bride "becoming her situation and fortune" had cost him five hundred pounds, and he was having to find three thousand pounds for Walter's captaincy. But he could afford it. Indeed, he had offered Charles and Surtees a foreign tour—Paris, the Rhine, Brussels and Holland.

He was not getting on well with his four *Tales of the Crusaders*. He had got stuck, very inappropriately considering the situation in his own home, with *The Betrothed*. Ballantyne thought highly of the next one, *The Talisman*. He had a most invigorating Saturday call at Abbotsford from Ballantyne and Constable.

Constable was meditating what Lockhart called nothing less than a revolution in the art of bookselling—cheap editions of classics. There would be all the Waverley novels and the *Life of Napoleon Buonaparte* by the Author of *Waverley*.

NOTES

1. Letters, VII, 279, 285, 301.
2. Ibid., 411–15, 498–505.
3. Lockhart, III, 513; IV, 141. Dr Carson has seen the cancelled pages. They contain part of Hannah Irwin's confession.
4. Letters, VIII, 32, 44–46, 50.
5. The Schetky family were well known to Sir Walter. John Christian Schetky had provided illustrations for *The Lay* (1808). The family was of Transylvanian origin, Von Schetky of Hermannstadt, and John Christian's mother was Maria Reinagle, daughter of Joseph Reinagle, musical composer. Tradition affirmed that Johann Georg Schetky, who died in 1824, aged ninety-five, had settled in Edinburgh after the "affair" of 1745, and had been employed by Clementina Sobieska, mother of Prince Charles Edward.
6. The Edgeworths' Scottish tour is the subject of valuable articles from family manuscripts in *Review of English Studies*, New Series, Vol. 9, R. Butler (1957), pp. 23–40, and *Review of English Literature*, Vol. IV, Christina Colvin (1964), pp. 55–63. The first collection contains letters from Ireland from Maria and Harriet, the second two letters from Harriet. See also, Letters, VI, 84, and *Maria Edgeworth, Life and Letters*, Augustus Hare, 1894, an edition published Boston 1895. Sophy's description of the visit to Mrs Dugald Stewart is very unflattering, and it seems that Maria had taken the measure of this informant's jealousy. Mrs Stewart, once renowned for her charm and looks, was living sadly with her paralysed husband and unmarried daughter in Kinneil House, provided for them by the Duke of Hamilton. Lady Anne Maria Elliot, daughter of Lord Minto who had invited herself, was liked by the Scotts, but accepted generally as a gossip. The story about Lady Scott being a daughter of Lord Downshire was said to have been spread by "a cast mistress". Grierson, in a footnote to Letters, X, 38, says that Scott's letter to Sophia, 39, "contains the only reference we know to a weakness of Lady Scott on which Lady Charlotte Bury and others have occasionally commented."

7. Reprinted in *Miscellaneous Prose Works*, IV (1827), 343. Letters, VIII, 292. Lockhart, IV, 180.

8. Letters, VIII, 209–10, 238–9, 248–50.

9. Ibid., VII, 471–8, 483–512. Mrs Hughes's accounts of her visits to Abbotsford contain many anecdotes available from other contemporary sources—Scott's Smailholm memories and those of his first romance, opinions of Americans, Royal visit, Radiant Boy, etc.

XVI

"The Muffled Drum"

1825–1826

"I must drop the curtain on a scene of un-
clouded prosperity and splendour. The
muffled drum is in prospect."
(Lockhart, *Life*, IV, 232)

I

THE SPRING OF 1825 WAS EARLY AND LOVELY. ANNE, WHO HAD TO
write to tell Miss Millar that Papa was sorry he had no suggestions to
make about a new post for her at present, said that at Abbotsford they
had large plots of hyacinths and jonquils in full blow before the doors.
Charles had been staying at Stowe with the Duke of Buckingham. Dr and
Mrs Hughes had given him an introduction. Mrs Thomas Scott had gone
with her girls to stay with an invalid brother at Cheltenham. Their uncle
feared there would be little company there for them, except yellow-faced
gentlemen and blue-stockinged ladies. Anne had been to a Fancy Ball in a
Spanish costume lent to her by a Spanish Donna. Papa was having Mr
Graham Gilbert paint her in this dress. The library and drawing-room
were now finished and both were magnificent. The entrance hall was very
large and fitted up with painted glass and armour. There was a splendid
harp in the library. Her father, who felt that she had not been taken
about as much as Sophia had been, had offered her the chance of going to
Ireland to visit the young newly-marrieds there. There had been only
one Lion of any consequence in Edinburgh this spring—Marshal
Macdonald, Duke of Taranto. Sir Walter had met him at a dinner given
by Staffa and had been the only person there not a Macdonald. The
Marshal had no English and was off for South Uist, bleakest of the

Sir Walter Scott, 1822
By Sir Henry Raeburn.
By permission of the Scottish National Portrait Gallery.

Hebridean islands, the home of his ancestors, a pious expedition about which Sir Walter had grave doubts. He would find a great many relatives, all very poor. Chantrey came to Abbotsford in May and departed the happiest man in the world, having killed two salmon. Charles had gone off to shoot the red deer with Glengarry. He did not seem likely ever again to travel on holiday *en famille*. Surtees and he had become regular guests at country houses. "What the Duke said to me, and *what I said to the Duke*," repeated Anne writing to Ireland.

In the end, the party that set off from Castle Street in a light barouche on July 9th was only Sir Walter, his son-in-law and his younger daughter; Lady Scott had wished to go but hated the ocean, bad beds and night journeys. She was going to the seaside at Helensburgh with Sophia and little John-Hugh who was recovering from whooping-cough. They were now at Germiston, where "I calculate," wrote Sir Walter to Charles, "upon his recovery with the greater certainty that I am well assured there is no medical man within reach. Sophia is rather too great an encourager of the art of Aesculapius." Sir Walter's party sailed from Glasgow to Belfast, and Anne had a sad first experience of sea-travel. She was not a country girl, and now that she was the only companion to parade for walks, her father had to scold her for going in thin slippers and silk stockings through dirty paths, and in lace veils through bushes and thorn brakes.

The principal impression received by the travellers before they drew up at 10 St Stephen's Green, Dublin, was that Ireland was rightly called the Emerald Isle. The soil was rich but not intelligently cultivated, the peasants were beggarly in dress and appearance beyond description. Scott saw the battlefield of the Boyne. The house taken by Captain and Mrs Scott of Lochore (he had been gazetted on June 25th) gave his father a bit of a shock. It was palatial. It had been represented as an economy as it was divided between them and another officer and lady—the MacAlpines. It was furnished with what Sir Walter described as a great deal of antiquated finery. Lockhart reflected that the founders of these large and noble houses around the most extensive square in Europe, had little dreamt that they should ever be let at an easy rate as garrison lodgings.

Jane looked perfectly well and had nothing worse to contend with than servant troubles. She was frightened of going down to her own kitchen, and when she had done so perforce one night had found her staff and that of the MacAlpines all carousing together, and all punch-drunk except her extremely talkative, imperious, personal maid,

K

Mrs Rebecca, whom she had brought with her from Shandwick Place. Her father-in-law was not easy that the young couple had bought a gig. He had somehow got to the bottom of the extraordinary inertia of Charlotte's sister-in-law, Mrs Carpenter. She had lost her health for life owing to an accident in a gig, when pregnant. He decided to offer Jane a pair of carriage horses. Lockhart thought he had never seen the old man look so full of fond joy and pride as when he looked around him as he sat for the first time at his son's table.

Their first week in what Sir Walter called Pat-land was one of increasing ovation. On the evening of their arrival, the Dublin Royal Society sent a deputation to invite the famous visitor to a public dinner. Next morning the Provost of Trinity College announced that the University wished to confer a Degree (Doctor of Laws). The scene at the theatre was rather embarrassing. The piece was *Much Ado* and poor Benedict and Beatrice were unable to make themselves heard for shouts from a packed house wanting *Sir Walter Scott!* He had to stand up and utter a few words before Shakespeare could be resumed.

He was invited by the Lord-Lieutenant to dinner at Malahide Castle. When he came out from attending ceremonies in the city, the crowd gathered to see him blocked the street so that his carriage got away with difficulty, and proceeded at a funereal pace, followed by a mob huzzaing like that at the wheels of a conqueror. He was told that the city was desolate, but its classical buildings were splendid beyond his utmost expectations. Before he left, his figure was observed in a characteristic attitude, hands linked behind his back, looking at the bookstalls before the custom house on the quay. It was a relief to get away for an excursion to see the beauties of County Wicklow. The mere wood, water, and wilderness had not so much charm for a north as for a south Briton, but these were intermingled with a brilliancy of verdure which never accompanied them in his own land. The Surgeon-General put them up at his villa, and the Attorney-General did the honours at Old Connaught, his seat near Bray. Sir Walter climbed up to St Kevin's Bed and could not help laughing while on the precipice, at the thought of old Constable's face if he could have seen the future historian of Boney resting like a Solan goose on a craig, with only one foot fixed and a drop of thirty or forty feet below him into very deep water. They had to return to Dublin for a lunch offered by the Lord Lieutenant, elder brother of the Duke of Wellington, a controversial figure. "The Marquess's talk gave me the notion of the kind of statesmanship that one might have expected in a Roman emperor, accustomed to keep the whole world in his view, and

to divide his hours between ministers like Macaenas and wits like Horace."
After his collation Sir Walter did not need dinner, but he had a quiet
hour with Jane, hearing her plans. She had been married nearly six months
but had nothing confidential to tell him.

At Edgeworthstown at last, they had counted upon three or four days
in which to relax. The weather had been sticky hot from the moment they
had landed, and they arrived looking as if they had been powdered. Indeed,
although people in a carriage could converse, they could not see one
another well, for the clouds of white dust. But there was a party there for
them every night. The Great Maria had thrown her net wide. The school
band played Scottish airs after dinner. He was cheered to see that villagers
walked in the park, and this country house accepted responsibilities. He
was shown the school founded by Maria's half-brother. There were
about equal proportions of Protestant and Roman Catholic pupils. "Here
we found neither mud hovels nor naked peasantry, but snug cottages and
smiling faces all about."

When they set out south for Killarney on Tuesday, August 2nd, the
party had been augmented by Captain and Mrs Scott of Lochore and Miss
Maria and Miss Harriet Edgeworth. (Sophy had been married last year
and Harriet was going to be, next year.) They filled two low, light
carriages. Anne was bearing up well and Jane seemed alert at everything
except talking much. Limerick welcomed them with bells, and Sir Walter
did not think that even Scottish hospitality could match that of Ireland;
but he was increasingly saddened by the poverty of the peasantry compared to the beauty of the scenery. He hoped that this country was
convalescent. At any rate he could assure Mrs Jobson by letter that her
son-in-law's occupation led him into no danger. To Laidlaw he told
more. Large bodies of armed police in green uniforms, armed to the
teeth, passed and repassed them. "It is not pleasant to see this, but it is
absolutely necessary for some time at least, and from what I can hear, the
men are under strict discipline and behave well." They were travelling
through a most beautiful and plentiful country in the full pride of
harvest, but not a sickle was being put into the fields. The blue Killarney
lakes were remarkable and the purple Gap of Dunloe was dramatic, but
he did not really think they surpassed Loch Lomond. He went on the
principal lake with Miss Edgeworth, and their boatman, informed what
redoubtable figures he was carrying, gallantly said that he no longer
regretted he had not been able to go to the hanging.

At picturesque Cork they had a reception necessarily on a smaller scale,
of the sort offered in Dublin. Sir Walter duly made an expedition to kiss

the Blarney Stone. He had intended only to change horses at Cashel, and meanwhile take a glance at the place. But when he perceived the wealth of sightseeing material there he ordered dinner and rooms for the night. He was asked when dinner was to be served and said, "Not till after dusk should have rendered it useless to linger among the ruins." They had only three bad shakes on the tour. Two were when travelling after dark, which they tried to avoid. There was an ominous-sounding row between a postilion and a keeper at a toll-gate who was slow in appearing at 2 a.m. It passed off, and they drove on. A much worse quarrel blew up between their drivers when they had lost their road. Captain Scott produced his pistol and threatened to shoot, upon which two of the men cut the harness and fled. The third alarm was in a narrow defile where blasting was in progress and they were waved on with a long queue of humbler vehicles. The detonation went off when the first carriage was less than twelve yards from the spot. Changing horses was always a Hogarthian scene, and Lockhart was furious at the contrast between the naked, clamorous beggars who seemed to spring out of the ground like swarms of vermin, and the boundless luxury and merriment surrounding the estates of the few magnates who condescended to inhabit their ancestral seats. His father-in-law "with the habitual hopefulness of his temper" said that he had received great kindness and a very warm reception from the inhabitants of a country which wanted nothing but internal peace to render it the almost richest portion of the Empire.

II

The travellers reached home on August 26th. After showing Anne Killarney, Scott took her on to Windermere and Ullswater. They crossed to Holyhead, and on their road, in reply to a pressing invitation, called in upon a couple of oddities, the Ladies of Llangollen. Lady Eleanor Butler and the Honourable Miss Ponsonby had flouted convention by going off together to settle in Denbighshire. They were now very old, and with their men's clothes and hair-cuts and lurching gait, looked like a pair of crazy old sailors. But they were prized in their neighbourhood where they did much good, so Lockhart thought it would be unkind to mock at them. His charity was to run out over Wordsworth.

They stayed first with Professor John Wilson whom they found in an unaccustomed rôle, "Admiral of the Lakes". He took them on to Mr Bolton who had assembled a distinguished company including Canning (looking poorly, but on a ride he came alive), and Wordsworth, "so old,

I begin to think I must be getting old myself". They went for enjoyable cavalcades in the woods, and on the lake by moonlight, and ended up with a splendid regatta in Elysian weather. Scott was enchanted by the placid beauty of the waters, still as a mirror, and reflecting hills and trees as distinctly as if they were drawn on its surface with a pencil. From Rydal Mount, Wordsworth took them to visit Southey in his library with an unrivalled view. Southey looked pale and rather sickly. To Wordsworth, Lockhart took one of his instinctive dislikes. He poured it all out in his next letter to Sophia.

> This I remark, once for all. The Unknown was continually quoting Wordsworth's poetry, and Wordsworth ditto, but that the great Laker never uttered one syllable by which it might have been intimated that your Papa had ever written a line, either of verse or of prose, since he was born.

(Scott had written to Morritt that during their two days together Wordsworth's conversation had been like a fountain in the desert.)[1]

He took up his usual round at Abbotsford without an hour's delay. Peeping into the lion's den, Lockhart had previously been pleased to note "the white head erect, and the smile of conscious inspiration on his lips, while, his pen held boldly, and at a commanding distance, glanced steadily and gaily along a fast-blackening page of *The Talisman*". But he was now having to read a mountain of small print and difficult manuscripts. Buonaparte was much more demanding. He came out looking jaded. Lockhart apologised for having to interrupt him to show him a letter from Murray. It was mysterious. It introduced "my most particular and confidential young friend, Mr Disraeli". There was quite a well-known Disraeli in literary circles, rather an old coxcomb, Scott thought, author of *Curiosities of Literature* and much else; but he must be sixty. The figure to present himself at Chiefswood on September 24th gave Lockhart and his father-in-law a shock. Mr Benjamin Disraeli, in his twenty-first year, was something new on Tweedside—a dandy. He was ridiculously overdressed and had the most elaborate manners. Evidently the old coxcomb had bred a worthy young coxcomb. He speedily explained that Mr Murray had in mind a newspaper to be called *The Representative*, an ultra-Tory organ to rival *The Times*. Lockhart was crestfallen. He had heard that Murray was not perfectly satisfied with a nephew of Coleridge who had recently succeeded Gifford as editor of the *Quarterly*. It seemed he had guessed wrong. The young ambassador spoke as if he had them in his bestowal, of a great position at the English bar, and a seat in Parliament. After discussion with Sir Walter, Lockhart wrote to Murray declining to be interested in *The Representative*, but saying he would be coming up to London and would see him. For he had heard meanwhile that Coleridge was indeed leaving the *Quarterly*. When he arrived at Albemarle Street, the editorship was immediately offered him. He would get a thousand pounds a year, and, with articles, this might easily mean fifteen hundred. If he became a regular contributor his income might rise to three thousand. There had been a misunderstanding. Only his general advice and assistance would be asked on *The Representative*. There was no doubt in the minds of either Scott or Lockhart that the post was desirable. It would mean moving to London, and the moment was quite inopportune, as the happy return of her husband from his Irish and English tours had resulted in Sophia becoming pregnant. But the doctors would not answer for the fate of little John if he spent another winter in Edinburgh. Scott prudently arranged that a legal contract should be drawn up. It was very necessary, for no sooner had the news spread than there were complaints from several sources that Lockhart was not suitable for the post. In view of his past record, even Croker had been against employing him. But Murray, apparently swayed by the young Disraeli, pooh-poohed all objections. To Scott the deprivation would be great. He would no longer be able to say to Dalgleish, at the end of a fine day, "Now, since I have done so well, I will call at Chiefswood and give my dear Mrs Lockhart a startle." He would also lose his best literary companion.

During these weeks of anxiety, guests had been arriving steadily. The Ashestiel Russell cousins came first. Colonel Russell had returned from India. They stayed ten days and were followed by Captain Basil Hall and his lady. Hall always sat on the edge of his chair bursting with eagerness to break in on conversation. But he was intelligent, and his sister Lady De Lancey's diary of her Waterloo experiences sounded useful for Boney. He was bringing that, and could get the accounts of Captain Maitland of H.M.S. *Bellerophon*. A legal group meant a full house—Lord and Lady Gifford, the Chief Baron and Lady Shepherd, and what Scott with helpless good nature noted simply as "two friends of Lord Sidmouth". Judging from the Journal of her Scotch Tour kept by Miss Angel Heath who came with her brother and sister-in-law for the weekend from Saturday, 22nd October, he did not know much more about them. They missed by a day Mrs Coutts again, but this time bringing her rejected suitor the Duke of St Albans, aged twenty-four, and his sister Lady Charlotte Beauclerk. (Scott guessed correctly that the duke, who was "very spooney", would eventually be accepted.) He had been disappointed to miss Tom Moore in Ireland. He came the day after the intending bride and bridegroom and stayed three days, during which he sang like a cherubim. The weather had broken, but Scott took him to call upon the Laidlaws and the Misses Ferguson, and had Sir Adam and his lady to dine and partake in the music-making. The poets were delighted with one another, and Scott recounted, and Moore wrote down, all the familiar anecdotes about Smailholm, the beginnings of *Waverley*, and Jeanie Deans, and Muckle Mouthed Meg and Lord Castlereagh seeing the Radiant Boy and Mungo Park dreaming of Africa on Tweedside. They talked of Campbell (*Hohenlinden* very remarkable, *The Pleasures of Hope* and longer set pieces, very inferior). Scott praised Wordsworth's manly endurance of his poverty. He had given them dinner in his kitchen. They agreed that he was disappointingly vain of his poetry. Rather to Moore's surprise his host made no secrecy about the authorship of prose works. He was now on the life of Buonaparte, but was also writing another novel—Civil War date, to be called *Woodstock*. They talked much of Byron, and Scott heard to the point of emulation that Byron had left a diary. They parted, in Scott's words, "Friends for Life".

The carriage taking Moore to the Jedburgh coach was instructed to drop a young Russian nobleman and tutor who had turned up last night, at Melrose Abbey. This seemed the only recorded occasion on which Scott did not accompany a guest to act as showman. He had taken Moore and he had taken the Heaths—both in north-east wind, in which Miss Anne Scott had shivered and shaken. Miss Angel Heath, like a great many female visitors, found the whole scene sprang to life when the Wizard of the North stepped into his own drawing-room.[2] But she was very unkind about her hostess. "Rouge and what appeared to me to be pearl powder, and a black curled crop wig usurped the place of those endearing young charms which in their zenith must have enthralled the heart of 'the great magician'." Lady Scott received them courteously and kindly, but was in appearance, manner, "and I opine character, the last person whom the great genius of the age would have selected for the partner of his joys, the soother of his griefs . . ." Lady Scott, in very early youth,

> had probably the attraction of a certain piquante sort of beauty accompanied by a little foreign coquetry, which to some men is alluring, but of mind, or a possibility of meeting him on any of the higher subjects with which his intellect must have been occupied,

she must have been utterly devoid . . . And yet, such as she was, she had for more than thirty years, the love of one of the most kind and tender as well as the most gifted beings of his age.

Nobody knew that Lady Scott, who had swollen ankles and was short of breath, was making gallant efforts. She had been in bed for a week at the beginning of October, kept her room much, and rose to play her part as hostess when she could. Her husband wrote to Ireland that he was not happy about her.

Captain Scott of Lochore had been appointed an aide-de-camp to the Lord Lieutenant. Sir Walter said he would learn very good manners. It was about all he could say in praise of Lord Wellesley who had just married for the second time, but openly, an American lady, a Catholic widow, surely a masterpiece of tactlessness in his position. Scott had seen her, and thought that she would play her rôle with elegance.

There was to be no Abbotsford Hunt this year. "The crowd became rather too great and so many of the old stagers are gone; besides I have no young folks to head the field." The Duke of Buccleuch, who was now at Cambridge, and had been touring Europe with a tutor in the long vacation, had written to offer what would once have been accepted with rapture—a brace of greyhounds from Drumlanrig. They were declined with thanks. "Times are so much changed with me that I have given up coursing almost entirely." He had been shaken by a bad fall when he had put Sybil Grey at that fabulous prehistoric trench the Catrail up behind his house. He had not broken anything, but he was bruised and disconcerted. Lockhart thought that he afterwards talked of this accident with "a somewhat superstitious mournfulness". He was still very hardy. He told Dalgleish that he had never had a great-coat but once, and that had been upon his travels, but he would not like to say how many shepherd's plaids he had worn out. As to gloves and mitts, he never had them upon his hands unless at a funeral. But he liked to have a few pairs by him for the good of the trade. He took a kindly interest in local commercial ventures—had shares in the Berwick and Kelso railroad, the Edinburgh Oil Gas Company, and Flint glass manufacturers. Constable had been upset by hearing that Hurst and Robinson, with whom he was so closely allied, had fallen victims to the current speculation fever and were gambling in hops. This was the firm that had held up Constable's Miscellany by objecting that if all the Waverley novels went into cheap editions they would be heavy losers. Who would pay a pound for *Waverley* if they could get it in the series for six shillings? This was annoying, for

Scott had written to Sir William Knighton, and His Majesty had graciously consented that the whole series might be dedicated to him. Constable still thought that no announcement had created so much excitement in the world of letters as that of *Napoleon Buonaparte* by the Author of *Waverley*. Actually, Scott had been obliged to lay it aside after finishing the first volume until he had caught up with his research for the next. It was agreed that the Miscellany should at present publish only the *Tales of the Crusaders*, and the first number should come out on New Year's Day, 1826. Before that date Hurst and Robinson had withdrawn all objections.

Young Walter from Canada seemed to have determined to behave like a ghost—that is to say would not speak until conjured to do so. When he did write it was to say that he had contracted some debts. The sum did not sound very alarming—a draft for sixty pounds would settle it and leave him something for future expenses; but the resemblance to his poor father's career was intimidating. He was sent a kindly but severe letter and warned that once he was in India he must live within his income. He sailed from Gravesend for Bombay in February and never again offended.[3]

Sir Walter arrived in Edinburgh for the winter Session on November 11th. The Lockharts were now well ahead with their plans for the Great Remove. Well-meaning people filled Sir Walter with warnings about the dangers awaiting young nursemaids in London. He had seen the one who was going to take charge of his frail and most engaging grandson and his mind was at rest. Sophia's stout Aberdonian was about five and forty and so harsh-featured that she might walk in any park with all the safety of Hecate. He knew he would miss the Lockharts grievously. They spoke of keeping on Chiefswood and coming for summer holidays. He kept silence but could not see it being managed. They meant to settle, for Johnnie's sake, near one of "the Lungs of London". While they were in the throes of packing up, Lockhart got a letter from a London friend, a lawyer, William Wright of Lincoln's Inn, which he posted on to Castle Street. It arrived there on November 19th. It said that Constable who had been south for three weeks and returned home to take to his bed, at his country house at Polton, had been refused credit by his bankers. Scott took the bull by the horns and went round to Princes Street at once to see Cadell in whose prudence he put faith. Cadell listened gravely and then showed him a letter from their London bankers, Messrs Dixon, acknowledging a draft from Constable for two thousand pounds, discounting a large number of bills and concluding with declaring themselves highly satisfied with the way in which their business was managed at a time when money was short.

Cadell said that if Sir Walter liked he could see two thousand five hundred pounds' worth of bills which they had kept out of the market for fear of seeming to push their bankers. Scott asked what about the hops? Cadell admitted it was true that Hurst and Robinson had made one immense profit "out of the bookselling line". He did not think they had engaged in any other. Scott wrote the whole to Lockhart that night, and told him he might pass it on to Murray, whose name he had not mentioned, of course, nor that of Lockhart. His letter was in the post before he received an unexpected call from Cadell. He had communicated with Ballantyne and with Constable. Young Thomas Constable, the elder son in the firm, was certain that Murray had been the London friend and that Sir Walter had been informed by his son-in-law, "J.C.L. is a serpent and will sting us one day very acutely". Cadell was only to ask if Sir Walter's authority was likely to propagate the rumour.

Scott had bought two small volumes, nine inches by eight, bound in vellum and furnished with strong locks. In these he intended to jot down henceforward, morning and evening, anything topical—not necessarily remarkable. He had begun to add to his literary output something intimate, unpretentious and stalwart which would establish him as one of the first diarists in the English language and an heroic figure.[4] His hour was well chosen. He made his first entries on November 20th— quite amusing. Two days later their tone utterly changed:

> Here is a matter for a May morning, but much fitter for a November one. The general distress in the city has affected H. and R., Constable's great agents. Should they GO it is not likely that Constable can stand, and such an event would lead to great distress and perplexity on the part of John Ballantyne and myself. Thank God I have enough at least to pay forty shillings in the pound, taking matters at the very worst.

Next day the sad chronicle continued:

> Constable has been here as lame as a duck upon his legs, but his heart and courage as firm as a rock. He has convinced me that we will do well to support the London House. He has sent them £5,000 and proposes we should borrow on our joint security £5,000 for their accommodation. J.B. and R. Cadell present. I must be guided by them and hope for the best. Certainly to part company would be to incur an awful risk.

Cadell paid another of his evening visits on November 25th. He was blessedly reassuring but after he had gone Scott wrote down some resolutions in the Journal:

No more building;
No more purchases of land till times are quite safe;
No buying books or expensive trifles.

He was depressed that he now needed, when working, to wear spectacles continually. He thought that perhaps 39 Castle Street had become darker because of "the vast number of houses built beneath us to the north". He still dined out, though less than of old. When Lady Scott and Anne went to the theatre to see the inimitable Mathews, he stayed quietly at home. He was not in the mood for a whole evening of laughter. But his sense of humour was still lively. "People make me the oddest requests." Amongst his large post came several from young students at Oxford or Cambridge, total strangers, who had outrun their allowances. Someone signing himself the Captain of Giggleswick School wanted to establish a magazine called *The Yorkshire Muffin*. He was seventeen and must be entreated to forbear. A soldier of the 79th thought Sir Walter could oblige him by getting him discharged from a wicked and profane service. Sir Walter would have to exhort him to bear with it rather than take the very precarious step of desertion.

The visitations of a family friend, Robert Gillies, were an affliction. Lockhart said the poor man was *in extremis* owing to his imprudence. All agreed that money given to him would be thrown away. He wanted Sir Walter to help him by insuring his life. He was offered Chiefswood, rent free, while he supported himself in making translations from the German for booksellers. Charlotte was against having him and his tribe (for he was married and had children) so near to Abbotsford. Mercifully, he was off on another hare.

A Danish naval captain wrote to say that he had dreamt Sir Walter had made him a gift of money enough to transport himself to Columbia to assist in liberating that province. Well—dreams went by contraries.

The Lockharts came to stay for their last few days before they left to conquer England—a heroic little group, reminiscent of classical statuary— the handsome father, difficult, rigid, full of courage, the mother serene as ever, great with child; the ill-favoured handmaid attendant upon the brilliant little boy. "O my God! that poor delicate child, so clever, so animated, yet holding by this earth with so fearfully slight a tenure. Never out of his mother's thoughts, almost never out of his father's

arms, when he has a single moment to give to anything. *Deus providebit.*"
In the end they went off without farewells at seven o'clock in the morning.
He was grateful. "I hate red eyes and blowing of noses." Anne, who knew
how much he would miss her sister's singing after dinner, was practising
Scots songs. He had thought she cared only for foreign music. "God
bless her!"

He was glad when a thaw came and he could walk to the Court again
through the rain.

> No man that ever stepped on heather had less dread than I of catching
> cold; and I seem to regain, in buffeting with the wind, a little of
> the high spirit with which in younger days I used to enjoy a Tam
> O'Shanter ride through darkness, wind and rain—the boughs
> groaning and cracking over my head, the good horse free to the road
> and impatient for home . . .

But disaster seemed to be escalating in the London money market. On
December 18th Ballantyne came in early. Sir Walter wrote in his Journal
after that call:

> My extremity has come. Cadell has received letters from London
> which all but positively announce the failure of Hurst and Robinson,
> so that Constable and Co must follow, and I must go, with poor
> James Ballantyne for company. I suppose it will involve my all . . .
> This news will make sad hearts at Darnick . . .

He had always realised Abbotsford had been "my Delilah". He counted
his blessings.

> My children are provided; thank God for that. I was to have gone
> there on Saturday in joy and prosperity to receive my friends. My
> dogs will wait for me in vain. It is foolish—but the thoughts of
> parting from these dumb creatures have moved me more than any
> of the painful reflections I have put down. Poor things, I must get
> them kind masters; there may be yet those who, loving me may love
> my dog because it has been mine. I must end this, or I shall lose the
> tone of mind with which a man should meet distress.

But he could not quite end yet.

> I find my dogs' feet on my knees, I hear them whining and seeking
> me everywhere—this is nonsense, but it is what they would do if
> they knew how things are. Poor Will Laidlaw! poor Tom Purdie!

this will be news to wring your hearts and many a poor fellow's besides to whom my prosperity was daily bread.

He had something more that was sad to relate.

Another person did not afford me all the sympathy I expected, perhaps because I seemed to need little support; yet that is not her nature, which is generous and kind. She thinks I have been imprudent, trusting men so far. Perhaps so—but what could I do? I must sell my books to someone and these folks gave me the largest price, if they had kept their ground I could have brought myself round fast enough by the plan of the 14th December.

(That was a plan to raise ten thousand pounds on Abbotsford. His son's marriage contract allowed him to charge so much on the estate.) But now it was done too late. "The magic wand of the Unknown is shivered in his grasp."

III

Sophia wrote from London. They had taken a six months' lease of a handsome furnished house, 25 Pall Mall. It was not in a park, but the amenities included a key to the gardens in the centre of St James's Square. His nurse had brought a little bag of meal to make porridge for Johnnie in hostelries on the Great North Road and whole inn-yards had assembled to watch the operation. The Aberdonian was of the opinion "England was an awfu' country to make parritch in". Sir Walter asked to be told which variety of meal Johnnie favoured so that Abbotsford could provide.

Christmas at Abbotsford was quiet. Anne was bearing up bravely, her mother was still incredulous, and they could hardly be blamed, for a false ray of hope had dawned again before they left Castle Street. Cadell had come in late to say Hurst and Robinson were standing out; stocks had risen. Sir Walter added to a joyous entry (for he too had dared to hope), "This was a mistake." He wondered, as he wrote his story of joys and fears, would this little volume be taken some day after he was gone, out of its ebony cabinet at Abbotsford or in some obscure lodging house where one or two old friends would look grave and whisper, "Poor gentleman. A well-meaning man. Nobody's enemy but his own. Thought his parts could never wear out. Family poorly left. Pity he took that foolish title."

They generally went to the Scotts of Harden for Christmas dinner. Luckily, this year they had asked if they might come the day after. On December 24th Sir Walter was suddenly seized with a pain as if a dagger had been plunged into his entrails. Dr Clarkson said he was not dying; it was gravel. He prescribed remedies which included a fire in the dressing closet, and rest. Scott slept for twelve hours. The Fergusons and the Russells came over to Abbotsford for Hogmanay. Unpleasant news from Edinburgh damped the evening for Scott. He must, and had, attempted to supply Ballantyne again. He was even more anxious about Constable. The post on January 1st brought the ugly possibility that Captain Scott's regiment might be ordered to India. Walter, he supposed, would want to go, and Jane was not likely to dissuade him. She had been complaining of her husband dining in his mess so often. Scott thought he would get on better with *Woodstock* if he did not have what he could only describe as "those cold sinkings of the heart". A veteran Sandy Knowe relation had died—Aunt Curle. He could not attempt to get to the funeral, though he had admired her. He loathed funerals. (The Scotts of Raeburn were tough. When his cousin Barbara Scott came over to see Lady Scott next May she insisted on walking back to Lessudden, a distance of at least six miles, and though the carriage was ordered, she would not enter it.) So little fit to be put in the Journal was happening that he had to fill out a letter to Jane describing Spice, the Dandie Dinmont, getting stuck in a flue of the garden wall, after a *cat*.

He was not very pleased that a young artist called John Knight was sent up to paint a portrait of him for Terry. He was not surprised that in the result he had pinched nostrils. Sophia had thought the picture by young Charles Leslie the best likeness she had ever seen. There was deep snow underfoot now and he needed Tom Purdie's shoulder on his daily walk. The Skenes arrived, and Skene joined the walkers. Mathews, and his son, who had inherited the talent for mimicry, came for a night. Upon the whole the empty, anxious days passed pleasantly enough—work till one or two, then a walk in the snow, lighter work or reading, late dinner and singing or chat. But on January 14th all his cold sinkings returned on receiving a letter from Constable, headed Osborne's Hotel, Adelphi. It was so odd and mysterious that it struck him as being the sort of stuff that men write when they want the recipient rather to apprehend something disagreeable which they have not avowed. But without explanations which time alone would bring, he could only guess. He was cheered by a fine walk, the sun dancing delightfully on "grim Nature's visage hoar". They returned to Castle Street on January 16th and got in late "through cold roads to as cold news". Hurst and Robinson had suffered a bill of a thousand pounds to come back upon Constable.

He sent a message round to Skene's house and that best of friends was with him before 7 a.m. Skene found him in his study, surrounded by papers. He held out his hand and said, "Skene, this is the hand of a beggar." The darkest day ever known at Castle Street followed. Ballantyne arrived looking black, "good, honest fellow": then Cadell, Hogarth, John Gibson. All advised his making a Trust of his property.

Dalgleish did not hear of his master's failure till the afternoon, and brought in dinner as usual. As he was taking off the cover of the tureen, Sir Walter asked him to leave it and added that he would ring the bell when they were done. It was rung within ten minutes. Nothing had been touched. But Dalgleish could see that "all was not right with them for they were sitting with millincolly countenances". The same thing happened at tea. No soiled cups. Supper was ordered away before it was brought in, and all went to bed early. Next morning over breakfast it was the same story. About noon, her ladyship sent for him. "Dalgleish, I suppose you have heard what has happened to Sir Walter?" "Yes, my lady." "Well, you will have to look out for a situation, as we will be obliged to part with all our servants and the carriage and horses." "I am very sorry to hear it, but I shall not leave you." About an hour later he reappeared with a dish of mutton chops. Lady Scott asked what was this? But Miss Scott said, "What a fine chop, do have one, Papa, since Dalgleish has been so kind." They partook. About six weeks later Lady Scott sent for him again, and this time it was to tell him that he might let the servants know that things would be the same as before. Sir Walter had entered into a Trust.

IV

Sir Walter Scott's creditors met on January 20th, 1826, at the Waterloo Hotel, Edinburgh, and his lawyer, Mr John Gibson, produced a draft of a private Trust deed. The best thing to come out of the very bad business was that people were behaving so nobly. Friends had arrived to assistance with such speed—Skene, Colin Mackenzie, Morritt, Forbes, Adam, Rae. It was a shock when he realised that someone staring at him was not come to commiserate. It was young Mr Knight to finish his portrait.

The Duke of Buccleuch had offered to take the whole of Sir Walter's losses upon himself. Little Mr Pole, who had taught the girls the harp, sent to offer five or six hundred pounds—probably his all. "But I will involve no friend, rich or poor. My own right hand shall do it." His entire acquaintance seemed to have poured into his house since his tragedy became known, rather as if paying a formal call upon a death. Will Clerk's sister, Elizabeth, had died suddenly. For a moment he wished it could have been "S.W.S." but dismissed the idea as unmanly. He said that his wife and daughter were sad but patient. Only the Journal was told that on the day following the fatal 18th, after dinner, and again after supper, there had been "painful scenes".

He had to convince these dear creatures that it was useless waiting for miracles; they must consider their misfortune as certain. He had to write without delay, to those closest to him, suiting his explanations to the recipient. He assured Mrs Jobson that her daughter's fortune was safe. (Miss Edgeworth had heard that that dear warm-hearted little Janie had offered her whole fortune, as if it were a gooseberry.) Scott read in the gazette that the stately firm of Mr Barber, the Nicolson nephew who looked after Mrs Carpenter's affairs, had been amongst those "to go to the wall". But this time, eternally unlucky Mrs Carpenter was lucky. He expanded at length to his dear Mrs Hughes and the worthy Doctor, who had written delicately to enquire. He admitted that he would certainly lose a very large sum by the failure of his booksellers, whom all men had thought worth a hundred and fifty thousand; but he did not think he really deserved profound commiseration as he had made an arrangement for settling his affairs which satisfied all concerned and would leave him, if not as comfortable as he had been, still far richer in point of income than generals and admirals, who had led armies and fleets. "My family are all provided for, in present or in prospect; my estate remains in my family, my house and books in my own possession." He was giving up his Edinburgh house and would live at his club while the Courts sat. They would be cutting down on staff, which must mean on casual strange guests, "useless visitors"; but if they managed economically, he hoped that, in five years, if the public continued to buy what he wrote, he would get back more than he had lost. He was a little concerned for his younger son. He thought of trying to get him into some diplomatic line for which his habits and manners seemed to suit him. Most people thought that because Sir Walter Scott had entertained so lavishly, he was dependent on constant society. "I am by nature a very lonely animal . . . And now let this matter be silent for ever. It is a bad business, but might have been much worse."

He noted whimsically, on Valentine's Day, that it was a month since anyone except of his immediate family had dined in his house. And even now, he had asked Mr Scrope, who had a lease of The Pavilion, Melrose, only because Lady Scott's gratitude for a gift of game from Tweedside had become ungovernable.

He had refused to consider bankruptcy which would have been the easiest course. There was the danger that the marriage contract, settling Abbotsford on Gilnockie, might be questioned. He had, even so, a terrible night after he had been told that Abbotsford might be stripped from him "together with all". "Naked we enter the world and naked we leave it—blessed be the name of the Lord." The Bank of Scotland had laid claim, on behalf of Constable's estate, to *Woodstock* on which he was still at work, and *Boney*, his gold-mine, hardly begun. These bad things were not allowed to happen, and he managed to get a clause in the Trust removed which had said that everything he wrote now must go to his creditors. He wanted to be free to perform by-jobs, to review, and to assist needy authors.

Cadell entered into a horrible quarrel with Constable, and Scott had himself a sad last interview with the ailing man who wanted to continue publishing his books without Cadell ("the clock without the pendulum"). He was still amazed by Constable's failure. "I really believe they have not had any capital for twenty years but were entirely trading on credit." He still could not believe that if Constable had not left his last journey to London so late the banks would have obliged him. Lockhart had been to see him immediately on his arrival and had thought him on the verge of insanity.

Sir Walter wrote to warn Laidlaw that he would have to give up the farm and dispose of his stock as soon as possible. He told others that he had always loathed farming. He was keeping Peter Matheson and the carriage for the sake of Lady Scott, and Bogie in the garden, but they must sell their produce now. As for Tom Purdie "he and I go to the grave together". He said that he felt like the Eildon Hills—"quite firm though a little cloudy".

He was surprised to find that he was the one who cared most about leaving the Edinburgh house. Anne sat silent and uncomplaining while coaches carrying her fellow *belles* sped past outside bound for the ball-room. (She wrote to Charles that she was sick of hearing of nothing but pounds, shillings and pence, and the prospect of six months annually shut up in the country with her ladyship, who was very cross, did not attract her.) But Lady Scott seemed to view her seclusion without horror. What she did not like was being "let down" in the eyes of Edinburgh. Only to the Journal and his elder daughter could Sir Walter confess that he was "subject to attachment even to chairs and tables". So many of these inanimate objects recalled happy memories. Some of them were not valuable. He had seven or eight paintings by a poor young lady who could not paint given him by a kind old lady who had bought them out of sheer kindness. They would have to be sold in the house for what the large gilt frames would fetch. "Walter Scott in youth with his dogs", by Sir Henry Raeburn, was also large. Skene said he could give it a home till his friend wanted it. The dog Camp was dear, but not to everyone. He got rid of him on "true" Jock Stevenson, bookseller. Sharpe took his Piranesi engravings, which were not in very good condition owing to smoke, but had belonged to the old sailor uncle at Rosebank. They could go in Sharpe's office. To Gibson, who was being a model of efficiency, he presented his father's cabinet, likely to be of use to a lawyer. Skene was a perfect Good Samaritan. When Scott got to books and manuscripts, he exhausted himself. Skene took him for walks in the new Princes Street pleasure gardens. He wanted Scott to live with him during his Edinburgh months, not at the Albyn Club. He was refused. So were the suggestions of legal friends of a seat on the Bench.

The TO SELL notice was up; he saw it every time he went out and came in; but he had pleaded with Gibson not to show any false delicacy, and to advertise the contents as "lately the property of Sir Walter Scott". He had heard a passer-by saying he did not mind giving a pound for a chair that had been his. Gradually, he created the inevitable depressing disorder, and rooms became almost uninhabitable. He could not get his partner to express any wish about keeping or jettisoning ornaments once her pride. He had dreaded his first appearance at the Court since his failure, but it had passed off quietly. The best-mannered people had said nothing—greeted him just as usual. He had, until absolutely immersed in the packing-up, been at his desk fairly regularly. Lockhart had sent him a book to review—the diary of Samuel Pepys, Secretary to the Navy in the days of the Merry Monarch. The fellow had curious turns of phrase. Now that he had signed away his freedom, Sir Walter said he could only hope that, like the regicides so winningly described by Pepys on their way to be hanged, drawn and quartered, he would appear "as cheerful and comfortable as any gentleman could be in that situation".

Like Macbeth, he was vexed by "thick-coming fancies". Cadell caused a sensation by taking refuge in the debtor's sanctuary at Holyrood. He was threatened with the Calton Hill jail by the Bank of Scotland. He had withdrawn nine hundred pounds the day before Constable and Co. stopped payment. He was able to return to his office when he had proved that he had surrendered the money to the creditors in general. Neither Scott's sense of humour nor his flood of begging letters had failed. He gave the palm to the lady who had heard (alas!) that he was a lover of speculation. She wanted him to let her use his name as the author of a novel for which she would ask only half profits, to be devoted to launching a patent medicine which she had invented "for the benefit of little babies". "I dreaded to have anything to do with such a Herod-like affair and begged to decline the honour of her correspondence."

Patriotic fervour had driven him on to engage in another by-job. Signing himself "Malachi Malagrowther", he contributed three articles for the *Edinburgh Weekly Journal* attacking the Government's decision to limit the Bank of England to the issue of notes of five pounds and upwards, and remove note circulation altogether from private banks. In Scotland coin was scarce and the note system had, he held, worked well. But the true intention of the Government was to give all three kingdoms uniform currency. As a nationalist, not an economist, Scott sounded a clarion call. His victory put him in the wrong with valuable Tory friends. Lord Melville would not call him Dear Walter for two months. Canning spoke against him in the Commons, and Croker produced a Government-inspired reply. The Whigs did not thank Sir Walter for his opposition, and the repercussions were to be rather regrettable. But he felt he had shown the world he was not to be "poor manned". *Blackwood's* had published the articles as a pamphlet and it had sold seventy-two pounds' worth.

He was now longing to be gone, but Charlotte and Anne were not quite ready. He had persuaded his wife to have an inspection by a leading specialist before she went into the country—Abercrombie. It was agreed that he should go ahead and warm up Abbotsford for the arrival of the invalids—for Anne too had been in bed, a development which had filled him with horror. He closed the door of the house which had been his home for almost twenty-five years with the words of the Gaelic lament "I return no more", and wrote in the Journal, "So farewell, poor 39, and may you never harbour worse people than those who now leave you."

NOTES

1. Letters, IX, 187–214. Lockhart, IV, 285–308. Edgeworth, *Life and Letters*, and Diary (National Library of Scotland), *Sir Walter Scott's Tour*.
2. *A Scotch Tour with my brother and his wife*. Angel Heath, 40 pp., typescript lent to London Library.

3. Walter, son of Tom Scott, retired from India with the rank of General in 1875. He settled in Dresden with his sister Mrs Cumine Peat (Eliza, a widow since 1848), in 1867. A daughter of Eliza married Baron Ernst von Oppell, and General Scott assisted them in reconstructing their estate of Halberdorf near Schirgiswald, in Saxony. He died there in 1876.

4. The original manuscript of the Journal is in the Pierpont Morgan Library, New York. Two volumes revised by John Guthrie Tait from a photostat were published Edinburgh, 1939–46. The edition quoted here is that published and edited by David Douglas, 1890. In 1972 Eric Anderson's edition had valuable notes. The Journal begun by Scott in 1825 was kept by him until he could no longer hold a pen and is, except for his letters, t he most valuable source for the last seven years of his life. The story that Scott ruined himself building Abbotsford, though widely believed, is mistaken. Letters, IX, 345–50, 357–63, 369–94, 398–444, 448–56. John Buchan, 283–95: Lockhart IV; Life, Chapter LXVII and The Ballantyne Humbug (Edinburgh, 1839). Archibald Constable, 3 vols (Edinburgh, 1873). Lockhart's inaccuracies have been pointed out by Grierson, Life (1938), and Professor Edgar Johnson, Sir Walter Scott, 2 vols (1970). Scott's Journal, Vol. I, gives a day-to-day account by Scott himself.

XVII

"Right Hand"

1826–1827

I

ON SATURDAY, OCTOBER 21ST, 1826, MR THOMAS MOORE, SKIPPING along Pall Mall with his usual verve, heard at Number 25 that Sir Walter Scott had not yet returned from Windsor. He went on and got a dinner from Samuel Rogers, and that night at his lodgings in Duke Street found a kind note in a familiar small hand asking him to partake of a family dinner at Mrs Lockhart's today, or at all events come for breakfast tomorrow. He could not do either, but he went next day in the evening, taking with him Sir Thomas Lawrence who had begged him to mention he was within call. Lockhart had at once sent to ask Lawrence. It was no novelty to see Sir Walter Scott in London in deep mourning. He was a devoted family man, and Scotland like Ireland excelled in insistence on such habiliments of woe. (All the same, when summoning the sons for the funeral in Dryburgh Abbey, he had warned them to get their mourning in Dublin and Oxford.) One of the two black-robed daughters present provided a good hot supper—Lockhart's wife. Miss Anne Scott had been taken ill at the theatre last night, and indeed looked so poorly that it was surprising to hear that she was just off with her parent to Paris to collect material for the life of Napoleon Buonaparte. Scott looked tired too, but talked a good deal about Coleridge and Hogg. He tried to recall some verses by the Ettrick Shepherd, but unsuccessfully.

Moore was back again for breakfast the next morning and when he said in his unrepressed way, "How I should like to go with you!" both Scotts seemed to him to catch at his words. They were sailing from the Tower on Thursday and would only be away ten days. Up to the last moment Moore could not make up his mind. Rogers had been rather typically blighting, and had said it would be "an extraordinary frisk". Longman, on the other hand, had seemed highly pleased. (Longman was publishing *Woodstock*—John Gibson, on behalf of the Trustees, having struck a very hard bargain.) In the end, however, he did not accept, though Sir Walter said he had applied for his passport and had a seat in the carriage. Moore had himself thought it rather brave to ask such a political reprobate as himself, especially since Sir Walter was "so high with the King". They insisted that this was a business trip; they would not be dining out at all. He went to the play with them, *Peveril of the Peak*, and Miss Scott said, "One confuses the stories of these novels, there are so many of them . . . 'pon my word, papa must write more." A sure proof, thought Moore, that the mask was about to be thrown off entirely. She was rather satirical about her father's plans of retrenchment. "Papa is a bad hand at economising; all his great plans have ended in selling my horse!" To the last Moore was not quite sure whether Scott might not have gone to the Passport Office in Portland Place and added his name, and that some shabby dog there had dissuaded him. He would not put it past the Colonial Secretary.

The Scotts rose at five on Thursday morning and were in the packet by six. The weather which had been overpoweringly hot was still fine and until the very end they had an easy passage. They got a good dinner and much courtesy at Dessein's classic hotel at Calais, as her parent had told Anne they would. She was evidently doing all she could to be helpful.

Charlotte had lasted exactly eight weeks after they had got her home to Abbotsford. Abercrombie had prescribed digitalis and although at first it had seemed to help her she had been obliged to give it up. The date when Scott must leave for Edinburgh came. Dr Clarkson said she might linger some weeks and gave her laudanum which made her drowsy. When her husband went in to say *au revoir* to her she was in a deep sleep. Four days later he heard that she had died peacefully. He had sent to Cheltenham for his Canadian niece Anne, a fine responsible lass, and it had been very necessary, for his Anne had fainted and had hysterics persistently. She wrote to Sophia that she thought she had heard their mother murmur something like the words "Lord Downshire" and "father", and almost her last coherent speech had been that she would never see Sophia's boy again. Scott told Sophia, "Whatever were her failings they hurt only herself and arose out of bodily illness, and must be weighed against one of the most sincere, loyal and generous hearts that ever blood warmed." His spring and summer had been such as he prayed no honest man might be called upon to endure. There had been a terrible period after which he had heard that Little John had spinal disease and must lie flat, indefinitely. Sophia had taken him to the hot baths at Brighton. Scott foresaw that she might die in childbirth. But she bore a second son, a fortnight or three weeks too early, and though he was not at first expected to live, he took a grip on life and became a splendid child. He was baptised Walter Scott on the day before Charlotte died.

Scott had not much wanted to go down to London this year, or to France, but there was no doubt he did need information; it would be an outing for Anne, and Gibson had assured him that a Jewish bill-broker, Mr Abud, had graciously agreed to institute no legal proceedings for four or five weeks. His Edinburgh lodgings (Mrs Brown, 6 North St David Street), which at first sight had been so suitable, had proved but a whited sepulchre. He would have done better to go to the Albyn Club, but there was the difficulty that they could not take Dalgleish. This devoted servitor began within a few days to quarrel with Mrs Brown. She had the furniture from the parlour removed between midnight and 3 a.m. one fine night. Sir Walter threatened her with the beadles, and Dalgleish, in sorry triumph, brought back the author's papers, all ink-splashed—a week's work to set right. His misery reached its lowest ebb in the long light nights of June. Charles had come to see him safely into Mrs Brown's lodgings and, he was afraid, had found him weeping on the evening of their arrival. His tears were not easily checked—such as he had described of Alan Fairford in *Redgauntlet*, a throttling passion of terrible violence before the storm broke. Pretty soon he discovered with disgust that he had been much deceived. This was a dirty house. With the warmer weather the bugs became bold. He had never known such a thing in any of his homes. Charlotte had kept all in a state of sparkling cleanliness. He remembered how she would have been in and out of his room half a score of times to see if the fire burned, and to ask a hundred kind questions.

On Monday, June 7th, he noted in the Journal that as he had passed a piper on the way to a consultation with the Dean of Faculty and Constable's creditors, he had given the fellow a shilling to play *Pibroch a Donuil Dhu*—for luck's sake. That night he hardly slept. A dog howled without ceasing. "Poor cur, I daresay he had his distresses, as I have mine." Yet the Trustees had not been unsympathetic. He remembered how he used to come home from such business meetings and poor Charlotte had dressed her face in sadness or mirth to suit what expression she saw on his countenance. He had gone in to see her once only after death. He would hardly have known her. He missed her still almost hourly. Once he woke thinking he heard her calling him by a pet name.[1]

That sharp-sighted sailor, Captain Basil Hall, turned up at 6 North St David Street the next Saturday. He was pleased to see an old friend at the door. But he was horrified when he saw, on the landing outside Sir Walter's sitting-room, a tray with a single plate, and glasses for a solitary person's dinner. Only a few months past Sir Walter Scott had been surrounded by his family, and wherever he was, his headquarters were the focus of fashion. Now his wife was dead, his son-in-law and favourite daughter were gone to London, and his grandchild was said to be staggering, poor little fellow, on the edge of the grave. His elder son was married, and at a distance, "and report spoke of no possibility of the title descending".[2] But except that Sir Walter was in widower's mourning and his face was a little woebegone, he seemed essentially unchanged. He closed a volume of the *Moniteur* and came forward to ask immediately about a book of African travels by a service friend whom Hall had seen recently in London. He was made of stern stuff, and had that morning finished volume three of Napoleon. He was not so unhappy while absorbed in composition.

He had given up trying to extract any bashful whisper of a forthcoming happy event from Jane. His warnings of the dangers to young newly married ladies of dashing about in gigs had met with no response. She had become a fearless swimmer, a perfect mermaiden, from their new quarters at Athlone.

> I wish [he confessed to Morritt] that Walter could have made me a grandfather. But he tells me there are no such productions ever made in the regiment. So I told him to negotiate a change with all possible despatch and leave a corps where there was no means of striking a balance for the folks that they might send out of the world by those who they might be the means of bringing into it.

II

He showed Anne the very handsome Gothic church at Abbeville, and the magnificent cathedral at Beauvais and by Sunday, October 29th, they were well lodged in the Hotel Windsor, Rue de Rivoli. Within four days

Monsieur Meurice wrote to say that he was ready to hang himself that Sir Walter and Mlle Scott had not sought accommodation at his hotel, almost next door. But they were very snug and well fed where they were. On their first morning they hired a coach and left cards on Count Pozzo di Borgo, Lord Granville, British Ambassador, and M. Gallois, to whom their introduction had been supplied by Tom Moore. This old gentleman was the author of a History of Venice and quite invaluable. It rained. Nobody was at home, not even that old pirate Galignani at his library. None of the clerks at this establishment had the least idea who Sir Walter Scott was, but when the whisper spread, the place was in a commotion. The Louvre was closed (Monday), but he showed his companion the splendid outside, and they had an exploratory drive round the most famous quarter of the capital. They went to the Comédie Française. This was splendidly French. The piece was the tragedy of Fair Rosamond. Two or three ladies were carried out in strong hysterics. A monsieur with splendid moustaches (Scott hoped a husband), was extremely assiduous to a beautiful young lady taken very ill in the box next to theirs.

Monsieur Gallois arrived early the next morning, and sightseeing began in earnest. Anne saw the Museum, Notre Dame, the Palais de Justice and the quayside. At their hotel Count Pozzo di Borgo awaited them. He was personable, inclined to be corpulent, with handsome features and all the fire of a Corsican patriot in his eyes. He was anti-Buonaparte. He had been a perfect Old-Man-of-the-Sea to the late Lord Minto, once Viceroy of Corsica, but had wonderful powers of survival and was now in Paris as Russian Minister. Lord Granville's secretary came to invite the travellers to dinner tomorrow. They went to see *Ivanhoe* that evening at the Odéon, and Scott could not help remembering wryly how he had dictated some of this story to Will Laidlaw at Abbotsford while in agony with the stone.

The news of his arrival had now spread and an extraordinary assemblage of old wives, the Dames des Halles, waited upon him with a bouquet the size of a Maypole and a speech of welcome to Paris, all honey and oil. (Ten francs.) At the Collège Henri IV, M. Chevalier was ten years older than when they had last met, but had all his previous charm and vivacity. The Jardin des Plantes was closed, but they saw one "lioness", walking about at large, and were introduced. Madame de Souza was the authoress of romances Scott had not read, must have been beautiful and was still good-looking and very agreeable. She was the mother of the Comte de Flahaut, who was said to have been the son of Talleyrand, the lover of two queens (Caroline Buonaparte and Hortense Beauharnais), and had

ranged himself happily with the heiress daughter of furious old Admiral
Lord Keith. The Scotts received the most distinguished kindness from
Lord and Lady Granville, but this was not surprising considering that
their recommendation had come from Windsor. The British Embassy
was already known to Scott since his Waterloo-year visit. It had belonged
to Boney's favourite sister, "if its walls could speak they might tell us
mighty curious stories". Quite a number of their fellow guests were old
friends, or had been to Abbotsford, and those who had not were eager to
be introduced.

He was instructed where to stand to see the Royal Family pass to and
from chapel through the Glass Gallery at the Tuileries. The king coming
out from the service did him the honour of stopping to say a few civil
words, which created a sensation. Smiles, bows, curtsies rained on them
from the courtiers and court ladies in the procession. The Dauphine,
whom Boney had said was the man in the family, looked indeed as if she
had a good deal of character though her features were not beautiful. She
was very attentive in her devotions. Madame de Berri, the other daughter-
in-law, from whom the succession to the throne must come, yawned once
or twice. She was by no means pretty, having a cast in one eye, but a
lively-looking good-humoured blonde. Charles X, of course, Scott had
known in exile at Holyrood House—very debonair—and was to know
there again. His opinion of the Bourbon dynasty after a week in Paris
was that it had probably come to stay, let the Whigs say what they
may.

He had to give up his Journal for the last days of his stay, for French
hospitality became outrageous, and he could not refuse to sit for his
portrait to a Madame Mirbel who cried when he said he would not. She
worked while he wrote. She turned out to be useful. Her uncle, General
Monthion, had been *chef de l'état major* to Boney. As far as the business of
his visit went, he had done well. He had seen again the Orangerie from
which Boney had entered on an important stage in his career, and had long
interviews with Pozzi di Borgo, Marshal Macdonald (a splendid dinner
to follow), Marshal Marmont, the Duke of Fitz-James, grandson of
James II, M. de Molé, Minister of Justice to Boney, and the Marquis
de Lauriston. He had made the acquaintance of Mr Fenimore Cooper, the
American novelist, who wanted to help him with suggestions for publishing in America.

At the salon of Princess Galitzin, grand-daughter of Marshal Suvarov,
he was greeted by a whole covey of Russian princesses arrayed in tartan.
The lady most interesting to him was the Comtesse de Bouffleurs—

upwards of eighty and with the manners of a court lady of the days of
Madame de Sévigné. She had herself been the correspondent of Horace
Walpole.

He wrote to Ballantyne that the information he had received from conversation with Boney's friends and foes had been mostly confirmatory. He
might now attempt to draw his character with a firmer hand. He told
Mrs Scott of Harden that Anne had seen more fine folks and heard more
fine speeches than ever in her life before. She had bought a French bonnet
the size of a shovel.[3] Her father had bought a wadded dressing-gown.
His first act on arriving in Pall Mall had been to get a good London
hat.

III

They clattered into Oxford by the London road at six o'clock on the
evening of November 20th. It was, of course, dark and there was no
moon, so he was not able to see the view from Magdalen Bridge which he
used to think one of the most beautiful in the world. The expense of his
trip had been much more than he had hoped, but he knew that to rough
it would be penny wise and pound foolish. However, he had gained in
health, spirits and new ideas. He had stayed another ten days in London
on his return from Paris, and worked regularly at the Colonial Office,
Admiralty and Foreign Office on Boney material made ready for him.
Perhaps his greatest haul had been from the Duke of Wellington—"a
bundle of remarks on Boney's Russian campaign, written in his carriage
during his late mission to St Petersburg". It was furiously scrawled and
the Russian names, always difficult, were hard to decipher but it would do
yeoman service. His social life had opened with calls on the old ladies in
Piccadilly (rather sad as three of their nephews had been ruined in the
recent financial crash), the Duke of York (desperately ill and gone quite
thin), and Lord Melville (blessedly unchanged). Croker came to breakfast,
and the facetious Theodore Hook to whom Scott had hesitated to introduce Lockhart for fear of rows. Sophia gave a little "blow out" to which
came Sir Thomas Lawrence and Mistress Joanna Baillie. Lawrence was
finishing his portrait of Sir Walter Scott for Windsor. Everyone said it
was very fine. The sitter thought it a wonder how the artist had managed
to make so much out of an old weather-beaten block. They had to go out
to Putney to dine with Lady Stafford, who had Rogers and Tom Greville
to meet them and expressed herself sincerely desirous to be of service to
Sophia. He breakfasted with honest Allan Cunningham, and went, duty

bound, to attend the couch of Lydia White who had once stayed at Ashestiel, in her prime as a literary lioness. She was as eccentric and talkative as ever, unable to stir, rouged, jesting and dying.

The Duke of Wellington's simple frank manners absolutely captured Anne. He had a good party for them—the Peels, Arbuthnots, Lady Bathurst and a daughter, Vesey Fitzgerald and Croker . . . But Scott was shocked that one gentleman gave at superfluous length an account of the disgrace of a well-known peer in a gambling transaction. Peel asked him confidentially for an opinion of the candidates for the Scottish gown, and he was amused to see that his recommendation (his old friend George Cranstoun) took his seat as Lord Corehouse before the end of the month. He was grateful to Rogers for presenting him to Madame D'Arblay, the celebrated authoress of *Evelina* and *Cecilia*, an elderly lady, with no remains of personal beauty, but with a gentle manner and pleasing expression. The best conversation he heard in London was at dinner at Peel's, who afterwards showed them his picture gallery. The worst incident had been another consultation of specialists over his little grandson, who though extended on a paralytic chair had greeted "Ho-Papa" with unquenched enthusiasm and listened with rapture to a very expert story-teller recounting the adventures of his namesake Gilpin.

He had, of course, spent dutiful hours with the old Downshire man of business at Pentonville in case something left to Charlotte's mother by an unknown Welsh gentleman might mean something for his children—four thousand pounds was worth four hours' patient listening. Longmans had agreed willingly to his making what he could in America. He received before he left Pall Mall a cryptic intimation from that old coxcomb, Sir William Knighton. It meant he need worry no more about a post in the Foreign Office for his younger son. Lockhart had been extremely concerned lest repercussions of the Malachi letters might have closed the door for applications to such influential characters as Lord Melville and Croker. But Scott from the first had gone straight to the top—applied to the king.

He had the happiest memories of his visit to Windsor. Lockhart had told him that he had heard that, when the news of Sir Walter Scott's failure had been broken to His Majesty, he had been melancholy all evening. He had been invited to stay all night after dinner at Royal Lodge, the king's mock-Gothic retreat in the park. Though ridiculed by connoisseurs as much too big for the cottage style which it attempted, it was delightfully situated. (He had told Morritt after seeing the king's architectural exploits at Brighton, that while he was taking his cure there he might burn down the Chinese stables, and if the fire should embrace the whole Pavilion it would rid the world of an eyesore.) There had been no company at Royal Lodge, beside the royal retinue—Lady Conyngham, her daughter and two or three ladies. After they left the dinner table, there had been soft music from a band ambushed in a neighbouring conservatory. The king had made him sit beside him and talk—perhaps too much; for His Majesty had the art of raising one's spirits and making one forget he was in conversation with anybody except a particularly accomplished, amusing and sympathetic gentleman. Scott decided that George IV was in many respects the model for a British monarch. He had little inclination to try experiments except through his ministers, sincerely desired the good of his subjects, was kind to the distressed, and moved and spoke "every inch a king". It was to be deplored that he was not generally popular and did not nowadays show himself much in public.[4]

Scott had been chilled and saddened in London by the low standard of morals in almost every rank of life, especially at what he called the top. Lockhart had told him one horrible story of incest and even secret murder. Lockhart had thought Charles had better think of the Church since he did not want to sit for an honours degree at Oxford, where he had been enjoying himself. But this suggestion had roused Charles to a desirable interest in his future. On the morning after his dinner at Royal Lodge, Sir Walter had gone for a walk with Sir William Knighton and had much confidential chat. Scott had said that there was really nothing he wanted except to recommend Charles, when he had taken his degree, to be attached to some diplomatic mission.

Surtees and Charles had mustered, at the Oxford hotel where they had taken rooms for him and Anne, a good fire and a good dinner. Next day they breakfasted with Charles in his rooms at Brasenose College. "How pleasant it is for a father to sit at his child's board! It is like an aged man reclining under the shadow of an oak he has planted." The boys had collected young companions to act as guides for a tour of the lions of Oxford, and Surtees gave them luncheon with the best ale Sir Walter had ever drunk in his life, at his rooms in University College. The Vice-Chancellor called, but missed them. At All Souls, Scott called on Charles Douglas, heir to his brother Lord Douglas, for an hour's chat. But Oxford was now full of sad memories. Young Reginald Heber, who had shown them his Newdigate poem so many years ago, was dead, in a foreign clime. The fate of Richard Heber had caused Scott such horror when he had eard of it, that he had to write to Lockhart for confirmation. It made him almost doubt the existence of moral virtue. Heber had voluntarily resigned his seat in Parliament, changed his name and left the country. Scott realised that if this man had offered to take either of his young sons for a tour on the Continent he would have thought of it as nothing but the greatest kindness.[5]

After Oxford, they went on to Cheltenham and made the sad discovery that easier circumstances do not always improve people. Mrs Tom Scott had been left ten or twelve thousand pounds by her brother and was not nearly as agreeable as she had been as a poor relation. Scott had come happily prepared to give advice on the marriage settlement of his favourite niece, Anne, who was engaged to a Dr Allardyce. It was not quite plain sailing, as he had four children and had divorced his wife. (A few months later the match was off. The unprincipled mother had returned to England and was interfering about the children.) Three days after his return home Scott heard from Allardyce that Colonel Huxley, husband of Jessie, the eldest Tom Scott daughter, had committed suicide. There seemed absolutely no reason. Scott worried over this for weeks. Huxley had been just about to sail from Halifax. He was to have come with all his family to Abbotsford for Christmas.

The Laird of Abbotsford arrived at his gates for the festive season, so afflicted with rheumatism that he could not suppress a howl as he was helped out of his carriage. His children and neighbours had rallied as they had done all through the summer. The Lockharts were coming, the Captain and Jane from Ireland, all to stay, and the Skenes, Laidlaws, Russells and Fergusons, to feast and dance. Once more the sound of the pipe and the harp was to be heard in his lonely halls. Fate was against him. He got to Mertoun to dine with the Scotts of Harden as usual on Christmas Eve, but he had not been able to struggle up the little spiral staircase outside his study to his bedroom the night before, and had been obliged "to take up my lodging in the chapel room as it is called. We were late in setting out and I have rarely seen so dark a night. The mist rose like volumes of smoke on the road before us."

IV

By January 3rd, 1827, he told the Journal he was mending slowly, and was determined not to mark down any more griefs and groans. He was tired of chronicling "fomentations of camomile flowers, leeches and embrocation, plasters and unguents". Two things were for the best—he lost no good weather by being confined to his chair, as the ground was covered by snow, and if he could summon sufficient stoicism he had a good opportunity to get on with Nap. But as he could scarcely stand, he was awkward at consulting books and maps.

The guests came and went, and he managed by dint of "handing and chairing" to get to the dining-room and drawing-room, but he could not attempt an expedition to Mr Scrope at the Pavilion. He only once had to retire to his bed from the dinner table. Still, the valiant Blücher coach carried regularly packets of Boney for Ballantyne, and he dauntlessly prepared to return to take up his duties in Edinburgh, his holidays over. Two Tweedside landlords exchanged greetings in a wintry scene. "Coming through Galashiels we met the Laird of Torwoodlee, who, on hearing how long I had been confined, asked how I bore it, observing that he had once in his life (Torwoodlee must be between sixty and seventy) been confined for five days in the house, and was like to hang himself."[6]

Sir Walter Scott was never again to descend to the squalor of Mrs Brown's two rooms and Dalgleish to look after him. He had taken the whole house at 3 Walker Street, and was interested to see that some of the furniture had obviously come from the sale at Castle Street. He remembered Charlotte choosing it. The old home had rather hung on the market and he had been obliged in the end to agree to a price he thought three hundred pounds short of its value. He now brought up with him Anne and two maids. John Nicolson, in service at Abbotsford from boyhood, footman for some years past, quiet, efficient and observant, was going to replace the devoted but dreadful Dalgleish. At last the old man had been persuaded to consider retirement. He had rejected all Captain Basil Hall's kind offers of another situation. Scott had long thought that with his extraordinary rueful countenance he would have made a fortune in the employ of any creditable undertaker. He was almost illiterate, but he knew what he meant to do. He was going to be an author.

> Memoirs of Sir Walter Scott
>   by Willm. Dalgleish
> During his services in Sir Walter's
>   from 1822–1829.

Walker Street, Sir Walter guessed, was almost a mile and a half from the Court, but he thought the exercise would be beneficial, and by the end of January he proudly noted, "My rheumatism is almost gone." He thought nothing of Dr Ross's medicines but found a chamois-leather knee-cap helpful. Basil Hall had brought in to call upon him the lion of the moment, Mr Audubon, the ornithologist, an American by naturalisation, a Frenchman by birth, but less of a Frenchman than Scott had ever seen—no dash or glitter. He had simple manners, and was slight in person and plainly dressed. Scott wished now that he had been to look at Mr Audubon's exhibition. After two days the author-artist reappeared, bringing some of his bird pictures—absolutely of the first order. Another of Sir Walter's callers was not quite a stranger and not quite out of his teens, "Young Murray, son of Mr M. in Albemarle St breakfasted with me. English boys have this advantage, that they are well-bred and can converse when ours are regular cubs. I am not sure if it is an advantage in the long-run. It is a temptation to premature display." He repeated the observation during the spring recess at Abbotsford when Mr Bainbridge's boys from Gattonside came over, "invited to see the armoury, which I stood showman to". He had to admit that southern boys were well-mannered and sensible. Perhaps the sun brought them forward. But he had been anxious that his grandson should not become a perfect little English-speaking boy. Sophia set his mind at rest. Johnny and the Terry children were sharing a governess with the name of Miss MacTavish.

He was pleased by a letter from the Baron von Goethe. Who would have thought, thirty years ago, that he should correspond and be on something like an equal footing with the author of *Goetz*—the Ariosto and almost the Voltaire of Germany?

This was the season for dinners in Edinburgh, and invitations came thick and fast. He accepted less than of old, but was regular at the Bannatyne and Royal societies. An incident in February took him by surprise. He had agreed to take the chair at a subscription banquet in aid of the Edinburgh Theatrical Fund—at least three hundred guests were expected. As they assembled, little Lord Meadowbank, who was going to propose the vote of thanks, bustled up to ask permission to refer to him as the author of *Waverley*. Since the formation of the Trust revealing all his connections with Constable, the secret was out. He replied, "Do just as you like—only don't say too much about so old a story." But Lord Meadowbank was dramatic, referring to him as "the Great Unknown, the minstrel of our native land—the mighty magician who has rolled back the curtain of time . . . We owe to him as a people a large and heavy debt of gratitude. It is HE who has called down upon their struggle for glory and freedom, the admiration of foreign lands," etc. Before the speaker had ended, the company had mounted upon tables and chairs and the storm of applause was deafening. Scott's reply was that like another criminal of more consequence—one Macbeth—he pleaded guilty.

I am afraid to think what I have done;
Look on't again, I dare not . . .

"The wand is broken, and the book buried. You will allow me further to say, with Prospero, it is your breath that has filled my sails." The affair was widely and he thought very badly reported.[7]

But he was far from retiring. He had got to the retreat from Moscow in *Boney*. In Edinburgh weather was suitable—hard frost, and snow flying past his windows. The little room in which he was writing seemed snug in comparison with what he was describing. He put into the Journal, rather occasionally, happenings in Court. A breathless assemblage had gathered to gloat upon a horrible case. A woman of rather the better class, a farmer's wife, had been tried for poisoning her maid-servant.

> The unfortunate girl had had an intrigue with her son, which this Mrs Smith (I think that is the name) was desirous to conceal, from some ill-advised puritanic notions, and also for fear of her husband. She could find no better way of hiding the shame than giving the girl (with her own knowledge and consent, I believe) potions to cause abortion, which she afterwards changed for arsenic, as the more effectual silencing medicine.

But as this tale of horror was unveiled, one of the jurymen fell down in an epileptic fit. It was impossible to proceed. The woman appeared again a fortnight later. She was, in Scott's opinion, clearly guilty, "but as one or two witnesses said the poor wench had hinted an intention to poison herself, the jury gave that bastard verdict, *Not proven*". In spite of his admiration for everything Caledonian, Sir Walter hated that verdict. "One who is not proven guilty is innocent in the eyes of the law."[8] The woman's face was one to make a heart stand still. As they were moving out Sir Walter told Henry Cockburn and others, "Well, sirs, all I can say is that if that woman was my wife I should take good care to be my own cook."

On March 3rd he told the Journal of "Very severe weather, came home covered with snow. White as a frosted plum-cake, by jingo! No matter; I am not sorry to find I can stand a brush of weather yet; I like to see Arthur's Seat and the stern old Castle with their white watch-cloaks on." On Tweedside, Haig of Bemersyde, who had been five years in balmy Italy with his family, had been absolutely stuck in a drift, on a hill with a famous view overlooking his property, a great favourite with Sir Walter. Deserted by their postilion and horses they had been obliged to stay all night there.

L

The Royal Society of Literature desired to show recognition of his many works of pre-eminent genius, both in prose and verse. He wished it could have been a pension for poor Hogg. He sent the secretary's letter on to Lockhart asking him to attend in his place. Anne seemed to think the medal should be set in a substantial bread-basket, for dinner or break-fast rolls. He had thought of a salver. Sophia would make some enquiries and would know best.[9]

He got down to Abbotsford in the middle of April and the middle of a great thaw, which set rivers streaming. Tom Purdie and the dogs received him with unsophisticated feelings of goodwill. An old friend was missing. Mr Hinzie, the old tom-cat, long drunk with power, accustomed to dominating all the small fry and even the enormous Maida, had been speedily despatched by Nimrod, the staghound, sympathetically sent by Glengarry at the time of Sir Walter's worst financial troubles. Dalgleish, for the last time, had packed up books in the Edinburgh lodgings, and they had not arrived, so the Laird could do nothing but reviews for Lockhart and calls on neighbours. He drove over to Huntly Burn with Anne, and Tom Purdie tugged him through the remaining snow wreaths as they walked home together through the plantations. He took up *Boney* again. He was pleased, when he went out on the heights without Purdie on a stormy day, to find he could still face the gale staunchly. Tom would have made him keep to the sheltered ground. He expected falls these days in the slippy heather, but nobody was ever the worse for that, and when he came in glowing, he worked hard and got a whole bundle of proofs and copy ready for the Blücher tomorrow. He walked with Colonel Russell for nearly three hours in the woods and enjoyed "the sublime and delectable pleasure of simply feeling well". His cousin was a patient and appreciative audience on his favourite subject of laying out ground. Amongst the by-jobs awaiting attention was an article on Planting of Waste Lands.

He was surrounded by artists. He thought highly of William Allan, but Mr Scrope's friend, the Rev. John Thomson of Duddingston, he believed was the best landscape-painter of their age. Sir Walter had two younger men to help him now with copying—Andrew Shortreed, a fine lad, at Abbotsford, and Robert Hogg in Edinburgh, a nephew of the Ettrick Shepherd, modest and clever. Shortreed was a little forward, struck with Miss Anne Scott's fine eyes.

Scott returned to Edinburgh with rather a sinking heart. Abbotsford was beginning to look so beautiful; but a new opportunity for outdoor exercise presented itself. The Committee of the Princes Street Gardens had sent him a pass-key. He used it for the first time on coming out of Court on May 22nd and walked up to Shandwick Place to call on Mrs Jobson. She was going to Ramsgate, and he had his eye on her house for his next quarters. This extraordinarily rash experiment was arranged, and against all reasonable expectation was a success.

On June 7th he wrote the proud words "This morning finished Boney". A happy summer awaited him. The Lockharts had taken seaside lodgings in Portobello, and came up by steamer. Lockhart believed that his father-in-law's almost daily expeditions to dine and stroll on the beach with them was a source of constant refreshment at a critical period. *Boney* had occupied him for two years. In his gloomier moments he referred to the book as "my millstone", but he had vastly enjoyed his task. The Journal had become full of notes on highlights of his hero's career. "Got Boney over the Alps"; "Finished Jena. I believe it has taken me more time to write it than Boney took to win it!" He saw again from the description of an eyewitness, the roadside first meeting of the impatient Emperor with his gauche Austrian bride. He got Boney to Elba . . .

But it was not to be imagined that while he waited for production of this lengthy chronicle he was idle. Before he had actually tied it up he was off on what was to be his most famous and best-selling by-job, a history of his native land for little Johnnie, *Tales of a Grandfather*.

> The morning was damp, dripping and unpleasant; so I even made a work of necessity and set to the Tales like a dragon. I murdered M'Lellan of Bomby at Thrieve Castle; stabbed the Black Douglas in the town of Stirling, astonished King James before Roxburgh; and stifled the Earl of Mar in his bath in the Canongate.

He sent proofs to Johnnie as they came in, and the young critic returned comments by Mrs Hughes. "He very much dislikes the chapter on Civilisation, and it is his desire that you will never say anything more about it, for he dislikes it extremely." His Aunt Anne had sent him a paint-box, and letters to his grandfather now included highly coloured sketches of his family. The dedication of *Tales of a Grandfather* was waggish. "Humbly inscribed to Hugh Littlejohn Esq". Published in December 1827, the first edition ran out at once.

It was a pity that the Lockharts' arrival could not have been postponed until after Scott had been for what he called "my antiquarian skirmish beginning in Fife". The members of the Blair Adam Club with whom he visited St Andrews, the manor houses of Elie and Balcaskie and Wemyss Castle, included Will Clerk, Adam Ferguson and Thomson, and they picked up the Lord Chief Baron and Lord Chief-Commissioner at Charlton, home of the Anstruther Thomsons. He did not go up St Rule's Tower at St Andrews, as on former occasions. He sat down on a gravestone and remembered how he had come there thirty-four years past on fire for a suitor's visit to Fettercairn and carved in Runic characters on the turf beside the gate the name of his *chère adorable*. "But my friends came down from the tower and the foolish idea was chased away."

Ten days after his return to Edinburgh, Cadell burst in just as he was sitting down to dinner, in high spirits about *Napoleon*. Orders were pouring in. Altogether skies were brightening. Lord Stafford, whom he had met with Lady Stafford on their way up to Dunrobin as he came south, wanted to join the Bannatyne. So did Lord Melville and Colin McKenzie. Charles arrived from Oxford having taken his degree—penniless but that could be mended. Sir William Knighton was informed. The only thing to be desired now was an appointment for Lockhart, and in that he had utterly failed, try as he would. A long correspondence with Canning about a post in the Excise had ended in that statesman behaving as handsomely as possible. He admitted that he had been quite mistaken in supposing that Mr Lockhart had written against him. But then Lord Liverpool had a stroke, and Canning, after breaking with Peel and Wellington, became Prime Minister for four months before dying, worn out. Lockhart had kept his father-in-law well informed about "the beautiful mess they were making in London". Scott could only wish that his beloved son-in-law had not such a brilliant talent for getting on the wrong side of important characters.

July at Abbotsford was idyllic. The Lockharts joined him, and to his great joy Johnnie was so decidedly improved he could sit on his Shetland pony, Marion, who had been running in the lush grass almost hidden, looking like a black Newfoundland dog. Little Walter Scott Lockhart was a very fine child.

The problem of the emus was a little vexing until the Duke of Buccleuch, kindly as ever, offered them a home at Dalkeith. They were an unsolicited gift from a protégé, George Harper of Darnick, just returned from Sydney and apparently, though possessed of every virtue, the birds were as large as ostriches. Enquiries at the Tower of London menagerie had brought the disappointing reply that His Majesty was already provided.

July was very warm on Tweedside. Scott regretted that the only room which he mistakenly believed to have a southern aspect was his study.

I have been baking and fevering myself like a fool for these two years in a room exposed to the south; comfortable in winter but broiling in the hot weather. Now I have removed myself into the large cool library, one of the most refreshing as well as handsomest rooms in Scotland, and will not use the study again until heats are past.

He heard of two deaths at once. Lady Diana Scott, widow of Walter Scott of Harden, had still had an acute mind at ninety-two. She had been remarkably kind to him as a boy. Archibald Constable, upon reflection, he could not think had been very kind to him. When he had first heard, the year before last, of the possibility of Constable failing, he had felt as if the skies were falling. Now he received the news of the death of someone who had once meant much to him, almost without regret. Except for the last five thousand pounds sent to bolster up Hurst and Robinson he considered now that Constable had not injured him intentionally. (He did not recollect that Cadell and Ballantyne had been equally pressing about the Abbotsford mortgage.) "He was a prince of booksellers; his views sharp, powerful and liberal, too sanguine however, and like many bold and successful schemers, never knowing when to stand or stop . . ." He had been very vain, and not without reason, he had not been what is termed literary, but he knew the rare volumes in his library not only by the eye but by the touch. He could be violent when his adversary was not of too much consequence; but on the whole had been generous and not bad-hearted. "I have no great reason to regret him; yet I do. If he deceived me, he also deceived himself."[10] Two evenings later he heard from Gibson the most welcome tidings that Lord Newton had decided that the profits of *Woodstock* and *Napoleon* should belong to the author. This removed the most important part of his dispute with Constable's creditors. He had never heard of anyone not being able to sleep for happiness. Now the *Chronicles of the Canongate*, on which he was at work, would be all pure gain. "The money realised will pay one-third of all I owe in the world— and what will pay the other two-thirds? I am as well and as capable as when these misfortunes began."

He cut wood with Tom Purdie for four hours one morning, laying the foundation for future scenery. Mr Adolphus, who had always known who must have written the novels, came for three nights. Anyone less enthusiastic might have been daunted by the fact that during most of his stay it rained so hard that one could scarcely go out; but he noticed plenty indoors, and even out. The plantations had grown much since his last visit three years ago. Sir Walter's favourite afternoon walk was through them, conversing while he used his knife. Going uphill he would sometimes stop, leaning on his stick, and pour forth some sonorous stanza of an old poem applicable to the scene. Nimrod had a habit of standing statuesquely on knolls at effective intervals. So many books in the library were enriched by marginal comments in Sir Walter's own hand, that a wet morning amongst them was almost as good as speaking to him in person. He did sometimes appear from his study to look up some point, and his young guest heard with pleasure, after a long silence, the sound of an uneven step and a stick. He invited Adolphus into his writing-room, gave him the publications of the Bannatyne Club to look through, and resumed writing—almost certainly the book for the grandson. Peace reigned unbroken except by the rattle of rain against the windows, and the dash of the author's pen across his sheet. There did not seem to be any rule against his being interrupted, and he sometimes was, by a flurry of little dogs barking, and a merry outcry from one of the grandchildren which would cause the enormous dogs, who slept at their master's feet, to stir and give a mimic growl.[11] Bran was the gift of Cluny Macpherson.

Mr Adolphus left, and Sir Walter resumed calling upon neighbours and dining. The Fergusons had a brother, a colonel from India, staying, and a naval brother, fresh from the Spanish Main; both were full of information. Scott had become quite an admirer of that honest John Bull, Mr Bainbridge, the *nouveau riche* from Liverpool who had bought Gattonside. He turned up his plate at the breakfast table and said it interested him for he had started life in a china shop. After they had left Castle Street a bill had come in for china and glass ordered by Lady Scott—nearly four hundred pounds. But Sir Walter's service at Abbotsford was beautiful—full-blown roses with golden foliage.[12]

At last, in the very end of August, he did something he ought to have done long ago—called at Fleurs Castle. This was a little awkward. Four months after the death of Charlotte, a pompous idiot whom he did not know at all well, Sir John Sinclair, had written to say how beautiful it would be if Sir Walter Scott should propose to the Dowager Duchess of Roxburgh. There was historical precedent. Addison, an author, had made a match with the Dowager Countess of Warwick. Sir John was a regular visitor at Fleurs, and after receiving a reply which should have been a quietus, wrote again from that address regretting Sir Walter's want of enterprise. He was there with his daughters when the party from Abbotsford turned up this year. Scott had taken the Lockharts and Allan. "The great lady received us well, though we have been very remiss in our duty." Sir John had been quite right though in saying that she was not averse from re-marriage. In November she went to the altar with Colonel O'Reilly of the 41st Regiment.[13] But folly seemed to run in the Sinclair family. In 1830, a son, the Rev. John, wrote to tell Sir Walter that his sister nourished affection for the author of *Waverley*. ("The Lord Deliver us!")

Lord Goderich was not supposed to be likely to stay in office long as Prime Minister. In early October Scott accepted an invitation to go down to Ravensworth Castle where the Duke of Wellington would be making what was practically an electioneering campaign in the neighbourhood. He met several old friends, including Lawrence and Lord Lothian. In Durham when the Duke arrived late there were bells and cannon and drums and trumpets and a fine troop of yeomanry. Scott thought the enthusiasm of the ladies and gentry was great but otherwise the crowd was lukewarm. The stately Prince-Bishop looked ill, but was very civil, proposing the health of the author of *Waverley* in a splendid old baronial hall where a hundred and fifty banqueters had a hot dinner, and bright moonlight streamed in through Gothic windows. At Sunderland the crowds were immense—many seamen. When the Duke left to stay with the new Lord Londonderry at Seaham, Scott went on to Alnwick where the Duke of Northumberland drove him through his park, laid out by the celebrated Brown, and very ill-planted with non-indigenous clumps of birch and Scottish firs, instead of the magnificent oaks which grew so freely in this part of the country. To complete this, the late Duke had not had them thinned. People would not buy wood where coal was so cheap. Scott thought his host and hostess agreeable and high-principled, perhaps a little formal; they would scorn to be fashionable.

Two troubles, both of which contained elements of the ridiculous, vexed his autumn. He had always foreseen that General Gourgaud would not like what he had disclosed about him in his life of Boney. He went in to see Will Clerk to ask if he would act as second if Gourgaud challenged him, and Will agreed. Scott had Buonaparte's own pistols taken from his carriage at Waterloo and would be glad to use them on a lying minion. He was not at all dismayed when poor Ballantyne wrote to warn him Gourgaud was a crack shot, a *mauvais garçon* and a *beau sabreur*. Even Cadell was in a funk. Sir Walter published in the *Edinburgh Weekly Journal* a letter of serious length giving chapter and verse for all his allegations. He had seen the St Helena correspondence at the Colonial Office and could prove from his own hand that Gourgaud had informed British Ministers that his old master's health was good, his confinement was easy and his finances were ample. Later he had told French audiences that the Emperor had been treated by Sir Hudson Lowe with the utmost harshness. Gour-gaud was a deplorable creature. General Bertrand, much the best of the exiled Emperor's *suite*, had said that he pilfered candle-ends and cold victuals. But Sir Walter would not bring in evidence that might mean trouble for Bertrand. The St Helena papers made sorry reading, but fascinating. He did not allow Gourgaud to concern him too greatly. He wrote the second volume of *Tales of a Grandfather*, smoked his cigar with Lockhart after dinner, and then whiled away the evening over one of Miss Austen's inimitable novels. The French press was hot about the insult to a national hero (Gourgaud really had twice in the days of Boney's prosperity saved his life), but Gourgaud made no interesting attempt to refute Scott's devastating letter and did not come to London.[14]

On October 24th Scott was suddenly vilely low in spirits. He felt as if something melancholy or horrible was about to happen. He tried to walk it off. After a page and a half he did not attempt to write any more. Anyway they were going to dine at Mertoun. Here he heard young George Scott had gone up in a balloon. He laughed and said that he would never have expected honest George of something so flighty. He walked along her riverside with Mrs Scott and wished her lord and master could have had something of her taste for planting. Nothing could have been more normal. When he got home he found another letter from Lady Jane Stuart, mother of his first love. He had heard from her a week before, but merely a formal request on behalf of a friend for permission to quote. "Methinks this explains the gloom which hung about me yesterday. I own that the recurrence of these matters seems like a summons from the grave." She now said that she would like to meet him. The house to which she had retired as a widow was in Maitland Street very close to Shandwick Place, and she had often seen him pass her windows. He felt as if he ought to have stopped it at once, but during the next black month he did call upon her four times, and they were very sad together.

For his second cause for worry that autumn was agonising, and came upon him almost at once. He was disturbed cutting trees on the last day of October, by the arrival of Mr Gibson with a melancholy look. It was Abud again. His firm had never recognised the Trustees arrangement and possessed two Hurst and Robinson bills amounting to £1,760. Scott's decision was instant and adamant. He refused for the second time to go bankrupt. This would undo all the careful and beneficent work of the Trust, and leave him in the position which he had disdained nearly two years ago. But Abud had already begun legal proceedings, ordering him to pay the debt or go to jail. To avoid that he could either fly to the

Isle of Man as Brother Tom had once done, or retire to the precincts of Holyrood as Cadell had once done. He decided upon Holyrood; this course would protect his other creditors.

Lockhart believed that during the next weeks Sir Walter actually made preparations for quitting Shandwick Place and driving down to the Abbey to declare himself a debtor willing to pay but at present unable to do so. The Trustees tussled with Abud, making handsome counter-offers, but he was determined on his pound of flesh. Gilnockie came up from his quarters at Canterbury to offer sympathy and any possible aid. The Lockharts offered to take in Anne, in spite of the fact that Sophia expected her next child about Christmas. Their father replied that he believed Anne would wish to stay with him. He had chosen the Abbey on her account. He had a hopeful week while the Trustees started what he called a new hare. Abud's firm were gold-refiners; their payment had been in ingots at an inflated value; they might be guilty of usury. Abud's Edinburgh agents looked queer and talked of throwing up the business. But it was hardly to be expected that so long-sighted a firm had not foreseen such an accusation. The Trustees filed a bill of suspension, and uneasy peace settled. When the case against Abud came on they lost and paid. They did not want to dissolve the Trust. The ghost of Abud was not finally laid till February 1828, but Scott had long known the Trustees' intention. Not until the death of Sir William Forbes on October 24th did he learn that his old friend had settled with Abud privately—to the cost of three thousand pounds, Lockhart believed.

November 1827 was a black month. Scott's two latest publications, *Miscellaneous Prose* and *Chronicles of the Canongate*, sold disappointingly. This did not disturb him so much as the possibility that it might interfere with a plan for getting from Constable's creditors the copyrights of all his poetry and all the novels from *Waverley* to *Quentin Durward*—a collected edition, "the Magnum Opus". Cadell bought this gold-mine on December 17th jointly for himself and Scott at eight thousand five hundred pounds. The Trust had just paid its first dividend, six shillings to the pound. Scott had been earning at the rate of twenty thousand pounds per annum for his creditors. A suggestion from him that he might rest on his oars for a bit was unwelcome to Cadell and Ballantyne. In renewed spirits he started another novel, *The Fair Maid of Perth*.

He arrived at Abbotsford on Christmas Eve.

My reflections on entering my own gate were of a very different and more pleasing cast than those with which I left my house about six weeks ago. I was then in doubt whether I should fly my country or become avowedly bankrupt, and surrender my library and household furniture with the life-rent of my estate to sale . . . But I could not have slept sound as I now can . . . If I achieve my task I shall have the thanks of all concerned, and the approbation of my own conscience. And so I think I can fairly face the return of Christmas Day.[15]

NOTES

1. Letters X, 27, 35–39. Journal, I, 1–202. Lockhart, IV, Chapter LXX, covers Scott's daily life in 1826 until the death of Charlotte.
2. Journal, I, 213–26. Lockhart, V, 6–8. Dalgleish, 215, 223.
3. Scott's 1826 London and Paris visits are covered by Journal, I, 276–311; Lockhart, V, Chapter LXXI; *Journal of Thomas Moore*, Quennell (1963), 141–5.
4. Journal, I, 278–9.
5. Journal, I, 312. Letters, X, 100, 229. Richard Heber alarmed his widowed sister-in-law by saying he was coming home to live at Hodnet in Shropshire, a few months after his flight; but he stayed abroad till 1831, and lived in seclusion until his death in 1833. His fabulous library was dispersed in sales over three years. Scott never ceased to wish that he would return to take up his old place in the world, and clear his name; but this it appeared was not possible.
6. Journal, I, 340.
7. Letters, X, 173. Lockhart, V, 93.
8. Journal, I, 335, 361.
9. Letters, IX, 185.
10. Journal, II, 11–13.
11. Lockhart, V, 131–3. Mr Adolphus has got the big dogs wrong. Bran did not turn up at Abbotsford until 1830.
12. Letters, X, 26.
13. Letters, 103; Journal, II, 235.
14. Letters, X, 276–82. Journal, I, 137; and II, 26, 30, 36.
15. Letters, 301–8, 317–18, 375. Lockhart, V, 154. Journal, II, 57–94.

XVIII

"We Must Take What Fate Sends"

1828–1832

I

MR JAMES FENIMORE COOPER, PASSING THROUGH PALL MALL ON A
fine spring morning of 1828, made a welcome discovery. "I saw a mer-
maid combing her hair before a small mirror, as the crest on a chariot
that stood at a door, and I at once thought I recognised the arms of Sir
Walter Scott. On examining closer, I found the bloody hand, which left
no doubt that the literary baronet was in town."

He was quite right, and although he was disappointed that neither Sir
Walter nor his daughter seemed to remember him when they met in a
drawing-room a few days later, happy relations were soon re-established,
and on hearing that the intelligent American was Consul for Lyons, Sir
Walter asked him if he could discover the birth certificate of the late
Lady Scott. It was needed for an inheritance left to her mother and now
falling to his family. Mr Fenimore Cooper was able to perform this within
the month. The fact was that Sir Walter on this trip south was being
lionised as never before and had been working too hard. He had not
really been very keen on coming south this year, as he had no pressing
duty connected with research for any book; but his family had much

encouraged him to quit his desk. Anne needed a holiday and there was a new grandchild for him to see in the Lockharts' new house—Charlotte Harriet Jane, born on New Year's Day, named for her grandmother, the late Duchess of Buccleuch and Mrs Scott of Lochore. Charles was now boarding with the Lockharts, and going to the Foreign Office daily in high spirits. Sir Walter made Sophia an allowance for his keep. The party from Abbotsford—Sir Walter, Anne, her personal maid, Mrs Cissy Street, and John Nicolson on the box, had done a little sight-seeing *en route*. At Carlisle Cathedral Scott had taken his daughter to stand on the spot where he had married poor mama. He had shown her Kenilworth Castle in April showers. The ruins which had been much neglected on his last visit in 1815 were now preserved and protected. Since the publication of a Waverley novel they had been a tourist attraction. Scott was shocked to find decent children begging here, a thing uncommon in England; but that had been the same last time.

Lord and Lady Warwick (obviously in low water owing to the late Lord Warwick), received them kindly and gave them lunch. They finished up the day at Stratford-on-Avon. Scott had never yet succeeded in seeing the monument to William Shakespeare in the church there. They found Charlecote where traditionally Shakespeare had been sent to gaol for stealing Sir Thomas Lucy's deer, still in the possession of Lucys and still with verdant pastures in which numerous herds of deer were reposing in the shade. Mr Lucy said that his ancestor had been living at the time of Shakespeare's trespass in another mansion.[1] They proceeded by Edgehill (a fine prospect of splendidly rich country), by Buckingham (ancient but ugly) and Aylesbury, through the wealth of Shakespeare's England, in the pretty springtime. They got to town about midday on April 9th.

After a brief trial of Wimbledon (too far from Albemarle Street for the Editor of the *Quarterly*), Lockhart had settled his family in a house which he was to occupy for a quarter of a century. 24, Sussex Place, Regent's Park (Outer Circle), was just inside Clarence Gate. It was, of course, comparatively new (begun in 1812), and might have been in Edinburgh—terrace upon terrace of handsome houses in the classic style. The park was not open to the public so was blessedly peaceful, and proud nurses paraded favoured infants in competitive fury.[2] Mrs Margaret Carpenter the artist had said that Johnny Lockhart—a regular little St John—was the most admired. He looked to his grandfather sadly white, but his mother said he had so much enjoyed the History of Scotland that he had tried to dirk his younger brother with the scissors. Lockhart was gorgeously unchanged, quite as devastating in literary criticism as ever,

When his father-in-law asked him "Pray who writes *Pelham*?"—a novel published this season which he had found very interesting—Lockhart replied, "*Pelham* is writ by a Mr Bulwer, a Norfolk squire and horrid puppy. I have not read the book from disliking the author, but shall do so since you approve of it."

Scott opened his London campaign by calls on the Dumergues and at Albemarle Street. Mr Murray was thinking of a Family Library and wanted a collection of Scott's essays on planting (which had appeared in the *Quarterly*), perhaps prefaced by a sketch of the life of Evelyn, and also really any biography Sir Walter would choose. But the reply was that the only Life he could do easily was Mary Queen of Scots, "and that I decidedly would not do, because my opinion, in point of fact, is contrary both to the popular feeling and my own."[3]

Gilnockie was now stationed at Hampton Court. He had been disappointed not to be ordered to India, or to Portugal, to start another Peninsular war, against the Regent, Dom Miguel, who was aiming at a tyranny. Jane and he came up to dine at Sussex Place and asked the whole family down to them, Sunday first. Scott walked himself tired paying calls, and began to recollect that he could not stand London late hours. When proofs from Edinburgh came in, he fell upon them and sent off the last of *The Fair Maid of Perth* after a morning's work. Next day he got the lamentable news that Terry was bankrupt. Some people thought he had been badly treated by his partner over the theatre, but some that he was just a hopeless case. Scott grew mournful thinking of his other failures. "It is written that nothing shall flourish under my shadow, the Ballantynes, Terry, Nelson, Weber, all came to distress." Rather an unexpected publication with his name as author had appeared this January—a slim volume of sermons. He had written them for poor George Huntley Gordon, when a candidate for the ministry. This was the afflicted son of the half-pay officer with whom he had ridden over the field of Waterloo. Gordon, who was quite deaf, had not succeeded in getting a parish. Scott had found him various jobs, but he was now in debt. He had asked permission to sell the two discourses. Scott would much rather not, but they had brought in two hundred and fifty pounds.

When the visitors from Abbotsford had been at Sussex Place less than a fortnight, a blow fell. Johnnie was taken ill. He was feverish and could not stop coughing: he was spitting blood. That he had never done before. Sophia rushed with him to his specialist, Dr Yates of Brighton, and Anne accompanied her. Mrs Scott of Harden was to have taken Anne to Almacks, and she had brought a new gown. As soon as he could, Lockhart followed them, so Sir Walter, who had come to London to see his family, and looked forward to his after-dinner talks with Lockhart, was left with just young Charles. Lockhart went up and down during the next weeks. He fetched the younger children. Scott saw many old friends and made several expeditions to people and places unknown. As he had been elected Professor of Antiquities, he went to Royal Academy dinners. He went to the Literary Society, the Royal Society, and the Roxburghe. He dined with Sotheby, where Coleridge's manners horrified Mr Fenimore Cooper. He said not a word until he had gobbled his dinner. He was rude about the navy, though his host had a son in the Royal Service. When the ladies retired, he fairly talked everyone down—first upon the Samothracian Mysteries and next Homer. Sir Walter had sat immovable as statue, muttering only "Eloquent", "Wonderful" or "Extraordinary". He told the Journal, though, that he had never been so be-thumped with words.

He went down to the Duke of Devonshire's Palladian villa at Chiswick. A numerous and gay party walked in the highly ornamented gardens. He was reminded of a picture by Watteau. An immense elephant, under the charge of a groom, was led up and down, giving an air of Asiatic pageantry to the entertainment. It was a Saturday, and he was due to dine at Holland House for the first time for twelve years. He gladly agreed to change there into a demi-toilette and stay all night, sooner than drive back to London and then out again.

On Sunday morning, Rogers and he wandered about the Kensington lanes and might have been twenty miles from a town. Sir William Knighton had returned from abroad and sent a warning that he was to be summoned to a small private party at Windsor. He also wanted Sir Walter to sit for a portrait to Northcote, an ancient painter like an antiquated mummy. Scott needed Sir William's good offices for Lockhart, so could not refuse. He was already having to sit for Haydon, for Colvin Smith, a cousin of Robert Gillies in Edinburgh, and Chantrey. He was, as usual, received very kindly at Royal Lodge, and heard that the dedication of the Magnum Opus would be welcomed.

He had another royal summons—to dine with the widowed Duchess of Kent, a very pleasing and affable lady. Her brother, Prince Leopold, kindly recognised him and spoke of Abbotsford. He was presented to the little Princess Victoria, the heiress apparent to the throne as things now stood. She was fair, like the royal family, but did not look as if she would be pretty. He hoped they would change her name.

He went down to Brighton and found it twice the size it had been in 1815—a Vanity Fair, a city of invalids and loiterers. It almost broke his heart to look at Johnnie—yet he was better. The younger children—so unlike, blonde and solid—were in "high kelter". He was happy at Sophia's quiet table and only sorry he must leave her so soon. Almost his last outing was to take a party of lions and lionesses down to Hampton Court again—Samuel Rogers, Tom Moore, Wordsworth, wife and daughter. The band played and Tom thought that the Hampton blues were all eyes for the author of *Waverley*; the other scribblers were not worth a glance. Scott just saw Southey, when deep in the business of tearing up papers, writing thanks and paying bills. It appears sadly probable that this was the occasion when he tore up one, or perhaps two letters about medals sent him by Goethe, via Scotland, dated April 15th and May 23rd. The writer's name was not yet well known in literary circles—Thomas Carlyle, who did not forget or forgive.4

Scott reckoned that, upon the whole, though his holiday had been expensive, and Johnnie's illness had taken away much of the pleasure, he had not done so badly. He had been able to place Lockhart "on the right footing and in the right quarter". He had picked up a lot of interesting information about current affairs (The Duke of Wellington, Mr Peel, Lord Bathurst, Lord Sidmouth, Croker). He had remembered to tell the Journal that Emily, Lady Londonderry, had said you must never feed a beast with a glove on your hand: it affronted the animal; and that Coke of Norfolk had told him that Withers, who had published a *Letter to Sir Walter Scott exposing certain fundamental errors in his late Essay on Planting* had never been employed at Holkham except upon some very small twenty-acre jobs. He had got a commission for young James Skene, and got Andrew Shortreed a free passage to India. He had to use a fisherman's simile for his good luck in placing two sons of Allan Cunningham. Both John Loch, a Director of the East India Company, and Lord Melville had promised cadetships, so he had caught two trouts, one with the fly and the other on the bobber. He had gone with Lockhart to see Miss Jane Nicolson and it looked as if the sum coming from Mme Charpentier's estate would be nearer five than four thousand. He had been able to help Terry materially. Finally, he had managed to protect his Darnick neighbours and himself against the New Road bill.

He took Anne on the first days of their journey home into the narrow lanes of Hertfordshire to see three of the great houses of that county. At Moor Park, now the property of Lord Grosvenor, Thornhill's entrance hall was handsome in the French style. The Grove, Lord Clarendon's seat, was much smaller, but had a fine park and, he was told, pictures. Cassiobury (Lord Essex) adjoined The Grove, and was very old, and picturesque.

The river Colne rather crept than ran through its grounds. They made a detour to inspect a scene of horror. There might be the plot for another by-job in it. At Gill's Hill, Mr Weare had been murdered by a boon companion in his villainy, Mr Thurtell, and his body flung in the pond, right up close to the house—now ruinous. The whole gang had been bad lots and a terrible old hag, whom Scott gave half-a-crown, looked just right in her setting. She told them that the landlord had pulled down the house because no respectable person would live there. But there did not seem to be one redeeming feature amongst the participants; they had not even been clever. He read William Napier's *War in the Peninsula* on his journey. He had mentioned several times in his Journal his admiration for the singing of Mrs Arkwright in London drawing-rooms, but it was left to Lockhart to write down a disturbing incident connected with one of these concerts. " 'Capital! Capital!' whispered Sir Walter as the song-stress closed some verses which, like most of her performances, she had herself set to music. 'Capital words! whose are they? Byron's, I suppose.' "He was astonished when I told him they were his own in *The Pirate*. He seemed pleased at the moment, but said the next minute, 'You have distressed me—if memory goes all is up with me—for that was always my strong point.' "

II

He got home on June 2nd and next day did almost nothing—that is to say he packed up some books to take to Shandwick Place, walked in his beautiful young woods with Tom Purdie and the dogs, looked in on Miss Ferguson, and read a famous trial after dinner. (There might be a plot for a by-job in it.) He had to return to Edinburgh at once. Cadell breakfasted, in great spirits about the success of *The Fair Maid of Perth* which had come out during the London trip. Day after day passed in regular routine. He wrote now both before and after dinner and said he had become a sort of writing automaton. This made him so stiff that he now had difficulty in getting into and out of a carriage. He had also what he called rheumatic headaches. Ballantyne sent a note complaining of his handwriting. Niece Anne had come for a prolonged stay and was company for his Anne. He had begun another foreign novel, *Anne of Geierstein*. On July 8th, 1828, he locked up his Journal and put it away until January 1829.

Lockhart thought he was almost as serene during the next two summers as he had been during the golden years. The supply of guests also began to resemble that of his days of prosperity. Charles went off for a continental tour to improve his languages. Gilnockie was persuaded not to go to northern Germany for his rheumatism, but to try the south of France. At Nice he might meet Mrs Carpenter, Miss Hooke and Morritt in-laws. Johnnie, on the other hand, was making a marvellous recovery, and was now running about again. Sophia spoke of taking a lease of Chiefswood for next summer. It had been let to a retired army couple; Captain Thomas Maitland later author of two entertaining books, *Cyril Thornton* and *Man and Manners in America*. Mrs Maitland, born Anderson, was a grandchild of Robert Anderson, the gentleman who had shown Prince Charles Edward the eastward path on the night of the battle of Prestonpans.[5]

Scott would have preferred his grandchildren to come to him, at Abbotsford. Lockhart admitted handsomely, "The house is certainly perfect, both for beauty and comfort." It seemed to him crammed more than ever with gifts of cups, pictures, books, candlesticks, etc. Chantrey's bust had arrived in the drawing-room; Cadell had sent a clock, very magnificent, Louis Quatorze.

The Duke of Buccleuch's coming-of-age festivities took place at last, to Scott's relief. They had been postponed twice. Lord Melville, godparent, had fallen off his horse and broken a shoulder; then the Duchess-Dowager had died. The duke had expressed himself very nervous about his speech, but in the event was most manly and courteous. Nothing would have held Sir Walter from attending, though he described himself rather unflatteringly, "I am getting very unlocomotive—something like an old cabinet that looks well enough in its own corner, but will scarce bear wheeling about, even to be dusted." He expected a full house for the turn of the year—Skenes, Morritt and a niece, Sir James Stuart of Allanbank who drew horses beautifully.

Lockhart had a promising idea to discuss. His Majesty had been left the *Stuart Papers*, which Scott had seen in 1815, by the last of the royal Stuarts, Cardinal York. "The Invisible" wrote that His Majesty would be delighted if Sir Walter Scott and his son-in-law would edit them. A Commission had been appointed to look at them but seemed to have done nothing. The Duke of Wellington advised, "Dissolve the Commission, by God!" But there was no hurry.

Scott had in hand for 1820, besides polishing off, *The Swiss Tale*, and getting the first volumes of the Magnum Opus into the world, an article for the *Foreign Quarterly Review*, "to give Gillies a lift", a biography for Mr Murray's Family Library, and two reviews (one heavy) for Lockhart. He had allowed his old play *The House of Aspen* to appear in a publication called *The Keepsake*. It was, rather to his surprise, to be produced in Edinburgh, at the theatre. For other occupation, the Duke of Buccleuch had empowered him to bid for any pictures he thought good at the Moray Place sale of the late Stuart of Dunearn. Scott showed surprising expertise, even considering that he had artist friends, particularly a young one called John Graham, in George Street, to whom he had been sitting. He regretted losing a Reynolds of Lord Rothes, but did not much mind missing a Watteau sketch. He described at length to the duke an avenue by a Dutch painter, Hobbema.[6] "I believe an uninteresting scene of the kind was never better painted." Charles Kirkpatrick Sharpe said he was well out of the Reynolds. The face had been much re-touched. Scott thought a picture for the duke must be as unsuspected as Caesar's wife. He had bid up to a hundred and fifty pounds. Lord Haddington had got it for a hundred and sixty. From another source, Scott strongly advised for Bowhill "Newark Castle" by Thomson of Duddington, at present in the spring exhibition.

He was worried about Ballantyne, whose wife had died. The poor man seemed to have become rather queer—in the religious line.

In March, Mons Meg was reinstated at Edinburgh Castle and rockets were fired off with pompous ceremony. One alighted on the bonnet of Miss Anne Scott, and her father was proud of her. Although her head was ablaze she neither shrieked nor ran. Charles Kirkpatrick Sharpe put out the fire dexterously. All present agreed that Blood did tell. The shrubs in the Princes Street gardens, down below where Good Samaritan Skene had taken him for gentle walks when his first grief for the loss of Charlotte had been almost overpowering, were now of good size and gay with leaf and blossom. "I too, old trunk as I am, have put out tender buds of hope which seemed checked for ever." He was very well satisfied that his own woods were growing so gallantly. He was selling hurdles, palings, pit-props, bark for tanners and staves for herring-barrels in response to a pretty bobbish demand.

The first of the Magnum Opus volumes came out and Cadell was panting to supply the demand. Two of Scott's chronic losers were still turning up with hard luck tales. He was educating one of Terry's sons at the High School. "The Lord forgive you," he wrote to Lockhart, "for letting Gillies loose on us." Lockhart said that he had given Gillies some supplies but that what he really needed to do was to throw up an absurdly expensive, and not yet paid for, London house in Connaught Square. Unfortunately his wife was a perfect sheep. (He returned to London after a few months and did not reappear in Edinburgh for eighteen years, but

that did not mean that Scott had heard the last of him.) Scott met this
spring a character whom he had successfully evaded in London, Mr
Edward Irving, the celebrated preacher. He reminded Sir Walter of the
devil disguised as an angel of light, so ill did his terrible squint harmonise
with his dark, tranquil features. He spoke with much simplicity—real or
affected. He boasted much of the tens of thousands who attended his
ministry in his native town of Arran. Scott longed to remark what a distinguished exception he was to the rule that a prophet was not esteemed
in his own country. Later this season he had a visit from Henry Hallam,
who brought a son, Arthur, considered a wonder at Cambridge. Wonders
would never cease! Mrs Carpenter, and one supposed Miss Hooke, had
decided to return to India. Major Scott of Lochore was back at Hampton
Court again, fearing his lungs were affected, but refusing to take proper
advice. ("Now, dear lad, remember what Sophia used to say to you
when you went to the dentist, and BE A MAN.")

Sophia and her family, escorted by Charles, arrived in the middle of
June by steam-boat. Poor Johnnie was a pitiable specimen but the
younger children were, at a glance, true Scots. Young Walter ("Wa-Wa")
had splendid apple cheeks, blue eyes and flaxen hair, and got lost in the
woods five times a day, running about like a little Puck. "Cha" was now
a little girl, not a baby. She liked presenting herself alone to the author
in his study, sure of her welcome. She might not be going to be beautiful,
but she had grace and charm. Her grandfather wrote down three times
that he foresaw she might be the brightest of the family. The Hamiltons
had Mrs Hemans staying, and neither of Scott's daughters took to her, but
she, for her part, was in a seventh heaven. "With Sir Walter Scott by my
side in the Dowie Dens of Yarrow reciting every now and then, some
verse of the fine old Ballad."

The great event of that happy summer was the engagement of the
Duke of Buccleuch. Mrs Hughes, last year, had brought wonderful
London gossip of his progress as a young man about town. On receiving
a notification that he had been elected a member at Crockfords he had
returned thanks but begged to decline. A vile veteran female gambler had
tried to induce him to play at unlimited écarté; the stake was high when
limited. When he refused she said scornfully, "Be it known to all and
sundry that the poor Duke of Buccleuch with a hundred thousand a year
refuses to play at unlimited écarté." He replied, "You are very liberal—
but why not give two hundred thousand? And even then the Duke of
Buccleuch would not play." One of the Sheridan girls, a beautiful bold
piece, had said, "Duke, they say you mean to marry me or my sister, I

hope it will be me." To Sir Walter, the young man said, "I hope when I do marry I shall not disgrace myself, and depend upon it my friends shall not have the first intelligence from the newspapers." He wrote now from Longleat, the seat of Lord Bath, to announce his intended marriage with Lady Charlotte Thynne, the youngest of three daughters of the house. Sir Walter was delighted, for he was able to tell the intended bridegroom that a member of the Thynne family had been a most attached friend of his ancestor the Duke of Monmouth, who was actually in the coach with him when he was murdered in Pall Mall of which there was a curious representation in Westminster Abbey. He hoped that the fair bride would love old Scotland.[7]

The only sad event of the year at Abbotsford was the sudden death of Tom Purdie. He had complained, or rather spoken of, a sore throat but gone off to his cottage as usual, and next morning risen and sat at table with his head on his hand. It was not for several hours that his family discovered that he was dead, without a sigh or a groan. He had been invaluable to Scott for twenty-four years. Abbotsford seemed melancholy without him and the children.[8] Scott was relieved to get to Edinburgh. The snows began early that winter. To his shame, for the first time in his life coming down from the Mound Sir Walter Scott had to hold by the railings.

On the afternoon of February 15th when he got back from work, cold and tired, he found a caller waiting. He remembered that he had promised old Miss Young to get ready for publication some memoirs of her father, a dissenting minister from Hawick. He bent his head over what she had brought, for half an hour. When he rose to see her out, he failed at the first effort. He just got up the stairs to the first floor where Anne was sitting with Violet Lockhart. He could only look at them. This was the scene of his most successful social moment, the fine Edinburgh drawing-room where his beloved Gilnockie had been married to the pretty heiress of Lochore. Anne afterwards described his expression as "peculiar and dreadful". She felt he was trying to break some very bad news. She cried, "Johnnie gone? Is it Sophia? It is Walter!" He did not reply. He fell like a tree.[9]

III

On June 29th the solemn sound of minute guns broke the peace of a beautiful summer's day as Scott walked over the battlefield of Prestonpans with Cadell and Ballantyne. From Lockhart and other sources he had known that the death of George IV was fully expected, but besides regret for a sovereign who had been very kind to him he had to mourn the passing of an era. For Reform was coming, do what he would, and he was opposed to it in almost every form except Catholic Emancipation.

He had made a swift and apparently complete recovery from what he described to Laidlaw and his family as vertigo or a fit of giddiness. Cadell was now enthusiastic over the idea of his beginning a new novel, though not quite so jubilant when he learned that it was to be Byzantine in setting and eleventh century. Guests were coming to Abbotsford again, a good many foreigners, who had not heard that he was at all impaired in health. He had almost refused Bloody Lass, "a young Lady Blood-hound with very grim features and large bones adorned with an absurd puppyish innocence". Charles had brought her on approval. But he had already a new outsize dog, Bran, sent him by Cluny Macpherson, and there had been some violent battles at first between him and Nimrod, mostly to be attributed to their rivalry for the favours of Di Vernon, the crossbred pointer. She had belonged to poor Tom Purdie, and tender-hearted Sophia had expected she would die after following her master's coffin to the grave. But she now formed one of the solemn procession escorting the Wizard of the North on his daily rides. He had for some seasons past been reduced to what he sadly described as a quiet pony. Douce Davie, named after the Covenanter in *Old Mortality*, was of humble origin, dun with black mane and legs and accustomed to a rider of un-certain balance. He had belonged to a jolly old laird in a neighbouring county, and had a distinguished reputation for his skill in carrying his master home safely when dead drunk. He had a disconcerting habit when he saw a tempting stretch of water on a warm day: he not only drank his fill, he liked to lie down in it. Scott bought another quiet pony at St Boswell's fair for the children. Nectanabus, called after the dwarf in *The Talisman*, was sturdy.

Only one piece of business had called him to London this spring, the congenial prospect of inspecting the *Stuart Papers* at St James's Palace. His family had pressed him to come to Sussex Place but he had pleaded that he was off on the Essay on Demonology for Mr Murray's Library. Only to the Journal had he disclosed that he envisaged with nightmarish clarity the possibility of being overtaken on the road by another seizure, depriving him of his speech and even consciousness. For although the doctors had spoken only of a stomach upset, and after two days he had been himself again, thanks to a course of pills and strict dieting, he knew in his heart that he had seen the writing on the wall. When he had received a packet of letters with mourning seals from Rome earlier this month, he had to read through twice one from Anna Jane Clephane before he realised that it was to inform him that her sister, now the Marchioness of Northampton, had died in childbirth. It was perfectly clear, and he had heard the sad news some weeks before.

He had decided to resign his clerkship of Court. He would get a retiring allowance, but would lose five hundred pounds of income; but he would be saving considerably since he need not keep on an Edinburgh house. He refused, after consultation with his Trustees, to apply for a pension. He had also refused the Lord Chief Commissioner's suggestion that he should become a privy councillor. "When one is old and poor, one should avoid taking rank." He reckoned that by 1832 he would have paid off his debt. He was much touched by a letter from Morritt urging him, now that at last he could cast anchor for a little longer, to come bringing dear Anne to Rokeby for a visit of indefinite duration.

He thought he would be very happy at Abbotsford, with plenty of walks in summer, and billets of wood in winter. He had named a plantation Jane's Wood in compliment to his little daughter-in-law, and a path "The Bride's Walk" where she had once got nearly bogged down. He had ordered seats to be placed at strategic intervals between Abbotsford and Chiefswood.

The Continent was very unsettled. When Charles X arrived in Holyrood House again after the July Revolution in Paris, Scott wrote a letter for the *Edinburgh Weekly Journal* pleading that the ex-king and his family might be treated with courtesy in spite of his unfortunate record, which he believed was mainly the fault of bad ministers. After the great fire of 1824 in Edinburgh, Charles X had contributed magnificently. France had not quite departed from royalty. Louis Philippe of the Orleans branch announced himself the Citizen King. Courtiers of resounding name from Holyrood House were entertained at Abbotsford; the Duchess of Angoulême and some of her ladies came incognito and unannounced, out of delicacy, Lockhart believed, having heard that the famous author had poor health and straitened means. In September Scott noted, "the usual number of travelling Counts and Countesses and Yankees, male and female". A Polish lady, the wife of Count Ladislas de Potocki, was strikingly pretty. Cadell came to say that the Trustees had agreed on another dividend, three shillings in the pound. *Letters on Demonology* had been published on 21st September and there was talk of another edition.

He heard from Lockhart that the Duke of Wellington had been

obliged to call out the troops against the London mob. Major Scott of Lochore, in command of his regiment stationed in the Midlands, received a letter from a character signing himself Captain Swing, threatening to burn down the barracks and cut the throats of the hussars. The Duke of Wellington resigned and William IV asked Earl Grey to form a ministry. Now a Reform Bill was certain. Scott longed to rush into politics. Neither young Robert Shortreed nor Mr Adolphus had noticed anything amiss with him when they had stayed. Lockhart thought he had a nervous twitching of the mouth. Only the Journal knew that, on going up to bed after entertaining old Lord Meadowbank, he had found himself flat on the floor again. Nobody had come in, and after what he reckoned to have been only a few minutes he had gathered himself up, and afterwards slept soundly. He had written to Abercrombie and Rose, but they had nothing further to suggest than rest and a restrictive diet. A miserable half-glass of mountain dew, during a long session with a great talker, had been too much for him, these days.

After a fortnight's reflection he had written to tell Cadell frankly what had happened. Both his parents had died of paralytic strokes, and as he gathered that *Count Robert of Paris* was not approved, he was willing to lay it aside and retire—perhaps abroad. This letter, followed by others in the same strain, struck them with dismay. A week before Christmas, Cadell and Ballantyne arrived to tell him that his Trustees had resolved to give him, in grateful acknowledgment for the unparalleled exertions he had made, and was continuing to make, his furniture, plate, linen, paintings, library and curiosities of all kinds at Abbotsford. This made a very happy evening. The first volumes of the Magnum Opus were already making huge sales, and they had persuaded a leading *avant garde* artist from England, J. M. W. Turner, to come up to Edinburgh and Abbotsford next spring to make illustrations for the *Collected Poems*. James had been too cowardly to tell Scott how bad he thought "the poor Count" was. They had fixed their visit to come when they could bring the good news of the Trustees' generosity. They had also brought the latest Malachi letter in proof. But it could not be issued in its present form. It would wreck the reputation of their most valuable author. Fortunately, it was much too long for the *Edinburgh Weekly Journal*.

On the morning after their arrival things went unhappily. Laidlaw was present. For some time Sophia had been pressing upon her father the suggestion that this excellent man should return to live at Kaeside. He had quietly reappeared. As a convinced Whig, naturally the trumpetings of Malachi were anathema to him, but he afterwards told Lockhart that in his opinion no composition of Sir Walter's happiest days contained anything better than the bursts of indignant and pathetic eloquence which here and there appeared in his political effusion. A painful scene followed. Cadell said Scott was out of date, owing to his failure to read newspapers and periodicals, and that his old Tory views had already been expounded by many of the party and successfully answered by the Liberals. He feared for the Magnum Opus if Scott's reputation was assailed. Ballantyne hesitantly agreed with all Cadell said. The meeting ended with a compromise satisfactory to nobody—that the pamphlet should be published separately and anonymously. Lockhart heard that Scott's temper gave way and the unfortunate manuscript was consigned to the flames.[10]

He dined as usual at Mertoun where young Henry Scott, "a Heart of Gold", was preparing for the third time to be elected Member for Roxburghshire, but there was no question of Christmas gaiety with the Fergusons this year. Miss Bell died on the morning of December 24th. It was a bitter cold day. Anne drove her father over to Huntly Burn to comfort the bereaved family, and that night Scott wrote a long letter to his elder son. The gift from the Trustees of the plenishings of Abbotsford meant the possibility of another ten thousand pounds. He could now make some more proper provision for his younger children. He must execute a new Will. He attended Miss Bell's funeral. "In a cold day I saw poor Bell laid in a cold bed." He got to Selkirk and to Jedburgh to perform duties as Sheriff. There were about a hundred and twenty special constables to be sworn in. The weakness of his voice and the confusion of his head when he attempted to address them gave him a shock. "Really a poor affair." He had a long day trying youths for sheep-lifting at Galashields, and returned home half-starved. Swanston, one of his foresters, was now attending him in place of Purdie for walks in unpleasant weather.

On January 11th, after his walk, he tried in vain to get on with *Count Robert of Paris*. Will Laidlaw dropped in and in the most natural manner offered his services. Gradually, as the snows began to fall thicker, Laidlaw began to come for some part of every day. The book began to move bobbishly. But Sir Walter must get to Edinburgh. On the last day of January he ordered the carriage for the next morning, but the snow was so deep he cancelled his intention. Nevertheless, with daylight he set out, alone but for John Nicolson. He would never forgive himself if he left his younger children unprovided for. None of his family seemed to be very strong. Walter had his cough and fears of lung trouble, Anne was in bed again, with a persistent sore throat. Charles had been considerately sent to Naples *en poste*; a good climate for rheumatism. Sophia, with her "pet" doctors had always been "a confirmed coddler", but this summer she had certainly done something to her back which made her screech with pain. At Chiefswood she had been hobbling about on crutches. Her complaint too was diagnosed as rheumatism.

Poor Malachi had been much relieved by a very handsome letter from the Lord Chief Commissioner, saying that the new monarch would do all possible to promote the interest of Sir Walter Scott's second son (another strong reason against engaging in opposition politics). William IV had seemed at first to be chiefly bent on doing everything exactly opposite from his late brother. He had been going to have a cheap coronation. He had, in view of the hard times, rather wished not to have one at all. Carlton House was pulled down, and a new club, the Athenaeum, had gone up in its place. Sir Walter Scott's second son had been elected a member and said it was a perfect palace.

When Mr Cadell heard that Sir Walter Scott was at Mackenzie's Hotel in Castle Street, deadly cold and unable to sleep for the noise, he appeared at once to invite him to do his move to Atholl Crescent. He got more than he expected, for the roads became impassable for ten days. Sir Walter was touched when he perceived in the room prepared for him, some of the furniture evidently bought at the sale at "poor old 39". He proceeded to write in the mornings and conclude his testamentary affairs. John Nicolson, suppressing deep emotion, signed as a witness, and the document was lodged with Cadell. When Sir Walter dined with the Skenes, with Lord Medwyn and Adam, he went and returned in a sedan chair. He also took the opportunity of calling at the establishment of Mr Fortune, an ingenious maker of surgical aids. He chose and ordered a brace to assist his lame leg. It certainly did that, but once he had got accustomed to the thing he needed it, and it took three persons to get him into the saddle. It was the same over having Laidlaw to write for him. All the time, snow-bound in Edinburgh, he needed friend Laidlaw's assistance. His pen as well as his tongue stuttered. Edinburgh looked most desolate this New Year—hackney coaches with four horses strolling about like ghosts, no foot passengers except of the lowest very poor class, people who had to get somewhere. He needed to be more mobile. He would have to speak when the foundation stones of two bridges were laid quite soon over the Tweed and the Ettrick.

His letter of thanks to Cadell for his visit was in good spirit.

I got out here about half past four on Wednesday, and set like a tiger to work. By next carrier comes a box for Atholl Crescent. A

well-meaning German Baron has sent me some German cases of
liqueurs which would be as much as my life is worth to meddle
with. I intreat you would relieve me of the temptation.[11]

IV

On the evening of December 17th, 1831, H.M.S. *Barham* (of fifty
guns, Captain Hugh Pigot) dropped anchor in Naples Bay. A boat from
the British Legation[12] presently came out to her, and Charles Scott saw
his father for the first time for almost a year. He knew that Sir Walter
had caught a chill (though on a beautiful April day) laying the foundation
stone of a bridge over the Tweed, and had suffered a third and most severe
paralytic seizure; but he had understood he was much recovered. He was
shocked by the change. Doctors had been unanimous that his parent should
not risk another winter in Scotland. Friends had been active. Croker had
written from the Admiralty to Lockhart to say that he was sure that a
passage could be arranged. Cadell had heard from Charles, and later Anne,
suggesting that they should try Basil Hall. That active officer had been to
the Admiralty immediately. The result caused emotional paragraphs in
the British press. The Sailor King had ordered a frigate, known as "the
Beauty of the Navy", to convey the Author of *Waverley* and his family
to Malta. The *Barham* had been named for an octogenarian First Lord
with strong Scottish connections, who had been in office in the year of
Trafalgar. Wordsworth, who had been staying at Abbotsford to almost
the last moment, had produced a sonnet with a lovely dying fall:

> Lift up your hearts, ye mourners! for the might
> Of the whole world's good wishes with him goes;
> Blessings and prayers in nobler retinue
> Than sceptred King or laurelled Conqueror knows
> Follow this wondrous potentate. Be true,
> Ye winds of ocean, and the midland sea,
> Wafting your charge to soft Parthenope!

The party which Charles beheld leaning over the side by lantern-light on
that December night was Sir Walter, Major Walter Scott of Lochore and
Miss Anne Scott. Walter's wife had come down to Portsmouth to see
them off but had not sailed. She had suffered so dreadfully on her frequent
experiences of coming to and from Ireland that she could not face any
more. She was going to stay with her mother at Brighton. Even allowing
that her husband had been particularly sick coming from Malta, he looked

green tonight. Charles returned the next day bringing letters and an invitation from his employer to dine as soon as possible. The bay was still very rough, and in any case passengers could not land until they had performed a week of quarantine. When they were released, Charles suavely directed them to an hotel while they inspected various lodgings. They chose a *suite* in the Palazzo Caramanico where there was an English couple—a son and daughter-in-law of Lord Ashley—already established.

Callers began to arrive. Sir William Gell, archaeologist and artist, was the author of several elegant works and had been knighted after a mission to the Ionian islands.[13] He was six years younger than Scott, but also lame, and possessed a carriage, designed by himself, which was a boon to his fellow invalid. Scott could not have found a more enthusiastic guide to the classical treasures of the neighbourhood. They had met years before staying with the Abercorns at Stanmore. Gell introduced Mr Keppel Craven, a son of the late Lord Craven, whose *Tour in the south of Italy* Scott had just been reading. Both gentlemen had been in the household of the late Queen Caroline on her scandalous Italian excursions, and had gone to London to give evidence on her behalf. They still were very fine men. Anne Scott looked at them and decided that both were wicked. But the Naples court, and English hangers-on, had never been remarkable for purity. Sir Walter Scott accepted calmly the kind offices of two invaluable and polished expatriates.

He was presented to the new King of Naples and the two Sicilies, and they chatted for five minutes, without, he was sure, either understanding a word the other said. King "Bomba" was, like the late George IV, grotesquely stout, but much younger. Sir Walter wore the uniform of a brigadier-general of the Royal Scottish Archers. Lockhart was hurt to hear that people had thought this comic. It had been ordered for the London christening of the heir of the young Duke and Duchess of Buccleuch, and he had never worn it as the event had coincided with the November riots last year, and had been postponed. Scott had not been entirely enthusiastic at the thought of Italy. He knew little of painting and less of music. He had never been a classic. But the weather, when the Tramontana ceased to blow and the sun came out, was delicious.

He had felt much better already as the *Barham* glided along the north African shore, and Malta had been so enjoyable he had almost regretted he had not stayed there longer than a month. He had found a most interesting companion in the Right Hon. Hookham Frere, who, since his own country house was under repair, was living in San Antonio, in the village of Pietà, highly picturesque, with many flowers and oranges. It had been the scene of an amour of the celebrated Lady Hester Stanhope.

One of the late Lord Kinnedder's daughters and her husband had been amongst the first to welcome the Scotts. A Skene son was here, on military duty. The society of Malta was superior to that of Naples from the British tourist's point of view, in that it was almost entirely retired intelligentsia or serving officers. Frere was a typical fixture, "captive of the enchanting climate and the romantic monuments of old chivalry". Sir Walter gazing about him in Valetta was heard to say, "This town is really like a dream," and "It will be hard if I cannot make something of this." He went to the Church of St John twice, and on his second visit even clambered down into the crypt to see the tomb of the Grand Master who had given its name to Valetta. He went also out to the old capital Mdina, a walled city: he attended a ball where everything possible was Scottish, held in the splendid great room of the Auberge de Provence. After a banquet with the Chief Justice, Sir John Stoddart, he was so unwell that his daughter, fearing the worst, had come running for Dr Davy, a brother-in-law of Lady Davy. On board the *Barham* it was easy to see that he observed a strict diet; but feeling himself so much better he was apt to forget.

Their rather hurried departure for Naples was because Captain Pigot could only just get them there; he was ordered elsewhere. Although she could not really like Gell, with his "Brutus" hair-style and cold cynical blue eye, his almost daily arrivals with his low carriage solved a problem for Anne Scott. Keppel Craven generally accompanied them on horseback. He was a brilliant child of a broken home and amongst the richest persons in the Neapolitan English colony. He had bought a large convent beautifully situated above Salerno where he entertained lavishly. Anne's trouble was that nobody was in charge of this party. Major Scott of Lochore, as eldest son should have been, but he was quite in her black books. He had gone off alone to a ball on their first night in Malta; he was continually out all day dining at messes, and his swearing at waiters and bills in the mornings put her out of all patience. Worst of all he had been so insufferable to her maid Celia and their father's valet Nicolson that she had feared both might leave.[14] "You can have NO IDEA," she wrote to Sophia, "what it is to travel with him."

Sad news from the Lockharts came early in the New Year of 1832. Little Johnnie was gone at last. He would have been eleven next month.

Sir William Gell took Sir Walter Scott's sightseeing in hand. He perched the Author of *Waverley* on a heap of ruins from which he might see the remains of the Thermae, commonly called the Temple of Serapis.

He took him early to the Lago d'Agnano and Sir Walter was evidently much taken with the autumnal foliage still lingering on the trees. It reminded him of a lake in Scotland. He took him to dine with the Archbishop of Tarentum, a prelate in his ninetieth year, and in a boat to see a ruined Roman villa at the very tip of the Posilipo promontory. Upon the whole, he was disappointed with Sir Walter's reaction to Pompeii— it was that of a poet not an antiquary. He exclaimed repeatedly, "The City of the Dead," without any other remark. But he did sit upon a table for some time to study the mosaic representing the combat of Alexander and Darius. It had been discovered only last October.

He came himself one morning to Gell's house to tell him he had received news of a piece of good luck from Scotland. All his debts were paid and his two last novels, *Count Robert of Paris* and *Castle Dangerous*, had gone on to second editions. His Magnum Opus, the forty-eight volumes of his novels, brought in five thousand a year. He generally patted the head of Sir William's carriage dog, saying, "Poor boy, poor boy," but this time he assured the animal that now he would be able to keep as many big dogs at home as he chose. He said he was far advanced in another novel, *The Siege of Malta*, and a short story.[15] He had given up writing poetry because Byron beat him (he pronounced it "bet"), but might take it up again. He was much interested in an old English manuscript, *The Romance of Sir Bevis*, in the Royal Library. It might do for a Roxburghe Club volume. He was tremendously polite to the Italian sent to make a copy for him, always asking him to stay to breakfast and even to dine. His courtesy, to high and low, was old-fashioned. He always greeted Gell's valet with some pleasantry, and although so disabled, always rose to receive visitors, male and female. When a Russian lady asked him for a set of verses for her album, he sat down at once and wrote three stanzas. "As I am now good for nothing else, I thought it as well to be good-natured." But that had been in Rome . . .

Sir William did not accompany Sir Walter to Paestum. Mr Charles Scott had been there three times already with parties from the Legation, so should be capable of finding the way from La Cava, the home of an English spinster lady of courage and benevolence.[16] The travellers— filling two carriages—returned very fatigued after the drive of fifty-four miles. It had rained all day. Sir Walter told his Journal that the large swampy plain from which the tremendous ruins arose was inhabited by many wild buffalo. He thought the first temple one of the most awe-inspiring pieces of classic architecture that he had ever seen, and though weary, had beheld magnificence beyond compare. Miss Whyte of La Cava had got them an invitation from the Abbot of the Monastery of La Trinità della Cava. This was another of the highlights of Sir Walter's Italian tour. He was quite delighted with the manuscripts in the convent. A young Neapolitan painter who happened to be on the spot was engaged by Dr Hogg, one of their party, to make copies for Sir Walter of the pictures of the Lombard kings in an old book in the library. Vincenzo Morani also made sketches of Sir Walter and Sir William looking at the manuscripts.

Sir William knew what had happened while Sir Walter was in Rome because when the Scotts prepared to move on there he happened to be going at the same time. Major Scott of Lochore had returned to his regiment. Anne told Sophia he had been flirting with Mrs Ashley. Charles had become so diplomatic that it was almost impossible to get him to give a straight answer to anything. Sir William Gell and Mrs Ashley both booked rooms for the Scotts in Rome. Charles wrote to Lockhart that Anne disliked him as well as Walter, and her hostility to him was increased by seeing that he was determined not to quarrel with her. Charles was shocked by his father's delusions. So were the family at home and Cadell. Happy in the conviction that all his debts were paid, he wrote to ask that a harpsichord might be sent to Cadell's girls. He wanted Laidlaw to look out for two good-looking horses and a couple of clever ponies. He thought again now of buying the estate of Faldonside, to the south of Abbotsford. But sometimes a dread that he was not yet quite clear crept over him, and then he was silent, looking wretched. Lockhart deleted from Gell's reminiscences sad complaints by Sir Walter that he had been treated very badly by some partner—Ballantyne?

Anne was not happy. Writing to Miss Millar about Papa's attack of apoplexy on April 16th of last year she had added:

> By the way, I must tell you that after *mature deliberation* I have rejected my little —— But he has got over it and is going to be married, which I am glad of, to a lady with a great deal of money, which I found *afterwards* would be very necessary, so I am sure it will be all for the best.[17]

V

The Scotts entered Rome about seven o'clock on the evening of April 17th by the Porta S. Giovanni and paraded the streets for some time, in moonlight. Nobody knew the address of the lodgings booked for them by Mrs Ashley and Sir William Gell, or indeed whether they had not been doubly booked. It was Holy Week and the streets were vociferous. Their journey had been uncomfortable. Scott had bought for two hundred pounds a carriage said to be English, taking three inside and two outside. Charles, whose opinion had not been asked, since his sister knew best, guessed that the vehicle was worth about half. A wheel stuck before they ever got away and then fell off, which meant they must return to the miserable village of S. Agata where they had breakfasted, and put up for a night. But they were lucky in their passage over the dreaded Pontine marshes; brigands had been kept in awe by the escort of Jerome Buonaparte, ex-King of Westphalia, who was on his road from Rome to Naples.

By sheer chance they met a servant who guided them to the Casa Bernini in the Via di Mercade,[18] where Gell had seen to it that a good fire and refreshments awaited them. Scott, having felt himself so well, in mind and body, had been intending to go on for the Ionian Isles where Sir Frederick Adam, a son of the Lord Commissioner, was Governor. He wished exceedingly to see Rhodes, Capua, and perhaps Greece, before returning home by the Rhine valley and Weimar, where he had hoped for an interview with Goethe. These plans were frustrated. Two days before he left Naples he heard that Sir Frederick had been appointed Governor of Bombay. Goethe had died on March 26th. Lockhart heard that from that hour "all his fine dreams of recovery seemed to vanish at once". "Alas! for Goethe," he exclaimed. "But he at least died at home— Let us to Abbotsford."

Sir William Gell, when drawing up a programme for Sir Walter, had unselfishly decided that it would be useless to include too much of Imperial Rome. Scott, when asked what he particularly wished to see, mentioned the house where Benvenuto Cellini claimed to have slain the Constable of Bourbon with a bullet fired from the Castle of St Angelo. This was easily achieved and was often referred to in conversation. He sat to the Danish sculptor, Thorwaldsen, who produced a most unlike bust. A Captain Cheney of a Shropshire family and a close friend of the Clephanes, an art collector and connoisseur, had a house, the Villa Muti, at Frascati, for many years the residence of Cardinal York. Cheney had asked Gell what were Sir Walter Scott's favourite subjects and got the reply:

He was the Master-Spirit of the history of the Middle Ages, of feudal times, of spectres, magic abbeys, castles, subterraneous passages and preternatural appearances, but that perhaps he was more animated on the history of the Stuart family than on any other topic.

Cheney afterwards confessed that he had suspected Gell's picture of being overcharged, but that he had soon been convinced of the contrary. Sir Walter was taken out to Frascati by Gell on a fine May morning, a very rough twelve miles, particularly between Velletri and Albano, but arrived in good spirits and was gratified by seeing portraits of Charles I, James VIII and Henry IV and a crowd picture of the fête given when the last Stuart was made Cardinal. In this Sir Walter thought he identified Scottish followers, including Cameron of Lochiel. Cheney had been grieved at first sight by the stricken look and carriage of the author. He seemed at times to retire into a dream-world of his own. "It was only when warmed with his subject that the light blue eye shot from under the penthouse brow, with the fire and spirit that recalled the Author of *Waverley*." At dinner at the Villa Muti he surpassed himself in wit and gaiety. Miss Scott told their host that she had not seen him so happy since he left home. His talk ranged over admiration for Cervantes, Boiardo, Ariosto and Dante. He gave a droll imitation of Mrs Siddons dining with the Lord Provost.

Gell understood that Scott had come to Rome so that his daughter could admire some of the "ecclesiastical shows" of Holy Week. He saw to it that the party from Abbotsford were well placed amongst the thousands in the Piazza outside St Peter's on Easter Sunday to see the Pope come out to bless the faithful. Benedict XVI had heard that Scott was in Rome and had expressed interest. Cheney asked if Scott wished to apply for an audience and got a tactful answer. "He respected the Pope as the most ancient sovereign of Europe, and should have great pleasure in paying his respects to him, did his state of health permit it." Gell was afterwards criticised for not having taken Scott to see some of the treasures of the Vatican, but he envisaged with dismay Sir Walter in the endless corridors, galleries, and staircases of that vast establishment. Although so lame, he hated being helped, and was liable to stumble and overbalance. Gell got him into the darkness of St Peter's, where the floor was most uneven, by a side entrance, and had taken the precaution, unknown to Scott, of attaching a glove to the point of his stick. Scott beheld Canova's monument to the last of the Stuarts for which George IV had paid.

His daughter, it appeared, wished to visit the Protestant cemetery.

One of her girlhood's playmates, Lady Charlotte Stopford, a daughter of the late Duke of Buccleuch, had been buried there. On their road Scott was interested in the house of Cola di Rienzi and liked the little Temple of Vesta better than many of the more imposing Roman remains. He was so much taken with the description of his family manuscripts by the Duke of Corchiano that he considered staying in Rome to take a preliminary look at them before, perhaps, a return next year. He met the Duke at one of the few banquets which he attended in Rome. It was very late and very splendid. The hostess was the widow of the banker Torlonia who had been created a duke by Buonaparte. The eldest son of the house owned an outstanding mediaeval castle twenty-five miles from Rome, and on May 9th, Gell set off for it taking Sir Walter, in his "droska". Don Michelangelo Gaetani, heir to another remarkable fortress, at Sermoneta, occupied the box on Scott's carriage. He was an artist and amusing caricaturist and his ancestors had been not only one of the most ancient, but one of the most turbulent, of noble Roman families in the Middle Ages. His conversation was full of fascinating anecdote: he was invited to Abbotsford.[18]

Bracciano seemed to present an insuperable difficulty. No wheeled vehicle could ascend to its entrance. But Scott, enchanted by the appearance of the place, was off at top speed on his stick. A steward had been warned and conducted them through suites of grand apartments, some still retaining the old furniture and silk hangings of the houses of Orsini and Odescalchi. The steward had a large dog, a Great Dane, and when the animal came fawning up to Sir Walter he was gravely told that he was a proper accompaniment to such a castle, but that the visitor had a larger dog at home, though maybe not quite so good-natured to strangers. The notice taken of his dog seemed to gain the heart of the steward, and next morning Cheney found Sir Walter seated in a deep recess of a window overlooking the lake from which the tremendous Gothic castle of black lava towers took its name. Scott had already made another tour with the custodian and animal, having risen early.

He was leaving for home on the next day, Friday, May 11th. He had consulted with Gell and had been advised to go through Milan and the Tyrol for Basle where he could pass by water to Rotterdam and London. To inspect a splendid mediaeval tomb, that of the Emperor Maximilian I in Innsbruck, was an object he mentioned repeatedly. As he was now writing for hours together, which she had been warned he must not do, his daughter saw no point in his doing that in Italy, and faced the long journey home as bravely as possible. He had written what Lockhart

M

believed might be the last words in his handwriting, in his Journal, a month before, but later a person from Leamington found in the visitors' book in the little inn at Ferni a typical entry of May 12th, "Sir Walter Scott—for Scotland".[19]

VI

"After the 11th of May," wrote Lockhart, "the story can hardly be told too briefly." In Florence Scott visited the church of Santa Croce, the Pitti Palace and the Grand Ducal library (to enquire for manuscripts about Malta). He admired the snow and pines of the Apennines because they reminded him of Scotland, but did not make any sightseeing expeditions in Bologna. In Venice, where they stayed at the Hotel Leone Bianco very comfortably for four nights, he visited the Accademia, the Arsenale and the Palazzo Mocenigo, once the home of Byron. He looked at the Bridge of Sighs and scrambled down the dungeons under the Palace of the Doges. At Verona his hotel was close by the tombs of the Scaligers, but only Charles saw them. They crossed the Alps by the Brenner. The Goldene Sonne at Innsbruck was a very poor hostelry and only Charles saw the tomb of Maximilian. They had better accommodation in Munich. Now they were in a landscape where memories of Buonaparte were attached to every city—Ulm, Augsburg . . . A man in a bookshop at Frankfort tried to sell Scott a lithograph of Abbotsford. "I know that already, sir." They embarked on the Rhine at Mainz at 6 a.m. on June 8th and though he was feeling the effects of so many hours of jolting and noisy travel, Scott roused himself to admire the succession of ruined castles and monasteries gradually disclosed on either bank of the river. After Cologne there was nothing much to see and he became miserable and impatient at his slow progress. Shortly before they arrived at Nimeguen he had his most severe cerebral haemorrhage yet, bringing paralysis. He was carried ashore, but as he recovered consciousness he insisted on being put on board a small steamer about to sail for Rotterdam.

By evening on June 13th he was safe in a back bedroom on the second floor of the St James's Hotel, Jermyn Street, with Doctor Robert Ferguson by his side. Next morning came two royal physicians, Sir Henry Halford and Dr Holland. He knew the Lockharts, but for the most part he lay in a stupor, or fancied himself still in the slow steamer. He seemed to improve bodily, and Ferguson thought he had never seen anything more magnificent than the symmetry of his torso as he lay with his chest and neck exposed. Major Scott arrived, Mrs Tom Scott (he knew and thanked her), Cadell from Edinburgh. When John Richardson got out something about having recently seen the woods at Abbotsford, he understood eagerly. Hardly a day passed without enquiries from every member of the royal family. Walking home one night, Allen Cunningham was stopped by a party of working men at the corner of Jermyn Street. "Do you know, sir, if this is the street where he is lying?" It was not until July 7th that the doctors allowed him to travel and he was wrapped in a dressing-gown and carried down to his carriage. It was a calm, clear afternoon, and a number of gentlemen on horseback were amongst the crowd which had quickly gathered. Ferguson noticed that Mrs Lockhart, trembling from head to foot, could not stop crying. At Newhaven, the proprietress of the Douglas Hotel in St Andrew's Square was Mrs Douglas, once housekeeper at Bowhill. The last stage of the long journey began early. As they ascended the vale of the Gala he murmured a name or two, "Gala Water, surely, Buckholm, Torwoodlee". They rounded the hill at Ladhope, and the beloved unmistakable outline of the Eildons burst upon him. They could hardly keep him in the carriage; and when he saw, at length, his own towers, only a mile distant, he sprang up with a glad cry. But the Tweed was in flood and they had to go the long way round by Melrose bridge. When they lost sight of Abbotsford, he sunk into a stupor again.

Laidlaw was waiting at the porch and helped to get him out of his chair and into his bed, which had been prepared for him in a downstairs room.[20] Suddenly he recognised him. "Ha! Willie Laidlaw! O man, how often have I thought of you!" The dogs began to steal in and fawn upon him and lick his hands. He fell asleep peacefully.

But he was only sixty-one and of powerful physique. It became apparent that he was not going to fall asleep for ever so easily. For several days after the happy return he was able to be pushed out in a Bath-chair by Laidlaw and Lockhart to look at the garden. The roses were in high beauty. The grandchildren helped—"Wa-Wa" aged seven, "Cha" four. He was wheeled into the hall, the library, and left alone there for a little by the central window so that he could look out at the river. He asked his son-in-law to read to him from the guid book, and the fine voice of Lockhart was heard in the fine room. "Let not your heart be troubled; ye believe in God, believe also in me. In my Father's house are many mansions, if it were not so, I would have told you. I go to prepare a place for you."

When he had been home nearly a week he shook off his plaids in the garden and accused himself of "sad idleness". "Take me into my own room and fetch the key of my desk." The daughters laid paper and pens in their usual places. He smiled and asked them to leave him. Sophia put the pen into his hand, but his fingers would not close upon it. He sank back amongst his pillows, silent tears rolling down his face. "Friends, don't let me expose myself—get me to bed." He did not rise again but he could not die. He had nightmares. During the local elections last year he had insisted on going to Jedburgh to support Harry Scott of Harden, though that was a safe seat. The trials of the body-snatchers, Burke and Hare, had filled the press and the mob had coined a new ugly word for a villain who had gone to the gallows. The Sheriff's carriage was stoned to shouts of "Burke Sir Walter". At the time he had added stoutly in his Journal, "Much obliged to the brave lads of Jeddart", but evidently the wound had been deep. Lockhart heard with horror the words "Burke Sir Walter" escaping from his lips. Sometimes he fancied he was out happily with Purdie giving orders about trees. He chanted cadences which he must have heard in the churches of Italy. From being gentle as a lamb he became a classic difficult patient, something quite out of character. His daughters were worn out. Helpers came to relieve them from Mertoun House and Ashestiel. Lockhart had asked William Allan to come to take some sketches of Abbotsford which he foresaw he might soon be leaving for ever. Allan also helped in the watching.

While Lockhart was dressing on the morning of September 17th, Nicolson came into his room saying the master had woken completely conscious and was asking for him. His eye was clear and calm. "Lockhart," he said, "I may have but a minute to speak to you. My dear, be a good man, be virtuous, be religious, be a good man. Nothing else will give you any comfort when you come to lie here." Lockhart, perceiving that the end was very near, asked, "Shall I send for Sophia and Anne?" "No, don't disturb them. Poor souls, I know they were up all night—God bless you all." Outside the locked gates of Abbotsford, reporters noticed the arrivals of the doctors and nearest relatives, Major Scott from Ireland, Mr Charles from London. At about half past one on the afternoon of September 21st the end came almost imperceptibly. All his children were there.[20]

Lockhart noticed, with senses sharpened by the realisation that he was beholding something historic, how beautiful was the scene. It was a perfect early autumn Scottish day, so warm that all the windows were open. It was so still that he could hear distinctly the sound of all others most delicious to the ear of Walter Scott—the gentle ripple over its pebbles at Abbotsford of the Tweed.[21]

NOTES

1. Journal, II, 155.
2. The façade of 24 Sussex Place is still as Scott and Lockhart knew it, but the house behind has been rebuilt and is now occupied by the London Graduate School of Business Studies.
3. Lockhart, V, 211.
4. Grierson (Life, 288) mistakenly believed Scott destroyed the letters. They are in the National Library of Scotland, MS. 3906, H 208 and 256. It is also possible that Scott had heard of Carlyle as a devotee of "Mr Irving, the celebrated preacher".
5. Hughes, 311, 325.
6. Letters, XI, 121. Journal, II, 232.
7. Hughes, 287.
8. Letters, XI, 256, 262.
9. Letters, XI, 297–8, 321, 334. Lockhart, V, 262. Journal, II, 355.
10. Letters, XI, 433–40. Lockhart, V, 297–302. Journal (II) fails between July 18th and December 20th, though there are a couple of pages simply labelled "September". Scott's suggestions in his pamphlet seems to have begun with the reimposition of Income Tax.
11. Letters, XI, 449, 456–9. Lockhart, V, 309–11. Journal, II, 317–75.
12. Contrary to general belief, the diplomatic representative at the court of Naples and the Two Sicilies was not an ambassador (nor had Sir William Hamilton ever been one). Mr William Noel Hill, afterwards Lord Berwick, was British envoy-extraordinary and minister-plenipotentiary.
13. *Sir Walter Scott in Italy*, 1832, edited Dr James Corson. William Gell's reminiscences cover Scott's Naples and Rome visits admirably; but it must be borne in mind that they were produced in answer to a request from Anne Scott on behalf of Lockhart, for his Life of her father. Mrs Davy, wife of Dr Davy, supplied Lockhart with Malta accounts. In Malta, Scott refused offers from the Governor and lodged in Beverley's Hotel, Strada Ponente (later West Street), Valetta.
14. On Anne's death in 1833 her maid Celia Street was absorbed into the Lockhart household. John Nicholson became butler to Morritt at Rokeby.
15. Lockhart gave a foundation of the plot of Il Bizarro in his Life (V, 384–6) but hoped neither of these novels would ever see the light.
16. Miss Whyte, in December 1824, having heard that an English honeymoon couple had been captured by brigands at Paestum, set out alone from La Cava to try to succour them. No surgeon would accompany her. She was too late, both had been murdered.
17. Millar, Letters, XII, 41–47, 133. Lockhart, V, 371–416. Journal, II, 430–74.
18. Michelangelo Gaetani, afterwards Duke of Sermoneta, who accompanied Scott on May 9th to Bracciano when aged eight and twenty, unveiled in the spring of 1882, on the façade of the Casa Bernini, a tablet commemorating Scott's stay there.
19. Lockhart, V, 400–16, quotes the descriptions, sometimes overlapping, of Cheney

and Gell dealing with Scott's Roman stay. Charles Scott found a letter to a Professor Scopenhauer of Berlin University dated from Mainz on June 3rd regretting that Scott was not well enough to return his call. Letters, XII, 48.

20. The room in which Scott died is now the dining-room.

21. Lockhart, V, 416–29. Grierson (Life, 299) throws doubt upon Lockhart's story of Scott's last message to him, since Mrs Scott of Harden had suggested to the biographer by letter how desirable it would be that he should include remarks of a religious tendency made while Scott's mind was clear, "such as I heard he said occasionally 'Oh, be virtuous! It is one's only comfort in a dying state!' and anything of that kind." But this only proves that Scott had made such remarks at some time towards the end.

Appendix

Who was Lady Scott?

CHARLOTTE SCOTT DIED IN 1826. AS EARLY AS JULY 1833, LESS THAN fourteen months after the death of her husband, an unsigned article in *Chamber's Edinburgh Journal*, "The Land of Scott, The Marriage of Sir Walter Scott", declared that she and her brother had been children of the Marquess of Downshire by Madame Charpentier, a very beautiful woman, wife

> of Monsieur Charpentier of Paris, an individual who held the lucrative office of provider of post-horses to the royal family of France. The Rev. Mr Burd [*sic*] Dean of Carlisle, who had been his early friend, had recommended to the young nobleman "almost his only continental acquaintance" and the unhappy result had been an elopement follows by a liaison, after which M. Charpentier had transmitted his children to their mother and all had lived "under the general protection of Lord Downshire".

After her death, Lord Downshire had placed the girl in a French convent and got the boy a valuable appointment in India, with the understanding that he should make an annual payment to the girl.

There was a curious mixture of fact and fiction in the article, apparently by Robert Chambers, republished in his 1871 edition of his *Life of Sir Walter Scott*. Some of the facts show signs of having come from the same source as those in the *Centenary Memorial*, also published in 1871, but with differences.

In 1836–37 Lockhart brought out his famous biography of his father-in-law and was immediately attacked as "uncandid" in his account of Lady Scott's origins.

> She was the daughter of Jean Charpentier of Lyons, a devoted royalist who held an office under government, and Charlotte Volère, his wife. She and her only brother, Charles Charpentier, had been educated in the Protestant religion of their mother; and when their father died, which occurred in the beginning of the revolution, Madame Charpentier made her escape first to Paris and then to London where they found a warm friend and protector in the late Marquess of Downshire, who had, in the course of his travels in France, formed an intimate acquaintance with the family and spent some time under their roof. M. Charpentier had, in his first alarm as to the coming revolution, invested £4,000 in English securities— part in a mortgage upon Lord Downshire's estates. On the mother's death, which occurred soon after her arrival in London, this noble-man took on himself the character of sole guardian to her children, and Charles Charpentier received in due time, through his interest, an appointment in the service of the East India Company, in which he had by this time risen to the lucrative situation of Commercial Resident at Salem. His sister was now making a little excursion under the care of the lady who had superintended her education, Miss Jane Nicolson, a daughter of Dr Nicolson of Exeter, and grand-daughter of William Nicolson, Bishop of Carlisle, well known as the editor of *The English Historical Library*. To some connections which the learned prelate's family had ever since his time kept up in the diocese of Carlisle, Miss Carpenter owed the direction of her summer tour.[1] (1797)

This was extraordinarily full of error; but Sir Walter and his family had been so reserved about Lady Scott.

In 1827 Scott had written to Lockhart that he was sending his younger son, Charles, to see

> Mrs Jane Nicolson, a woman of great cleverness and at one time of great personal beauty. She came from France with Madame Charpentier and her children and therefore can tell more than anyone about their family history into which I never enquired; there was, I

believe, domestic distress and disagreement between Madame Charpentier and her husband—at least I have conjectured so much. Mr Slade of Doctor's Commons and the elder Miss Nicolson know most about the matter.

Scott thought it would be a pity for his children to lose the chance of a legacy apparently left to Madame Charpentier, and Charles was duly briefed.

Miss Jane Nicolson is the only person I know who can explain the circumstances of Mrs Charpentier's coming to England, as she was with her at the time. She will expect to be treated with great formality, and as your poor Mama's earliest friend she is entitled to it.

By October 1827 neither Charles nor Lockhart had been able to draw the necessary affidavit from the old lady but Scott himself in the following May told Lockhart he had succeeded and was getting it made and lodged in Chancery "while she is in the humour and has the power of making it".[2] A chance meeting with Fenimore Cooper, American Consul to Lyons, resulted in his getting his wife's baptismal certificates from that city.

In Addenda to his 1848 edition, Lockhart attempted a reply to his critics. He had not thought it necessary to allude to the story that Lady Scott was a child of Lord Downshire while any of her own children were living

and I presume it will be sufficient for me to say now that neither I, nor, I firmly believe, any of them, ever heard from Sir Walter or from his wife, or from Miss Nicholson [sic] who survived them both, the slightest hint as to the rumour in question. There is not an expression in the preserved correspondence between Scott, the young lady and the marquess that gives it a shadow of countenance. Lastly, Lady Scott always kept hanging by her bedside, and repeatedly kissed in her dying moments, a miniature of her father which is now in my hands; and it is the well-painted likeness of a handsome gentle-man—but I am assured that the features have no resemblance to Lord Downshire or any of the Hill family.

He no doubt did not know that Anne Scott had written to his wife, Sophia, that on her death-bed she thought she had heard their mother murmur something like the words "Lord Downshire" and "father".[3]

Lockhart's "lastly" did not give the quietus to the rumour "of early prevalence". Miss Maria Edgeworth before she had ever met Scott's wife had heard it, and also mention of "a cast mistress of Lord Downshire" visiting Edinburgh, as the authority. This sounds remarkably like Miss Jane Nicolson. With the Centenary of Scott's birth the story burst into print from several quarters, and a paper war raged. John Buchan, whose Centenary biography carried away the palm, would have nothing of the Downshire scandal ("some have without reason suspected a closer relationship"). He had not seen Sir Herbert Grierson's biography. Grierson's article, "Margaret Charpentier, the mystery of Lady Scott's parentage", published in the *Glasgow Herald*, and his correspondence with Donald Carswell, were brought out simultaneously in that paper, and *The Scotsman*. Dr Crockett entered the fray. "Who was Lady Scott?" "Lady Scott's origins". He was sure that Lady Scott and her brother could not have been children of the Marquess of Downshire. Donald Carswell thought otherwise. Dr Crockett persevered. "New light on Lady Scott". "Fresh documents".[4]

By 1938 Grierson, in his biography *Sir Walter Scott, Bart.*, had indeed seen some fresh documents. They had been shown to him by Mr James Glen. Jane Nicolson, that enigmatic and slightly sinister figure, was the youngest of three daughters. Another was housekeeper to Charles François Dumergue, a French émigré whose first wife had been a Charpentier. Dumergue was so successful in his profession of surgeon-dentist that he was appointed to the royal family. Jane Nicolson had been installed by Dr Samuel Johnson's Mrs Thrale to look after her girls when she left England upon her marriage to Signor Piozzi. But Jane had either been dismissed by the daughter who became Viscountess Keith, or had retired. There was a story in the family that she had been Piozzi's mistress.

Grierson was able to divulge some reliable information about M. Charpentier. He discovered that in 1771 Maria Edgeworth's father had boarded in an agreeable house on the ramparts with the family of the head of the Military Academy at Lyons, M. Charpentier, who had been controller of the Embassy at Constantinople for twenty years, and had a young wife, beautiful, lively and domesticated. At that time Marguerite Charlotte, born December 16th, 1770, must have existed. Jean David, afterwards Charles, followed her by two years. By the time that Noël Felicien Marthe, of whom nothing more is heard, was baptised, Edgeworth had left. It is perhaps remarkable that he never mentioned the infants in his memoirs but allowances must be made for him. He h a himself, by three wives, fifteen children.

Élie Charlotte Volère, Madame Charpentier, was found by Grierson next in a strange context. A young Welsh landowner, Wyrriot Owen, attempted before his death, as a bachelor, in 1789, to make some provision for her. (This was the Chancery case vexing Scott in 1827.) Two years earlier, her daughter Margaret Charlotte, aged seventeen, and her son Jean John David (fifteen) had been baptised at St George's, Hanover Square, together with a Dumergue daughter, Antoinette Adelaide. Madame Charpentier had by then been resident in Paris, but St George's, Hanover Square, had been her parish previously. Lord Downshire, then still Lord Hillsborough, had married in 1786. His arrangements before this event looked quite normal for a young nobleman about to tidy up his private life. He sent a French lady back to France and made long-sighted provision for her children. Nothing is more probable than that he had been at the age of seventeen to a military academy at Lyons. (His cousin, Arthur Wellesley, did the same at the same age, though his choice was Angers.) Unfortunately it has never been traced that Lord Downshire did anything of the kind, though Lockhart speaks confidently of "travels in France".

In April 1787, a French Abbé de Chazelle wrote from Paris, by the hand of an amanuensis, to Lord Downshire (still Hillsborough), about the debts accumulated by a poor lady, often ill, and without any resources until her quarterly allowance from my lord arrived. Miss Nicolson (now in England) would bear witness as to all the abbé had done for Madame Charpentier. She died in 1788, said to be a widow.[5]

Lockhart was therefore quite wrong when he composed his romantic tale of the Charpentier family flying from the French Revolution. The Fall of the Bastille did not take place until 1789 by which time Charlotte was nineteen and her mother had been dead for a year. The foresight of Charpentier in investing in English securities and a mortgage of Downshire estates is nowhere substantiated; yet at the time of her marriage to Scott, Charlotte did apparently own considerable chattels. Her guardian had made it plain that she had no capital, but she had plate which he was trying to get "sent over", and she had already sent four cases to Scotland by waggon from London, one of which contained a French porcelain tea-service. The plate cannot possibly have been sent from France. The Battle of Cape St Vincent had taken place on Valentine's Day, followed by Camperdown in October, and even so influential a man as Lord Downshire could not have managed such a business as the import of plate. Nor was he any longer so influential. Without qualifying exactly as one more mystery figure connected with Scott's marriage, it must be admitted that very little can be discovered about the guardian for whom Charlotte obviously felt deep reverence and affection as well as gratitude. Although it cannot be ruled out as impossible, it is most unlikely that he had been her father before he was turned seventeen, but his provision for her and her brother were certainly remarkable.

His father, Wills Hill, first marquess, had been a very well-known figure in high society, occupying a succession of posts under government, amassing a large fortune, and a record number of peerages. Good portraits of him are available. Charlotte's guardian came to grief over Ireland. He made an enemy of Castlereagh (a very bad enemy), was dismissed from his regiment of militia, from the privy council and from being lord-lieutenant of County Down. He had opposed the Act of Union. Charlotte was always uneasy when he had to go to Ireland.[6] He died in 1801 in retirement, it was said of a broken heart, aged forty-eight. A son who succeeded got the family back upon an even keel, and when the aged Marchioness of Salisbury, his aunt, paid him a visit, she was received with much ceremony and loyal addresses, which she preserved in her albums. She outlived Scott and sat with the Duke of Wellington in the front row at Hatfield House when the Sir Walter Scott *Tableaux Vivants* were produced there in 1833. Her daughter-in-law, Frances Mary Gascoyne-Cecil, "the Gascoyne heiress", was a Scott enthusiast and appeared as Edith, from *The Talisman*. Sir David Wilkie had provided sketches for the costumes.

The second marchioness entertained the Lockharts at Hatfield, and found Mr Lockhart "very agreeable, not the less so for his bitterness", and Mrs Lockhart "simple and natural with plenty of Scotch shrewdness". There are several allusions to the Lockharts in her diaries; she dined with them in Sussex Place; she was deeply grieved by the death of Sophia in May 1837. But there is not the slightest trace that she suspected a blood-relationship with her husband's family—Lord Downshire having been her husband's uncle. Scott had lost touch with them by 1813 when he told Lady Abercorn that the father of the present marquess had been "our good and affectionate friend. I never had an opportunity of seeing the rest of the family."

NOTES

1. Letters, XII, 64, 68–69, 76.
2. Letters, X, 413.
3. Letter from Anne Scott to Sophia Lockhart, May 21st, 1826, f. 127, National Library of Scotland.

4. Corson, Bibliography, 598–605.

5. Grierson, Life, 46–53.

6. Letters, XII, 64, 68–69, 76. There is a very fine portrait of the first Marquess of Downshire at Hatfield House, by Rising, after Romney, a Downman sketch, and a miniature. No portrait of the second marquess has been identified at Hatfield House. A large collection of family miniatures were mentioned by the first marchioness, some of them by number, in her will. But with her, when she was burnt to death, went nearly all her personal possessions, and the clue to the identities of about half of the Hill and Cecil miniatures.

There may exist an unidentified portrait of the second Marquess of Downshire in the collection at Murlugh House, Co. Down, now leased to the Church of Ireland. Dr Dexter collected three portraits: an illustration of him aged about twenty-one in *The History of the Grand Lodge of the Free and Accepted Masons of Ireland*, Vol. I; a second, without name of artist or engraver, but looking old and haggard; the third is that reproduced in this book, by H. D. Hamilton, a crayon sketch in the possession of Mrs Conway.

The author wishes to thank the Borough Librarian of Richmond-upon-Thames, the County Archivist of Berkshire, the Public Record Office of Northern Ireland, Mr J. W. Stubbs of the Freemasons' Hall, London, and the Grand Secretary of the Grand Lodge A.F. & A. Masons of Ireland for kind assistance in her search for material about Lady Scott's guardian; also the late Dr Elizabeth Dexter, Miss Angela Lewi at the National Portrait Gallery, and Miss Clare Talbot, Archivist, and the late Mr Kingsley Adams, for information about the collection at Hatfield House. The Albums of the first Marchioness of Salisbury escaped the conflagration of November 27th, 1835, as they were in the library. They contain many sketches by members of the Hill family. The diaries of the second marchioness form part of the Cecil Papers.

Index

Index.

Index

In this Index W.S. = Walter Scott

Abbotsford: W.S. buys land and a farm, Newarthaugh or Cartley Hole, 168; begins to enlarge, 169; rejects Stark's plans for, 171, 183; buys association-objects and furniture for, 173, 215, 270-1, 336; employs Sanderson and Paterson on the cottage at, 174, 191; "Conundrum Castle", 224; Blore's plans rejected, 215; William Atkinson's adopted, 218; W.S. moves into enlarged old cottage, 223; happy hospitality, at, 240 et seq.; additions to, 254; foundation stone of final building laid, 267; John Smith of Darnick employed, 247, 255, 279; Chinese wallpaper for, 271; porcelain service for, 326; painted glass and armour, 288, 320; panelling, 276; ball at in honour of engagement of heir, 284; settled upon Gilnockie, 285; W.S. will not consider bankruptcy as this might endanger marriage-contract, 305; Christmas at, 280, 318; plantations at, 322, 325-6, 342, 355; W.S. returns to die at, 356

Abercorn, Anne (born Lady Anne Gore), wife of 1st Marquess of: her character and career, 147 (n.); entertains W.S. at Stanmore, 128; and in St James's Square, 135; sends a cap to his wife, 137; asks him if he was ever in love, 158; sends acorns for Abbotsford, 172; writes to him, 130, 139, 142, 154, 157; W.S. writes to, 174, 211; a widow, 224; told of Sophia's engagement, 236; orders portrait of W.S. by John Watson: going abroad, 237

Abercorn, John James, 1st Marquess of: "Le Marquis de Carabas", 103; character and appearance of, 128; takes a great liking to W.S., 134;

Abercorn, John James—*cont.*
   behaves with magnanimity to Tom
   Scott, 138; *The Lady of the Lake*
   dedicated to, 158; his absurd pom-
   posity, 178
Abercromby, George, 40, 42
Abercromby, James, 40
Aberdeen, George Hamilton Gordon,
   Marquess of, 133
Abud, Mr, bill-broker, his persecution
   of W.S., 311, 328–9
Adam, Dr Alexander, as Rector of
   Edinburgh High School, "taught
   Latin, some Greek and all virtue",
   28; has high hopes of the French
   Revolution, 50
Adam, Sir Frederick, 198
Adam, Sir William, Lord Chief
   Commissioner of the Jury Court in
   Scotland, 192, 198, 220; tells W.S.
   Prince Regent wishes to give him a
   baronetcy, 222, 234 (*n.*)
Adolphus, John Leycester, proves W.S.
   must be the author of *Waverley*, his
   descriptions of W.S. and Abbots-
   ford, 278, 283, 325–6, 330 (*n.*), 343
Alexander I, Czar of Russia, W.S.
   presented to, 203
Allan, William, W.S. would rather he
   was given the job of a portrait than
   Raeburn, 228, 240; orders portrait
   of Gilnockie from, 256; thinks
   highly of, 322; makes sketches of
   Abbotsford while W.S. dying and
   helps in watching, 356
Alvanley, Lady (*born* Anne Wilbra-
   ham Bootle), widow of Richard
   Pepper, Baron, W.S. escorts in
   Paris, 203; she smuggles a shawl for
   Charlotte, 204; is snobbish to Mrs
   Coutts, 283; dies in Edinburgh and
   W.S. finds her daughters futile, 284
Animals owned by W.S. *Cat*: Mr Hinze

of Hinzefeld, brindled Tom, 214;
   handwriting of Cornet Scott looks
   as if it had been performed by, 232;
   demolished by Bran, 322
Dogs:
Camp, "Kiki", "The Black Child",
   coloured bull-terrier, 88–9, 93;
   painted with W.S. by Saxon, 1805,
   94, 97 (*n.*), 98, 104–5; by Raeburn,
   122; failing health of, 143; dies,
   147; his portrait, 306
Percy and Douglas, greyhounds, gift
   of Laidlaw, 98, 106, 173; painted
   by Raeburn with W.S., 122, 173
Wallace, terrier, gift of Miss Dunlop
   of Dunlop, 154, 161–2
Lady Juliana Berrers, greyhound
   bitch, gift of Mr and Mrs George
   Ellis, 173–4
Maida, deer- or wolfhound, gift of
   Glengarry, 214, 217, 228, 240; dies
   and has epitaph on his grave outside
   Abbotsford, 282; the dog on the Scott
   Memorial, Princes St, 214
Marmion, greyhound, gift of Terry,
   216
Ourisk, Kintail terrier, 242
Fifi, Lady Scott's spaniel, 242
Spice, Dandie Dinmont, 302
Nimrod, staghound, gift of Glen-
   garry, 322, 326
Bran, deerhound, gift of Cluny Mac-
   pherson, 326, 341
Bloody Lass, bloodhound bitch, 341
Horses:
Lenore, 62, 72, 78
Brown Adam, 87, 122
Captain and Lieutenant, 122
Daisy, 205–6
Sibyl Grey, 228, 240, 278, 296
Douce Davie, 341
Nectanabus, 341
Pigling, 240

Apreece, Mrs, later Lady Davy (*born* Jane Kerr, grand-daughter of William Kerr of Kelso and Antigua), goes on Hebridean holiday with Scotts, 162

Arbuthnot, Mrs Charles, Harriet (*born* Fane), said by W.S. to be the most beautiful woman in Paris 1815, 204; in London 1821, 246

Argyll, George William Campbell, 6th Duke of: attacked by Macleans for neglect of Iona, 164; President of Highland Society, 263

Ashiestiel, 9; invariably spelt by W.S. Ashestiel, 59, 71; he takes lease of, 114–21, 124 (*n.*); happy at, 129; certain spots at associated with composition of *Marmion*, 139; "flitting" from, 175 *et seq.*

Atkinson, William, architect of St John's Wood, famous for his patent cement, designs Abbotsford, 218, 238, 269 (*n.*)

Audubon, John James, ornithologist, naturalist, and artist, his pictures of the first order, 320

Austen, Jane, W.S. reviews *Emma*, 211–12, 233 (*n.*), 328

Baillie, Joanna, her *Plays of the Passion*, 89; W.S. visits, 128; she visits Castle St and sticks up for Mrs Scott, 142; her drama *The Family Legend*, 152, 156, 163, 173, 195, 239, 315

Baillie, Dr Matthew, brother of Joanna, prescribes with sagacity for Wilkie, 218; W.S., Duke of Buccleuch, and Mrs Charles Carpenter, 245–6, 250

Bainbridge, George, of Gattonside, *nouveau riche* neighbour of W.S. at Gattonside: unpretentious, 282, 326 has bright sons, 320

Baird, General Sir David, a severe disciplinarian ("God pity the poor lad that's chained to our Davie"), Gilnockie objects to, 249

Ballantyne, James, at school with W.S., 30; jilted, 59; journalist, 63; W.S. shows poems to, 84; Ballantyne prints them, 89, 90, 97; moves to Abbeyhill, Edinburgh, 102, 119; to Canongate, 120; John Buchan's opinion on relations of W.S. with, 125 (*n.*); Ballantyne & Co., 145; moves to Herriot Row 1823, 145; threatens nervous breakdown over unsaleable productions by other authors, sent him by Scott, 165; W.S. nicknames him Aldiborontiphoscophornio, 166; warns W.S. their firm is going on the rocks, 177, 178; no adequate study of the Ballantyne-Scott relationship yet published, 181 (*n.*), 189–90; burns to hear about Waterloo, 205; marries, 211, 213; fears illness of W.S. very serious, 217; suggestion that "The Great Unknown" should call a halt repelled by him, 255; involved in failure of Constable, 300; W.S. sends supplies twice to, 302; looks black, 303; in a funk on hearing W.S. threatened by General Gourgaud, 327; goes very queer, 338; his row with W.S. over Malachi pamphlet, 344; complaints of, in senescence by W.S., 350

Ballantyne, John, at school with W.S., 30; sings a poem by W.S. on acquittal of Lord Melville, 131; taken on at Ballantynes at £200 p.a., 142; W.S. assists to found publishing firm in opposition to Constable, 145; moves to South Hanover St, 145; nicknamed by W.S. Rigdumfunnidos, 166; sends W.S. sudden

Ballantyne, John—*cont.*
demands for expenses, 170; Grierson discovers letters dealing with the crisis, by John, *Open Not, Read Not*, 180 (*n.*), 206, 212, 213; W.S. weeps at funeral of, 250

Bannatyne Club, W.S. first President of, 271, 280

Beaumont, Sir George, patron of the arts, 195, 218

Beechey, Sir William, portrait-painter, 200

Bell, Sir Charles, 196

Bell, George, 196

Belsches, Lady Jane (mother of "Greenmantle"), afterwards Belsches Stuart, 46; favours suit of William Forbes, 58; writes to W.S., 60, 328

Belsches, Sir John, afterwards Belsches Stuart, 46, 53, 54, 58

Belsches, Williamina, afterwards Belsches Stuart, first love of W.S., "What a romance to tell", 38, 45–48, 52–53; marries Sir William Forbes of Pitsligo, 58; dies, 59, 60, 103; W.S. admits she was original of Matilda in *Rokeby*, 46, 177, 180 (*n.*)

Belzoni, Giovanni Battista, excavated second Pyramid of Gizeh, 237

Bird, Dr and Mrs, friends of Miss Jane Nicolson, 65, 66, 74, 75; their son runs away from Charterhouse, 133

Blackwood, William, Edinburgh agent of John Murray, receives news of Waterloo from Murray, 196; secures for Murray first series of *Tales of my Landlord*, says the Ballantynes are thieves and Constable is proper person for them, 213; founds *Blackwood's Magazine*, 225

Blair Adam Club, 283, 324

Blücher coach carries Boney MS. to Ballantynes, 319, 322

Blücher, Gebhard Lebrecht von, Field Marshal, W.S. sees in Paris, 202

Boodle, Mr, solicitor to Marquess of Northampton, W.S. arranges marriage settlement for Miss Maclean-Clephane with, 193

Boswell, Sir Alexander, eldest son of biographer, 255

Boswell, James, second son of biographer, 194, 238

Boulton, Matthew, engineer, meets Scotts at Dumergues, 102

Bowhill, W.S. visits with Dalkeiths, 114; visits continually to comfort Duke Charles, 189; thinks of "The Twelfth" at, when in Paris, 202; William Atkinson engaged to make a library at, 218; house overheated, 226; W.S. says his horse turns automatically to go there, 229; Hutson, head keeper from, comes over to Abbotsford and talks to W.S. for an hour, 241

Braxfield, Robert Macqueen, Lord, 43, 47

"Broughton's Saucer", 38–39

Bruce, Robert of Langlee, visits Brussels and Paris with W.S., 197–204

Buccleuch, for Charles, 4th Duke of, and Harriet, wife of, *see* Dalkeith

Buccleuch, Elizabeth, wife of Henry, 3rd Duke of, heiress of George, Duke of Montagu, 91, 102, 229, 337

Buccleuch and Queensberry, Henry Montagu-Douglas-Scott, 3rd Duke of, 63, 72, 81, 83, 85; W.S. dedicates *Minstrelsy of the Scottish Border* to, 90; a dog-lover, 91; has simple funeral by his own desire, 172

Buccleuch, Walter Montagu-Douglas-Scott, 5th Duke of Buccleuch and

Buccleuch, Walter—*cont.*

Queensberry, succeeds at age of thirteen, 229; W.S. visits at Eton, 239; and Ditton, 243; entertains George IV at Dalkeith, 262–4; a promising youth, 264; "a most delightful young man", 278; offers W.S. a brace of greyhounds, 296; offers to take the whole of Sir Walter Scott's losses upon himself, 303; comes of age, 337; empowers W.S. to buy pictures for him, 338; chased by the girls, 339; marries Lady Charlotte Thynne, 340; W.S. orders a uniform of a brigadier-general of the Royal Scottish Archers in which to appear at the christening of the duke's heir, 347

Buchan, David Erskine, 11th Earl of, *eccentric*: calls to tell invalid W.S. of his splendid programme for his funeral at Dryburgh, 229–30; his own grave all ready there, 276

Bullock, George, antiquarian furniture dealer and interior decorator, employed for Abbotsford, 215; extraordinary experience there on the night of his death, 223

Burns, Robert, W.S. sees, 31; meets, 39

Byron, George Gordon, 6th Baron, accuses W.S. of writing for pelf, 153, 156; apologises, 175; sends for *Rokeby*, 177; delighted with Hogg's *Queen's Wake*, 182; historic meeting with W.S. at 50 Albemarle St, 194; dines with W.S. "as playful as a kitten", 205; leaves England, 212; touched by review of *Childe Harold* by W.S., 216; W.S. refuses to interfere in the matrimonial troubles of, 216; but invites Lady Byron to Abbotsford, 219; W.S. sends family news to, 255–6; hears of death of, 281; hears of Diary of, 295

Cadell and Davies, publishers, 79, 97, 120

Cadell, Robert, partner in Constables, 178, 242; his interviews with W.S. over Constable's failure, 297–9, 300, 301, 303; quarrels with Constable, 305; takes refuge in debtor's sanctuary but emerges, 306–7; in high spirits over life of Boney, 324, "Magnum Opus", 329; rescues W.S. from Mackenzies' Hotel, 345; comes to London to visit him at St James's hotel, Jermyn St, 355

Campbell, Lady Charlotte (*born* Campbell), daughter of 5th Duke of Argyll, married (1) Colonel Jock Campbell of Shawfield, (2) Rev. E. Bury, 79, 92, 96, 102

Campbell, Thomas, recites "Hohenlinden" to W.S. in a stage-coach, 96; a difficult guest, 100; recommends John Murray to W.S., 121; Washington Irving, 219; W.S. talks of to Moore, 295

Canning, George, statesman, 93, 128, 133, 135, 146; W.S. longs to hero-worship, 157; becomes Prime Minister but for only four months, 324

Carlisle, W.S. visits his *fiancée* at Palmer's lodgings, (83 later 81) Castle St, 66 *et seq.*; is married in Cathedral at, 75; makes sentimental visits to, 205, 332

Carlyle, Thomas, sends W.S. two letters, 335

Caroline of Brunswick, Princess of Wales, wife of George IV, Scott visits and admires, 129, 131; hears

Caroline of Brunswick—*cont.*
she has been indiscreet, 135; her unconventional manners, 136; she obliges him to tell "Scotch stories", 153; wishes to set up her court at Holyrood, 246; wishes to share her husband's coronation, 253

Carpenter (Charpentier), Charles (Jean David), brother-in-law of W.S., Resident at Salem, Madras, 66, 68, 72, 101; marries Miss Isabella Fraser, 115; dies leaving a fortune to children of W.S., 227

Carpenter, Mrs Charles (*born* Isabella Fraser), sister-in-law of Lady Scott, marries Charles Carpenter, 115; miscarries after a carriage accident, 135, 290; arrives in London from India a perfect neurotic, 242–6, 250; brings valuable gifts for Scotts, but the expected inheritance from her husband disappointing, 251; considers re-marriage, 257; visits Abbotsford, 257; does not lose her capital in collapse of Barber & Co., 304; tries Nice, 337; decides to return to India, 339; outlives W.S. and all his children, 268 (*n.*)

Carpenter (Charpentier), Margaret Charlotte, *see* Lady Scott (wife of W.S.)

Castlereagh, Viscountess (*born* Lady Emily Hobart), afterwards Marchioness of Londonderry, 135; W.S. asks her for Swift MSS., 157, 158; is invited by her to Versailles, 203; tells W.S. never to feed an animal in a glove, 335

Castlereagh, Robert Stewart, Viscount, afterwards Marquess of Londonderry, 146, 157; tells W.S. of his vision of the Radiant Boy, 203; 239; his appearance at coronation of

George IV, 253; commits suicide, 258

Cathcart, Robert, partner in Constables, 178

Celtic Society, W.S. becomes President of, 250; reviews a parade of, 260, 261

Chantrey, Sir Francis, sculptor, 238; kills two salmon at Abbotsford, 289; W.S. considers his bust by "one of the finest things he ever did", 238

Charlecote, visited by W.S. with Anne, 332

Charles X of France, entertained at Abbotsford, 31; at Dalkeith, 91; civil to W.S. at the Tuileries, 314; at Holyrood House again, 342

Charpentier, Élie Charlotte (*born* Volère), mother of Lady Scott, 68, 316, 359–65

Charpentier, Jean François, father of Lady Scott, 68, 359–64

Chiefswood, originally Burnfoot, Lockhart cottage on Abbotsford estate, 247; Sophia entertains at, 275; leaves for London, 297; W.S. offers to Gillies, 299; let to Captain Thomas and Mrs Maitland, 337

Christie, John, Lockhart's second in affair of honour, 243, 268 (*n.*)

Clarke, Rev. James, Librarian and Domestic Chaplain, 192

Clarke, Mary Anne, mistress of Frederick, Duke of York, 146

Clarkson of Selkirk, Dr Ebenezer, 234 (*n.*), says W.S. has gravel, 302; attends Lady Scott, 310; attends W.S. on his deathbed, 356

Clerk of Eldin, James, midshipman, 40

Clerk of Eldin, John, father of John, Lord Eldin, naval strategist, antiquarian, 48; builds cottage at Lasswade, 80

Clerk of Eldin, John, Lord Eldin, Judge, son of John Clerk of Eldin and Susannah Adam, *Eldin upon Stair*, 280

Clerk of Eldin, William "the baronet", grandson of Sir John of Penicuik, antiquary, 33; an original of Darsie Latimer in *Redgauntlet*, 37; studies Law, 40; introduces W.S. to his Penicuik cousins, 42; 43, 45, 46; character of, 48; his nickname, 49; comments on W.S., 51, agrees to be his second in an affair of honour, 327

Clerk of Penicuik, Sir John, 4th Baronet, entertains W.S., 42; 51; landlord at Lasswade, 80

Cockburn, Mrs Alison (great-grand-aunt), reports enthusiastically on W.S. aged five, 23; 41

Cockburn, Henry, Lord, 28, 63, 321

Cogswell, Professor Joseph, from Harvard, stays at Abbotsford, 229

Coke of Norfolk, Thomas, 1st Earl of Leicester, discusses with W.S. his *Essay on Planting*, 335

Coleridge, Samuel Taylor, 92, 104, 107, 153, 234

Compton, Countess, *see* Maclean-Clephane

Compton, Spencer, Earl, afterwards 2nd Marquess of Northampton, introduced by Morritt to W.S. and by W.S. to Mrs Maclean-Clephane, 193; marries Miss Margaret Maclean-Clephane, 193, 195, 196; sketches "Conundrum Castle", 226; takes his family to Italy to economise, 226; his wife dies, 342

Constable, Archibald, "Old Crafty", 84, 91; publishes *Edinburgh Review*, 108; character and appearance of, 120; commissions Raeburn portrait of W.S., 122; offers £1,000 for *Marmion* unseen, 132; W.S. does "by-jobs" for, 137; dislikes being "pushed" by, 143; quarrels with, 145, 152; Ballantyne suggests to W.S. they must go "cap in hand" to, 177–8; a hard bargain is driven, 178, 190, 197; is offered *A Child's History of Scotland* and the *Annual Register*, 236; Edgeworths find "rather sleeky and silky": he tells Maria he has the MSS. of forty-five Scott novels, 275; upset by the conduct of Hurst and Robinson, 296; W.S. hears alarming rumours about from Lockhart, 297; confirmed, 300, 303; W.S. has sad last interview with, 315; his comments on hearing of death of, 325

Constable, George, character of Jonathan Oldbuck in *The Antiquary*, drawn from, 24; believed by W.S. to be a suitor for Aunt Jenny Scott, 29; gets W.S. a lexicon, 54

Constable, Thomas (son), says Lockhart is a serpent, 298

Cooper, James Fenimore, recognises the crest on the chariot of "the literary baronet", 331; obliges W.S. with making enquiries at Lyons, 331, 361; Coleridge's manners shock, 334

Coutts, Messrs, Sir William Forbes enters firm of, 57–58; W.S. visits in London, 82; Sir Edward Antrobus partner in, 205; Gilnockie offered a draft on, 232

Coutts, Mrs (*born* Harriet Mellon), actress, later Duchess of St Albans, says other women guests horrible to her at Abbotsford but W.S. kind, 203; accepts Duke of St Albans, 294

Crabbe, Rev. George, 175; two ludicrous incidents of at Castle St, 260, 261; 268 (*n.*)

Cranstoun, George (afterwards Lord Corehouse), 40, 46, 104, 316

Cranstoun, Helen, *see* Mrs Dugald Stewart

Cranstoun, Jane Anne (afterwards Countess Purgstall), 41, 54–56, 80

Craven, Hon. Keppel, author of *Tour in the South of Italy*, escorts W.S. family around Naples, 348

Croker, John Wilson, politician and journalist, 153, 179; says Prince Regent and W.S. two of the most brilliant story-tellers he ever met, 192; advises Lockhart to call an enemy's bluff, 243; hears from George IV "all about our friend Scott", 267

Cunningham, Allan, Clerk of the Works to Chantrey, his tribute to W.S., 238; 245, 315; W.S. gets jobs for two Cunningham sons, 335

Dalgleish, William, butler, 254, 268 (*n.*), 282; is proud of his literary ability, 283; graphic account of the Scott family ruined, 303; attends W.S. as widower loyally but not tactfully, 311; retires to write his memoirs, 319

Dalkeith, Charles, Earl of, afterwards 4th Duke of Buccleuch and Queensberry, brother-officer of W.S. in Volunteers, 72; greets W.S. at Hermitage Castle, 91; has camp for Volunteers, 99; W.S. stays with at Langholm, 121; approaches Lord Melville on behalf of W.S., 127, 132, 133; stays at Ashestiel, 171; succeeds his father, 172; welcomes W.S. and family to Drumlanrig, 178; lends W.S. £4,000, 178; broken in health after loss of his wife, 189; goes abroad with Adam Feguson, 227; dies at Lisbon, 229; last letters to W.S. ask him to sit for a portrait with Maida to Raeburn, for the new Bowhill library, 228; W.S. sends a cuirass to from Brussels, 199

Dalkeith, Harriet, Countess of (*born* Townshend), afterwards Duchess of Buccleuch and Queensberry, wife of Charles, 4th Duke, "my fair patroness" waves greetings to W.S. from battlements of Hermitage Castle, 91; suggests introduction of the goblin page in *The Lay of the Last Minstrel*, 104, 110, 119; loses her elder son, 140; dies in childbirth, 189

Dalzel, Professor Andrew, W.S. studies Greek under, 30; Heber visits, 83

"Dandie Dinmont", 49

D'Arblay, Frances (*born* Burney), W.S. finds has "a gentle manner and pleasing expression", 316

David, Jacques Louis, "Buonaparte's first painter" has the most villainous countenance W.S. ever saw, 202

Davy, Sir Humphrey, 123, 142, 163, 195

Dick, Dr, late of East India Service, now at Darnick, 227, 231, 234 (*n.*)

Disraeli, Benjamin, afterwards 1st Earl of Beaconsfield, surprises Abbotsford, 293–4

Doisy de Villargennes, Adelbert Jacques, French prisoner of war entertained at Abbotsford, 179, 181 (*n.*)

Donaldson, Hay, solicitor, recommended to Lord Montagu by W.S., 241

Douce, Francis, antiquary, Ritson will not bow to in British Museum, 94; lends W.S. manuscripts, 103

Douglas, Dr Robert, minister of Galashiels, W.S. buys a farm and land from, 168–9, 174; addresses some of *Paul's Letters* to, 197–204

Douglas, Lady (*born* Lady Frances Scott), wife of Archibald, 1st Baron, W.S. meets at Bothwell Castle, 83; in London, 135; takes Charlotte to visit at Bothwell, 139; at Buchanan House, 156

Downshire, Arthur Hill, 2nd Marquess of: guardian of Charlotte Carpenter, 65; consents to her marriage with W.S., 69–72, 81; dines with the Dumergues to meet W.S., 82; godfather to Sophia Scott, 85; dies, 93; Charlotte has grateful memories of, 130; *see also* Appendix, "Who was Lady Scott?", 359–65

Dryburgh Abbey, 19, 73, Lady Scott buried at, 309

Dumergue family, "Our Piccadilly friends", Charles, surgeon-dentist, 70, 71, 74, 78, 93, 102, 133, 135, 191, 203–4; Miss Sophia chooses trousseau for Charlotte, 70, 74; godmother to Sophia, afterwards Mrs Lockhart, 85; sends her superb Brussels lace wedding veil, 239; disastrous visit to Abbotsford, 239; W.S. calls on, 333; *see also* Appendix, "Who was Lady Scott?", 362

Dundas, Henry, 1st Viscount Melville, statesman, 80, 126; hounded out of office, 127, 129; acquitted of perjury, 137; visited at Melville Castle by W.S., 131; 132, 143; restored to privy council, 147 (*n.*), 159; dies, 169

Dundas, Robert Saunders, 2nd Viscount Melville, 97 (*n.*), 147 (*n.*), 159, 166, 222, 224, 225, 229, 239, 265, 307

Dundas, Robert, Lord Arniston, the elder, Lord Advocate for Scotland 1789, 83, 85, 242

Dundas, Rt Hon. William, politician, 3rd son of Robert Dundas, Lord Arniston, the younger, 93, 119, 222

Dunvegan, W.S. stays at, 187

Durham, Shute Barrington, Bishop of: gives the Scott family breakfast, 175; gives banquet for Duke of Wellington, 326

Edgeworth, Misses Harriet and Sophy, their devastating comments on the Scott circle at Abbotsford, 273–7; but weep on leaving, 278, 287 (*n.*)

Edgeworth, "The Great Maria", sends W.S. effusive letter of congratulation on *Waverley*, 189; compared by W.S. with Jane Austen, 212; her visit to Scotland, 272–8; Lockhart's description of, 278; her comments on Lady Scott, 273, 277, 286 (*n.*); entertains the Scotts at Edgeworthstown, 291

Edinburgh Academy, 280

Edinburgh Annual Register, a loser from the start, 152, 166; W.S. contributes a sketch on Buonaparte to, 170; Constable refuses to take over from Ballantynes, 177

Edinburgh High School, W.S. attends, 27–28, his son "Gilnockie" attends, 150

Edinburgh, residences of W.S. in: 25 George Square, 18, 37; 50 George St, 71, 73; 10 South Castle St, 78; 39 South Castle St, 95, 306 *et seq.*; 6 North St David St, 311; 3 Walker St, 319; 6 Shandwick Place, 323

Edinburgh Review, W.S. contributes to, 108, 119; Jeffrey reviews *Marmion* in, 141

Edinburgh, Scott Memorial, Princes St, 214

Edinburgh University, W.S. attends six sessions at, 30 *et seq.*, 44

Edmondstone of Newton, John James, 40, 55, 185 *et seq.*

Edmondstone Dr, author of a *History of Shetland*, goes on lighthouse cruise, 185 *et seq.*

Ellis, George, diplomatist, and man of letters, called by W.S. "one of my two sheet-anchors", and Mrs (*born* Anne Parker), "Ladyfair", 93; W.S. reads *The Lay of the Last Ministrel* to under an oak in Windsor Park, 103; Ellis provides W.S. with introductions for Daniel Scott, 114; goes to Bath for gout, 128; W.S. visits at Sunninghill, 137; Ellis at Bath again, 154; reviews *The Lady of the Lake* for the *Quarterly*, 161; sends W.S. a greyhound, 173; dies, 194

Encyclopaedia Britannica (supplement), Constable staggers under burden of, 189 (W.S. contributed articles on Chivalry, 1814, the Drama, 1818, and Romance, 1823)

English Bards and Scots Reviewers, 153, 156

Eldon, John Scott, 1st Earl of, 132

Erskine, Charles, W.S.'s Sheriff-Substitute, 88, 123, 126, 168

Erskine, Mary Anne (Mrs Campbell of Clathick), 41, 55, 57

Erskine, William (Lord Kinnedar), 42, 46, 54, 94–95, 104, 120, 123, 137, 176; weeps in Fingal's Cave, 188; part of *Paul's Letters* addressed to, 197; 223; loses his wife, 230; is "done to death by slanderous tongues", 259, 268 (*n.*)

Everett, Edward, Professor of Greek at Harvard, visits Abbotsford, 225

Ferguson, Professor Adam, entertains Burns, 39; charges at Battle of Fontenoy, 167 (*n.*)

Ferguson, Adam, "Linton", Captain, afterwards Sir Adam, son of Professor Adam, 40, 50, 65; reads *The Lady of the Lake* to the 101st regiment in the Peninsula, 162, 167 (*n.*); prisoner of war, 176; retires on half-pay, 211; comes to live at Huntly Burn, 218; appointed Keeper of the Scottish Regalia, 221–2; goes to Lisbon with Charles, Duke of Buccleuch, 227; marries, 247; his sisters, "The Three Witches", Margaret, Mary and Bell, 247–8; 344; presented to George IV, 262; knighted, 266; has a wine-red face, 275; suggests marriage of his wife's heiress-niece to Gilnockie, 281–4

Ferrier, Susan, authoress, 171

Fettercairn, home of "Greenmantle", 53–57

Fitzherbert, Mrs Maria, Scott meets at the Dumergues', 133

Florence, W.S. visits Santa Croce, Pitti Palace, Grand Ducal Library, 354

Florence, Monsieur, arch-cook of the Dukes of Buccleuch, 225; accompanies Duke Charles to Lisbon, 227; comes to Dalkeith for visit of George IV, 262

Forbes, Sir William of Pitsligo, "the formal cavalier", father-in-law of "Greenmantle", 57

Forbes, Sir William of Pitsligo, "Don Guglielmo", "Dot-and-carry-one", husband of "Greenmantle", 57; behaves nobly, 59, 62, 329

Fox, Charles James, statesman, 119, 126–7, 131

France, Revolution in, 50; General Buonaparte First Consul in, 87, 196; Experimental Peace with, 98; Britain declares war on, 103; Buonaparte becomes Emperor and invasion expected, 112, 122; but abandoned, 124; marches from strength on the Continent, 141; but not in Spain, 144, 147; divorces Josephine, 157; gets an heir, 170; failing in Peninsula, attacks Russia, 174, 176; is defeated, 177; sent to Elba, 184; escapes, 190, 195; defeated at Waterloo, 196; W.S. comments on state of the country in 1815, 200–4

Fraser, Luke, "a flogger", W.S. enters his second class at Edinburgh High School, 28

Frere, Rt Hon. Hookham, diplomatist, 128, 133, 144, 146, 148 (*n*.), 347

Friday Club (Fortune's Tavern), W.S. rude to Lord Holland at, 160, 167

Galt, John, 175

Geddes, Andrew, artist, produces a crowd-picture of the finding of the Regalia, 233 (*n*.)

George III, Scott sees going to chapel at Windsor, 136; death of, 236

George, Prince of Wales, afterwards Regent and George IV, said to be mortally sick, 136; W.S. hears has spoken bitterly of him, 153; hears *via* Lord Byron he is the Prince's favourite poet, 175; as Regent sends message that W.S. is to be given every facility to use royal library, 177; offers him post of Poet Laureate, 179; arranges "snug little dinner" for W.S., 191; devotee of Jane Austen's novels, 212; pro-claimed king, 236; "I shall always reflect with pleasure on Sir Walter Scott's having been the first creation of my reign", 238; obliged to W.S. for deflecting Queen Caroline from Holyrood, 246; his coronation, 251–4; entertains W.S. at Royal Lodge: melancholy all day when he hears of the financial troubles of W.S., 316–17; W.S. visits for last time, 334; death of, 341

George Square, Edinburgh, Scott family home, 18, 23, 27, 37

Gell, Sir William, escorts W.S. and family from Palazzo Caramanico, Naples, to Temple of Serapis, Lago d'Agnano, Posilipo, Pompeii, Royal Library, Library of La Trinità delle Cava, 349–50; and from Casa Bernini, Via di Mercade, Rome, to Castle of St Angelo, Villa Muti, Frascati, Piazza of St Peter's on Easter Day, monument to the last of the Stuarts, Temple of Vesta, and Castle of Bracciano, 350–3, 357 (*n*.)

Gibson, John W. S., 303, 306, 310

Gillies, Robert, his recollections of Lasswade, 94–95; his financial troubles, offered Chiefswood free, 299, 339

Gilnockie (son), *see* Scott, Walter, afterwards Sir Walter Scott, 2nd Baronet

Gilsland, spa, Northumberland, scene of W.S.'s wooing of his wife, 64 *et seq.*; revisited in 1805, 123

Glamis Castle, visited by Scott, 51–52

Glenbervie, Sylvester Douglas, Baron, entertained by Caroline, Princess of Wales, 136; sends acorns for Abbotsford, 172

Goethe, Johann Wolfgang von, W.S. corresponds with, 320; sent medals

Goethe—*cont.*
by, 335; fails to meet owing to death of, 351

Gordon, George Huntley, son of Pryse Lockhart Gordon, secretary to W.S., 222; Scott writes sermons for, 333

Gordon, Jane, Duchess of (*born* Maxwell of Monteith), wife of Alexander, 4th Duke, W.S. "no stranger to her Grace's activity", 96; W.S. meets at Stanmore, 133; claims to have assisted him over *Marmion*, 154

Gordon, Pryse Lockhart, Major, conducts W.S. over Waterloo battlefield, 198–9

Greenmantle, *see* Belsches, Williamina, afterwards Belsches Stuart and Lady Forbes

Grierson, Sir Herbert, editor of W.S. Letters, 9, 66, 147 (*n.*)

Hall, Captain Basil, R.N., 56; gives information for Life of Boney, 223, 294; his Journal, 284; visits W.S., widower, in horrible lodgings, 312; offers Dalgleish employment, 319; introduces Audubon to W.S., 320; pokes up Admiralty for frigate for W.S., 346

Hallam, Henry, brings a brilliant son, Arthur, to stay at Abbotsford, 339

Hamilton, Lady Anne, spinster sister of 9th Duke, lady-in-waiting to Caroline, Princess of Wales, 96; does not accompany her abroad, 246

Hamilton, Archibald, 9th Duke of: W.S. spends Christmas 1801 with, 96; Keeper at Holyrood House, 246

Hartstonge, Matthew Weld, 171, 172

Hastings, Warren, wants W.S. to write an epic poem on Lord Nelson, 130

Heath, Miss Angel, her weekend at Abbotsford, 294–5

Heber, Reginald (half-brother of Richard), wins a University prize, 105, 111 (*n.*); dies, 317

Heber, Richard, M.P., Fellow of All Souls, wealthy bibliomaniac, 83, 87, 89, 90, 92, 103; W.S. goes to All Souls with, 105; invited to Ashestiel, 131; stays there, 144; W.S. meets in London, 153, 195, 238; tragic fate of, 317–18, 330 (*n.*)

Hemans, Mrs Felicia, thinks herself in a seventh heaven at Abbotsford, 339

Hogg, James, "Jamie the Poeter", "The Ettrick Shepherd", W.S. introduced to, 99–100, 102; his strange behaviour at 39 Castle St, 109–10; has grand ideas, 117; 121; loses his flock, 143; dedicates *The Forest Minstrel* to Lady Dalkeith who sends him 100 guineas, 165; regrets W.S. leaving Ashestiel, 173; has success with *The Queen's Wake*, 183; absurd behaviour of, 208; is furious with James Ballantyne, 217; refuses to go to coronation, 251; Captain of Bowmen at St Ronan's Border games, 279

Holland, Henry Vassall Fox, 3rd Baron, invites W.S. to Holland House, Whig stronghold, 128; criticises conduct of W.S. in an appointment for brother Tom Scott, 159; W.S. wounded, 160; storm blows over and *Old Mortality* appreciated, 215, W.S. stays with, 334

Hood, Admiral Sir Samuel, Baronet, W.S. visits at Tonbridge, 153

Hood, Lady (*born* Mary Mackenzie, heiress of Earl of Seaforth), 153; re-married 1817, Rt Hon. James Stewart of Glasserton who

Hood, Lady—*cont.*
took the name of Mackenzie, 220, 233 (*n.*)
Home, George, Clerk of the Courts of Session, "as deaf as a post and as capable of discharging his duties as I am of dancing a hornpipe", Scott performs his duties unpaid for five years, 127, 133, 169
Home, John, author of *Douglas*, meets W.S. at Bath, 22; at Sciennes Hill House, 39
Hook, Theodore, W.S. dare not introduce Lockhart to for fear of rows, 315
Hooke, Miss, depressing cousin companion of Mrs Charles Carpenter, 243, 337, 339
Hopetoun, John Hope, 4th Earl of: entertains George IV at Hopetoun House, 265–6
Hoppner, John, portrait-painter, 200
Hughes, Canon and Mrs of St Paul's, 152, 245, 282, 304
Hume, Professor David, 40
Hunter, Alexander Gibson, partner of Constable, disliked by W.S., 143; dies, 178
Hurst and Robinson, "Constable's great agents", alarming rumours about, 296, 298; confirmed, 300, 301, 303, 325, 328

Innsbruck, W.S. disappointed in hopes of seeing tomb of Maximilian, 354
Iona, W.S. visits, 164
Irving, John, "Crab", 31, 33, 40, 42, 50
Irving, Edward, celebrated preacher, Scott longs to tell him what an exception he is, 339
Irving, Washington, 207–8, visits Abbotsford, 219; dines with Dumergues to meet W.S., 238

Jedburgh, Assizes at, 51, 66, 84, 87–88, 105; election cry at, "Burke Sir Walter", 356
Jeffrey, Francis (afterwards Lord Jeffrey), 38; editor of *Edinburgh Review*, 108, 132; has a brush with Charlotte Scott about his review of *Marmion*, 141; praises *The Lady of the Lake*, 161; W.S. hopes he will attribute the anonymously published *Bridal of Triermain* to Will Erskine, 176; guesses authorship of *Waverley*, 189
"Jessie" of Kelso, Walter Scott courts, 34–36
Jobson of Lochore, Mrs (*born* Stewart of Stenton), sister of Lady Ferguson, mother-in-law of Gilnockie, 275; considers Sir Walter Scott socially inferior, 281; but becomes quite fond of him, 323
Jobson of Lochore, Jane, afterwards wife of Gilnockie, *see* Mrs Walter Scott of Lochore

Keith, Mrs Anne Murray, of Ravelston (grand-aunt of W.S.), original of Mrs Bethine Balliol, in *The Chronicles of the Canongate*, 41; tells W.S. "Take back your bonny Mrs Behn", 272
Kelso, the most romantic village in Scotland, 29; W.S. takes shares in railroad at, 296
Kemble, John, 52, 89, 133, 143, 156, 171, 218
Knighton, Sir William, "The Invisible", 265, 274, 297, 317
Knole, W.S. visits, 153

Laidlaw, William, sends W.S. a brace of greyhounds, Percy and Douglas,

Laidlaw—*cont.*
98; introduces him to his cousin
James Hogg, 99–100; dines with
W.S. to meet Wordsworth, 107; to
meet Hogg, 109; arrives at Kaeside,
218; finds Lady Byron's mouth
indicates obstinacy, 219; involved
in the failure of W.S., 300; has to
leave Kaeside, 305; returns and is
invaluable, 343; his evidence on row
between W.S. and publishers over
Malachi pamphlet, 344, 357 (*n.*);
W.S. recognises on homecoming to
Abbotsford, 355

Landseer, Sir Edwin, painted every dog
at Abbotsford and ended up with
the owner, 282

Lasswade, W.S. has cottage at, 42, 79,
80, 94, 106; reluctantly leaves it,
109, 114–15

Lawrence, Sir Thomas, portrait-
painter, 135, 315

Lenore, translations of published by
W.S., 56; his charger named after, 62

Leopold, Prince of Saxe-Coburg, visits
Abbotsford, 231; W.S. meets at
Kensington Palace, 334

Leslie, Charles Robert, artist, brought
by Washington Irving to meet W.S.,
238

Lessudden, home of Scotts of Raeburn,
19; W.S. stays at, 26; his mother
stays at, 179; Barbara Scott refuses
the carriage and walks from to Abbotsford and back, twelve miles, 302

Lewis, Matthew Gregory, author of
The Monk, 79, 82, 85, 89, 103, 152

Leyden, John, 84, 91, 93, 95, 97, 98

Liddesdale, W.S. draws, 33; Hermitage Castle in, re-visits, 91; explores
district with Shortreed, 48–49, 83;
and alone for Border Ballads, 93, 98

Lindsay, Lady Charlotte (*born* North),
wife of Lieut.-Col. Hon. John Lindsay, daughter of 2nd Earl of Guild-
ford, one of the wittiest and most
agreeable women W.S. ever met,
133, 136, 153; her comments on
Lady Scott, 286 (*n.*)

Lockhart, Charlotte Sophia, (*born*
Scott), daughter, born Oct. 22nd,
1799, her father's darling, "my
little Scotch girl", 85; on holiday
with her parents, 143, 155, 163,
179, 219; remembers burial of
dog Camp, 146; clever, musical and
a good little nurse, 149, 150, 158;
has not read *The Lady of the Lake*, 161;
sent orders to illuminate Castle St,
181; stays with Joanna Baillie, 195;
beholds the Scottish Regalia, 221;
engaged to Lockhart, 235; married,
239; birth of John Hugh, 243;
settled at Chiefswood, 247; admired
by Villiers Surtees, 249; the Edgeworths, 277; has a daughter who
lives only two days, 280; her father
regrets her dependence on doctors
and medicines, 289; moves to
London with her family, 293; bears
a second son, Walter ("Wa-Wa"),
311; another daughter, Charlotte,
332; splendid children, 339, 355;
on crutches herself, 345; Dr Ferguson observes she cannot stop crying and trembling at the sight of her
father paralysed and semi-conscious,
355

Lockhart, John Hugh, "Little John"
(grandson), born Valentine's Day,
1821, 243; Hugh Scott of Harden
godfather, 246; precocious and fascinating but fragile child, 275, 289;
likes his "parritch", 301; a severe
literary critic of "Ho-Papa", 316,
323, 333; "never out of his

Lockhart, John—*cont.*
mother's thoughts, almost never out of his father's arms'', 300; must lie flat for spinal trouble, 311; improves and rides his pony, 324; spits blood, 333; recovers but a pitiable sight, 339; dies, 1832, 348

Lockhart, John Gibson (son-in-law), at Oxford, 177; his background, 236, 267 (*n.*); arrives at Abbotsford, 224; falls in love with Miss Scott of Abbotsford, 228; his story "of the moving hand", 225; becomes engaged to Sophia, 235–6; married, 239; sad affair of Mr John Scott, 243 *et seq.*, 268 (*n.*); birth of John Hugh, 243; a devoted husband and father, 273, 275, 279; very clever and with a Spanish hidalgo look, 277; horrified by contrast between poverty of peasantry and luxury of magnates in Ireland, 292; also by conceit of Wordsworth, 293; moves to London to become editor of the *Quarterly*, 293, 297; reports alarming London rumours about Constable to W.S., 298; confirmed, 305; W.S. tries in vain to get a government appointment for, 324; buys 24 Sussex Place, Regents Park, 332; his comments on *Pelham*, 333; his description of death of W.S., 356

Lockhart, Violet (sister of J.G.), 279, 340

London, "This immense Vanity Fair", W.S. visits April 1775 with Aunt Jennie, 22; March 1799 with wife, 55 Bond St (Dumergues), 82; April 1803 with wife, 15 Piccadilly (Dumergues), 102; Jan 1806 with Lord Somerville, St James's Hotel, 79 Jermyn St, 126; March 1807 on business alone, 5 Bury St, 132;

April 1809 with wife, Half Moon St (Dumergues), 151; March 1815 with wife and Sophia, White Horse St (Dumergues), 191; Sept. 1815 with Scott of Gala, Long's Hotel, Bond St, 205; March 1820 to meet Gilnockie and be dubbed Sir Walter (Dumergues), White Horse St, 236; Feb. 1821 with Robert Dundas, Waterloo Hotel, 85; Jermyn St, 242; July 1821, Old Palace Yard, staying with William Stewart Rose, 251; Oct. 1826, 25 Pall Mall with Anne (Lockharts), 309; Nov. 1826, 25 Pall Mall, 315; April 1828, 24 Sussex Place, alone (Lockharts), 332; October 1831 (Lockharts), June 1832, St James's Hotel, Jermyn St, 354

Longman, publishers, "The Leviathan of Paternoster Row", buy copyright of *The Lay of the Last Minstrel*, 118; refuse *Edinburgh Annual Register*, 152; 178; offered and accept *Guy Mannering*, 190; part-profit of *Paul's Letters*, 197; Woodstock, 310

MacBeith, John, butler to W.S., objects to Kemble calling him "Cousin Macbeth", 156; "a half-drowned baboon", 185–6; is dismissed, 224

Macdonald Buchanan of Drumakiln, Hector, W.S. visits at Ross Priory, 129; excuses himself from dining with "on account of the death of a dear old friend" (the dog Camp), 147; visits taking Charlotte and Sophie, 155

Macdonald, Jacques, Marshal Duke of Tarentum, son of Niel MacEachainn, Jacobite exile, 204; visits Scotland, 288–9; W.S. dines with in Paris, 314

Macdonald, Ronald, "Staffa", "a right and tight Highland chief", invites W.S. for Hebridean holiday, 162; 272; gives a dinner for Marshal Macdonald, 288

Macdonnell of Glengarry, Alexander, marries a sister of William Forbes, 59; gives W.S. "Maida", 214; welcomes George IV, 261, 262; Charles Scott shoots red deer with, 289

Mackintosh, Sir James, philosopher and political author, 102

Mackenzie, Colin, 102, 129, 130; has T.B., 133, 134, 197 (n.)

Mackenzie, Hannah, 162–4

Mackenzie, Henry, author of The Man of Feeling, 30, 80; guessed to be author of Waverley, 189, 211

Maclean-Clephane, Mrs Douglas of Torloisk, supplies W.S. with Highland data, 152; W.S. sees Torloisk, 164; visits, 188; her eldest daughter married to Lord Compton, 193, 196

Maclean-Clephane, Misses Anna Jane and Williamina Marianne, younger sisters of Margaret, 193, 240, 342

Maclean-Clephane, Miss Margaret, afterwards wife of Spencer Compton, 2nd Marquess of Northampton, has a profile like that of Minerva, 152; 164, 188; engaged to Lord Compton, 191, 195; "Do you know who has been father, brother, everything to me? Mr Scott", 196; stays with her husband and sons at Abbotsford, 226; sends Mrs Lockhart splendid wedding gift, 239; Spencer Scott, godson of W.S., at Abbotsford, 283; dies in childbirth in Italy, 342

Malta, W.S. appreciates, 347; stays at Beverley's Hotel, Strada Ponente (West St), Valetta, 357; visits San Antonio (Pietà), Church of St John twice, Mdina, attends ball in his honour, 348. "It will be hard if I cannot make something of this" (The Siege of Malta), 349, 357 (n.), unpublished

Marriott, Rev. John, comes to Ashestiel "to fish and rhyme", 132; tutor to Lord Scott, 140; but has to retire owing to "a pulmonary tendency", 134, 147 (n.)

Mary, Queen of Scots, 17, 29, 33, 91, 266, 271, painting of severed head of, at Abbotsford, 282; W.S. says he could easily do life of, but his opinion of is contrary both to popular feeling and his own, 333

Matheson, Peter, coachman, 117, 124, 175, 179, 229, 261, 305

Mathews, Charles, veteran actor, 205; admired by Dalgleish, 283; 299

Maturin, Rev. Charles, author, W.S. assists, 196, 211; his spectacular misfortunes, 233 (n.)

Melrose Abbey, 20; W.S. shows the Wordsworths, 107, the Heaths, Tom Moore, 295; stone from used at Abbotsford, 170; grotesques, 215; Duke of Buccleuch takes the lead in repairing, 265

Melrose, Battle of, 1526, 168, 268 (n.)

Melville, see Dundas, Henry, 1st Viscount, Robert, 2nd Viscount

Menzies, William, his story of "the moving hand", 225, 234 (n.)

Millar, Miss, governess to Scott family, 150; gets a shawl from Paris, 204; retires, 219; Sophia Scott writes to, 220, 227, 230, 267; Anne Scott writes to, 280, 288, 350

Miller, William, of Albemarle St, publisher, 120, 132, 137, 142, 146

Minto, Gilbert Elliot, 1st Baron, 100–1, 111 (*n.*), 127

Mitchell, James, tutors W.S. in French, 28, 55

Moira, Francis Rawdon Hastings, 2nd Earl of, "Old Honour and Glory", appointed Commander-in-Chief in Scotland, 108; 112; friendly to W.S., 127, 153

Mons Meg, W.S. obtains return of, 267; accident at ceremony celebrating this, 338

Montagu, Henry James Scott, Baron, brother of Charles, 4th Duke of Buccleuch, 140; sends lime-seed for Abbotsford, 172; W.S. consults repeatedly before and after death of Duke Charles, 189, 229; W.S. visits at Ditton, 239, 243; comes to Scotland for visit of George IV, 262

Moore, Lieutenant-General Sir John, regarded by W.S. as a Whig nominee, 144; retreats to Corunna and is killed in action, 145; defended by Castlereagh, 146–7

Moore, Tom, poet, rude about *Rokeby*, 177; reports on Scott at Lockharts' house, 310; sings like an angel at Abbotsford, 295; meets W.S. in London, 311 *et seq.*

Morritt of Rokeby, John Bacon Savrey, and Mrs (*born* Katherine Stanley), W.S. shows them the Border and Edinburgh, 143; visits at 24 Portland Place, 151; at Rokeby, 154, 175, 224; invites to Abbotsford, 169; receives acorns from, 172; Mrs Morritt ill, 178, 205, 214

Murray, John (II), publisher, 121; meets John Ballantyne at Ferrybridge and goes on to Ashestiel, 144, 145; W.S. visits at Albemarle St, 152; insists W.S. and Byron must not

misunderstand each other, 175; historic meeting arranged at 50 Albemarle St, 194; sends message of Waterloo victory to Blackwood, 196; W.S. offers part of profits of *Paul's Letters* to, 197; W.S. reviews *Emma* for, 211–12; spots W.S. as the author of *Waverley*, 213, 215; appoints Lockhart editor of the *Quarterly*, 294; hears Constables in trouble, 298; asks for biography of Mary, Queen of Scots, 333; Essay on Demonology for his Library, 341

Murray, John (III), aged seven, observes Byron and W.S., 194

Murray, Patrick, of Simprim, 40, 50, 55, 82, 87, 176

Murray, Sir Patrick, of Ochtertyre (cousin), 40

Napier of Ettrick, Francis, 8th Baron, Lord-Lieutenant of Selkirkshire, 83; dissatisfied that W.S. is a non-resident Sheriff of Selkirkshire, 91, 108–9

Newton, Gilbert Stuart, American artist, produces portrait of W.S. for Sophia, 283

Nicolson, Catherine (Mrs Barber), 257; her son's firm perishes, 304

Nicolson, Miss Jane, companion to Charlotte Carpenter, afterwards Lady Scott, 65 *et seq.*; accompanies W.S. and bride on their honeymoon, 75; managing and overbearing, 67; does not settle in Scotland, 80, 82; approves of Sophia Scott, 88; 124, 125 (*n.*), 257; a mystery figure, 360–2; W.S. visits, 335

Nicolson, Miss Sarah, housekeeper to Dumergues, W.S. entertains in Paris, 203; at Abbotsford, 214; kind to Jane Scott of Lochore, 285

N

Nicolson, John, efficient man-servant to W.S., 319, 332, accompanies W.S. on Mediterranean cruise, and never leaves him till the end comes at Abbotsford, 348–56; became butler at Rokeby, 357

"Old Play", favourite chapter-heading quotation invented by W.S., 204
O'Neill, Miss Eliza, afterwards Lady Becher, the sweetest Juliet ever seen by W.S., 195
Orkneys and Shetlands, W.S. visits in lighthouse yacht, 184–7
Opie, Miss Amelia, novelist, 195
Owenson, Miss Sydney (authoress), later Lady Morgan, asks Lady Abercorn if W.S. has ever been in love, 158

Paestum, W.S. thinks first temple at one of the most awesome pieces of classic architecture he had ever seen, 349
Park, Mungo, explorer, 93, 117–18, 125 (n.), 211
Paterson, Peter, "Old Mortality", 52
Paul, Sir George, philanthropist and prison reformer, 162–4
Peel, Right Hon. Robert, 258, 316
Pepys, Samuel, Lockhart sends W.S. his diary to review for Quarterly, 366
Percy, Dr Thomas, Bishop of Dromore, his Reliques admired by W.S., 30; sends him a ballad, 92
Pitt, William, recites passages from The Lay of the Last Minstrel at his dinner table, 119; dies, 127, 141
Platoff, Matvei Ivanovitch, Count, Hetman of Cossacks, embraces W.S. in the Rue de la Paix, 200, 203
Plummer, Andrew, W.S. succeeds as

Deputy Sheriff of Selkirkshire, 83, 85; the Misses Plummer, 99
Pole, Frederick, teaches Scott girls to play the harp, 231; hearing of Sir Walter's losses offers £600 "probably his all", 303
Portobello sands, reviews on, 108, 265; Skene's description of Scott composing Marmion while on duty in camp at, 139; W.S. visits Lockharts at summer lodgings in, 323
Pozzo di Borgo, Count Andrea Carlo, Corsican patriot, 100; W.S. gets Boney material from, 314
Pringle families of Haining, 83; of Torwood Lee, 117, 124, 319; Alexander of Whytbank, 117; visits Brussels and Paris with W.S., 197–204
Purdie, Tom, brother-in-law of Peter Matheson, coachman, 117; gets a present from Paris, 204; inherits his master's white hats and green jackets, 206; lifts him into his saddle, 229; marks the sheep S.W.S. when he hears of baronetcy, 237; 241; "poor Tom Purdie", 300; "he and I go to the grave together", 305, 322; but Purdie goes first, 340

Quarterly Review, Tory counterblast to Edinburgh, W.S. agrees with Murray to contribute to, 145; Canning contributes to, 157, 159; Ellis, 161; Waverley pronounced a "Scotch Castle Rackrent" in review of, 189; W.S. reviews Tales of my Landlord for, 215; Childe Harold, 216; Lockhart editor, 294
Queen Hoo Hall, 142

Rae, Sir William, 228, 242, 279

Raeburn, Sir Henry, portrait-painter, 122; paints W.S. for Constable, 122, 145; for Charles, Duke of Buccleuch, 228, 279; knighted at Hopetoun House by George IV, 266; dies, 274

Richardson, John, parliamentary solicitor, searching for fishing tackle to lend him, W.S. discovers mislaid MS. of *Waverley*, 180; called in by W.S. to advise on marriage settlement of Miss Maclean-Clephane, 193; at Abbotsford, 226, 230; in London, 239; trustee for Scott children, 257; visits dying W.S., 355

Richmond, Charlotte, Duchess of (*born* Lady C. Gordon), wife of 4th Duke of, 198

Ritson, Joseph, antiquary, 92, 93; a difficult guest, atheist, republican, anti-Scottish and a vegetarian, 94; quarrels with Leyden, 95; his sad end, 97 (*n.*); praises *Minstrelsy of the Scottish Border*, 103

Robinson, Crabb, "of *The Times*", 142

Rogers, Samuel, connoisseur and banker, 103, 195, 316, 334

Rose, Sir George, British Minister in Berlin (brother of William Stewart), 257

Rose, William Stewart, eccentric translator of mediaeval romances, 102, 108, 119, 132; W.S. visits Hampshire and Isle of Wight with, 133–4; meets in London, 153; stays with for coronation, 251

Roxburghe, Fleurs built for 1st Duke of, 29; John, Duke of, bibliophile, 82, 103, 177

Roxburghe, Harriet (*born* Charlewood), widow of James, 5th Duke of: Sir John Sinclair thinks W.S. should propose to, 326

Roxburghe Club, 349

Royal Society of Edinburgh, W.S. accepts Presidency with misgivings, 250

Royal Society of Literature, W.S. doubtful of but George IV interested in, 250; it sends W.S. a tribute, 322

Russell family of Ashestiel, Colonel William (uncle of W.S.), 71, 114; Colonel afterwards Major-General Sir James (cousin of W.S.), 114, 116–17, 294, 322; Miss Jane, 124 (*n.*)

Rutherford, Miss Chritty (Christian), aunt of W.S., he tells her that there is "no romance" in the composition of his fiancée though her temper is sweet and cheerful, 70–73; part of *Paul's Letters* addressed to, 197–204; dies suddenly, 231

Rutherford, Dr John, grandfather, 16

Rutherford, Dr Daniel, step-uncle, 33, 65, 81, 102, 231

Sandford, Dr Daniel, afterwards Right Rev. Lord Bishop of Edinburgh, baptises Sophia Scott, 85; marries Miss Margaret Maclean to Lord Compton, 196

Saxon, James, artist, paints W.S. with Camp for Charlotte, 122; portrait used as frontispiece for *The Lady of the Lake*; paints Charlotte, 161

Schetky, Miss, performs on the pianoforte at Mertoun, W.S. says ought to be annihilated, 276; her family well known to him, 286 (*n.*)

Scott, Anne (daughter), born Feb. 1803, 101, resembles her mother, 149; ill, 158; has hysterics, 231; grown very handsome, 231; found tart by Misses Edgeworth, 277; wishes she had been "Lady Anne"

Scott, Anne—*cont.*
278; goes to Fancy Dress Ball in Spanish costume, 289; not a country girl, 289; visits Ireland and the English Lakes, 289–93; bears up bravely over her father's ruin, 301, 303; but depressed at prospect of life in the country economising with her mother, 310; accompanies her father to London, Paris, Oxford, 310–18; captivated by Duke of Wellington, 316; her party to Almacks frustrated, 333; her courage, 338; witnesses her father's first stroke, 340; accompanies him to Malta and Italy, 346 *et seq.*; but finds both her brothers impossible travelling companions, 348–56; her fine eyes admired by Andrew Shortreed, 322; her frustrated romance, 350

Scott, Anne, *born* Rutherford (mother), a sterling character, loses many infants, 18, 33; "Wattie, my lamb", 52; writes kindly to his fiancée, 71–72; finds her manners gay, 78; attends her in her first confinement, 81; stays at Lasswade, 82; godmother to Sophia Scott, 85; receives gift from her son Tom, 138; only wishes his new career might have had nothing to do with money, 160; stays at Ashestiel, 171; stays at Abbotsford, 179; dies after a short illness aged eighty-seven, 231

Scott, Anne (sister), an accident-prone child, 27, 31; a Pre-Raphaelite type, admires Charlotte, 78; stays at Lasswade, 82; dies, 93

Scott, Anne (niece), daughter of brother Tom, has refused several officers in Canada, 280; helps at Abbotsford, 310; her engagement broken off, 318

Scott, Barbara, *born* Haliburton of Newmains, wife of Robert Scott of Sandy Knowe (grandmother), tells W.S. tales of his ancestors, 19–20; widowed and moves to Kelso, 21; dies, 28

Scott, Charles (son), born Dec. 1805, 124; running about, 133; rescued from a watery grave in the Tweed, 149; looks like a dancing dog in his first breeches, 166; an original, 171; nearly dies of measles, 171; "very clever and very idle", sent to tutor in Wales, 241; improves, 249; to be sent to Oxford, 257; page to George IV, 264; small for his age, destined for the Foreign Service, 273; "What I said to the duke", 289; at Brasenose College, 270, 315, 317; W.S. applies to George IV on behalf of an appointment for, 316–17; lives with Lockharts in Regent's Park and goes to Foreign Office daily, 323; *en poste* in Naples, 344; travels with W.S., Gilnockie and Anne in Italy, 346

Scott, Charlotte Sophia (daughter), *see* Lockhart, Charlotte Sophia

Scott, Daniel (brother), weakish and of unsatisfactory character, alcoholic, 78, 82; W.S. provides funds to send to West Indies, 114; reappears a broken and discredited man, W.S. refuses to attend funeral of, 124 (*n.*); confides his grief to Lady Abercorn, 131; Lord Byron, 175

Scott, Miss Jenny (aunt), takes infant W.S. to Bath, 21–22, Prestonpans, 23; Kelso, 26; her garden, 29, 34

Scott, Jessie (niece), son of brother Tom, marries Major Huxley, 232; he commits suicide, 318

Scott, John, *see* Earl of Eldon

Scott, John (brother), enters army, 38; on leave, 63, 74, 75, 78; lends W.S. £2,000, 142; retired and invalidish, 171; lends £2,000 for purchase of Abbotsford, 180 (*n.*); *Paul's Letters* addressed to, 197; dies, 210

Scott (Lady), Marguerite Charlotte, *born* Charpentier, wife of W.S., described by Lockhart, 65; accepts W.S. after a headlong wooing, 66; married, 75; gay and happy, 80; rides and drives, 80, 85 (*n.*), 90; "Who was Lady Scott?", 68, 69, 359–64; a faithful wife and loving mother, not an intellectual partner, 72; the marriage "something short of love in all its fervour", 158; gives birth to a son who dies next day, 81; to a daughter (Sophia), 85; a son (Walter), 95; another daughter (Anne), 101; another son (Charles), 124; her Gallic thrift, 124; rebukes Jeffrey for a bad review, 141; goes on Hebridean holiday, 162 *et seq.*; takes parties to Edinburgh theatre, 166; moves happily to Abbotsford but her charities much missed at Ashestiel, 173; goes to Twelfth Night party at Dalkeith with whole family, 182; her frustrated surprise for W.S., 205; longs for a conservatory, 218; has asthma, 222; "no sort of objection" to Lockhart as son-in-law but would have liked "a little more *stile*", 235; takes her daughters to drawing-room at Holyrood House, 263; unflattering descriptions of by Maria Edgeworth, 273, 286 (*n.*); later modified, 277; frightened of thunderstorms, 282; the ocean, bad beds and night journeys, 289; spiteful portraits of by Angel Heath, 294–6; and Mrs

Dugald Stewart, 277, 286 (*n.*); not sympathetic over her husband's ruin, 301, 305; in failing health, 296; persuaded to see Dr Abercrombie, 307; sinks into unconsciousness and dies peacefully, 310

Scott, Michael, magician, 20

Scott, Robert (great-grandfather), "Old Beardie", 21, 28; W.S. uses his sword, 223

Scott, Robert of Sandy Knowe (grandfather), Walter sent to, 18; dies, 21

Scott, Captain Robert, of the East India Company's service (uncle), visits W.S. at Bath, 22; retires to Rosebank, Kelso, 34; 48, 67; sends W.S. a cargo of pickled pork, 73; 84, 102; leaves him Rosebank, 114

Scott, Robert (brother), "haughty and imperious", enters Royal Navy, 27, 38; exchanges into East India Company's service, dies at sea aged twenty-three, 39

Scott, Thomas (uncle), plays "Sour plums in Galashiels" on the pipes, 20; gives Walter a pony, 26; takes over Sandy Knowe, 28

Scott, Thomas (brother), goes into partnership with his father, 40, 42; enlists as Volunteer, 50; 78, 82; marries Elizabeth MacCulloch, 84, 90, 102; unsatisfactory agent for Abercorn estates, 103, 128, 135, 138; levants to Isle of Man, W.S. gets him a post, 159; attempts to join a regiment, 159; appointed Paymaster, 70; regiment, 160; ordered to Canada, 179; guessed to be author of *Waverley*, 210; in trouble again, 232, 271; dies, 271

Scott, Mrs Tom (*born* Elizabeth MacCulloch), rather an ordinary girl,

Scott, Mrs Tom—*cont.*

84; a stalwart wife and mother, 138; her cousin, General Ross, helps Tom, 160; suspected of being author of *Waverley*, 189, 210; visits Scotland from Canada, 217; her husband in trouble there; widowed and invited to Abbotsford, 271; arrives, 279–80; left a legacy by brother and becomes bossy, 318; comes to London to visit dying W.S. on his return from Italy, 354

Scott, Sir Walter, birth of, 1772, has poliomyelitis, 17; happy at Sandy Knowe 1821, a Bath cure ineffective, 22; painful memories, 26; pugnacious and no scholar at Edinburgh High School, 27; a voracious reader and story-teller, 28; apprenticed to his father, 31; first sight of Highlands, 32; convalescent at Kelso, 34–36; collects chapbooks, 32, 44; and association-objects, 38; decides not to go into partnership with his father, 39–40; a comely youth, 40, 41; athletic, 42; Advocate, 43; falls in love with "Greenmantle", 46–47, 52–57; never forgets her, 59, 60; joins clubs and societies and regrets some were hard-drinking, 49; publishes translations from German, 56, a Volunteer, 62–63; meets and marries Charlotte Carpenter, 63–75; birth and death of first son, 81; birth of daughter, Sophia, 85; of son, Walter, 96; of Anne, 101; Sheriff-Depute of Selkirkshire, 85; refuses to resign from Edinburgh Light Horse, 109; happy at cottage at Lasswade, 42 *et seq.*; but moves to Ashestiel, 114–16; inherits and sells Rosebank, 114–15, 120; publishes *Minstrelsy of the Scottish Border*, an instant success, 97; *Lay of the Last Minstrel*, 118; birth of son, Charles, 124; "sleeping partner" with James Ballantyne, 120; edits Dryden, 120, 130; begins and throws aside *Waverley*, 123; visits Southey and Wordsworth, London, 125–8; becomes unpaid Clerk of the Court of Session, 127; decides to make literature his principal profession, 127; visits the Princess of Wales, 129; to London suddenly again, finds himself "a little Lion", 132 *et seq.*; quarrels with Constable and founds John Ballantyne and Co., 145; visited by John Murray II, 144; horrified by news of Corunna, 146; in London and much lionised, 151–4; *The Lady of the Lake* surpasses its predecessors in sales, 161; W.S. on holiday in Hebrides, 162; tells Brother Tom he might consider a good post in India, 166; buys a farm and land to be called Abbotsford, 168 *et seq.*; writes *Rokeby* under difficulties but "in my old Cossack manner", 174; distressed by industrial unrest, 176; turns over gradually from verse to novel-writing, "Byron beat me", 177, 190, 349; refuses to accept Poet Laureatship and suggests Southey, 179; circumnavigates Scotland in cruise in lighthouse yacht, 182–9; returns home to find *Waverley* published anonymously, most successful novel in world, 189; *Guy Mannering* greeted by public with rapture, 191; entertained by "our fat friend" (Prince Regent), certainly the first *English* gentleman of his day", 192; visits Brussels and Paris, 196–204; awed by Wellington, 202; poem on

Scott, Sir Walter—*cont.*

Waterloo, 206–7; buys Kaeside, 207; consults Duke of Buccleuch about a Barony of the Exchequer, 216; is violently ill with gall-stones for three years, 217 *et seq.*; finds Scottish Regalia intact, 220–2; hears Regent wishes to bestow a baronetcy, 222; has relapses, says he resembles "Death on the Pale Horse" in the Book of Revelation, 228; has heavy expenses placing his elder son in cavalry, 230; paying debts of Brother Tom, 232; but the Waverley novels a goldmine, 232; George IV dubs him Sir Walter, 239; delights in a literary son-in-law, 239; in the coronation, 251–4; in organising King's visit to Scotland, 258–66; but exhausted, 267; Brother Tom dies heavily in debt, and Gilnockie needs aid, 271; entertains Miss Edgeworth and nieces, 272–8; visits Ireland and is struck by the richness of soil and poverty of peasantry, 289; presence of many armed police, 291; shows Anne the English Lakes, 293; has a bad fall at the Catrail, 296; alarmed by rumours about Constable, 297, 300; confirmed, 303; begins his Journal 298, 308 (*n.*); too ill to go to Mertoun, 302; his friends rally and he enters into a Trust with his creditors, 303; refuses to consider bankruptcy, "my own right hand shall do it", 304; sells Castle St, 306, 319; articles signed Malachi Malagrowther sound a nationalist clarion call, 307, 344; a sad widower, 308–9, 311–12; visits London and Paris for research on Boney, 310–16; Royal Lodge, Windsor, 316–17; Oxford, 317;

admits authorship of *Waverley* at Theatrical Fund Dinner, 320; threatened by General Gourgaud, 327–8; upset by letters and interviews with mother of "Greenmantle", 328; threatened by Abud, bill-broker, 329; the "Magnum Opus" (collected edition) proposed, 329; has first paralytic stroke, 340; recovers well but resigns Clerkship of Court and refuses Privy Councillorship, 342; his Trustees behave handsomely, 343; makes provision for Anne and Charles, 344–5; William IV provides a yacht to take him to Mediterranean, 346; returns to die at Abbotsford, 356

Appearance, habits and manners: in infancy, 22; about thirty, 94; about thirty-five, 128, 137; at forty, 171; at fifty, 278; wears the "Maud" Low Country plaid, 117; awkward in Court dress, 245; has a quick heavy step, 238; his conversational look, 238; modesty, 239; whole scene springs to life when he enters his drawing-room at Abbotsford, 295; very hardy, eschews great-coats and mitts, 296; unrivalled at reading aloud, 283; his sense of humour never fails, 307; his phlegm, 283; large mail from strangers, lunatics, etc., 299; no bed-gown and slipper tricks, an early riser, 121; a devoted parent, 150, 154; unfailing assistant to fellow-authors, 155, 165, 202, 211; a compulsive sightseer, 205; his physical courage: in middle age climbs up a craig like a Solan goose, 290; and up a rope-ladder to Bell Rocks Lighthouse, 183; and into Fingal's Cave, 163; "It's commonly him that sees the hare sitting", 161

Scott, Sir Walter—*cont.*

Dislikes: his spectacles, 299; games of cards, 283; boarding schools for girls, 150; chestnuts or greys and bright bays, 224; "that bastard verdict 'Not proven'", 321; the Great North Road, 191; sedentary life, 130

Likes: talking to his staff, 241; holding Sunday services for them and his children, 115, 150; majestic beauty of Loch Corriskin, 188; King's College, Cambridge, 197; Place Louis Quinze, 199; Killarney, 291; to follow Peninsular campaign on maps, 170, 174; having many irons in the fire, 142; "by-jobs", 137, 142; study of the supernatural, 55

Sayings: "I belong to the Death-Head hussars of literature", 213; "If I did not see the heather at least once a year, I think I should die", 219; "Next to the love of truth comes the love of horsemanship", 150; "Like the Eildon Hills 'quite firm though a little cloudy'", 305; "Skene, this is the hand of a beggar", 302; "My own right hand shall do it", 304

Nicknames: Duns Scotus, Colonel Grog, 49

Principal pseudonyms: "Paul", 197; Jedediah Cleishbotham, 212; Malachi Malagrowther, 307

Principal portraits of, in order of date: miniature aged four, 22; miniature in uniform as fiancé, 69

Oil-portraits by James Saxon, 94, 122; Sir Henry Raeburn, 122, 145, 228, 306

Bust: "One of the finest things Chantrey ever did", 238

Oil-portraits by Sir Thomas Lawrence for Windsor, 244; Gilbert Stuart Newton for Sophia Lockhart, thought by her best likeness of her father, 282

Sketches by Sir David Wilkie, 233, 283; Andrew Geddes, 233; Landseer, 282

Oil-portraits by John Watson (later Watson Gordon), 237; John Knight, 302-3; Haydon, 334; Leslie, 282; Northcote, 334; Calvin Smith, 334; John Graham, 338; William Allan (many sketches posthumous), 356

Sketch: Vincenzo Morani, Italy 1832, 350

Principal publications: Minstrelsy of the Scottish Border, 33, 49, 91, 97; The Lay of the Last Minstrel, 103-4; edition of Dryden, 120, 142-3; Marmion, 140; editions of Swift, 142 et seq., 153; Somers, Tracts, 142, 155; Memoirs of Ralph Sadler, 137, 155; Captain Carleton, 142, 189; Robert Cary, 142; edition of de Grammont, 155; The Lady of the Lake, 158, 161, 166; The Vision of Don Roderick, 170; Rokeby, 176; Bridal of Triermain, 176; Waverley, 183; The Lord of the Isles, 189; Guy Mannering, 191; Paul's Letters, 194; Harold the Dauntless, 207; The Antiquary, 210; The Black Dwarf and Old Mortality (Tales of My Landlord), 213; Rob Roy, 217; The Heart of Midlothian, 217; The Bride of Lammermoor, 217; A Legend of Montrose, 217; Ivanhoe, 232; The Abbot, 240, 255; The Pirate, 245, 255; The Monastery, 255; Kenilworth, 255; The Fortunes of Nigel, 255; Peveril of the Peak, 270; St Ronan's Well, 272; Redgauntlet, 281; The Betrothed, The Talisman, 286; Life of Napoleon Buonaparte, 286-323;

Scott, Sir Walter—*cont.*

Woodstock, 295; *Tales of a Grandfather*, 323; *Chronicles of the Canongate, The Surgeon's Daughter, The Three Drovers*, 325; *The Fair Maid of Perth*, 329; *Anne of Geirstein*, 336; *Count Robert of Paris, Castle Dangerous*, 349; *The Siege of Malta, Il Bizarro* (unpublished), 357

Scott, Walter (father), a careful parent, 18; Mr Saunders Fairford in *Redgauntlet*, 37, 38; agrees to his son studying for the Bar, 40; interferes in his son's courtship of "Greenmantle", 53; unwillingly accepts his son's choice of Charlotte Carpenter, 71, 78; dies, 81; shows his son site of his future home, Abbotsford, 168

Scott, Walter (son), afterwards Sir Walter Scott, 2nd Baronet, "The Laird", "Gilnockie", 95, 101, 134; "a strapper", 149; dangerously ill, 158–9, 161, 171; has a tutor, 174, 175; contracts smallpox, 190; "a bold horseman and a fine shot", carries standard at Carterhaugh, 207; destined for cavalry, 224; 226, 230; unsatisfactory progress, 248; but shows courage, 249; writes to Dalgleish, 254; sent to the continent, 257; marries Miss Jane Jobson, 281–4; his father stays with at 10 St Stephen's Green, Dublin, 289; aide-de-camp to the Lord Lieutenant, 296; Basil Hall hears "no possibility" of the title descending, enquiries by W.S. answered foolishly, 312; W.S. visits in quarters at Hampton Court, 333; an invalid, 337, 339; stationed in Midlands, 343; accompanies W.S., Anne and Charles in Italy, 346; a dreadful travelling companion, "swearing at waiters and bills", 348; returns home, 350

Scott, Walter (nephew, son of Tom), 210; sent from Canada to Castle St and Abbotsford for education, 242; arrives well-behaved but silent, 249; cheered by Sophia Lockhart, 250; page to George IV, 265; at Addiscombe as cadet, 271; contracts debts, W.S. settles with warnings, sails for Bombay and never again offends, 297; his successful career, 308 (*n.*)

Scott, Mrs Walter (*born* Jane Jobson of Lochore), daughter-in-law, 263; insists on marrying Sir Walter Scott's handsome son, 281–5; generous and has "a pretty pensive face", 285; her father-in-law loves her, and regrets the marriage is childless, 289, 291; offers W.S. her whole fortune "as if it were a gooseberry", 304

Scott of Gala, John, visits Brussels and Paris with W.S., 197–204; offers to raise yeomanry, 232

Scotts of Harden (ancestors of W.S.), Auld Wat, husband of the Flower of Yarrow, Young Wat husband of Muckle-Mouth'd Meg, John, the Lamiter, 25; *see also* Lady Diana, Hugh, afterwards Baron Polworth, and Mrs Hugh

Scott of Harden, Lady Diana (*born* Lady Diana Hume), heiress of Hugh, last Earl of Marchmont, tells W.S. tales of the reign of Queen Anne, 42

Scott of Harden, Mrs Hugh (Harriet, *born* Von Brühl), first woman of fashion to "take up" W.S., 41; helps Hogg, 117; the Edgeworths find her well-bred, but her handsome sons "absolute bears", 276; however George goes up in a balloon and Henry becomes M.P., 345

Scott of Harden, Hugh, afterwards 6th Baron Polworth, 19; W.S. and family dine with annually at Mertoun on Christmas Day, 166, 171

Scott of Raeburn, William of Maxpoffle, 211, 248

Seward, Anne, "The Swan of Lichfield", 50, 101, 105, 119; "Walter Scott came like a sunbeam to my dwelling", 137; dies having appointed him her literary executor, 151, 155

Sharpe, Charles Kirkpatrick, antiquary and artist, 99, 101, 147, 153, 274, 306

Shelley, Lady (born Frances Winckley), wife of Sir John, 230

Shortreed, Robert, Sheriff-Substitute of Roxburghshire, takes W.S. on "raids", 48–49; reports W.S. in love with Charlotte Carpenter, 67; reports on her phaeton, 90

Siddons, Mr and Mrs Henry, 156, 166, 216

Siddons, Sarah, 142–3, 156–7, 216

Sidmouth, Henry Addington, 1st Viscount, statesman, 237, 250–1

Sinclair, Sir John, Baronet, thinks it would be lovely if W.S. proposed to Dowager Duchess of Roxburghe, 326

Sinclair, Miss Catherine, novelist and philanthropist, her brother John writes to say that she has a passion for W.S. (as widower), "The Lord Deliver Us!", 327

Skene, James of Rubislaw, "Good Samaritan Skene", 48, 54; marries a sister of "Greenmantle", 59; describes W.S. as a Volunteer, 62; 78, 139; visits Ashestiel, 117, 121, 131; W.S. tries to get his drawings published, 120; visits Abbotsford, 205; organises and advises on king's visit to Scotland, 261; a good Samaritan, 303; W.S. finds a post for his boy James, 335

Smith, John, of Darnick, Messrs, employed at Abbotsford and Chiefswood, 247, 255, 279

Somerville, John, Lord, a favourite Tweedside neighbour, 116, 117, 121, 127, 135, 197, 219, 230

Southey, Robert, "of a mimosa sensibility", 90, 108; W.S. visits at Greta Hall, 123, 178; tries to help, 141, 151; suggests he is offered Poet Laureateship, 179; W.S. re-visits and finds sickly, 293

Spencer, George John, 2nd Earl, 103, 127

Staffa, Isle of, W.S. visits Fingal's Cave in, 163

Staffa petit titre of Ronald Macdonald, 162

Stafford, Marchioness of (born Elizabeth, Countess of Sutherland), W.S. visits collection made by her husband's uncle at Cleveland House, 153; sends him acorns to plant at Abbotsford, 172; W.S. re-visits at Cleveland House, 195; Putney, 315

Stanhope, Lady Hester, 119

Stanmore, The Priory, W.S. is offered cottage at by Lady Abercorn, 128; stays at, 133; his summer-house at, 147 (n.)

Street, "Mrs" Celia, personal maid to Anne Scott, 332; accompanies her on Mediterranean cruise, Gilnockie rude to, 348; Lockharts absorb her into their household, 357 (n.)

Stewart, Prince Charles Edward, "The Young Adventurer", 21, 29, 38, 39, 123, 187, 192, 204, 236, 267 (n.), 286 (n.), 317

Stewart, Professor Dugald, W.S. attends for instruction in Moral Philosophy, 30; at Sciennes Hill House, 39

Stewart, Mrs Dugald (*born* Helen Cranstoun), tells Maria Edgeworth Lady Scott said to be a daughter of Lord Malmesbury, and intemperate, 277, 286 (*n.*)

Stewart of Garth, General David, 260, 261

Stoddart, Sir John, 92, 104; promises Wordsworth he will find W.S. "a rare mental treat", 106; W.S. given banquet by in Malta, 348

Stuart, Lady Louisa, spinster daughter of 1st Marquess of Bute, lifelong friend of W.S. from their first meeting, 83; W.S. writes to, 140, 142; introduces W.S. to Morritts, 143; 156; meets at Rokeby, 176

Stuart Papers, 192; W.S. and Lockhart asked to edit, 337; W.S. never able to inspect, 341

Surtees, Robert, antiquary, 137, 151

Surtees, Villiers, friend of Charles Scott, 249, 275; becomes a Judge of the Supreme Court, Mauritius, 268 (*n.*); gives W.S. at Oxford best ale he ever drank in his life, 317

Sweden, Prince Gustavus Vasa of, "Count Itterbourg", 236, 240, 267–8 (*n.*)

Swinton, "Mrs" Margaret (great-aunt), tragic death of, 44 (*n.*)

Terry, Daniel, actor, 156, apprenticed in youth to architect Wyatt, 157; recommends William Stark to build Abbotsford, 169, 171; appears as Lord Ogleby at the Haymarket Theatre, 173; marries Miss Na-smyth, 195; 205; collaborates with

W.S. in stage version of *Guy Mannering*, 211; 223; bankrupt, 333; W.S. assists, 339

The Club, W.S. elected to, 222

Thomas the Rhymer, 20, 84, 218; "the Edgeworth stone" in his glen, 276

Thomson, George, wooden-legged tutor of Scott children, 174; accepted by Lockhart as prototype of Dominie Samson in *Guy Mannering*, 180 (*n.*), 241, 256

Thomson of Duddingston, Rev. William, 322; W.S. advises Duke of Buccleuch to buy a picture by ("Newark Castle"), 338

Ticknor, Professor George, from Harvard, stays at Abbotsford, 228

Thorwaldsen, Bertil, sculptor, 351

Turner, J. M. W., comes to Scotland to illustrate *Collected Poems* of W.S., 343

Venice, W.S. comfortable at Hotel Leone Bianco and visits Accademia, Arsenale and Palazzo Mocenigo (home of Byron), 354

Victoria, Princess, afterwards Queen, W.S. invited to Kensington Palace and presented to, 334

Waldie, "Lady" of Kelso, a Quaker, lends young Walter books, 29; remembered in note in *Redgauntlet*, 30

Walter, Rev. James, Minister of Dunnottar, 52, 54, 56

Waterloo, W.S. visits battlefield, 198–9; produces poem on, 205

Watson, John (later Sir John Watson Gordon), portrait-painter, 237

Waverley begun and laid aside, 123; sent to James Ballantyne who is not enthusiastic, 165; found after move

Waverly—cont.
to Abbotsford and finished, 180; a resounding success though anonymous, 189 *et seq.*; only Morritt, Will Erskine, Lady Louisa Stuart in the secret, 183, 211

Weare, William, W.S. takes Anne to visit macabre scene of Gill's Hill murder of, 336

Weber, Henry, amanuensis, author, 144, 165, 185

Wellesley, Richard Colley Wesley, 1st Marquess, entertains W.S. at Malahide Castle, 290; marries, 296

Wellington, Arthur Wellesley, 1st Duke of, 87, 144; says there never was a general so ill-used as Sir John Moore, 148 (*n.*); 157, 162; W.S. longs to visit in the Peninsula, 170; his victories in, 174; wins Waterloo, 196; W.S. entertained by in Paris and admires his simplicity of manners and frankness, 194–202; dines with at Apsley House, 237; supports Lockhart's view in his "affair of honour", 268; gives W.S. material for life of Boney, 315; and a good dinner, 316; on tour in north, 327; "Dissolve the Commission by God!", 337; 342, 343

Wesley, John, W.S. aged twelve, listens to him preaching in Kelso, 29

Whale, Lancelot, teacher at Kelso Grammar School, 30

White, Miss Lydia, 143, 316

Whitebanklee, Clovenfords, W.S. lodges at, 88; recommends the Wordsworths to stay at, 107

Wilkie, David, sketches W.S. and family, 218, 233 (*n.*); presented by W.S. to George IV, 262

Williams, Rev. John of Lampeter, 242, 257; Rector of new Edinburgh Academy, 280

Wilson, Hariette, courtesan, W.S. remembers, 103

Wilson, Professor John, "The Leopard" and "Christopher North", invited to Abbotsford, 225; appointed to the choir of Moral Philosophy, Edinburgh University, 239, 262, 278

Woodhouslee, Tytlers of, 80

Wordsworth, Dorothy, visits the Scotts at Lasswade, 106; reports of W.S., "He is a man of very sweet manners, mild, cordial and cheerful", 107

Wordsworth, William, his *Lyrical Ballads*, 92; visits the Scotts at Lasswade, becomes "a friend for life", 106–7; W.S. meets in London, 137; gives temperate applause to *Marmion*, 140; attacked by Jeffrey in *Edinburgh Review*, 141; his comment on Joanna Baillie, 142; W.S. visits, 293; is given dinner in his kitchen, 295; his poem on departure of W.S. for Mediterranean, 346

York, Frederick, Duke of, Commander-in-Chief, second son of George III, 146; W.S. meets at "snug little dinner" at Carlton House, 191; his unfortunate campaign of 1799, 197; W.S. presents Gilnockie to, 237; writes to, 246, 253, 256; at coronation of George IV, 285; W.S. waits on, 314